Malcolm Surridge and Andrew Gillespie

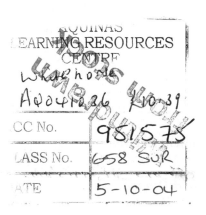
Hodder & Stoughton

A MEMBER OF THE HODDER HEADLINE GROUP

Contents

Introduction

What is A2?

A2 examinations are designed specifically for students who have completed the second year of their sixth-form studies in a particular subject. They build on the material covered at AS and add further topics specific to A2. The A level as a whole comprises the AS exams plus the A2 exams. The A2 exams consist of three papers; combined these A2 exams account for 50% of the A level.

As well as introducing new topic material, and in some cases new methods of assessment, the A2 is also different because there is more emphasis on the higher-level skills of analysis and evaluation. Whereas at AS level the weighting is heavier for the skills of content and application, at A2 these skills are less significant. This means that simply demonstrating knowledge is not as important – points have to be developed and evaluated to a greater extent.

AQA A2 examinations

- Unit 4
  Business decision making case study covering marketing, accounting and finance, people and operations management
  1½ hours   15% of the total A level marks

- Unit 5
  Either
  Business report and essay
  1½ hours   15% of the total A level marks
  Covers all areas of the specification
  or
  Project   Approximately 3000 words

- Unit 6
  Case study
  External influences and objectives and strategy
  1½ hours   20% of the A level marks

	AS UNITS (EXAMS)			A2 UNITS (EXAMS)			
Assessment objectives	1 %	2 %	3 %	4 %	5 %	6 %	Overall weighting of assessment objectives %
Knowledge and understanding	5	5	5	3	3	4 =	25
Application	5	5	5	4	3	3 =	25
Analysis	3.5	3.5	5	5	3	5 =	25
Evaluation	1.5	1.5	5	3	6	8 =	25
Overall weighting of units (%)	15	15	20	15	15	20	100

Table 1.1 *The weighting of skills in the AQA Business Studies Examinations*

OCR A2 examinations

Candidates choose one of the units below:

- further marketing (1 hour 30 minutes)
- further accounting (1 hour 30 minutes)
- further people in organisation (1 hour 30 minutes)
- further operations management (1 hour 30 minutes).

In each of these units candidates are expected to demonstrate an analytical and evaluative approach to the AS core in earlier modules and the content of the specific units chosen. The question paper is based on unseen case studies and consists of two compulsory questions.

Candidates also complete a **business project** or sit an examination called **business thematic enquiry** (1 hour 30 minutes, 90 marks). This assessment is based upon a report related to an unseen case study. The report focuses on a pre-issued theme which allows candidates to use knowledge from many parts of the specification. Candidates are expected to blend their knowledge, gained from local study, with the evidence in the case study in writing a report.

Business strategy unit (2 hours)

This is an entirely synoptic unit. It assesses the ability of candidates to use, explain, analyse and evaluate the whole subject core. It requires students to think in an integrated and strategic way about the way businesses operate and the way they react to change inside and outside the business.

Edexcel A2 examinations

- Unit 4
  Analysis and decision making
  1 hour 15 minutes   15% of the A level
  Students are required to answer structured questions. All questions are compulsory.

- Unit 5
  Either
  Coursework
  or
  Business planning
  1 hour 30 minutes   15%
  An unseen case study including 15 minutes reading time.

- Unit 6
  Corporate strategy
  1 hour 30 minutes   20%
  Students will be required to take a paper based on a pre-seen case study. The case study will be issued six weeks before the examination. There is 15 minutes reading time. All questions are compulsory.

	AS UNITS (EXAMS)			A2 UNITS (EXAMS)			
Assessment objectives	1	2	3	4	5	6	Overall weighting of assessment objectives %
Knowledge and understanding	4.5	4.5	6	3	3	4	25
Application	4	4	5.25	3.5	3.5	4.75	25
Analysis	3.5	3.5	4.75	4	4	5.25	25
Evaluation	3	3	4	4.5	4.5	6	25
Overall weighting of units (%)	15	15	20	15	15	20	100

Table 1.2 *Weighting of the skills on each unit for the OCR Business Studies A level*

	AS UNITS (EXAMS)			A2 UNITS (EXAMS)		
Assessment objectives	1	2	3	4	5	6
Knowledge and understanding	30	30	25	20	25	20
Application	30	30	25	20	25	20
Analysis	20	20	25	30	25	30
Evaluation	20	20	25	30	25	30

Weighting of the skills for the different units for Edexcel Business Studies

Answering A2 questions: higher-level skills

Compared to the AS level, A2 business studies places more emphasis on the higher-level skills of analysis and evaluation. Rather than simply identifying points and explaining them or putting them in context it is important to develop these further and weigh them up.

Analysis

Analysis occurs when you examine the effects of a particular point. For example, 'an increase in price may decrease sales' is simply making a point – to analyse this, this idea must be developed further 'an increase in price may lead to a fall in sales. The impact on sales will depend on the price elasticity of demand. The more price elastic demand is, the greater the fall in sales.' One technique which can often help to analyse is to make a point, explain what it means and then show why it matters using the structure: POINT, BECAUSE, THEREFORE. For example, if a question asks you to 'analyse the possible factors a firm might take into account when choosing where to set up' you might write 'a firm might consider the nature of the labour market (point) *because* if there is a high level of demand for particular skills but a low level of suitably qualified people available this may drive up wages (explanation) and *therefore* this might make this location less profitable than an alternative (analysis).'

Wherever you can, try to bring in business studies theory into your answers – this helps with analysis. If you are recommending a price change, for example, why not refer to the price elasticity of demand? If you are discussing a firm expanding why not consider economies and diseconomies of scale?

If you are discussing the reaction of employees to a particular proposal you could probably refer to motivational theorists.

By referring to business studies concepts you can develop your argument and examine a particular point in much more depth.

Evaluation

Evaluation occurs when you weigh up the relative importance of the points you have made or come to a conclusion in your answer (showing judgement). For example, you may argue that '*in this situation* factor X is more important than factor Y because of Z.' Or you may argue that 'X is most likely because ...' or '*in the short run* the firm may choose X because of Z but in the long run Y is more likely.' When you analyse your arguments you are developing your ideas in depth. To evaluate you must consider the arguments you have made – which one of them is the most significant? Under what circumstances would one of them become more or less important?

To evaluate you often want to consider the following factors.

■ What resources does the firm have – which of the various plans you have suggested is most realistic for this firm?
■ What are the firm's objectives – given what the firm is trying to achieve what is the most appropriate course of action?
■ How long does the firm have – are the consequences of any given change likely to be different in the short run compared to the long run?

When evaluating make sure you defend your arguments. Try to avoid simply listing points such as 'it depends on the size of the firm, the time span and the market'; take one or two of these and explain why your conclusion depends on these.

Integration

An important aspect of studying Business Studies at A2 level is to develop an integrated approach to the subject. Rather than seeing each aspect of the course in isolation you need to bring together your understanding of each area and appreciate how the different aspects of a business are interrelated. A decision by one part of a business is inevitably constrained by the resources elsewhere in the firm and at the same time will have an impact on the activities of those other functions.

Managing a successful business is not about getting the marketing right or getting the finance right, it is about getting all the different areas right! Management involves juggling all the different priorities, resources and demands of the firm and somehow bringing them all together into a coherent whole. Many of the problems of a business occur when its actions are not integrated ie when one part of the business acts without considering the impact on other areas of the firm.

The reason why business areas such as objective setting, strategic planning and communication are so important is because they provide a means of unifying the organisation and ensuring the firm acts as one and hopefully avoids the problems which can occur due to a lack of coordination.

When analysing the impact of change on a business or considering how a firm might react to a given situation it is important to take an integrated approach. This will add depth to your answer and highlight your understanding that a business consists of a complex set of different interrelated parts. Take an increase in demand, for example. Managers will need to consider

- has the firm got the capacity to produce more to meet this demand? If not should it reject the order or subcontract?
- what will the impact be on the firm's human resources? Will it need to recruit, for example?
- if the firm has to pay overtime to get the orders

produced what will this do to its costs, profits and cash flow?
- is the demand likely to stay high and if so is it worth/necessary investing in more capacity? Alternatively should the firm increase the price of the product?

Clearly an increase in demand has an impact on many different areas of the business and many factors have to be considered before managers decide on what actions to take. Although you are likely to have been taught about these different parts of the business separately at A2 level it is good practice to bring this understanding together.

Answering case study questions

When answering case study questions it is important to relate your response to the actual situation facing you. Rather than giving very general answers you need to focus on how the actual firm in the case is likely to react. This means you need to consider issues such as

- the firm's resources, eg what is its financial position? What is its liquidity? What is its gearing?
- its objectives ie what is it trying to achieve?
- the constraints it faces, eg what is its capacity?
- the markets in which it operates, eg what is its competitive position? Is the market growing or shrinking?

Good answers to case studies will always be rooted in the case itself.

Writing a business report

In the AQA unit five you are faced with a range of financial data. Your job is to write a report advising a firm about a particular decision. To write this report you need to analyse the data; this will not usually involve further calculations but rather using the data that is already there and interpreting it. The format of the report should include

■ the name and position of the person to whom the report is written
■ your name and position
■ the date
■ a title.

Your report should then contain sections with clear headings such as

■ the case for launching product X
■ the case against launching product X

or

■ the argument in favour of closing branch X
■ the argument against closing branch X.

Under each heading you should identify a few points and develop these. You should then come to a conclusion or recommendation advising the firm on the particular course of action which you think it should be taking.

Essay writing

To write an essay in business studies it is important to have a clear structure to your answer and to evaluate the points you have made. Read the question carefully, outline the various arguments you want to make and then make a judgement on their validity. Almost inevitably your answer will conclude that 'it depends'. Very few things in business studies are definite – they depend on all sorts of factors such as the firm's own strengths, the nature of the market and the external environment. The solution for one firm may not be appropriate for another. Your aim is to explore the validity of your arguments and consider when they are more or less appropriate, when they are more significant or under what circumstances they are relevant.

Marketing

Introduction

The subject matter for A level marketing is divided between the AS and A2 elements of the specification. The A2 course builds very heavily on the knowledge, concepts and skills of the AS material.

In the AS you studied topics such as

- market analysis. This includes market research and market segmentation
- marketing strategy. This includes niche and mass marketing, the product life cycle and product portfolio analysis
- marketing planning. This includes the marketing mix and the elasticity of demand.

On the A2 course you will revisit each of these areas and will hopefully develop a broader understanding of marketing in relation to the other functions of the business. You will also study new topics such as

- extrapolation and correlation
- marketing decision making
- the marketing budget
- sales forecasting.

Although there are clearly some new areas to be studied at this level the marketing element of the A2 course is heavily rooted in the work you did at AS. A key difference is that you will be expected to apply this understanding to the particular situation much more than you did at AS. You will need to think carefully about a particular firm's marketing objectives and strategy and relate this to its resources and the nature of its market.

MARKET ANALYSIS

Starting points

During the AS course you will already have come across the concept of market analysis. This involves an examination of market conditions and includes topics such as segmentation and market research. On the A2 course you will further develop your understanding of markets by considering

- asset-led v market-led marketing. These are two approaches to marketing and affect how a firm behaves and influences its success

- extrapolation. This is a method of predicting future sales
- correlation. This is a method of identifying relationships between different variables such as price and sales.

Having studies such topics you will have a better understanding of how a firm can analyse the determinants of its sales and estimate future sales.

Marketing

Marketing is the process by which a firm tries to anticipate and satisfy customers' needs and wants and at the same time meet its own objectives. A firm will aim to provide goods and services which customers want and in return it will usually seek to generate a profit. Marketing therefore involves an exchange process in which both sides hope to benefit.

Effective marketing requires a good understanding of customers' requirements; this is usually achieved through primary or secondary market research, although in some cases managers may rely on their experience and intuition.

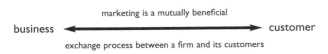

marketing is a mutually beneficial

business ←——————————————→ customer

exchange process between a firm and its customers

Figure 2.1

> ### Key terms
>
> ***Primary (or field) research:*** *data is gathered first hand.*
> ***Secondary (or desk) research:*** *the data already exists, eg it has been gathered by another organisation or is past data held within the firm.*

Market analysis

Market analysis occurs when a firm undertakes a detailed examination of the characteristics of a market. This is an essential part of marketing planning. Only by knowing the features of a market will a firm be able to plan effectively what to do next.

Figure 2.2

A market analysis will usually involve estimates of

- market size ie how big is the market? Market size may be measured in terms of the volume or value of sales. For example, in the soft drinks market a firm may measure the number of cans or bottles sold or the value in £ of the total sales. A firm must ensure the market is big enough to generate sufficient returns to make it worth competing in
- market growth: to what extent is the market growing? How big will it be in the future? Markets will grow at different rates. For example, the growth of demand for takeaway foods has been rapid in recent years whereas the growth in demand for high-fat foods has been slower. A firm will be reluctant to enter a declining market
- market segments: are there clearly identifiable groups of needs and wants within the overall market? If so, are these segments worth targeting?

By undertaking a market analysis a firm should be able to identify existing market conditions and identify possible opportunities and threats for the future. Opportunities may include particular segments which are likely to grow fast; threats may be markets which are about to decline.

Production-led, market-led versus asset-led marketing

It is important that all firms monitor their market conditions to ensure they offer customers what they want. If a firm identifies its customer requirements and tries to produce these goods and services, this is known as a 'market-led approach' – the decisions of the firm are determined by customer needs and wants. By contrast a production-led firm focuses on what it can do and hopes that once this is produced customers will want the goods it has made.

A production-led approach is much riskier than a market-led approach because it assumes customers' needs will coincide with what the firm itself wants to produce. Being production led will only tend to work if there is little competition (so customers have no other choice) or if the firm is fortunate enough to produce something customers want.

A market-led strategy is much more likely to be successful because it puts customers first and this should help ensure a firm produces something

Figure 2.3 *A production-led approach*

which the market actually wants. However, even this approach has potential problems: firms have to accept that they cannot always meet customer requirements. A market-led firm may end up entering markets where it has limited experience and no particular competitive advantage. This could stretch its resources, lead to poor customer service and damage the overall brand name.

Figure 2.4 *A market-led approach*

It is better, therefore, for a firm to compare what the market wants with what it can actually deliver. This is known as an 'asset-led approach'. Asset-led marketing matches a firm's skills and strengths with market opportunities; this should maximise its chances of success.

Figure 2.5 *Asset-led marketing*

Key terms

Market-led approach: a firm bases its decisions on customer requirements.
Asset-led approach: a firm bases its decisions on customer requirements and its own strengths.

EXAMINER'S ADVICE

When assessing a marketing strategy consider whether it really builds on a firm's assets. Mills & Boon publishes romantic novels – it may make more sense for this company to diversify into Valentine's Day cards or presents than to move into other publishing areas because its brand is so clearly linked to this type of occasion.

EasyJet has built a reputation for a cheap but reasonable service; this is now being extended into other areas such as car rental.

Business in Focus: Marks & Spencer

For many years Marks & Spencer was regarded as one of the most successful retailers in the country and was widely admired for its ability to provide good-quality products. In the late 1990s the company was struggling. One of its major problems was that it had a very centralised buying process. Rather than reacting to market trends Marks & Spencer relied on its head office buyers being able to anticipate future trends. This high-risk policy was exposed when its buyers failed to stock the goods that the customers wanted; the company's products looked out of date and expensive for what they were. The firm's competitors had spent years building up a global network of suppliers enabling them to change their stocks quickly as they spotted emerging trends. Marks & Spencer, however, had maintained its traditional supplier network and was committed for a whole season at a time making it sluggish to react to customer-buying patterns. The company had become a classic case of being too production rather than market led. The challenge facing the firm is to link market opportunities to its own strengths in the future and develop an effective asset-led strategy.

1 How might becoming more asset led change the way in which Marks & Spencer operates?

Extrapolation

Managers are naturally interested in how markets will develop in the future as well as their present situation. Just because a market is attractive at the moment does not mean it will always be appealing. New competitors, new laws, changes in technology and social change can all affect the success of a market in the future. In the 1950s the market for black and white televisions was growing; now this is a tiny market in the UK. In the 1960s the market for computer games was non-existent; now it is worth several hundred million pounds a year.

It is important therefore for firms to look ahead

when undertaking marketing planning. This way managers can identify any particular segments of growth or decline, and act accordingly. Obviously if a firm can plan ahead it is more likely to be successful than if it has to react to change once it has occurred.

One method of predicting future trends is known as 'extrapolation'. This involves identifying the underlying trend in past data and projecting this trend forwards.

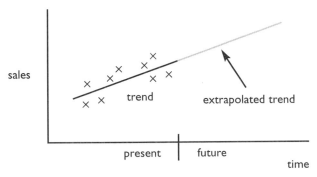

Figure 2.6

In figure 2.6, for example, the underlying trend in sales figures is clearly upwards. If we assume this trend will continue we can project it forward and estimate future sales.

Why is extrapolation important?

Firms must plan for the future. They will need to consider staffing levels, production levels and distribution strategies. All of these depend on the expected level of sales and so it is essential for firms to have some idea of likely sales. One way of estimating future sales is by using extrapolation. The past can provide a useful insight into trends – firms may identify particular times of the week or month or year when they are busy and take marketing actions accordingly. Extrapolation is therefore an important element of a firm's marketing planning.

Problems of extrapolation

Extrapolation is only likely to be effective if market conditions continue to develop in the future as they have in the past ie extrapolation only works if past trends actually continue. The problem is that many markets are very dynamic and change rapidly. The market for cameras, for example, has seen rapid

change in recent years with the arrival of the advanced photo system and digital cameras; in this situation extrapolation may be very misleading – examining the past may provide little indication of what is going to happen in the future. Sales can suddenly drop regardless of what has happened in the past, perhaps due to a recession, competitors launching a new product or a problem with production. In the 1990s farmers could hardly have predicted the collapse in the sales of beef due to the BSE crisis. In 2001 they could not have foreseen foot and mouth disease. Similarly Coca-Cola could not have predicted the short-term drop in sales in 2000 when it had to take some of its products off the shelves temporarily due to a health scare.

Extrapolated figures must therefore be treated with caution – their reliability depends entirely on the extent to which the future will imitate the past. Obviously firms can learn from past trends – retail sales are likely to increase in the run up to Christmas, holidays in Spain are more likely to be popular in the summer, central heating is likely to be used more when the weather is colder and so on – but they must also look out for future changes in the market conditions. Rapid developments in technology, for example, can lead to major changes in terms of what we produce and how business is conducted and this may make extrapolation more risky.

Correlation

When analysing market trends firms will attempt to identify whether there is any correlation between different variables and the level of sales. Correlation occurs when there appears to be a link between two factors. For example, a firm might discover a correlation between its sales and the level of income in its market – with more income consumer sales might increase.

Correlation analysis examines data to see if any relationship appears to exist between different variables. This is important for marketing managers because if they can identify the key factors which determine demand for their goods they can try and influence these or target their goods at customers who are most likely to buy.

In figures 2.7 and 2.8 you can see examples of different types of correlation

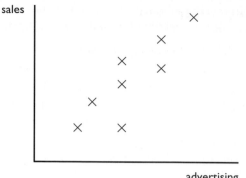

Figure 2.7 *This diagram shows a positive correlation between advertising and sales*

> **Key terms**
>
> A **scatter graph** plots a series of points on a chart.

'Positive correlation' means that there is a direct link between the variables. An increase in advertising, for example, might lead to an increase in sales and vice versa. The sales of a product might

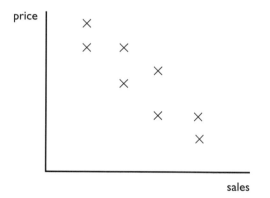

Figure 2.8 *This diagram shows a negative correlation between price and sales*

be positively correlated with income levels and the number of customers in the market.

A 'negative correlation' means that the two factors are inversely related; an increase in price, for example, is likely to lead to a fall in sales so price and demand have a negative correlation.

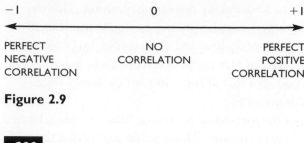

Figure 2.9

ɱ ATHS MOMENT

The correlation between two variables can have a value between -1 and $+1$.

If the correlation is $+0.6$, for example, this means there is a fairly strong positive correlation – eg there may be a positive correlation between the number of fliers sent out in a mailshot and the number of enquiries generated.

If the correlation is -0.2 this suggests a weak negative correlation; this type of relationship might exist between price increases and sales.

It is important to note that correlation analysis simply identifies an *apparent* link between the two factors; it does not show cause and effect. For example, there is often a strong link between coffee drinkers and smokers; people who smoke often drink a lot of coffee as well. There is a link between the two but this does not mean that drinking coffee actually makes you smoke or vice versa. It is important to treat correlation figures with some caution, therefore. Just because sales figures and the amount of money spent on advertising expenditure are both increasing does not necessarily mean that the advertising is boosting sales. In many cases firms feel that the high sales mean they can spend more on advertising ie sales may determine advertising spending and not vice versa. Alternatively the increase in sales could be coincidental – it could be caused by factors other than advertising.

However, the more times the correlation appears to exist – eg if the firm has regularly advertised and this has regularly increased sales – the more likely it is that managers will believe a link does occur.

Correlation and elasticity

The concept of elasticity is clearly based on the idea of correlation. The price elasticity of demand, for example, measures the strength of the relationship between price changes and changes in the quantity demanded; similarly income elasticity measures the relationship between changes in income and quantity demanded. A high price or income elasticity means that there is a strong correlation; a low elasticity means the correlation between the two variables is poor.

The price elasticity of demand will usually show a negative correlation because sales will fall when price increases (and increase when price falls). Income elasticity, however, may show a positive or a negative correlation. In the case of normal goods, sales increase with income so the correlation is positive. In the case of 'inferior' goods, such as cheap own-brand food, sales fall with more income (because customers switch to more luxurious products) and so there is a negative correlation.

Why is correlation important?

If a firm can identify the factors which seem to have most effect on its sales (eg the number of sales representatives it has, its spending on sales promotions or its distribution through particular types of outlet) it can then build this information into its marketing planning. For example, a firm may decide to change its marketing mix once it appreciates which elements of the mix are most important in determining sales. It may also affect which areas of the market are targeted. Imagine that a firm finds there is a strong correlation between income levels and demand for its service. It may then target areas of high income growth which should lead to faster growth in its demand. Similarly if a firm identifies a strong correlation between a particular customer profile and sales it might be able to focus more on this type of segment in the future.

EXAMINER'S ADVICE

Correlation and extrapolation are techniques used as part of marketing analysis to help a firm gain a better insight into its market. Although some successful marketing decisions are made using only intuition the majority of marketing successes are based on an examination of market conditions: what opportunities exist in the market? What is the market likely to be doing in the future? And what factors most influence demand? When discussing marketing planning you should stress the value of market analysis.

Moving averages

If you look at the following sales data and plot the figures on a chart, you will see that the sales are quite erratic during the year. In June, for example, sales are relatively high whereas in July they are lower.

	Sales £000
January	9
February	12
March	15
April	15
May	18
June	21
July	9
August	18
September	21
October	24
November	12
December	24

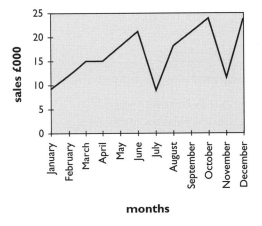

Figure 2.10 *Sales*

However, although the sales clearly change from month to month the overall trend is clearly upwards.

One way of plotting the underlying trend is to calculate the moving average. This looks at several periods at a time and averages out the data; by doing this the effect of particularly high or low figures is reduced because an average has been taken.

For example, for a three-month moving average we average out the figures for January, February and March. Then we average out February, March and April; then March, April and May and so on.

The three-month moving average highlights the underlying trend of the sales figures, as shown in figure 2.11.

	sales £000		three-month moving average £000
January	9		
February	12	(9+12+15)/3	12
March	15	(12+15+15)/3	14
April	15	(15+15+18)/3	16
May	18	(15+18+21)/3	18
June	21	(18+21+9)/3	16
July	9	(21+9+18)/3	16
August	18	(9+18+21)/3	16
September	21	(18+21+24)/3	21
October	24	(21+24+12)/3	19
November	12	(24+12+24)/3	20
December	24		

Table 2.1

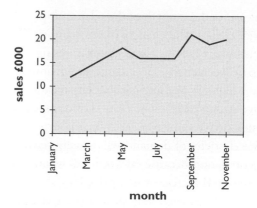

Figure 2.11 *Three-month moving average*

EXAMINER'S ADVICE

Note: a moving average can be calculated for different periods – it does not have to be calculated for three-month periods. It could, for example, be a four-month or five-month. Alternatively if the data are given in years it could be a three- or four-year moving average.

Progress questions

1 What is meant by 'market analysis'? *(2 marks)*
2 Julie Smethwick is thinking of setting up a shop to sell mobile phones. Explain two reasons why Julie might undertake a market analysis. *(6 marks)*
3 Distinguish between asset-led and market-led marketing. *(3 marks)*
4 Some firms forecast their sales using extrapolation. What is meant by extrapolation? *(2 marks)*
5 Explain two reasons why a firm might use extrapolation. *(6 marks)*
6 Explain the possible problems of using extrapolation to predict sales. *(5 marks)*
7 What is meant by correlation? *(2 marks)*
8 Susie Sue has noticed that the number of visitors to her hotel 'The Grand' in Liverton has been gradually declining in recent years. Explain how Susie might use correlation to help her with her marketing planning. *(6 marks)*
9 'Correlation simply shows a link between different variables. It does not show cause and effect.' Explain what is meant by this statement. *(4 marks)*
10a) What is meant by a moving average? *(2 marks)*
  b) Calculate a four-month moving average for the following sales figures.

Month	Sales £000	Month	Sales £000
Jan	50	Jul	70
Feb	60	Aug	75
Mar	65	Sep	80
Apr	70	Oct	72
May	45	Nov	80
Jun	50	Dec	78

Plot the actual sales and the moving-average figures on a chart. *(5 marks)*

Using the data what would you estimate sales would be in December the following year? Explain your reasoning. *(4 marks)*

Analysis and evaluation questions

1 Analyse the possible benefits to a firm of adopting an asset-led marketing approach. *(8 marks)*
2 Examine the possible advantages and disadvantages for a firm of adopting a market-led approach to marketing. *(12 marks)*
3 The managers of Strachan plc, a carpet retailer, are considering entering a new market overseas. Discuss the possible benefits to Strachan of undertaking a market analysis. *(12 marks)*
4 To what extent can extrapolation help a fast-food restaurant in its marketing planning? *(12 marks)*
5 Discuss the possible value of correlation analysis to a firm. *(12 marks)*

Case study 1

Hissam Khan has just been looking as his sales figures for the last few months. Hissam runs an agency which sells tickets for many of the major shows in London. Hissam cannot understand what has gone wrong. Earlier in the year everything had looked good. He had even started to think about moving to better premises and treating himself to a new car. The profit figures had been very impressive and when he had extrapolated on the basis of these numbers he had been convinced that this would be a wonderful year; he had already promised bonuses for all his staff.

Now when he looked at the recent figures he saw that recent sales have been very disappointing. He couldn't understand what had gone wrong. He had not put the prices up and the shows themselves had not changed in the last few weeks so why the fall off in demand? 'Look for the correlation' his dad always used to tell him and so he sat down and drew a few scatter graphs to try and identify what was going on. He did not hold out much confidence but surprised himself when he did notice quite a strong relationship between a couple of variables and his sales. The trouble was now that he had identified a correlation (thanks dad!), what was he supposed to do?

1 a) Examine the possible reasons why Hissam's sales might not have turned out to be as high as he thought they would be from extrapolation. *(8 marks)*

b) Discuss the possible consequences for Hissam's business of having lower than expected sales. *(12 marks)*

2 a) Outline **two** factors you might expect to be correlated with the sales of tickets for the major shows in London. Justify your choices. *(8 marks)*

b) Discuss the possible value of correlation analysis to Hissam. *(12 marks)*

Case study 2

Frankie Vialli is the managing director of a relatively small independent publishing company called Lemon Ltd which publishes a music magazine called *Scream* on a weekly basis. The sales of *Scream* for the last 12 weeks are shown as follows.

week	sales 000 magazines
1	35
2	33
3	34
4	32
5	35
6	31
7	30
8	32
9	28
10	36
11	32
12	30

As well as worries over recent sales Frankie is concerned about the way the market has been developing over the last few years. He feels there is increasing fragmentation in the market with new titles starting up fairly frequently to focus on niche markets. And to make matters worse Frankie thinks the whole future of the market is in doubt. 'The interest in music remains strong' says Frankie 'but whether this will continue to lead to high readership levels for music magazines is another issue. Factors such as the growth of the internet have to be thought about carefully.'

Frankie was well aware that *Scream* was no longer producing the high returns of the early 1990s when it was first established. The company had seized a significant share of the market in its early years with a very independent and somewhat rebellious look at music which its readers had liked. Some critics now complained it was too old-fashioned and rather tired. 'You've got to keep it real' said Bazza Hughes, editor of *Boom Boom*, one of the newer titles on the market. '*Scream* doesn't even whisper these days.'

Although the owners of Frankie's company had never been that interested in the money they realised that the business was in danger of no longer being viable unless it could boost its earnings. It had remained a one-product business and that product was no longer generating the profits it once did. 'Greater competition has kept our prices down whilst costs have soared' said Frankie. 'Our skills all lie in this field; the question is can we earn our keep?' He decided the time had come for a formal analysis of the market.

1 a) Calculate a three-weekly moving average for the sales figures in the table. Plot the weekly sales figures and the moving average on your chart.

(8 marks)

b) Using extrapolation estimate the expected sales of *Scream* in another 12 weeks' time.

(2 marks)

2 Frankie is thinking carefully about the future of Lemon. Discuss the possible value of market analysis for Frankie.

(11 marks)

MARKETING STRATEGY

Starting points

During the AS course you will have learnt about marketing strategy. You will have studied

- marketing objectives and strategy
- niche v mass marketing
- the product life cycle
- product portfolio analysis
- the concept of adding value.

In this unit you will learn about marketing decision making. This involves a consideration of how marketing decisions (such as the choice of marketing strategy) can be made scientifically and whether this is better than basing a decision on a hunch.

Introduction

Once a firm has undertaken market analysis it should have a good insight into the nature of its market and how it might develop in the future. Market analysis should provide information on the size of the market, the major firms competing within it and expected trends. Armed with this information the firm can decide its objectives and determine the required strategy to achieve them.

Figure 2.12

Marketing objectives are quantifiable marketing targets; these may focus on the

- level of sales
- composition of sales (eg the sales of one brand compared to another)
- timing of sales (eg in an attempt to smooth sales out over the year).

The marketing objective determines exactly what the firm is aiming to achieve in marketing terms. This will contribute to the overall corporate objective. The marketing strategy is the plan a firm adopts to achieve its marketing objectives.

> **Key terms**
>
> **Corporate objective:** *overall target of the organisation.*
> **Marketing objective:** *target of the marketing function which should contribute to the corporate objective.*

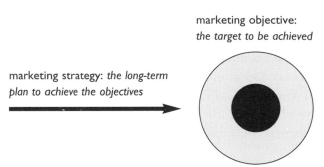

Figure 2.13

When deciding on a marketing strategy there are many issues to consider such as

- should the firm compete in a niche or try to compete head-on with the major players in a mass market?
- should the firm try to match competitors' offerings but sell them more cheaply (a low-cost strategy) or should it aim to differentiate itself and charge more (a differentiation strategy)?
- should it compete in particular regions, in the UK as a whole or globally?

Firms will make different decisions in answer to

these questions. Lobbs, for example, is an exclusive shoemaker producing expensive made-to-measure shoes – this is a niche, differentiation strategy. Clarks competes much more in the mass market. Asda offers a range of foods aimed at the 'average' customer and seeks to maintain a lower price than competitors'; this is a low-cost, mass market strategy. Waitrose offers a more exclusive range of goods at a higher price which is a differentiation strategy.

Figure 2.14 *A firm's marketing strategy determines what markets it wants to compete in and what products it wants to offer*

> ### Key terms
>
> **Niche market:** *this is a small segment of the market. Larger firms are not usually interested in a niche because it does not offer high enough returns.*
> **Mass market:** *this is the main part of any market; it offers firms the attraction of relatively high volumes.*

A firm's marketing strategy should aim to exploit its market opportunities and defend it against threats. It should naturally build on the firm's strengths and avoid entering market segments or offering products where its weaknesses will be exposed.

Determinants of a marketing strategy

When considering a marketing strategy a firm's managers should consider

- what is the firm trying to achieve ie what are its marketing objectives? There is no point cutting prices, for example, if the firm is trying to build an exclusive brand image. Similarly there is little point diversifying if the firm's objective is to focus on its core products
- what are the market opportunities? What market segments appear to be growing?

- what are the firm's strengths? What is the firm capable of achieving? Does it have any unique selling points (USPs)?
- what resources does the firm have? For example, what is its financial position? Will it be able to finance any plans for expansion, for example?

The marketing strategy should therefore be firmly based on an effective SWOT analysis which examines the Strengths, Weaknesses, Opportunities and Threats facing a firm.

> ### Key terms
>
> **Unique selling point:** *this is any aspect of a firm which differentiates it from the competition.*

Business in Focus: Motion Media – a SWOT analysis

Although videophones have been on the market for many years, they have not yet caught the imagination of the general public. However, a team of scientists at Motion Media have persisted in developing a range of videophone products.

Strengths

- The quality of the picture on a Motion Media device is remarkable for its clarity and colour. The industry has moved on since the early 1990s, when BT brought out an ill-fated videophone notorious for its poor quality.
- The price makes it practical for a big company to ask its managers to communicate by videophone instead of spending time and money travelling to meetings. IBM is one of Motion Media's customers.
- A recent project developing mobile devices for Orange has been good for Motion Media's cash position, reputation and knowledge base.

Weaknesses

- There is a serious question mark over whether callers really want to see the person at the other end of the line. There is a perception in some quarters that videophones are simply a gimmick.

■ Distribution is limited. At present, the videophones are sold through only a handful of retail outlets at the Link and BT Retail Business Centres. And they are still expensive for consumer products.

Opportunities

■ The company sells security devices that connect with its videophones, for people to watch over their property from a distance. Unlike the cameras in petrol stations, the evidence is beamed off site. This would enable one security guard to watch 100 sites from one office.

■ Videophones can be used to keep an eye on old people who might be vulnerable.

■ There have been successful pilots of telemedicine, whereby minor injury units are linked to accident and emergency departments for remote diagnostics.

Threats

■ Tandberg, a Norwegian rival, has produced videophones. Siemens, the German electronics company, has huge resources to promote its own model.

■ The biggest threat could be public indifference and a reluctance by retailers to stock the videophones. Public awareness is a problem. Very few people know videophones are available and those who have seen them in the past presume they are dreadful because there were some that were terrible.

The Financial Times

1 How might the above SWOT analysis influence Motion Media's future strategy?

Business in Focus

In 2000 First Choice defied the bloom that was occurring elsewhere in the holiday market by reporting a 47% increase in profits. This was partly due to a series of acquisitions which focused on higher margin specialist holidays. The UK's fourth largest tour operator aims to derive half its profit from activity and tailor made packages over the next three years.

Airtours, the second largest tour operator, reported a 30% fall in pre-tax profits. Meanwhile the profits of Thomson Travel group the largest package holiday company were halved.

First Choice's chief executive said: 'We are not looking to go head to head with the mass market players.' He said that the company would strengthen its operations in France and Spain and buy niche tour operators in fragmented southern European markets such as Italy.

The Financial Times

1 What factors might determine the future success of First Choice's strategy?

EXAMINER'S ADVICE

Students often place too much emphasis on the marketing mix and lose sight of the importance of the overall strategy. Whilst getting the price, product, promotion and distribution right is obviously important it is even more important to make sure you are competing in the right market to begin with. If the strategy is wrong and you are in the wrong market and competing in the wrong way it does not matter how good the marketing mix is, you are likely to fail.

Differentiation versus low-cost strategy

A differentiation strategy occurs when a firm attempts to clearly distinguish itself from its competitors. This should enable it to justify higher prices and earn bigger profit margins. For a differentiation strategy to be successful a firm must be able to offer goods and services which are perceived as better than the competition. This may be achieved by building a strong brand, patenting a new invention or developing a USP. The distribution of this type of product or service is often exclusive; the firm is likely to want to keep a tight control over distribution to maintain an exclusive image. The products are often innovative and the firm may invest heavily in research and development. The promotional strategy is likely to emphasise the difference between this product and rivals'.

Inevitably firms which do differentiate their offerings successfully may be imitated over time. Just look at the way in which Coca-Cola, Dyson and Pringles have been copied. At this point the firm will only be able to justify a higher price if it can continue to stress its role as the market leader or position itself effectively as the 'first of its kind' or the best. In 2000 Dyson, for example, ran an advertising campaign emphasising that 'if you want a Dyson you have to buy a Dyson' to emphasise its uniqueness; Coca-Cola often stresses it is the 'original'.

A Dyson

To be successful with a low-cost strategy a firm must be able basically to match its competitors' offerings but at a lower price. This means it must be able to deliver its products more cheaply than the competition. This may be achieved through economies of scale, special relations with suppliers or by removing some elements of the marketing mix – eg a firm may try to make distribution more direct and so be able to avoid the middleman's profit margins; alternatively it may provide fewer additional services – some supermarkets, for example, compete on price by keeping overheads low and offering a more basic service and a more limited range of goods in the store itself.

The Ansoff matrix and marketing strategies

The Ansoff matrix is another way of classifying different marketing strategies. Ansoff examines four strategies under the headings of 'existing' and 'new' products and 'existing' and 'new' markets.

PRODUCTS

		existing	new
MARKETS	existing	MARKET PENETRATION	NEW PRODUCT DEVELOPMENT
	new	MARKET DEVELOPMENT	DIVERSIFICATION

Figure 2.16

- *Market penetration:* this strategy occurs when a firm tries to sell more of its existing products to its existing customers. To achieve more sales the firm may adjust elements of its marketing mix. For example, it may increase its spending on advertising or cut its price. This is a relatively low-risk strategy which can be implemented in the short term.
- *New product development:* this strategy focuses on developing new products and offering these to existing clients. Firms operating in the soap, shampoo and washing power markets, for example, are continually developing new brands for their customers. This strategy is risky in the sense that new products often fail. Only one in ten new products launched survives the first two years.

  On the other hand managers should have a relatively good understanding of the market and their customers' buying processes, and so they may feel confident that their offering will be successful despite the high failure rate of others.
- *Diversification:* this strategy involves offering new products to new markets. For example, a chocolate company may decide to diversify into the soft drinks market. This is a high-risk strategy

because the firm may have only a very limited understanding of the production and marketing requirements of the new sector. If it is successful, however, it actually reduces the firm's risk because it is operating in two different markets. If sales decline in one market demand they may be sustained or even increase in another one.

■ *Market development:* this strategy occurs when a firm offers its existing products to a new market. For example, it may try and sell its products overseas or it may try and target new segments of its existing market. Many sportswear companies have successfully marketed their products as fashion items, for example. Chewing-gum companies have offered their product as an aid to giving up smoking, as something which helps prevent tooth decay and as a breath freshener; the product therefore had been offered to many new segments.

Business in Focus: new product development

In 1994 Unilever was forced to withdraw Persil Power from the shops because it appeared to rot the fabric it was supposed to be washing! Unilever's first major innovation after that was in 1998 when it introduced Persil Tablets.

Persil Tablets took the market by storm and propelled Persil back to the number one detergent brand in the UK. Within four months of being launched it took 9.3 per cent of all detergent sales. In overall market share, however, Unilever still trailed P&G, whose Ariel, Bold, Daz and Fairy accounted for more than 50 per cent of a market estimated at £850–£900 million a year, compared with around 35 per cent for Unilever's Persil, Surf and Radion.

A company spokesman said 'We are projecting from our figures that tablets could account for 20 per cent of the detergents market within two years.' P&G soon followed with its own version of the Persil tablets – Ariel Discs – which were test marketed in Grimsby and Cleethorpes for a few months.

Putting detergent into a tablet might sound like a simple matter, but Lever spent seven years getting the product right.

Much of the appeal of tablets, the company believes, is that they allow confused consumers to use their detergent in pre-measured doses. Lever says that research has shown that 70 per cent of those who use concentrated powders are over-dosing. This makes their wash more expensive and has been a contributory factor in the decline of concentrated detergents.

Detergents are definitely big business: collectively the soap companies spend £70m a year on advertising alone and more like £100m if you include other marketing paraphernalia such as special promotions, direct mail and sponsorship.

One reason for the Tablets' success – the premise is that they are completely idiot-proof – is the rise in single male households as men marry later and the incidence of divorce rises.

The Daily Telegraph and *The Observer*

1 What were the possible implications for Unilever of having to withdraw Persil Power from the market? (*20 marks*)
2 What factors are likely to determine the future success of Unilever's Persil Tablets? (*20 marks*)

Why change a marketing strategy?

It may be necessary for a firm to change its marketing strategy for a number of reasons:

■ for example; it may have changed its marketing objectives; rather than wanting more sales from a given product range it may seek to diversify
■ market conditions may have changed; the slowing up of the rate of growth in the PC market has led firms such as Intel and Microsoft to look for new markets to enter
■ competitors' actions; a head-on attack from other firms may force an organisation to move into a new segment or to focus on particular areas of its business where it has a competitive advantage. The threat of Wal-Mart attacking its core business arguably led to Boots moving more into

People in business: Peter Wood

Peter Wood turned the world of insurance on its head in the 1980s when he created a new way of distributing insurance: over the telephone. Now the man who founded Direct Line, the first insurer to sell policies over the phone, and who made £65m in the process is back. He has now linked up with Halifax the former building society turned bank to launch esure.com. This time he is using the internet to sell car and household insurance to small businesses. 'I am coming out to play, I see it in those terms. I do not need to work for money. Much more important is making this a success. I want this company to be fun.' His aim is to undercut rivals by 10 to 15% and turn esure into a top five insurer within the next few years. Wood, the man who introduced the adverts featuring the ringing red telephones on wheels, is scathing about the costs of UK insurers. 'The expense ratios of UK insurers are worse now than when I started. The average is 30.7% except for Direct Line which is around 10%. Insurance is not that complicated. You have got to have two things – a low-expense ratio and a low-loss ratio. If you manage to do that you will make money in good times and bad.' This strategy is an example of market penetration; through a new distribution system and lower prices esure hopes to gain more market share for Halifax.

Wood says he is not concerned about making another personal fortune having made £65m from Direct Line. This included about £20m when Royal Bank of Scotland bought his stake to take full control and a further £15m when he sold his stake in Privilege which specialised in insuring fast cars and higher-risk drivers to Royal Bank in October 1998.

Huge bonuses once made Wood the UK's highest-paid director. By 1993 Royal Bank was so embarrassed by Wood's bonuses that it paid him £24m to give up the scheme that made him £18m that year. 'People have said that I was lucky to get the £50m but that is nothing compared to the profit it made for Royal or the £2bn offer they were made to sell Direct Line a few years ago.' Analysts suggest he has a more difficult task ahead of him this time. In the 1980s banks and insurers underestimated completely the power of the telephone. This time people are aware of the potential of the internet. Wood is less worried – 'Halifax is a great brand ... Halifax also has 21m customers for us to target. The largest motor insurer has 2.3m. I do not think for us to get 2m from 21m is that hard a challenge.'

---

segments such as photography, optical and dental care

- the firm's own strengths; as a firm develops its staff, technology and product range it may find that its strengths create new opportunities and this brings about a change in strategy.

EXAMINER'S ADVICE

Remember, a change in marketing strategy will have major implications for other areas of the business. It may affect the numbers and skills of employees required, it may require additional funding and it may involve changes to the production system. A change in strategy must, therefore, be coordinated with the other functions.

Marketing decision making

Marketing managers face numerous opportunities and threats in the business environment and must therefore make decisions about the best course of action to take at any given moment. Their decisions will be influenced by the resources of the firm and its perceived strengths. In some cases managers will take decisions in a very scientific manner. They will gather data, analyse it thoroughly and select the best strategy. They will then review the results and make any changes accordingly. Scientific marketing decision making is rational and analytical; it is based on quantifiable data. This approach should reduce the risks of making the wrong decision.

Business in Focus: Pepsi's strategy

Under the leadership of Mr Roger Enrico PepsiCo has been radically restructured in recent years. The restaurant and bottling businesses have been sold off and the company can now focus once again on the two areas which made it great in the first place: salty snacks and beverages. These changes are part of an overall strategy of moving away from head-to-head competition with Coca-Cola. That is a big leap for a man forever associated with the cola wars of the 1980s when, after national taste tests, Pepsi-Cola pushed ahead of Coke in the US for the first time. Mr Enrico, Pepsi's boss even then, dismisses himself as 'young and brash' at the time, especially in writing a memoir that now seems embarrassingly premature: *The Other Guy Blinked: How Pepsi Won the Cola Wars.*

Pepsi's recent change plus an overhaul at Coca-Cola have widened the gap between the two companies; PepsiCo is now concentrating on developing snacks while Coke is committed more than ever to becoming an all-beverage company. Central to this is a notion that few consumers or even investors and employees have properly grasped: with Frito-Lay, PepsiCo expects to prosper by playing snacks and soft drinks off against each other, a strategy called 'Power of One'.

PepsiCo boasts it is the largest source of sales for retailers such as Wal-Mart because it supplies both the snacks and the beverages. "Just the simple things, such as putting the snacks across from the soft drinks, can increase sales by 3 to 4 per cent," Mr Enrico says. "The soft drinks bring the traffic in and the snacks give you the margin." This was the rationale that led Pepsi-Cola to merge with Frito-Lay, forming PepsiCo back in 1965.

At the time, Don Kendall, chief executive of Pepsi-Cola, uttered words Mr Enrico still repeats to this day: "You make them thirsty and I'll give them something to drink." Frito-Lay, which churns out Lay's potato and corn chips, Doritos, and other snacks, generates more than 60 per cent of the revenues and profits for PepsiCo. Six years ago it was barely 30 per cent.

Beverages are still a substantial part of the business but really only in North America, which accounts for nearly 24 per cent of profits.

The Power of One is, in many ways, also a recognition that PepsiCo could not win the war – any war – on colas alone. Its soft-drink sales outside the US are less than a quarter of Coke's and in some big markets, Mr Enrico admits, PepsiCo is unlikely ever to beat its competitor. "Are you going to see Pepsi with a 50 per cent market share in Germany and Coke a 20 per cent share? I don't think so," says Mr Enrico. Instead, he has selected a few countries – India, China, Russia – where PepsiCo has a better chance of winning. He took a particular interest in the once-bungled China operation, hiring Henry Kissinger, the former US secretary of state, to be his consultant. "We did not know what we were doing there before. We had no respect. Coke was the hero," he recalls. "That's why I got engaged. I was telling people they weren't spending enough money. I said we need to hire the best government relations person we can get, not the one we can 'afford'." The Power of One is also being deployed overseas. While PepsiCo is rejuvenating its soft drinks business in China, for instance, it has also been testing its potato chips on consumers. "The mayor of Shanghai said to me: 'Boy, I'm glad you guys came' because he loves potato chips. He said they tried to make their own potato chips but the potatoes were all wrong," Mr Enrico explains. "So we put in place this huge agri-programme there and when we launched Lay's in Shanghai with the first good potatoes that were coming out of the Chinese fields, we became the number one snack food in something like 30 to 90 days."

The Financial Times

1 Why do you think PepsiCo has changed its strategy?

However, the scientific approach to decision making can have some limitations or drawbacks

■ It is only as effective as the underlying data. If the information on which the analysis is based is incorrect then inevitably the decision is unlikely to be the right one.

■ In some situations the data may not be easily available or may be too expensive to gather. In

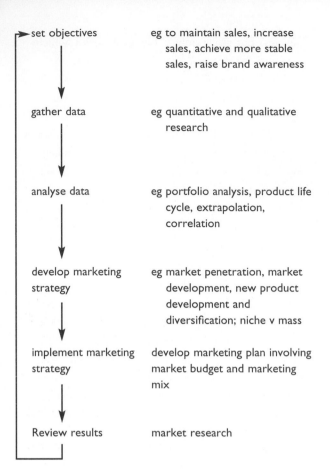

Figure 2.17 *Scientific marketing model*

such cases managers may rely on their experience or use their intuition and base the decision on a hunch.

■ Making a decision on a hunch can be quicker than using a more scientific approach (although it is riskier because it is not supported by quantifiable data).

*P*OINTS TO PONDER

Decisions are usually based on a combination of experience, intuition and data

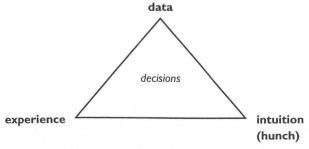

Figure 2.18

The most appropriate decision-making method will depend very much on the situation and the nature of the decision. In a stable market with plenty of information available and plenty of time to make a decision a scientific approach makes sense. If, however, a manager is eager to find a creative solution to a problem or if the situation is so unusual that there is not much information to go on, a hunch may be the answer. Many product breakthroughs are the result of the intuition of their designers or creators. In several cases entrepreneurs have argued that customers do not know what they want until they actually have it and so a scientific approach may not generate the right results!

Of course managers often use a combination of hunch and the scientific approach rather than one or the other, eg they may well gather and analyse data to narrow their options but when it comes to actually making the decision their own gut feelings are likely to play an important part as well. It is rare that any data gathered will provide a clear solution; the options have to be weighed up and interpreted and hunch can have an important role to play in this.

EXAMINER'S ADVICE

A hunch can work and be tremendously successful. However, gathering data usually reduces the risk. It is important to highlight the value of good information in your answers.

Business in Focus: the flawed market research of New Coke

In 1985 the chairman of Coca-Cola announced 'the best has been made even better.' After 99 years the Coca-Cola company decided to abandon its original formula and replace it with a sweeter version named 'New Coke'. Just three months later the company admitted it had made a mistake and brought back the old version under the name 'Coca-Cola Classic'!

Despite $4m of research the company had clearly made a huge mistake. The background to Coca-Cola's decision to launch a new product was much slower growth in its sales in the 1970s, especially compared to Pepsi. Pepsi was also outperforming Coca-Cola in taste tests. The relatively poor performance was even more disappointing given that Coca-Cola was spending over $100m more than Pepsi on advertising. The taste testing of the new recipe for Coca-Cola involved 191 000 people in more than 13 cities. Fifty-five per cent of people favoured New Coke over the old formula.

However, once the launch was announced the company was amazed by the negative response: at one point calls were coming in at a rate of 5000 a day. People were most annoyed by the fact that Coca-Cola dared to change the formula of one of the country's greatest assets.

What went wrong? Possibly one problem was that when undertaking the testing, customers did not know that choosing one cola would mean the other was removed ie that if they chose a new flavour the old one would be withdrawn. Also the symbolic value of Coca-Cola was perhaps overlooked.

I Coca-Cola did extensive (and expensive) market research and yet still made a mistake. Does this mean that market research is a waste of time?

*P*OINTS TO PONDER

'My gut will tell me within 20 minutes whether or not something's worth taking a risk. But I made *Lock, Stock* so cheaply that it wasn't even a risk. If you make a film for £2m or £3m you're going to get it back from TV and video around the world.'

(Matthew Vaughn producer of the highly successful film Lock, Stock, and Two Smoking Barrels.)

Overseas marketing strategy

One issue facing a firm when determining its marketing strategy is whether to focus purely on the domestic market or whether to expand overseas. Overseas expansion may be appealing because

■ the domestic market is saturated
■ the domestic market is subject to increasing competition
■ of the benefit from particular market opportunities overseas.

Entering a foreign market does of course bring various problems. Perhaps most importantly the firm is unlikely to know the market as well as its domestic market. It will need to ensure it fully understands market conditions including consumer-buying behaviour, legal and economic factors and the possible response of the competition. Given that the market is not known as well, entering an overseas market can be seen as risky.

Once the decision has been made to enter an overseas market a firm must consider the extent to which it will adapt its offerings to local conditions. Is it possible to market the product in almost the same way in every country (as Gillette does with its razors) or will the marketing have to be adjusted for each market? If a firm pursues a global strategy this means it is adopting essentially the same marketing mix wherever it competes. (If it operates in this way but only in Europe this is called a pan-European strategy.) A global marketing strategy has been adopted by firms in several markets such as jeans, soft drinks, cigarettes and luxury goods. A Rolex watch, for example, is positioned and marketed in a very similar way across the world. However, in some markets this approach may not be possible or even desirable; market tastes may differ very considerably requiring firms to adapt the marketing of their products accordingly.

One advantage of a global approach is that it offers marketing economies of scale (eg the firm can develop one advertising campaign and one approach to packaging worldwide). However, this type of strategy does not respond to the requirements of different national markets and so the firm may lose sales to competitors who focus more on local needs. On the other hand a more local approach may meet customer needs more precisely but may be more expensive and more complex to manage.

*P*OINTS TO PONDER

'A powerful force drives the world towards a converging commonality and that force is technology. It has proletarianised communication, transport and travel. ... the result is a new commercial reality – the emergence of global markets for standardised consumer products on a previously unimaginable scale of magnitude.'

Theodore Levitt

Progress questions

1 What is meant by a marketing objective? Give an example. *(3 marks)*

2 What is meant by a marketing strategy? Give an example. *(3 marks)*

3 Explain two factors which might determine a firm's marketing strategy. *(6 marks)*

4 Examine the possible reasons why a firm might change its marketing strategy. *(6 marks)*

5 Explain what is meant by the marketing model. *(4 marks)*

6 What is meant by scientific marketing? *(2 marks)*

7 Scientific marketing is based on information. Explain two ways in which a firm might gather information about its market. *(6 marks)*

8 Explain two possible advantages of scientific marketing decision-making compared to hunches. *(6 marks)*

9 Explain two possible disadvantages of scientific marketing decision-making compared to hunches. *(6 marks)*

10 Explain two factors a firm might consider before entering an overseas market. *(6 marks)*

Analysis and evaluation questions

1 Examine the factors which determine the marketing strategy a firm chooses. *(8 marks)*

2 Are marketing decisions based on hunches better than ones based on a scientific approach? *(12 marks)*

3 Discuss the possible advantages and disadvantages of basing decisions on hunches. *(12 marks)*

4 How useful is strategic planning? *(12 marks)*

5 Do firms need a marketing strategy? *(12 marks)*

Case study 1

Dave Clark works for Zeugma an independent record company responsible for some of the leading bands in the last five years. Dave is the man behind many of these groups having found them when they were unknowns and having helped them go on to great success. 'The thing you've got to remember in this game is that customers have got no idea of what they want. You've got to tell them what to like and spot what's going to be the next big thing. You want to know what's got me where I am today? Gut instinct. Ask music buyers what they want and you only get more of the same' he said in a recent interview.

His elder brother Chris works for a leading management consultancy firm specialising in marketing work. Chris disagrees completely with Dave (on this as on many other things!) arguing 'the solution to all problems lies in the data. If you want to make sure you get it right you need to take a scientific approach to decision making. When I was being trained they taught me all about the marketing model and that's what I have stuck to throughout my career.'

1 Outline the key stages of the marketing model. *(8 marks)*

2 Dave and Chris have both been successful in their own fields and yet have very different views of how to make a good decision. Who is right? *(11 marks)*

Case study 2

Heather Conelly had been managing director of Look Out, a major clothing retailer, for many years. During that time she built up many excellent contacts and gained a tremendous experience of different aspects of the industry. Look Out focuses mainly on young female buyers and positions itself as being highly fashionable.

Heather has recently been headhunted by the board of Broadshires plc which is another clothing retailer but one which has been struggling since the late 1990s. Broadshires has been a much more mainstream retailer than Look Out aiming at rather conservative dressers looking for value for money. The company has targeted middle-aged buyers and families. In the past its clothes have been perceived as good quality if a little traditional. In the past couple of years, however, they have been criticised for being overpriced and dull.

Heather has been brought in to Broadshires to turn the company around. 'We'll give you the authority and resources if you give us the results' said the chairman of the board of directors.

One of the first things Heather knew she had to do was to analyse the firm's market position and consider its marketing strategy. She called in the senior managers to get their views. According to one of them 'the problem is that we have to check our data so many times and submit so many proposals before we are allowed to do anything that by the time we do act it's too late. Our stores don't stock what the customers want because by the time we've gathered and processed all our data they've changed their mind.' Heather listened carefully although she did not necessarily agree; at Look Out she had always insisted that decisions were supported by 'hard facts'. 'Give me the facts and nothing but the facts' was actually one of her favourite sayings! Another of the managers also commented on the bureaucracy and the lack of flair in the company – 'we take too long to act and what we do is predictable not unexpected. In the fashion game you've got to surprise people.'

1 Discuss the factors which might influence the new marketing strategy which Broadshires adopts.

(12 marks)

2 Should all marketing decisions be supported by 'hard facts'?

(12 marks)

MARKETING PLANNING

Starting points

On the AS course you will already have learnt about the concept of marketing planning. This included topics such as

- the marketing mix (eg pricing, promotion, distribution and product strategies and tactics)
- the concept of the elasticity of demand (eg price elasticity and income elasticity of demand.

In the A2 course you revisit the marketing mix and so it is important that you review your AS materials on this part of the specification. When considering the marketing mix at A2 it is important to analyse it in the context of the firm's marketing objectives and strategy. We will also be considering how the plan must be coordinated with the other business functions such as operations, people and finance.

On the A2 course we will also study

- the marketing budget, eg how much should a firm spend on marketing? What should its sales targets be?
- sales forecasting – ie how can a firm estimate its future sales?

These two topics will further develop your understanding of marketing planning. Obviously the marketing mix that a firm develops will depend in part on the finance it has available and the target or expected level of sales.

Marketing mix

The marketing mix is the combination of factors which influence a customer's decision about whether or not to buy a particular good or service. There are many different factors which make up the mix (think of all the things which influence your decision to buy the latest CD or computer game) but they are often categorised under the headings of

- price ie the amount the customer has to pay for the product

- promotion ie the way in which the firm communicates about the product (eg advertising, sales promotion, mailshots and via its salesforce)
- place ie the way in which the product is distributed
- product ie the actual good or service itself – its features, specifications, reliability and durability.

This approach to the marketing mix is known as the 4Ps model (Price, Promotion, Place and Product). Although quite a useful way of thinking of the mix remember that there are in fact many different reasons why you might buy something which may not necessarily be under these headings – eg you may be influenced by the people selling the product, past experiences at the store, whether you have to queue and the ease of payment. These different factors all come under the general heading of the marketing mix.

The role of the marketing mix is to implement the firm's marketing strategy. The strategy determines what goods and services are to be offered and in what markets. The mix determines how these products are presented to the customer.

The marketing mix should be linked directly to the strategy. If the strategy is to position the product at the upper end of the market this will influence the price charged, where the product is distributed, how the firm promotes the brand and the actual design of the product itself. A premium product, for example, is likely to have some form of USP, to be relatively highly priced and to be distributed through well-selected distribution

Figure 2.19

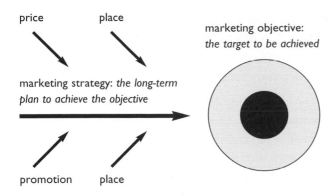

Figure 2.20

channels. If, on the other hand, the firm repositions the product towards the lower end of the market the product is likely to be sold at a lower price, to have a more basic design and to be more widely distributed.

The marketing mix will also be related to the particular stage which a product is at in the product life cycle. In the introduction stage, for example, there is likely to be a great emphasis on promotion to launch the product; the promotion will tend to be informative at this stage to let customers know that the product exists.

Later on the promotional budget may be reduced and the emphasis is more likely to be persuasive.

> **Key terms**
>
> **Product life cycle:** *this highlights the stages which most products go through during their life. These are: introduction, growth, maturity and decline.*

To be successful all of the elements of the marketing mix must be well integrated. This means that the price, promotion, place and product should complement each other. Imagine that when you go shopping you find a well-known brand selling at a very low price in a cheap discount store – you may be suspicious that it is a fake because the price does not fit with the brand image. Similarly a high-priced bottle of perfume will be unlikely to sell in a discount store because the elements do not fit together – the place is not complementing the price.

Marketing planning

Marketing planning involves developing the tactics necessary to implement the marketing strategy. It involves

- setting marketing targets
- developing the different elements of the mix to ensure they work together, planning what has to be achieved by when
- allocating funds to each activity ie deciding how big the overall marketing budget should be and how this should be divided up between different activities
- deciding on a time schedule ie what the firm hopes to achieve and by when.

> **Key terms**
>
> **Marketing budget:** *the total amount of money a firm allocates to marketing activities.*

Marketing planning is useful because

- by setting out in detail what it wants to achieve the firm should be in a better position to coordinate its activities
- managers can review the firm's progress by comparing the actual outcomes with the planned outcomes. If these are not the same it can analyse why and learn from this; this should then improve planning in the future

- the process of planning is useful in itself because it forces managers to think ahead and consider what might happen and what they need to do to succeed. This should make success more likely
- the plan should provide a sense of direction for all of those involved and help them to assess whether what they are doing is the right thing.

The possible drawbacks of marketing planning include:

- it is possible for the plan to become out of date because of changes in market conditions. In this case sticking to the plan can do more harm than good. Managers must be flexible and be prepared to review the plan regularly to see if it remains appropriate
- it may take up valuable time and delay decision making. The firm could spend so long planning that it actually misses out on opportunities.

*p*OINTS TO PONDER

'Paralysis by analysis' occurs when a firm takes so long analysing and planning that it never actually gets things done!

To evaluate a marketing plan managers must consider

- is it realistic? Can the firm actually achieve the goals which have been set?
- does it help ensure the strategy is achieved? To be

successful a plan must obviously help the firm to achieve its overall goals
- is it affordable? Does the firm have the finance necessary for it to work?

The ultimate test of any plan is, of course, whether it actually works! To some extent this is in the hands of the firm but it also depends on external factors. Even the most successful businessperson is usually willing to accept that luck played some part in his or her success. Succeeding when market conditions are against you is obviously more difficult than succeeding when the business climate is very favourable.

Marketing budget

A marketing budget is a quantifiable target which is set by a firm and which relates to its marketing activities. It may involve a target level of sales for a particular product (a sales budget) or set out the amount a firm intends to spend to achieve its marketing objectives (an expenditure budget). The sales budgets may include targets for the absolute level of sales a firm would like to achieve, or for a desired level of market share; they may also include targets for particular regions or for particular types of customers or distribution channels. Marketing expenditure budgets, by comparison, set out the desired amount of spending on activities such as advertising, sales promotions, paying the salesforce, direct mailings and market research.

The size of the sales budgets is likely to depend on:
- the level of sales a product has achieved in the past; a firm may extrapolate a future sales target based on past trends
- the expenditure budget; a firm may set a higher sales target if it is also intending to spend more on its marketing activities
- market conditions; actions by competitors and the state of the economy, may affect the firm's expected level of sales
- objectives and strategy; the target level of sales for a niche product is obviously likely to be lower than it is for a mass market product.

The size of the marketing expenditure budget will depend on
- the firm's overall financial position. The amount of money allocated to a particular function such

as marketing will inevitably depend on what it has available to spend in total. In a successful year it is easier to have a bigger budget than in an unsuccessful year. On this basis the marketing budget is likely to be lower when sales are lower and bigger when they are higher. This is often what actually happens within organisations although in many ways this is not a particularly sensible way to budget. In unsuccessful years the budget should arguably be higher (not lower) in order to improve the firm's sales, assuming of course that the firm can raise the funds needed to finance this. Unfortunately, though, the size of the budget does not just depend on what the firm would like it to be – it must depend on what the firm actually has available or what funds it can raise; as a result the budget may be lower at precisely the time when managers would like to increase it

- the firm's marketing objectives and strategy. The amount of money allocated for marketing activities should clearly depend on what the firm is trying to achieve and the returns it expects to gain from its plans. When first launching a product, for example, the promotional budget is likely to be higher than it is for a more established product. Similarly when first entering a new segment, spending on market research may be higher than in a 'normal' year.
- The amount the firm expects to receive back is also of critical importance: a firm is likely to be prepared to spend more marketing a project with a high rate of return than on one which has a low expected rate of return
- competitors. A firm's budget is very likely to be affected by the amount its competitors are spending. If its competitors increase their spending on product development or promotion, for example, a firm may feel it necessary to increase its own expenditure to maintain its competitive position.

Of course just because a firm has a large marketing budget does not mean that its marketing is necessarily more effective; the effectiveness of marketing activities will depend in part on the funds available but it will also depend on whether the right activities have been chosen in the first place and how effectively they are being implemented.

Setting the marketing budget

The marketing budget should be set in consultation with those who will be responsible for undertaking the activities it involves. The amount of money to be spent on marketing overall, for example, should be agreed with the marketing manager. Given that the marketing manager is the person who will be held accountable if the budget is not hit he or she would obviously be involved in deciding what the figure should be.

By involving the people who will actually have to achieve these financial targets the firm is more likely to gain their commitment. If instead people are simply told that they have to achieve certain targets without any prior discussion they are unlikely to feel much ownership of the budgets and as a result are unlikely to be committed to them. They may resent the fact they have not been involved in the process of setting the targets and consequently they may not be motivated to achieve them.

Furthermore the process of discussing the targets may well highlight important issues which the superiors need to be aware of; the people who implement the policies are the ones who are most likely to know what is and what is not feasible and it therefore makes sense to make use of their expertise.

However, it is important not to get involved with prolonged negotiations over the size of a budget if this delays decision making for too long. The process of budget setting can at times be quite slow and it is important to make sure it does not prevent managers from getting on with the job in hand.

Also superiors must be aware that subordinates may well try to set targets which suit themselves rather than the organisation. It is perfectly natural, for example, for people to exaggerate the likely costs of a project to make sure that they will be able to stay within their expenditure budgets. Similarly employees may set relatively low sales targets to make sure they are easy to hit.

It is also important for managers to consider the size of the marketing budget in the context of the overall spending and income of the firm. Resources diverted towards marketing are clearly not available for use elsewhere and so there is an opportunity cost which should be taken into account. As well as the overall size of the budget managers must also consider the timing of the payments and earnings in relation to the firm's overall cashflow position. A major marketing campaign, for example, may involve very heavy expenditure and managers must ensure this does not lead to liquidity problems.

Sales forecasting

A key element of a marketing plan is the sales forecast. This sets out targets for overall sales and for particular products and services. A sales forecast acts as a goal against which a firm can measure its progress. It also drives many other decisions within the firm. For example

- the production schedule will have to be closely linked to the sales forecasts to ensure the firm has the appropriate mix and number of products at the right time
- the sales forecast will also influence the cash flow forecast; only by knowing what sales are expected to occur can the finance department estimate cash inflows. Having compared the expected inflows with expected cash outflows the finance function can then decide if particular steps need to be taken such as arranging overdraft or loan facilities
- human resource decisions will also depend on the expected level of sales. Decisions about staffing levels and the allocation of staff to particular duties will inevitably be determined by the expected sales levels. Strong sales growth may require more recruitment, for example.

Producing a sales forecast

A sales forecast may be produced in a number of ways.

- It may be based on backdata (ie data from the past). The firm may look at sales levels in previous years, identify an underlying trend and extrapolate from this. A holiday company experiencing a fall in the number of enquiries in a particular month compared to past years may change its sales forecast downwards. This technique is useful, provided the trends identified in the past continue into the future. If, in fact, there has been a major shift in buying patterns (eg the timing of buying has changed) extrapolation could be misleading.
- The firm may use market research to try to identify likely future trends. The value of this research depends on whether it is primary or secondary and the quality of the information. If a small sample is used, for example, the forecast is less likely to be accurate than if a larger sample had been used.
- It may be based on the firm's best guess. Managers could use their own experience or hire industry experts for their opinion of what is most likely to happen. This approach to forecasting is common if the rate of change in the market is great or if the firm is facing a new scenario and does not have past data to build on.

p OINTS TO PONDER

One method of forecasting is known as the Delphi technique. With this method firms individually ask experts for their opinion of what will happen in the market. These views are analysed and summarised. The findings are then circulated to each expert to get their views. Once again the findings are summarised and sent out. The idea behind this system is that by asking each expert individually they will not be influenced by the others' views. By sending out the findings several times the group should gradually move towards a consensus of what will happen.

The method of forecasting used by a firm will depend on the nature of the product and the market situation. When the National Lottery was launched in the UK, for example, Camelot (the organiser of

Business in Focus

With 110 shopping days before Christmas the rush for 2000's hottest stocking filler began at midnight when Sony's much hyped Playstation 2 console became available to order. As demand was expected to exceed supply by up to four times the Japanese electronics giant decided to use an elaborate pre-ordering system to allocate the video games machines on a first come first served basis before they hit the UK stores.

Games fans were asked to leave a deposit at high street retailers such as HMV and Virgin to reserve the £299 console. There was a limit of one console per household. Customers received letters confirming they had joined the list. Then a second letter told them which week their console became available and a third letter told them exactly when and where to pick it up. The pre-ordering system made buying a Playstation almost as lengthy as buying a house!

Sony's marketing manager at the time said 'we are not sure about how many consoles will arrive in the UK by Christmas but we are hoping to get around 200,000.' At £299 each the company hoped to sell 100,000 on the first day of the release – five times as many as the first Playstation sold on its UK launch. This compares with Japan where 1m were sold on the first day of release. At 6.2bn mathematical operations per second the Playstation 2 can create three dimensional scenes with almost photo realistic quality. It is equipped with DVD and has a facility to connect to the internet. At the time of launch the games market was in the middle of a transformation with the arrival of four new console formats: Sony's Playstation 2, Microsoft's X Box, Nintendo's Dolphin and the Sega Dreamcast.

The Financial Times

1 Sony forecasted high sales and yet its planned production was not high enough to meet the expected initial demand. Why might this be the case?

the lottery) could have forecast sales by looking at existing national lottery systems in other countries and adjusting these data to take account of the differences in culture and the precise nature of the system in the UK. Camelot might also have used secondary research to identify gambling trends within the UK and primary research to identify customers' likely reaction to the lottery scheme. However, although the company probably used very sophisticated research techniques it is likely there was also an element of hunch in there too. After all, it was a completely new product within the UK and so there were no past data within this country to build on. Obviously once the lottery had been up and running for a few months the organisers were able to make better predictions of expected weekly sales because they were accumulating backdata and gaining a better insight into the market.

*P*OINTS TO PONDER

Health service managers are planning to avoid a repeat of the bed crises which have occurred in the past by using weathering reports to forecast when people will fall ill. The Meteorological Office has set up a unit using new technology to give doctors up to two weeks' notice of how many patients are likely to develop bronchitis, heart attacks and strokes. The service which claimed to be the world's first will allow hospitals and surgeries to prepare for increases in demand using warnings generated by a supercomputer.

In 1999 the National Health Service was caught out by sudden changes in the number of patients suffering respiratory and cardio vascular diseases. Meteorological Office experts say the timing was due almost entirely to changes in temperature and climatic conditions. According to a spokesperson 'there is a very close link between weather conditions and illness. We can predict almost the day when large numbers of patients will seek treatment.'

More patients die in Britain from weather related illnesses than almost any other country in western Europe. For every one degree fall in temperature 1.37% more people die; this is much higher than in other countries because the British are less well prepared; they do not dress warmly against the cold, their houses are less well heated or insulated and they take less exercise.

The Sunday Times

Test marketing

To help predict its future sales a firm may decide to try out a product or service in a test market. A test market is a representative selection of consumers which the firm uses to try out a new product. Having seen the results in the test market the firm can estimate how the product might sell elsewhere and product a sales forecast. By using a test market the firm can see customers' reactions before committing to a full-scale launch. If necessary, changes can still be made before the product is widely available. Many film companies, for example, show their films to a test audience before they go on general release to assess the public's reaction.

The disadvantage of using test marketing is that competitors have an opportunity to see what you are planning to launch. This gives them time to develop a similar product and race you to launch first on a wide scale.

A test market may also give misleading results. This might be because the test market chosen is not representative or because competitors' actions lead to misleading results. For example, rivals might increase their promotional activities in the test market to reduce a firm's sales and lead it to believe that the new product will not do well.

Why might forecasts be wrong?

Forecasts can only be predictions of the future. They may well be wrong because

- customer-buying behaviour changes suddenly, eg customers suddenly decide a product is unsafe or unfashionable
- the original market research was poor. This may be because the sample was too small or was unrepresentative. Alternatively it may be because

the results were wrongly interpreted; this could be because the firm was in a rush to launch the product. In some cases the research may actually have been ignored – managers may have been certain that they knew best and gone ahead with the decision regardless of the findings of market research

- the experts were wrong; even the best-informed people can misread a situation and make mistakes – just look at the predictions of so-called experts before any horse race or football match or look at the many different and often conflicting forecasts of growth in the economy that are often published in the papers.

Inevitably a firm's external and internal conditions are likely to change and this can make it extremely difficult to estimate future sales. However, this does not necessarily make forecasting a useless management tool. The simple process of forecasting makes managers think ahead and plan for different scenarios. This may help to ensure they are much better prepared for change than if they did not forecast at all.

Also even though a forecast may not be exactly accurate it may give an indication of the direction in which sales are moving and some sense of the magnitude of future sales which can help a firm's planning. Ultimately it may not matter much whether sales are 2,000,002 units or 2,000,020 units but it makes a big difference whether they are 2m or 4m in terms of staffing, finance and production levels ie provided the forecast is approximately right it can still be very useful even if it is not exactly correct.

It is also important to remember that sales forecasts can be updated. A firm does not have to make a forecast and leave it there. As conditions change and new information feeds in, the managers can update the forecast and adjust accordingly.

*P*OINTS TO PONDER

In 2000 the Hatfield train disaster led to a re-examination of safety on the railways. This led to many services being cancelled whilst the track was improved and also to a reduction in the speed at which many trains travelled. Soon after, floods caused problems to the train service. The effect of all this was to lead to a decline in the number of passengers by up to 50%. Companies such as Virgin which had invested up to £2bn in new trains found their original forecasts which had predicted a significant growth in sales were sadly optimistic. This highlights how unexpected events can make sales forecasts inaccurate and force the firm to re-examine its plans.

EXAMINER'S ADVICE

If you are given forecasted data in the exam do not be afraid to question its source. It can be important to know who has made these estimates and how the forecast has been drawn up. At the same time whilst being willing to question do try and appreciate the value of forecasting – if you were having a party you would want some idea of how many people were coming. You may get it wrong – you may find that some of the people you invited bring their friends or that your party clashed with someone else's but if you have no idea at all of how many might turn up you are more likely to find you do not have enough room, enough food or enough drink. The chances are that if you do try and forecast the number of guests you will not get it absolutely correct but it is likely to be roughly right; if you do run out of food and drink you know better for next time!

The reliability of forecasts

Forecasts are most likely to be correct when

- a trend has been extrapolated and the market conditions have continued as before
- a test market is used and is truly representative of the target population
- the forecast is made by experts (such as your own salesforces) and they have good insight into the market and future trends.
- the firm is forecasting for the near future. It is usually easier to estimate what sales will be next week compared to estimating sales in five years' time.

Marketing planning and other functions

The marketing plan will have a direct effect on other functions within the firm. A reduction in price to increase sales, for example, may require investment in production equipment and greater recruitment or training. A decision to cease production of a particular brand may leave the firm with excess capacity, less revenue and the need to make redundancies.

At the same time the marketing plan will also depend on these functions. For example, if a firm has a highly skilled workforce it may be able to build this into its promotional activities (think of football clubs and the way they promote their star players). The talents of the staff may also affect the design of the product – just think of the importance of designers in the software business. A firm's financial position is also important: a business with a strong financial position is more likely to be able to finance new product development than one with limited funds, for example. The production system can also make a difference: the capacity, the flexibility and the quality of the production will inevitably influence the nature of the marketing plan.

EXAMINER'S ADVICE

When assessing a marketing plan consider the objectives – does the plan actually achieve what the firm wants to achieve? Also think about the returns – is it worth the given level of investment? Also consider all the other functions of the business – is it possible to produce the desired sales levels? Can the firm achieve the right mix of specifications given the target price? Can it finance the promotional campaign?

Progress questions

1 What is meant by marketing planning? *(2 marks)*

2 Explain two factors which might determine a firm's marketing plan. *(6 marks)*

3 Explain two ways in which the other business functions might be affected by a change in a firm's marketing plan. *(6 marks)*

4 Explain what is meant by the marketing mix. *(3 marks)*

5 What is meant by a marketing budget? *(2 marks)*

6 Explain two factors which might determine the size of a firm's marketing budget. *(6 marks)*

7 What is meant by a sales forecast? *(2 marks)*

8 What is meant by backdata? *(2 marks)*

9 Explain two ways in which a firm might forecast its sales of one of its products. *(6 marks)*

10 Explain two problems a firm might face when forecasting the sales of one of its products. *(6 marks)*

Analysis and evaluation questions

1 ChillOut is a producer of frozen foods. Analyse the possible benefits of sales forecasting to a firm such as ChillOut. *(8 marks)*

2 Examine the possible reasons why a firm might change its marketing plan. *(8 marks)*

3 Xtreme plc produces computer software games targeted mainly at the 16–20 age group. Discuss the possible problems Xtreme might have forecasting its sales. *(12 marks)*

4 Which is the most important element of the marketing mix? *(12 marks)*

5 Discuss the ways in which a change in a firm's marketing plan can affect the other functions of the business. *(12 marks)*

Case study 1

Scrummy is a leading brand of crisps in the UK snack market. It was launched five years ago and now has a market share of 18%. It has a very distinctive packaging and a strong brand image. Scrummy sells at a price premium of nearly 10% compared to its nearest rivals. The product sells well throughout the year although sales are slightly higher in the winter months. Scrummy's manufacturer now wants to launch another product under the same brand name. At the moment the firm's marketing manager is trying to decide on the marketing expenditure budget for the new product.

1 Consider how the managers of Scrummy might decide on the size of the marketing expenditure budget for the new product. *(8 marks)*

2 Examine the key elements which might be included in a marketing plan for the product launch of the new product. *(8 marks)*

3 Discuss the ways in which the producer of Scrummy's forecast might forecast the sales of its new product for the first few years. *(11 marks)*

Case study 2

Charlotte Williams had been interested in the internet from the age of about 12. She would stay online for hours on end much to the annoyance of her parents who always told her she should be doing more school work and that their phone bill was way too high. In fact she did quite well at school although even she admits she probably could have done a little bit better if she had spent more time in front of her books and less time in front of the computer screen. 'You have to balance work and relaxation' she said 'but it's possible the balance swung a little bit too much one way! However, it was all good research.' And indeed it was, for when she left school she went on to set up her own website which was aimed at students her own age. She was helped by her best friend who was good at the programming side of things. On the website students could sign on, chat and pick up the latest news about what was happening on the music, fashion or film scenes.

The number of visits to the site grew very rapidly and Charlotte realised she actually had something which could be very big indeed. If only she knew how to market it properly she could make money by selling advertising space. It was obvious that this sort of site could be of great interest to firms wanting to target this age group. Charlotte was determined to make this one of the most popular sites on the net. 'My marketing objective is to make this the first site students visit when they want to know what's going on and I want to achieve this within the next three years.' She said. If only she knew how to develop and market it properly. Charlotte's mother who ran her own business told her that the best thing to do was to produce a marketing plan and then approach potential investors and advertisers.

1 Charlotte is considering producing a marketing plan for her new business. Consider the possible elements that Charlotte might include in her marketing plan. *(12 marks)*
2 Discuss the problems that Charlotte might have forecasting the sales revenue for her business. *(12 marks)*

Case study 3

Paul Santorini is the manager of a local branch of Supasave, a national supermarket chain. The managers of Supasave stores have considerable freedom over their ordering of goods and Paul is trying to decide how many items to order for the coming weeks. This obviously depends on the store's sales forecast; the forecast also affects many other aspects of the business. Paul is well used to producing such sales forecasts and is generally pleased with how accurate these prove to be; however, experience has shown they are not always correct and that he has to be ready to act quickly if they are too high or low.

1 Analyse the ways in which Paul might forecast sales of products within the store for the coming week. *(8 marks)*
2 Discuss the possible reasons why Paul's sales forecasts may prove inaccurate. *(12 marks)*
3 If Paul's sales forecast turns out to be too high
   a) examine the possible implications of this for his store *(8 marks)*
   b) discuss the actions he might take. *(12 marks)*

Case study 4

Fortunas is a leading publisher of business and economics books aimed at manages eager to know more about the business world and looking for promotion. Over the past 20 years the firm has built up a reputation for providing easy-to-read, entertaining books. Their best-selling titles include *Be a better manager – NOW!* and *Climbing the corporate ladder.* Fortunas has built up an established list of best-selling publications written by leading authors in their field; its overall sales are now around £87m. With increasing numbers of people apparently interested in understanding their own businesses more fully and getting promoted rapidly Fortunas' sales have grown rapidly. However, Jake Scott, the company's ambitious chief executive, is eager to push the company forward even faster. He wants to make his name at the firm and believes this is best done through sales growth. 'Investors always tend to look at the top line – you've got to keep revenue growing. We may be riding high on one wave but we've got to keep an eye out for the next one if we want to move forward' he said.

Jake is known as something of a 'ideas' man who tends to come up with at least five new ideas a day most of which are forgotten by the next morning but he is determined to push his latest idea through. He believes the company should attack the educational market starting with business textbooks aimed at sixth formers. 'We've gradually built our market share in the easy-to-read book market for managers – now let's move down to the 16-to 18-year-old market' he said at last month's planning meeting. 'It's not as easy as that' said Donna, the marketing manager. 'This market is very different from the one we're used to. Remember that the schools tend to buy the books for the students so we're selling to the teachers not the final consumer. In the past we've distributed through book shops and retailers such as WH Smith; this time we've got to convince the teachers to buy, which requires a very different type of strategy for our salesforce. Also we've got to help teachers to keep within their departmental budgets; sales could be very sensitive to government spending in this area. Also think how different our promotion will have to be. To make matters worse there's a lot of change in the market at the moment with the new AS and A level system.'

'Don't worry about it – one business book is pretty much like another and we're the market leader in the segment we are in. We've some of the best business writers there are. We've also got all the experience you could want in publishing – we know how to commission books, how to print and how to get books out at the right time. As for the changes in the market this means it is just the right time to enter.' Donna still looked concerned. 'Relax Donna' said Jake. 'I've looked at those charts you've shown me about the trend in this market and if we extrapolate forward it looks to me like we are bound to be on a winner. I've done some projections based on these trends and we can plan everything else around this. Once we've established ourselves in this niche we can then either broaden into other six-form areas or push up into universities. The other thing we need to do is to look more closely at our existing market to squeeze every last pound of profit we can out of it. I think a detailed correlation analysis could help us here.'

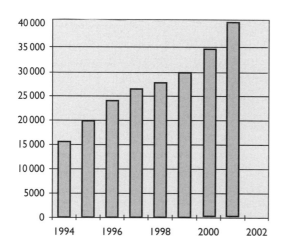

Figure 2.21 *Number of students entering for business studies A level*

1 a) Examine the value of extrapolation to a firm such as Fortunas. *(8 marks)*

  b) Discuss the ways in which a marketing analysis might benefit a firm such as Fortunas. *(12 marks)*

2 a) Analyse the factors which may be correlated with the sale of business studies textbooks. *(8 marks)*

  b) To what extent could correlation analysis help

Fortunas in its marketing planning within its existing market? *(12 marks)*

3 a) Examine the factors which might influence Fortunas' marketing strategy. *(8 marks)*

  b) Do you think Jake's strategy to enter the textbook market is right for Fortunas? *(12 marks)*

4 a) Examine the key elements of a marketing plan for a firm such as Fortunas. *(8 marks)*

  b) Produce a marketing plan for Fortunas if the firm decides to enter the textbook market. *(12 marks)*

Case study 5

'I knew I was right. The minute I thought of it I knew it was a winner. It was just an ongoing battle with the banks and investors at every stage to convince them this would work as well' says Zara. 'It was obvious that people were working harder and that there were more couples where both had jobs. People just don't have the time any more to get things done around the house. I was talking to some friends and they all agreed that what we needed was someone who would handle all the jobs around the house – basically if we needed some building doing or some decorating or there was a problem with the fridge or the cooker which needed fixing we would ring a number and they'd look after it. So I thought why not set it up? I was bored with my job in banking and it was time to take a few risks. The first thing I needed was a team of people who could be relied on to provide a good service. I spent a lot of time checking people out – they had to be good at what they did and good with customers. I knew from my own experience that people are suspicious of builders and repair people and always think they are being charged too much so we had to provided a professional and trustworthy image. I obviously couldn't hire people full-time at first so I paid them a retainer to ensure they dealt with my jobs first. I had no real idea of the size of the market at this stage, I just knew it could work and my friends thought so as well although they thought I was mad to do it!

'Business was slow at first but we learnt along the way – where to advertise, how best to promote the service. Basically I just tried something and saw if it worked – we soon learnt what was a waste of time. We got an idea of prices by ringing around and getting quotes from people out of the Yellow Pages. Obviously we were providing a premium service so I took their price and just added a bit on! At times we were probably lucky – we happened to start at the beginning of a boom which made it easier and gave us the chance to learn along the way. But we also listened to customers – I always followed up every job to make sure they were happy and to see what else they wanted. Half the time though customers don't know what they want until you give it to them! When we moved into more general personal services it was another piece of inspiration – I knew I was fed up taking things to the dry cleaners, getting my films developed, taking things to the rubbish tip and I thought if I would pay someone to do it so would others.'

1 a) Analyse the possible value of market analysis to Zara. *(8 marks)*

  b) Discuss the key factors an entrepreneur such as Zara might want to know about before entering a market. *(12 marks)*

2 a) Examine the benefits of sales forecasting to a firm such as Zara's. *(8 marks)*

  b) Discuss the possible problems for Zara of forecasting its future sales. *(12 marks)*

3 a) Outline the key elements of a scientific approach to marketing. *(8 marks)*

  b) To what extent can Zara's success be explained by a scientific approach to marketing? *(12 marks)*

4 How important is price likely to be in determining the success of Zara's business? *(20 marks)*

Finance and Accounts

Introduction

As with all topics in A2 business studies you will have studied some elements of this subject during your AS level course. The major elements you will have studied are as follows:

- classifying costs – eg fixed and variable costs
- the concept of contribution (selling price less variable costs)
- break-even analysis using calculations and charts
- the management of cash flow and the distinction between cash flow and profit
- sources of finance
- budgets and variance analysis
- an introduction to published accounts (this is **not** on the AQA AS specification, however).

The A2 specification for business studies builds upon the subject knowledge and skills acquired during the AS programme. It is worthwhile looking back over your AS materials before starting to study A2 finance and accounts. More specific advice is given on any prior knowledge required at the outset of each unit.

During your A2 programme you will study

- break-even in greater detail, including issues such as special order decisions
- company accounts in detail, considering their structure and interrelationships and topics such as depreciation, working capital and window dressing
- ratio analysis – a technique used to analyse company accounts
- investment decision making – looking at financial and non-financial factors considered by businesses before taking a decision on whether to undertake major investments.

CONTRIBUTION AND BREAK-EVEN ANALYSIS

Starting points

This unit builds upon work carried out as part of the AS course. Whilst studying AS, you will have encountered the following:

- the concept of contribution
- the notion of break-even output
- how to use contribution to calculate break-even output

- the construction of diagrams to illustrate break-even output
- reading profit and loss from break-even charts

This unit builds upon that work. It would be advisable to re-read the relevant sections from your AS book before commencing this unit.

Contribution

The concept of contribution was an important one within AS business studies and was used in calculating break-even point. We saw that it can be calculated by use of the following formula.

| sales | minus | variable costs | equals | CONTRIBUTION |

Contribution has two potential uses: first, it is available to pay fixed costs incurred by a business. Secondly, any contribution which remains after this transaction is profit for the business.

| contribution | minus | fixed costs | equals | PROFIT |

Contribution is also important in calculating break-even output and is a central element of the formula used.

Calculating contribution and profits

It is possible to consider contribution in two broad ways – either in relation to a single unit of output or in relation to the entire output of a particular product or business.

1 Contribution can be calculated for the sale of a single product. We refer to this as contribution per unit. It is calculated by using the formula

contribution per unit = selling price of one unit of output − variable cost of producing that unit

For example, the South Hams Brewery produces its beer at a variable cost of £1.50 a pint and sells it for £2.00 per pint. The contribution earned from the sale of each pint (or unit) will be 50 pence.

2 It is possible to calculate the contribution made by the sale of an entire product (or product range) over some period, say one year. Thus, if the South Hams Brewery sells 10 000 pints per month then it will generate £5000 in the form of contribution. The brewery uses contribution to pay fixed costs. Once fixed costs have been paid, the remaining contribution is profit.

Thus profit = contribution − fixed costs

If the South Hams Brewery sells 70 000 pints each month its revenue equals £140 000. Variable costs will be £105 000 at this level of output giving a contribution of £35 000 (£140 000 − £105 000). Fixed costs = £25 000.

Profit = £35 000 − £25 000 = £10 000

We can develop our example of the South Hams Brewery further to emphasise the way in which contribution is calculated and how it changes along with the level of output. The revenue, costs, contribution and profits earned at various levels of output are shown in table 3.1.

output per month (pints of beer)	revenue (at £2 per pint)	variable costs (at £1.50 per pint)	contribution £	profit (loss)
0	0	0	0	(25 000)
10 000	20 000	15 000	5 000	(20 000)
20 000	40 000	30 000	10 000	(15 000)
30 000	60 000	45 000	15 000	(10 000)
40 000	80 000	60 000	20 000	(5 000)
50 000	100 000	75 000	25 000	0
60 000	120 000	90 000	30 000	5 000
70 000	140 000	105 000	35 000	10 000
80 000	160 000	120 000	40 000	15 000

Fixed costs = £25 000 each month

Table 3.1 *South Hams Brewery – profits and contribution*

POINTS TO PONDER

The Post Office is seeking to increase its profitability by reducing fixed costs as it becomes subject to price controls once the newly formed Postal Services Commission becomes operative from 2001. Post Office executives believe that huge cuts in fixed overheads can be achieved by hiring private sector organisations to carry out activities such as security, training and personnel work.

The South Hams Brewery needs to produce (and sell!) at least 50 000 pints of beer each month in order to break even. At this point the contribution is just sufficient to pay the fixed costs faced by the business and thus nothing is available to provide profit. Hence, the business breaks even. At higher levels of output contribution is greater than fixed costs resulting in the business generating a profit. Confirm your understanding of this by calculating the monthly profit earned by the brewery if fixed costs rise to £30 000 and the firm sells 90 000 pints each month.

Contribution can be used to calculate the level of profits for a business producing a number of products. It can also provide managers with a clearer perspective of the performance of a particular business – or part of a business. We consider this more fully in the example of Marlborough Pottery later.

Contribution costing and pricing

Contribution costing

Contribution costing excludes fixed costs as a central part of the calculation. The principle of contribution costing is valuable in a business that has a number of products, or several factories or divisions. A product or division that earns sufficient revenue to cover its fixed costs is likely to be viewed favourably by the managers of the business. If this is the case then the product will generate a positive contribution and assist in paying fixed costs or providing profit.

In the example shown in table 3.2 products A and B generate a positive contribution that is available to pay fixed costs and provide profits. Product C incurs variable costs that are higher than the revenue earned and will not therefore help to pay fixed costs. It may be appropriate to abandon this product, but a final decision will depend upon a number of factors, including the following:

Product	A	B	C
Revenue (£m)	242	158	485
Variable costs (£m)	175	98	488
Contribution (£m)	67	60	(3)

Table 3.2 *An example of contribution costing*

Integrated Business: Marlborough Pottery

This company makes a range of products that are sold in gift shops throughout the UK. The business has a reputation for high-quality products and traditionally has sold to a market segment comprising older consumers, mainly female. Overall sales have declined slowly in recent years.

The company has three product lines: mugs and cups, plates and vases. The managers of the company have been concerned for some time that their business is not sufficiently profitable and is vulnerable to competition from larger European firms.

In particular the management team has been dissatisfied with the profits generated by the sale of vases. The production manager has argued that the line should be discontinued if the company is to improve its profitability. He argues that if the company's fixed costs are divided equally between the three product lines, it is obvious that vases are not a profitable item.

Product	mugs and cups £000s	plates £000s	vases £000s	total £000s
Sales revenue	575	450	227	1252
Less variable costs	352	326	189	867
Less fixed costs	101	101	101	303
Profit	**122**	**23**	**(63)**	**82**

Table 3.3

Other managers hold different views. The finance manager offers a different presentation of the data on cost and revenues. She argues that Marlborough Pottery would still face the same fixed costs and that to sell more mugs, cups or plates would require a price cut.

It can be seen (table 3.4) that all the products make a positive contribution. In other words their revenues or earnings exceed the variable costs of production (labour fuel, raw materials etc.). A decision to shut down the production of vases would reduce profits unless the production of other products could be

Product	mugs and cups £000s	plates £000s	vases £000s	total £000s
Sales revenue	575	450	227	1252
Less variable costs	352	326	189	867
Contribution	**223**	**124**	**38**	**385**
Fixed costs				303
Profit				**82**

Table 3.4

increased. Table 3.4 shows the contribution earned by each of the Pottery's product lines as well as overall profits. The financial consequences of this decision are illustrated as follows

Product	mugs and cups £000s	plates £000s
Sales revenue	575	450
Less variable costs	352	326
Contribution	**223**	**124**
Fixed costs		
Profit		

Table 3.5

Cutting what appears to be a relatively unprofitable line may not be worthwhile unless fixed costs will be reduced (eg through the sale of a factory) or the production and sale of other products increased. The concept of contribution has been helpful in calculating the profits of the business and also in making decisions based upon financial data.

1 a) Using the data in the case study, calculate the effects on the company's profits of a decision to discontinue the production of vases.*(5 marks)*
   b) Examine the assumptions that may have been made as a part of your answer to the previous question. *(10 marks)*
2 Discuss the marketing actions that Marlborough Pottery could take to improve its financial position. *(15 marks)*
3 The opening up of the European market is often presented as an opportunity as well as a threat. Do you think this is true of a company such as Marlborough Pottery? Justify your answer.

(20 marks)

- whether demand for the product may increase in the future, or if higher prices can be charged
- if the firm can increase its output of other products to use any spare capacity it may have, it may cease producing one product
- whether fixed costs will fall as a consequence of the decision
- the impact of the decision on the business – eg the effects on industrial relations, corporate image and productivity resulting from redundancies.

But would the business in table 3.2 make a profit? The answer to this depends upon the level of fixed costs incurred by the firm. The total contribution earned by the three products is (£67m + £60m – £3m) £124m. In these circumstances if fixed costs are less than £124m, the firm will make a profit. If they exceed £124m, a loss will result.

However, this approach to costing is based upon the business's ability to categorise its costs as fixed and variable. In many cases this is straightforward, but some expenses are most accurately classified as semi-variable. Thus, the costs of operating delivery vehicles contain fixed elements (insurance and vehicle excise duty do not vary according to the usage of the lorry) whilst fuel costs and drivers' wages are clearly variable. The existence of such semi-variable costs makes it difficult to calculate contribution accurately.

Contribution pricing

The concept of contribution is also useful when taking pricing decisions. If the manager or owner of a business sets a price in excess of the variable cost of producing the product, then each sale will make a positive contribution to fixed costs. If sufficient sales are made, the enterprise will earn a profit.

Thus the manager of a restaurant may calculate that the typical variable cost of serving a meal to a customer is £12. If the restaurant charges customers an average price of £25 for each meal, then it will make a profit so long as it attracts enough diners. It is certain that the revenue received from each customer will contribute £13 (£25−£12) towards fixed costs.

Contribution pricing offers firms flexibility when deciding upon the amount to charge for their products. Businesses that have well-established

products in high demand may be able to price significantly in excess of the variable cost of production. In these circumstances each sale makes a major contribution to fixed costs and profits. Fashion clothing is an example of a product where prices are set considerably above variable costs. Thus Ellesse might charge £40 for a T-shirt that costs £10 to manufacture. The contribution of £30 from each sale is necessary because the firm faces high fixed costs, spending heavily, for example, on marketing. Furthermore, products in the fashion industry have very short lives.

However, contribution pricing has its weaknesses. Whilst setting a price that generates a positive contribution may result in the firm earning a profit, this depends upon the business in question achieving sufficient sales. This is far from certain as this approach to pricing places relatively little emphasis on the state of the market. Using contribution as a guide for pricing may result in low levels of sales because competitors' prices are lower or their responses may be unpredictable.

*P*OINTS TO PONDER

BSkyB has imposed price increases of nearly 40% on pubs wishing to show its television service to customers. The company has increased prices to maximise the contribution from this aspect of its operations to help pay the £1.1bn that was necessary to win the contract to broadcast Premier League football. As a consequence Bass has withdrawn BSkyB's service from 1500 of its pubs and is considering the position of 1100 others.

Special order decisions

Businesses sometimes have to make decisions on whether to accept orders that are not on their normal terms. Thus a firm might receive a large order for its products at a price significantly lower than it usually receives. Alternatively a business might receive an order which offers a price above the usual, but which requires special features or a very early delivery date meaning the supplier is likely to incur additional costs in fulfilling the order.

Firms faced with the dilemma of whether to accept this type of order are encountering special order decisions. In these circumstances the concept of contribution can be applied to assist the business in reaching a decision on whether or not to accept the order.

(a) Prices lower than normal

It is not unusual for a firm to receive an order for a large quantity of its products at a price below that normally charged. Consider the following example.

Margaret Roberts Ltd is based in Wales and manufactures sweaters and other woollen garments for local shops at a standard price of £40. The sweaters are very popular with tourists and sell for high prices, particularly during the summer season. The cost of wool and the wages paid to knitters means that the average variable cost of producing a single woollen garment is £30. To the surprise of the managing director of the firm a large order is received from a national clothes retailer. The retailer requires 5000 sweaters and other garments, but is only willing to pay Margaret Roberts Ltd £32 per item. Should the firm accept the order?

Contribution is the key to this question. The firm would earn a positive contribution on each sale. Each woollen item sold would incur variable costs of £30, but would earn revenue of £32. Thus each sale would create £2 of contribution. Therefore, meeting the order would earn the business an additional £10 000 in contribution. This **might** mean profits would rise (or losses would fall) by £10 000.

But a number of factors need to be taken into account when taking special order decisions such as this.

■ Will additional fixed costs result from accepting the order? In the circumstances Margaret Roberts Ltd may have to hire additional factory space increasing fixed costs, meaning that additional contribution is required to meet these fixed costs before extra profits are earned. Thus if the firm has to pay an extra £10 000 in rent profits will be unchanged as a result of accepting the order. Having sufficient spare capacity is an important prerequisite of accepting such an order.
■ Might the order lead to higher variable costs?

Accepting a large order might mean that workers are paid overtime pushing up variable costs. Workers at Margaret Roberts Ltd might be paid higher hourly rates meaning that the variable cost of producing a single item rises to £35. In these circumstances the order would probably not be worth accepting.

■ Before accepting a special order decision (at a price below the norm) a business needs to ensure that the customer will not simply resell the product to other firms at the usual selling price thereby making a quick profit at the expense of the manufacturer.
■ A business may accept a lower price than normal, even if it doesn't produce a positive contribution, if it believes that it will result in more sales at higher prices in the future.

EXAMINER'S ADVICE

Questions on special order decisions are very common (and easy to set!). However, when responding to them it is important to consider non-financial factors as well as financial ones. Read the case study or stimulus material carefully to ensure you pick up on any non-financial factors the examiner may have included as clues.

(b) Prices higher than normal

It may appear a stroke of good fortune for a business to receive an order at a price above that usually levied. However, if the order requires products to have a specification higher than normal or to be delivered at short notice it is likely that the supplier will face higher costs. This may make the order unprofitable.

Once again contribution is the key to the decision. If the selling price exceeds the variable cost and no additional fixed costs are incurred, the order would be worthwhile and would result in increased profits. Thus if Margaret Roberts Ltd had an order for a new style of sweater which needed more expensive wool than normal and had to be complete within six weeks, the firm would need to

■ calculate the extra variable costs associated with the order – overtime for workers and more expensive materials, for example
■ consider whether they have sufficient spare capacity to meet the order – avoiding additional fixed costs

strengths	weaknesses
■ assists managers in multi-product firms in making decisions by giving an overview of the entire business ■ avoids the need for the arbitrary division of fixed costs ■ can provide a flexible basis for pricing decisions	■ pricing decisions based on contribution do not take market conditions into account ■ some costs are difficult to classify as fixed or variable ■ in the longer term fixed costs can change invalidating earlier decisions based on contribution

Table 3.6 *Contribution and decision making: strengths and weaknesses*

■ decide whether accepting the order would generate extra contribution and profits.

Business in Focus

In late November 2000 British Airways announced that it intended to sell *Go* its subsidiary airline noted for offering low-cost flights to European destinations. The announcement coincided with the company revealing improved profits for the previous three months.

A spokesperson commented: 'Thanks to everyone who works at *Go*, it is now a leading European brand. It has made a profit every month this year. However, given the strategic goals we have set for the group as a whole, now is the time for British Airways to gain the benefits of its investment and realise the considerable value it has created in *Go*.'

The company is seeking to concentrate on its most profitable routes (mainly long haul) and to allow franchises to operate flights to European destinations.

Adapted from FT.com

I The sale of *Go* is part of a long-term strategy by British Airways. To what extent does this decision indicate that historical data (such as that provided by contribution figures) is relatively unimportant in influencing corporate strategy?

BREAK-EVEN

Key terms

Break-even is that level of production at which a firm's sales generate just enough revenue to cover all the costs of production.

*The **margin of safety** is the amount by which a firm's current level of output exceeds the level of output necessary to break even.*

At break-even level of output a business will make neither a loss nor a profit. From identifying this level of production or output the managers of a firm can make two other important judgements.

1. At levels of production below break-even output the business will make a loss ie costs will be higher than revenues.
2. At higher production levels revenues will exceed costs and a profit will be made.

POINTS TO PONDER

Even some of the world's largest firms can struggle to break even. The US giant Wal-Mart is arguably the largest retail group in the world, yet does not expect to break even on its European operations until the end of 2002, several years after entering the competitive European retail market.

Break-even analysis is a simple technique that can be used by managers with relatively little financial knowledge or training. Firms may use break-even analysis to

- determine whether a proposed business idea may be viable
- assess the likely impact of change on the level of production
- support an application to a financial institution for a loan.

Break-even output may be determined through a calculation or by the construction of a diagram.

Whichever approach is used, the concept of contribution plays an important part in the process. The formula used to calculate break-even output is set out as follows.

$$\text{Break-even output} = \frac{\text{fixed costs}}{\text{contribution per unit}}$$

POINTS TO PONDER

Ladbroke, the betting and hotels group, has announced that the contribution from *Easy Play*, its football-based lottery game, is just breaking even. The company commented that it was disappointed with sales of the product that only generate sufficient contribution to cover its fixed costs.

Alternatively the level of production required to break even can be determined and illustrated and shown on a graph as in figure 3.1.

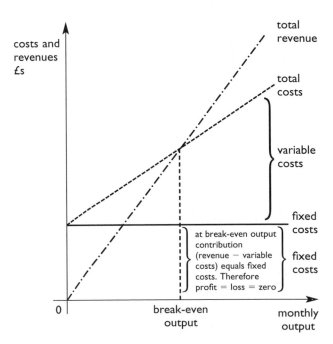

Figure 3.1 *Determining break-even output by use of a chart*

Business in Focus: Somerfield admits defeat in store wars

Supermarket group Somerfield has announced that it is to sell about 500 of its 1422 stores as it admitted that it could no longer compete with Tesco and Sainsbury's for the 'big trolley shopper'. The 500 or so stores that the company plans to sell during the last financial year contributed about half of the group's £5.9bn sales and half its contribution to fixed overheads.

The company intends to focus on approximately 850 convenience stores and expects to shed over 1000 jobs amongst its 4500 head office and distribution staff. The stores earmarked for disposal by Somerfield made an estimated contribution of approximately £300m over the last financial year. The Somerfield management team value the stores at £560m, but realistically only expect to raise £400m for the sale.

Adapted from the Electronic Telegraph, *19 November 1999*

1 Discuss whether it is a sensible decision for a business to sell assets for £400m that arguably generate £300m in contribution annually.

Using break-even analysis

Break-even analysis can assist managers in planning and operating their businesses. We saw earlier in this unit that it may help in deciding whether a business proposal is viable, plays a role in raising finance and assesses the profitability of various levels of production. However, break-even can deal with more complex circumstances including

- analysing the impact of a changing environment (alterations in costs or prices, for example) on the profitability of the business
- deciding whether to accept an order for products at prices different from those normally charged.

In spite of its relative simplicity break-even provides managers with an effective and clear method of analysis and can assist in making decisions such as setting prices or accepting one-off orders.

Break-even analysis can show the consequences for a business in terms of changing profits (or losses) that may result from changes in fixed and variable costs or alterations in the firm's selling price. This is important for many businesses operating in environments which alter frequently. It is too simplistic for firms to assume that costs will remain constant or that prices in their markets will not alter over a period of time. Using it in conjunction with a number of 'what if' scenarios can increase the value of break-even analysis in financial planning and decision making.

Table 3.7 illustrates the general effects of changing costs and prices on the break-even point of a business. To calculate the precise effect of changes at a particular level of production it is necessary to conduct calculations or to construct a break-even chart.

The use of break-even analysis: a case study

Maria Elphick owns and managers the famous *Elphick's* restaurant in Soho in west London. *Elphick's* has a worldwide reputation for serving high-quality meals. Maria recently opened a second restaurant nearby called *Elphick's Too*. This restaurant is in a beautiful Georgian property and is large enough to accommodate 750 diners each month (a maximum of 30 diners over 25 evenings each month). The new restaurant is expected to result in the financial data in table 3.8

type of cost or revenue	amount (£s)
average selling price per meal at *Elphick's*	£60
variable costs per meal – ingredients, fuel, wages	£35
monthly fixed costs such as rent and rates	£10 000

Table 3.8

Using this information and the formula repeated as follows, Maria calculated the number of meals (or diners) she will need in *Elphick's Too* each month if the restaurant is to break even.

change in business environment	effect on break-even chart	impact on break-even output	other effects
rise in variable costs	total cost line **pivots** upwards	greater output necessary to break even	due to rise in costs greater revenue (and so more customers and sales) is necessary to break even
fall in variable costs	total cost line **pivots** downwards	smaller output required to break even	each sale incurs lower costs so that a smaller number of customers is needed to cover total costs
rise in fixed costs	fixed cost line and total cost line move upwards in a parallel shift	greater output required to break even	business incurs greater costs before earning any revenue, so more sales will be required to cover total costs and break even
fall in fixed costs	fixed cost and total cost lines make parallel shift downwards	smaller output is necessary to break even	the business's overall costs are lower and hence fewer sales will be required to break even
rise in selling price	revenue line **pivots** upwards	break-even is achieved at a lower level of output	each sale will provide the business with greater revenue whilst costs are unaltered. Hence fewer sales will be necessary to break even
fall in selling price	revenue line **pivots** downwards	break-even is reached at a higher level of output	every sale will earn the business less revenue so, as costs are unchanged, more sales will be required to earn sufficient revenue to break even

Table 3.7

$$\text{Monthly break-even output} = \frac{\text{fixed costs}}{\text{contribution per unit}}$$

$$\text{Monthly break-even output} = \frac{£10\,000}{£25}$$

$$= 400 \text{ diners}$$

This position is shown in the form of a break-even chart in figure 3.2.

Maria is conscious that rental values of properties in the Soho area of London are rising rapidly. She appreciates that the rent of the Georgian building in which *Elphick's Too* is located is likely to rise and that this will increase her overall costs reducing the profitability of the new enterprise. Maria is concerned that a substantial rise in fixed costs (to say £12 500 each month) might make the business unattractive in financial terms.

Figure 3.3 illustrates the effect of a rise in fixed costs on *Elphick's Too*. The chart highlights that a rise in fixed costs results in Maria's restaurant requiring a greater number of diners (500 rather

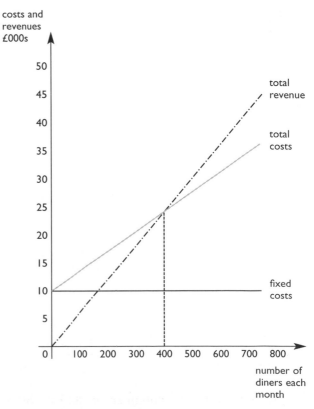

Figure 3.2 *Break-even output at* Elphick's Too

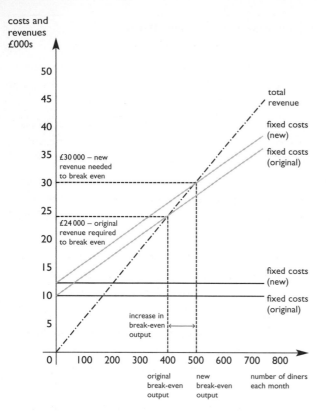

Figure 3.3 *Break-even output and rising fixed costs*

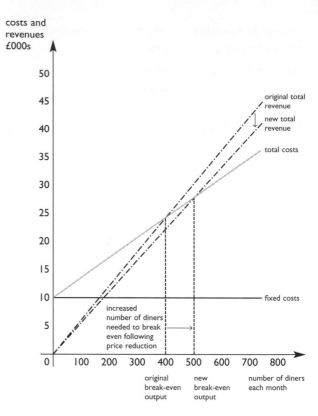

Figure 3.4 *Break-even output and reduced prices*

than 400) to break even. This occurs because given the increase in costs faced by *Elphick's Too*, the restaurant will need to earn higher revenue to cover its costs. Originally with fixed costs at £10 000 a month a revenue of £24 000 was sufficient to break even. With the increased level of fixed costs, Maria needs to attract enough diners to give the restaurant a monthly income of £30 000 and a contribution of £12 500 to ensure that break-even is achieved.

Maria's other fear is that she may be forced to reduce her prices because of increasing competition from other restaurants in west London. She believes that it may be necessary to cut the average price of a meal in *Elphick's Too* from £60 to £55. Maria recognises that if she lowers her prices the restaurant will need to attract more customers to break even. Alternatively the level of profit earned from a given number of customers will fall. The effect of reducing prices are shown in figure 3.4 (assuming original costs apply).

Had Maria been in a position to increase her prices, a smaller number of diners would have been needed to break even.

EXAMINER'S ADVICE

Don't forget that break-even analysis has a number of weaknesses. It is best suited to analysing static situations where change does not occur frequently. It is also based on the major assumption that businesses sell all that they produce. This is unlikely to be true.

Business in Focus

Some entrepreneurs do not make use of break-even analysis because they believe that it is too simplistic to analyse complex and ever-changing business situations. Larger firms who trade and sell in a number of international markets may make little use of the technique because they feel it has little relevance to a multinational business.

1 Discuss whether break-even analysis is only of use to small firms selling in local markets and to new businesses as part of their financial planning.

Progress questions

1 Explain the distinction between profit and contribution. *(4 marks)*

2 Marshall's of Ipswich sell two products. Product A generates £13m in sales revenue and variable costs of £8.5m. Product B earns £11m and incurs variable costs amounting to £12m. Given the firm has fixed costs of £2.5m what are its profits? *(5 marks)*

3 Would you recommend that Marshall's stops producing product B? Explain your answer. *(9 marks)*

4 Why is it more likely that a business's contribution will exceed its fixed costs as it increases its level of output? *(6 marks)*

5 Explain **two** problems a firm might encounter when using contribution pricing. *(6 marks)*

6 Alan Williams Ltd have received an order for 20 000 thermos flasks at a price of £3.50 each. The company's normal selling price is £5 and the variable cost of each flask amounts to £2.90. Should the company accept the order? *(10 marks)*

7 Assume that Alan Williams had been offered £2.75 per flask. Outline the circumstances in which it might have been worthwhile accepting this order? *(6 marks)*

8 Cook's Nurseries manufacture and sell bird tables. The variable costs associated with each table are £20 and annual fixed costs are estimated at £10 000. How many tables would the firm need to sell each year assuming a selling price per table of
   a) £30
   b) £40? *(8 marks)*

9 With reference to the previous question, state what happens to the volume of output required to break even when each of the following changes occurs:
   a) fixed costs rise
   b) the cost of timber falls
   c) the price of bird tables rises. *(3 marks)*

10 Outline **one** weakness and **one** benefit of break-even analysis to a small business *(6 marks)*

Analysis and evaluation questions

1 'The major advantage of contribution costing is that it avoids the need to divide up fixed overheads between the cost centres within a business.' Evaluate this statement. *(15 marks)*

2 Discuss the value of the concept of contribution to a business taking financial decisions *(15 marks)*

3 Analyse the non-financial factors that a business should consider before accepting a lower than normal price for its products as part of a special order decision. *(12 marks)*

4 Contribution pricing is of little use to managers because it ignores the market. To what extent do you agree with this view? *(15 marks)*

5 Evans & Sons manufacture mobile phones. One of the firm's phones is making a negative contribution. Examine the factors the managers of Evans & Sons should take into account before taking a decision to cease producing this particular mobile phone. *(12 marks)*

6 The chief executive of *music.com* has commented 'Break-even analysis is not a dynamic model and cannot cope with changing markets such as the high-technology one in which we trade.' To what extent to you agree with him? *(15 marks)*

Case study

'Cambridge is the most beautiful city in the world' Adam commented looking out across the grounds of King's College. 'I consider myself lucky to have spent most of my working life in such a wonderful environment.'

'A sentimental attitude to architecture will not improve the financial position of our business!' his wife responded acidly. Corena was holding the latest letter from the company's accountants in her hand. She had picked it up from the desk where Adam had cast it, not wanting to read the contents. 'Let me read an extract from this' she said and did so without waiting for Adam to reply.

We feel we must advise you that some tough decisions need to be made if your company is to survive. There are aspects of your business that are potentially very profitable, but it is no longer profitable to make some instruments, notably violins. There is not sufficient demand for these instruments to justify their continued production. The high standard of craftsmanship in each violin is not reflected in the prices you are able to charge. The following trading figures for the last six months highlight the problem.

£000s	guitars	flutes	violins
Sales revenue	*267 500*	*141 750*	*79 000*
Direct or variable costs	*178 300*	*107 425*	*91 000*
Contribution	*89 200*	*34 325*	*(12 000)*

With your fixed costs averaging out at £50 000 for the six months in question, it seems sensible to review your production and to take the steps necessary to improve the profitability of the business.

'There you are, the accountants recognise the situation. You are the only one who refuses to see it. The picture has been the same for 18 months or so and you have done nothing. Our profits have continually declined and you have sat and fiddled –

with instruments we cannot afford to make any longer!'

'But it is not so simple' Adam said after some hesitation. 'Our business has a highly skilled workforce who have been with the business for years. They are always busy and would not understand if I made some of them redundant. In many ways (and I mean financially too) ceasing production of violins could make the situation worse.'

1 a) Calculate the profits of the business for the past six months. *(5 marks)*

   b) Analyse the possible actions that Adam and Corena may take to improve the financial performance of violin production. *(10 marks)*

2 Examine the *financial* case for **and** against the continuation of violin production. *(15 marks)*

3 Discuss the non-financial factors that Adam and Corena should take into account before taking a decision on whether or not to cease production of violins. *(20 marks)*

BALANCE SHEETS

Starting points

The balance sheet was not a topic for consideration at AS level. Consequently this unit will develop this important financial statement assuming no prior knowledge.

Key terms

Assets *are items owned by a business, eg cash at the bank, vehicles and property.*

Capital *is the money invested within a business. Capital is used by most businesses to purchase a variety of assets including vehicles, machinery and property.*

Creditors *are individuals and organisations to which a business owes money.*

Liabilities *represent money owed by a business to individuals, suppliers, financial institutions and shareholders, eg funds owed to external parties such as suppliers and banks.*

Liquidity *measures the ability of a business to meet its short-term debts.*

Working capital: *in technical terms this is a firm's current assets less its current liabilities. Working capital provides businesses with the cash to finance their day-to-day spending.*

What is a balance sheet?

A balance sheet is a financial statement recording the assets (possessions) and liabilities (debts) of a business at the end of an accounting period. The balance sheet only represents a picture of a business's assets and liabilities at a moment in time: it is commonly described as a 'snapshot' of the financial position of an organisation. Because of this, balance sheets always carry a date on which the valuation of assets and assessment of liabilities took place.

POINTS TO PONDER

Vodafone is the UK's most valuable company, according to its balance sheet published in November 2000. The company worth was recorded as £160bn.

By recording assets and liabilities the balance sheet sets out the ways in which the business has raised its capital and the uses to which this capital has been put. The balance sheet provides a great deal of information for those with an interest in a business and is the primary financial document published by businesses.

Key balance sheet relationships

1. ASSETS = LIABILITIES

   This is the fundamental relationship that explains why balance sheets 'balance'.

2. TOTAL ASSETS = FIXED ASSETS + CURRENT ASSETS

   Businesses need to invest in a range of assets if they are to operate efficiently.

3. LIABILITIES = SHARE CAPITAL + BORROWINGS and OTHER CREDITORS + RESERVES

   Businesses raise capital from a variety of sources.

Figure 3.5 *Balance sheet relationships*

Balance sheets are an essential source of information for a variety of business decisions and for a number of stakeholders.

- **Shareholders (and potential shareholders)** may use balance sheets to assess a business's potential to generate profits in the future. Thus, they may examine the extent and type of assets available to a business. A high proportion of assets such as machinery and property may signify a potential for profit, depending upon the type of business.

- **Suppliers** are more likely to use a balance sheet to investigate the short-term position of the company. Thus, they may consider cash and other liquid assets a business holds and make a judgement about whether the business is likely to be able to pay its bills over the coming months. This may help a supplier reach a decision on whether to offer credit to the business in question.

■ **Managers** will be interested in a balance sheet as an indication of the performance of the business. Thus, they may extract information to help them reach a decision on how to raise further capital for future investment. The amount of existing loans may be one factor influencing this decision.

EXAMINER'S ADVICE

It is valuable to consider information about businesses and their performance from a number of perspectives. Although shareholders and investors might be the most obvious stakeholders examining a company's balance sheet, other groups have an interest too. And, of course, they are likely to be looking for different things on the balance sheet.

The precise information drawn from the balance sheet will depend upon the stakeholder and the nature of their enquiry. However, it is important to appreciate that this particular financial statement contains a great deal of information.

POINTS TO PONDER

English cricket finally came clean in 1999. The game's governing body the England and Wales Cricket Board finally published a balance sheet. The ECB's predecessor (the Test and County Cricket Board) had always insisted on keeping its financial situation secret. The ECB is not a company and is not legally obliged to publish its balance sheet.

What represents a 'good' balance sheet is difficult to determine. This will depend upon the circumstances of the business. However, in the course of this unit we will develop a number of key elements within a balance sheet that are worth considering when using this document to assess the financial position of a business.

Assets

An asset is simply something that a business owns. Thus assets are what a business uses its capital to purchase. There are two main categories of assets that appear on the balance sheet. The distinction between the two categories is based upon the time the assets are held within the business.

1 **fixed assets**. These are assets owned by a business that it expects to retain for one year or more. Such assets are used regularly by a business and are not bought for the purpose of resale. Examples of fixed assets include land, property, production equipment and vehicles.

2 **current assets**. This category of asset is likely to be converted into cash before the next balance sheet is drawn up. Therefore, stock and debtors (individuals or organisations who owe the business money) are examples of current assets as they are only retained by the business for a short period of time.

POINTS TO PONDER

Concorde is one of British Airway's most famous aircraft, because of its ability to fly passengers at supersonic speeds. The company operates a number of these aircraft, yet they have no value according to British Airway's latest balance sheet.

There is another classification of assets, which although it does not affect the balance sheet directly, is still important:

1 **tangible assets.** These are assets that have a physical existence and have been traditionally included on a balance sheet. Tangible assets include
   ■ land and property, which is frequently the most valuable asset owned by a business
   ■ machinery and equipment; a tangible asset that is likely to be of importance to manufacturing industries.

2 **intangible assets.** These assets do not take a physical form. Examples include

■ patents and other rights – eg the mobile telephone companies have paid the UK government substantial sums for licences to operate cell phones. These licences represent a valuable intangible asset for companies such as Vodafone

■ goodwill. This is the value of established custom and a good name to a business

■ brands. These can be included on a balance sheet if they were purchased or can be separately valued. However, many brands can fluctuate in value as they may have a relatively short life.

Since 1998 intangible assets have only been recorded on the balance sheet if they can be separately identified and money was spent upon their acquisition. This regulation brought UK accounting practice into line with international standards. It would be appropriate for mobile telephone companies to present their licences as intangible assets.

Liabilities

A liability is a debt owed by the business to organisations or individuals. Another way of thinking of a liability is that it shows the sources of capital the business has raised in order to purchase its assets. As with assets there are a number of categories of liabilities:

■ **current liabilities.** In many senses these are the equivalent of current assets. They represent debts owed by the business due for payment within one year or less. Examples of such short-term debt are overdrafts and tax due for payment. Creditors (organisations such as suppliers to whom the business owes money) are normally classified as a current liability because payment is normally due within a short period of time

■ **long-term liabilities**. These are debts that a business does not expect to repay within the period of one year. Mortgages and bank loans repayable over several years are common examples of this type of liability

■ **shareholders' funds.** It may seem strange that the money invested into the business by its owners (shareholders in the case of a company) is

a liability. However, if the company ceased trading, shareholders would hope for the repayment of their investment. Thus these funds (called shareholders' capital) are liabilities. If the business is not a company, but a sole trader or partnership, this form of liability is referred to simply as 'capital'.

Why does a balance sheet always balance?

The balance sheet is well named as at all times the assets held by a business must match its liabilities (including capital borrowed from its owners). Why is this the case?

Firstly, there exists what accountants call the 'dual aspect' of constructing a balance sheet. Thus any transaction that is recorded on the balance sheet

Assets

Fixed – property
machinery
vehicles

Other – investments in
subsidiaries

Current – cash
stock
debtors

Liabilities

Current – taxation due
– creditors
– dividends due

Long-term – bank loan
– mortgage

Shareholder's – shareholders'
Funds capital
– reserves
(accumulated
retained
profit)

Figure 3.6 *The balance sheet always balances*

has two effects that cancel out each other. The following examples highlight this point.

- If a business borrows £575 000 to purchase vehicles, the loan will appear as a liability as it is owed by the business to a bank or other financial institution. However, at the same time the business will have additional assets recorded on its balance sheet (in this case vehicles valued at £575 000). Thus this transaction will not cause the balance sheet to become unbalanced.
- Alternatively the business might sell a fixed asset for cash. In this case the business will have fixed assets of a lower value, but its holdings of cash will rise by the same amount. In these circumstances the value of total assets is unchanged and the balance sheet still balances.

Another feature of the balance sheet ensuring that it continues to balance is reserves. Reserves are simply profit accumulated during previous years' trading and not paid out to the owners of the business. This accumulated profit is **not** held in the form of cash but is invested into a range of assets that are useful to the business and hopefully generate further profits. If a business is successful, purchases more assets and grows, then its value will increase and so will the value of the assets. It may borrow money to achieve this growth; if it does, liabilities will grow at the same rate. However, if it funds its growth out of profits, then the matching liability will be recorded as reserves indicating that the owners' stake in the business has risen in value. Remember that the owners' funds in the business are a liability as this represents money lent to the organisation.

Integrated Business: how much are the dot.coms worth?

A striking feature of the activities of many of the world's major stock markets is the rapid increase in market values of a number of companies with few tangible assets. In some cases the market value of a company (market share price × number of shares) is ten times the value of the assets recorded on the balance sheet.

From where does the remaining 90% of the company's value come? The answer is it is in the form of intangible assets. It is possible to argue that physical assets are no longer the most important factor in creating a competitive advantage. One of the most important examples of intangible assets is intellectual capital. Knowledge is now a major source of competitive advantage, not just for high-tech and dot.com companies, but increasingly for manufacturers of traditional products. World-class manufacturers operate in an environment of continuous improvement and employee empowerment. In such an environment knowledge and brain power are a company's greatest assets.

The high values attributed to dot.com companies occur because the markets give a value to a business's intellectual assets that do not appear on the balance sheet. Intellectual capital includes patents, copyrights, trademarks and brand names. Accounting practice is to value these on the basis of historical cost, rather than current market value. Human capital such as employee know-how and capability to innovate is also included in the market valuation of the dot.com companies.

1 Outline the various types of intangible assets that may exist within a dot.com company. *(6 marks)*
2 Analyse whether a business based heavily on intangible assets represents a riskier investment for shareholders. *(9 marks)*
3 'The leaders of dot.com companies must use democratic styles of leadership if their businesses are to prosper in the international economy.' To what extent do you agree with this view? *(15 marks)*
4 'The increasing importance of intangible assets means that the balance sheet is an irrelevance for modern high technology businesses.' Discuss. *(15 marks)*

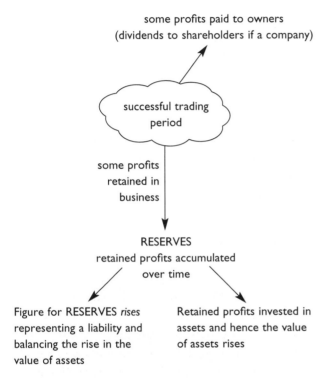

Figure 3.7 *Assets, liabilities and reserves*

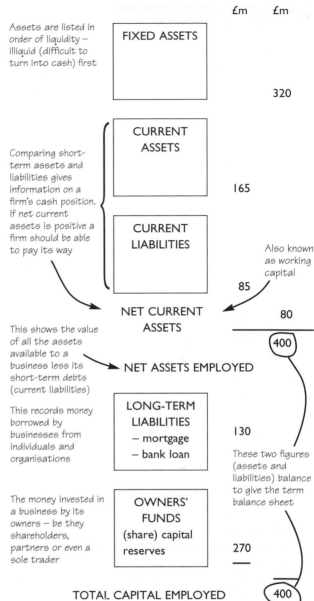

Figure 3.8 *The basic structure of a balance sheet in a vertical format*

Structure of a balance sheet

There are two possible formats in which the information on a balance sheet can be presented:

1 **the horizontal format**. This presents a business's assets and its liabilities alongside one another. This style of presentation is now relatively uncommon

2 **the vertical format**. This is the most common format and all public companies are legally obliged to present their balance sheets in this way. In this unit we will only consider the vertical format of the balance sheet.

The precise layout of balance sheets can vary a little according to the type of business, although the structure is similar for all businesses. All balance sheets list assets – fixed first followed by current assets. Next, current liabilities are recorded allowing a firm to calculate its working capital (simply current assets less current liabilities). Finally, the last section records the sources of finance both borrowed and provided by the owners.

*P*OINTS TO PONDER

The fall in the price of new cars has hit the balance sheet of troubled car manufacturer MG Rover. The stock of cars held by the company was originally valued at £740m during takeover talks. Since then analysts believe that falling high-street car prices have reduced the value by up to 20% – a decline in value of £148m.

A company is owned by shareholders and the owners' funds section is termed capital and reserves and will, of course, make reference to shareholders' capital. In contrast a partnership or sole trader will have a capital section setting out the funds put in during the year and the drawings made in the form of salary.

Some of the most fundamental differences between the balance sheets of private and public limited companies are shown in table 3.9. Most examination questions tend to use a relatively simplified format to make the figures easier to interpret. This is illustrated in the case of J Sainsbury plc, later in this unit.

The rules for presenting balance sheets are set out in the Companies Act of 1985.

Reading and interpreting balance sheets

Professional managers, potential investors and accountants can gain a great deal of information about a company from reading its balance sheet. In this section we will consider the balance sheet of one of the UK's best-known supermarket chain Sainsbury's to illustrate the uses of this financial statement.

There are a number of features on the balance sheet that are worth examining in assessing the performance of the business in question. It is possible to make some assessment of the short-term financial position of the business as well as its longer-term strategy from reading the balance sheet.

(a) The short term

Assessing a business's short-term situation entails examining its ability to pay its bills over the next 12 months. The balance sheet sets out a business's short-term debts (creditors due within one year or current liabilities) and also the current assets it has available to pay these creditors. The net position of these two factors is recorded as net current assets/liabilities. This is also known as working

item within balance sheet	public limited company (plc)	private limited company (Ltd)
money borrowed (thus a liability) over a period in excess of one year	creditors – amounts falling due more than one year	long-term liabilities
money lent by owners to the business	share capital	shareholders' funds
the total assets employed by the business	total assets less current liabilities	net assets employed
the figure against which capital is balanced	this figure is termed **net assets** (which is total assets less all creditors whether due for payment within one year or over a longer period)	private limited companies balance their capital against the net assets employed figure and so long-term liabilities are included as liabilities rather than being deducted from assets prior to a balance being made

Table 3.9 *Differences in the balance sheets of public and private limited companies*

	2000 £m	1999 £m
Fixed assets		
Intangible assets	310	–
Tangible assets	6 667	6 450
	6 977	6 450
Current assets	3 575	3 600
Creditors due within one year	(4 720)	(4 549)
Net current liabilities	(1 145)	(949)
Total assets less current liabilities	5 832	5 501
Creditors due after one year	(1 041)	(812)
Total net assets	4 791	4 689
Capital and reserves		
Share capital	1 860	1 839
Reserves	2 931	2 850
Total capital employed	4 791	4 689

Adapted from *J Sainsbury plc Annual Report and Accounts*, 2000 [www.j-sainsbury.co.uk]

Table 3.10

capital. If a business has more current assets than current liabilities it has a positive figure for working capital and should be able to pay its debts in the short term. However, if current liabilities exceed current assets, this may cause liquidity or cash problems, depending upon the type of business. Working capital is an issue we shall consider more fully in the next unit.

Business in Focus: Sainsbury's short-term position

Sainsbury's liabilities over the next year exceed the assets it has available for the same period. Potentially this could be a problem. The scale of this deficit has risen since the previous year. However, as a supermarket, Sainsbury's knows its customers will pay as they shop and that they will enjoy a steady inflow of money over the year assisting its cash position.

(b) The long term

This can be examined in a number of ways.

■ Movement of fixed assets: a sudden increase in fixed assets may indicate a rapidly growing company, which may mean that the company's financial performance might improve over the medium term.
■ Considering how a business has raised its capital may also be valuable. As we shall see in a later unit, it is risky for a company to borrow too much. Thus a company raising more through borrowing (creditors due after one year) than through share capital and reserves might be vulnerable to rises in interest rates.
■ Reserves provide an indication of the profits earned by the business. A rapid increase in reserves is likely to reflect a healthy position with regard to profits.

Business in Focus: Sainsbury's long-term position

Sainsbury's has increased its intangible assets because it took over other, smaller supermarkets and has to include the goodwill associated with these businesses on its balance sheet.

The overall increase in fixed assets shows that Sainsbury's has achieved some growth in the scale of its business. Sainsbury's has raised a relatively small proportion of its capital through long-term borrowing (creditors due after one year). In this respect at least the company is not a risky investment.

Sainsbury's reserves have risen by a small amount suggesting a relatively modest performance in relation to profits.

POINTS TO PONDER

UK football may not be the best in Europe, but the country's clubs have stronger balance sheets than many of their continental rivals. A recent survey by accountants Deloitte and Touche revealed that

Manchester United is the richest club in Europe and that eight other UK clubs made it into the top 20.

Window dressing balance sheets

Public limited companies are under considerable pressure to present their financial performance in the most favourable terms possible. There are a number of methods by which a company can improve the look of its balance sheet – these processes are called 'window dressing'.

■ Some companies borrow money for a short period of time to improve their cash position just before the date on which the balance sheet is drawn up. This action may enhance the company's apparent ability to pay its short-term debts.
■ An alternative method of improving a company's cash or liquidity position is through the use of sale and leaseback. This entails the sale of major fixed assets and then leasing them back. Many retailers have negotiated sale and leaseback deals on their high-street properties.
■ Businesses may maintain the value of intangible assets on the balance sheet at what might be excessive levels to increase the overall value of the organisation. This tactic is only possible when the assets in question (eg goodwill or brands) have been purchased.
■ Capitalising expenditure. This means including as fixed assets items that might otherwise have simply been regarded as an expense and not included on the balance sheet. Thus a firm might spend heavily on computer software and include this as a fixed asset on the basis that it will have a useful life of several years. This action will increase the value of the business.

*P*OINTS TO PONDER

Abbey National, a former building society converted to a bank, is planning a deal to sell and leaseback its extensive holding of high-street properties. This deal may raise £500m for Abbey National as its 750 branches pass into the ownership of another organisation. Other banks, eg Lloyds TSB, are expected to follow this example.

There is a fine line between presenting accounts as favourably as possible and misrepresenting the performance of the firm, which is illegal. The authorities have made several adjustments to accounting procedures in order to restrict the extent of window dressing.

Business in Focus

The 1985 Companies Act gave the government new powers to ensure that companies adhered to accounting standards when constructing their financial statements such as the balance sheet. The Act established the Financial Reporting Review Panel (FRRP) to investigate cases where company accounts may not provide a 'true and fair view' of the company's position. The FRRP will investigate any complaints about financial reporting and will take legal action if necessary.

For example, in 1992, the FRRP took on the conglomerate Trafalgar House and forced it to amend its accounts. The company never really recovered from the adverse publicity and was eventually taken over.

The 1985 Act also established the Accounting Standards Board to monitor accounting practices and advise on necessary reforms to procedures.

1 Given the controls created by the 1985 Act and the possibility of bad publicity from window-dressing accounts, do you think this activity is outdated?

Importance of the balance sheet

The balance sheet is often referred to as the premier financial statement. It is important for a number of reasons.

■ The fundamental use of the balance sheet is to provide a measure of the value or worth of a business. If a series of balance sheets over a number of years is examined, a clearer picture of a business's growth may emerge.
■ A balance sheet paints a picture of the sources of capital used by a business. This allows stakeholders analysing the statement to assess

whether the company has borrowed an excessive amount of capital making itself vulnerable to rising interest rates.

- It is also possible to see if the business has used expensive sources of short-term finance (eg overdrafts) to purchase fixed assets. A well-managed business would normally use cheaper long-term sources (eg bank loans or mortgages) to finance the purchase of this type of asset.
- The balance sheet illustrates the cash (or liquidity) position of the firm and allows an assessment to be made of its ability to meet its debts or liabilities over the next few months.

However, the balance sheet is not a sound basis for analysing the performance of a business. Any effective analysis would require that other sources of information be used alongside the balance sheet.

- The profit and loss account (which is the subject of a later unit) is another very important financial statement. A profit and loss account records a firm's income, expenditure and ultimately profit or loss over some trading period. A much fuller analysis can be made of a business's financial performance by reading the profit and loss account in conjunction with the relevant balance sheet.
- Any financial statement is a historical document recording what has happened in the past. This is not necessarily a good indication of what may happen to the same business in the future.
- A balance sheet records financial information. It does not provide any real insight into the quality of the management team, the degree of competition provided by rival firms and any change that may be taking place in the external environment. For example, a sudden alteration in tastes and fashions would not be seen on the balance sheet until after the change has occurred.

Progress questions

1 Distinguish between an asset and a liability. *(4 marks)*
2 Explain **two** reasons why a business should draw up a balance sheet. *(6 marks)*
3 Merrills Industries manufacture biscuits and other convenience foodstuffs. Identify **three** stakeholder groups who may have an interest in the company's balance sheet. Outline the likely nature of their interest. *(9 marks)*
4 Explain **two** factors that lead to a business's balance sheet always balancing. *(6 marks)*
5 Outline how the information recorded on a business's balance sheet can be used to assess the cash or liquidity position of the enterprise. *(7 marks)*
6 Explain the difference between the net current assets and the net assets of a public limited company. *(6 marks)*
7 The capital employed by Gujarati Products plc is £540m. The company has long-term borrowing of £310m. What are the possible implications of this situation? *(6 marks)*
8 Smith & White's reserves rose by £54 million last year. Outline the possible causes of this change. *(6 marks)*
9 Explain **two** ways in which a company might improve the look of its balance sheet through window dressing. *(6 marks)*

10 Describe **three** other sources of information, apart from the balance sheet, which would help a potential investor to assess the financial performance of a business. *(6 marks)*

Analysis and evaluation questions

1 'The balance sheet is of little use to assess the financial position of a business.' To what extent do you agree with this statement? *(15 marks)*
2 Examine whether the inclusion of intangible assets on a balance sheet makes it a less reliable indicator of the wealth of a business. *(12 marks)*
3 'Methods of window-dressing balance sheets are well known and changes in accounting regulations means that it is more difficult to hide financial problems. Because of these factors, window dressing is no longer an issue.' Discuss this view. *(15 marks)*
4 Analyse the possible value of a balance sheet to an investor considering purchasing shares in a high-street retailer. *(12 marks)*
5 A recent article in a national newspaper described one of the UK's high-street banks as having a 'strong balance sheet'. Discuss what the journalist may have meant by the use of this term. *(15 marks)*

Case study

Paul Ollington is one of Chester's best-known figures. He has been local councillor for more than 20 years and has been a major contributor to local charities. However, he is perhaps most easily recognised as the owner of Ollington & Smart Photographers with two shops in Chester and a further outlet in nearby Malpas.

Ollington's Photographers has been in business for over 30 years. Paul bought out his former partner several years earlier. However, Paul is now near retirement age and has to take a decision over the future of his business. In recent years Paul has been less motivated by his work as principal shareholder and managing director of the small business. Paul's accountant has urged him to sell the business given that the operator of a chain of photographic shops, Smith Photographic plc, has made an attractive offer. 'You may not receive an equal offer again, Paul, and if you are serious about selling you should not turn this down. You have said you are facing more competition and that people are producing more of their own photographs using computer software. This is a moment for a positive decision: you need to change the direction in which the business is going.'

Paul was not decisive. 'I agree the position of the local economy has not been particularly strong over the last couple of years, but I have worked with several of my current employees for many years. I would hate to see them lose their jobs as a result of a takeover by Smith or another major firm. What's more, the sales figures have held up quite well in the circumstances. I need to think carefully about this.'

	2001 £000	2000 £000
Fixed assets	180	192
Current assets		
Stock	48	60
Debtors	6	10
Cash	3	5
Less current liabilities	(62)	(72)
Assets employed	175	195
Mortgage	95	95
Share capital	25	25
Reserves	55	75
Capital employed	175	195

Table 3.11 *Ollington & Smart Photographers – balance sheet as at 31 March*

1 Identify **two** stakeholders who may have an interest in the balance sheet of Ollington's. In each case explain the possible reasons for their interest.
(6 marks)

2 Analyse the benefits that Ollington's may gain from taking action to window dress its balance sheet.
(10 marks)

3 Smith Photographic is considering the purchase of Ollington's. Consider the disadvantages of using a balance sheet as the basis of such a decision.
(14 marks)

4 Paul's accountant has commented that there are strong reasons why he should sell the business at this time. Discuss the case for and against this view.
(20 marks)

WORKING CAPITAL AND DEPRECIATION

Starting points

Working capital was not a part of the specification of AS business studies. However, it does relate closely to the management of cash flow, which was a significant element of AS finance and accounts at AS level. Some key points relating to cash flow are set out as follows.

■ Cash flow is the movement of cash into and out of a business over a period of time: an inflow of cash results from the sale of products whilst an outflow is caused by purchases of items such as raw materials, components and labour services.

■ Cash flow forecasts state the inflows and outflows of cash that the managers of a business expect over some future period.

■ By forecasting expected inflows and outflows of cash, managers can identify periods when the business may experience cash problems. This allows appropriate action to be taken in advance.

■ Careful management of cash is a major part of effective financial management.

Key terms ➤

Current assets are items owned by a business that can readily be turned into cash. Examples include cash, money owed by debtors and stocks of raw materials and finished goods.

Current liabilities are short-term debts of a business, usually repaid within one year. Examples include a business's overdraft and money owed to creditors.

Liquidity measures the ability of a business to pay its debts on time. A liquid business holds a high proportion of liquid assets, eg money held in bank accounts and debtors.

Working capital is current assets minus current liabilities.

What is working capital?

Working capital measures the amount of money available to a business to pay its day-to-day expenses, such as bills for fuel and raw materials, wages and business rates. Much attention is given to the capital firms choose to invest in fixed assets, but of equal importance to the success of a business is the capital set aside to finance regular transactions.

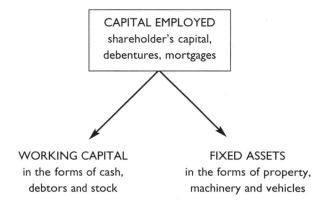

Figure 3.9 *A business's capital*

Working capital is what remains of a business's liquid assets once it has settled all its immediate debts.

It is possible to calculate the working capital of a business from its balance sheet by using the following formula.

Working capital = current assets − current liabilities

On a balance sheet working capital is usually labelled as net current assets.

EXAMINER'S ADVICE

In some circumstances current liabilities might be greater than current assets. In this case, working capital (which will be negative) will be labelled on the balance sheet as net current liabilities. As it is a negative figure it is likely to be in brackets.

```
┌─────────────────────────┐         ┌─────────────────────────┐         ┌─────────────────────────┐
│ WORKING CAPITAL         │         │ LIQUID ASSETS           │         │ CURRENT LIABILITIES     │
│ Essential, to pay for   │    =    │ (or current assets)     │  less   │ (debts payable in the   │
│ day-to-day expenses and │         │ – cash in the bank      │         │ short term)             │
│ keep the business       │         │ – debtors due to settle │         │ – debts repayable to the│
│ operating               │         │   their accounts soon   │         │   bank, eg overdraft    │
└─────────────────────────┘         │ – stock – raw materials │         │ – creditors – who expect│
                                    │   and components        │         │   to be paid in the near│
                                    └─────────────────────────┘         │   future                │
                                                                        │ – tax due to Customs and│
                                                                        │   Excise and Inland     │
                                                                        │   Revenue               │
                                                                        └─────────────────────────┘
```

NB An overdraft only represents a current liability if the bank calls for it to be repaid

Figure 3.10 *Working capital*

Too much working capital?

It is too simple to argue that a business should hold large amounts of working capital to ensure it can always pay its debts in the short term and has spare assets in a liquid form (cash and debtors). Holding excessive amounts of working capital is not wise. The nature of liquid assets such as cash and creditors means that they earn little or no return for the business. Therefore a well-managed business will hold sufficient liquid assets to meet its need for working capital, but will avoid having too many assets in such an unprofitable form.

*P*OINTS TO PONDER

The UK's high-street banks were left with a cash mountain after revellers on Millennium Eve failed to draw as much as expected from cash machines in the run up to the big night. Banks were left with an estimated £8bn of cash, which they are actively seeking to turn into more profitable assets.

A number of factors influence the amount of working capital a firm needs to hold:

■ the volume of sales – obviously a firm with a high level of sales will need to purchase more raw materials, pay a greater amount of wages and so on. Therefore, its need for working capital will be correspondingly higher

■ the amount of trade credit offered by the business. If a firm offers customers a lengthy period of time before they are required to pay, this increases the business's requirement for working capital. In effect companies allowing trade credit offer their customers an interest-free loan

■ whether or not the firm is expanding. In a period of expansion working capital requirements are likely to rise as the business purchases more fuel and raw materials. If a business expands without arranging the necessary working capital it is described as overtrading

■ the length of the operating cycle (ie the amount of time that elapses between the firm first paying for raw materials and receiving payment from customers). Some manufacturing industries (eg shipbuilding) have long operating cycles and a corresponding greater need for working capital

■ in a period of inflation, when prices rise rapidly, firms will require greater amounts of working capital to fund the increased costs of wages, components and raw materials.

As a rough guide, a firm holding current (or liquid assets) of twice the value of current liabilities would normally have sufficient working capital. It is also important for a business to have a significant proportion of its working capital in the form of cash. Cash, the most liquid of assets, is essential to pay the most immediate of bills.

Working capital cycle

The operating cycle of a business referred to earlier can be illustrated by drawing the working capital cycle. This shows the time taken from a business receiving an order to receiving payment. In some manufacturing industries this can be a long period of time, up to one year. Conversely, other businesses such as supermarkets enjoy a short operating cycle and therefore their working capital cycle is also of shorter duration.

- The working capital cycle commences with a business receiving an order or deciding to produce goods in the expectation of selling them. Thus a supermarket may purchase fresh fruit and vegetables or a shipbuilder may receive an order

for a vessel and commence construction. The first action will probably be the purchase of raw materials and components causing an immediate outflow of cash, unless trade credit can be negotiated.

- Producing the goods (or displaying them in the case of a supermarket) will incur further costs and outflow of capital in the form of wages and costs of heating and lighting, for example.

- Once the goods are manufactured further costs may be incurred if a customer is not found for them immediately. For goods of high value, or goods requiring specialist storage (eg frozen foods) holding stocks may cause a considerable outflow of cash.

- Even once a customer is found and a sale agreed, payment might not be received immediately if the firm offers trade credit. It is not unusual for a business to offer 30 or 60 days' trade credit, lengthening their credit cycle and their need for working capital. This delay can be made worse if customers do not pay on the agreed date.

The components of the working capital cycle illustrate why some firms have lower requirements for working capital. Using the example of a supermarket, they do not have a prolonged production period and customers pay on the day they make the purchase, frequently using cash. Thus supermarkets are able to operate with smaller volumes of working capital.

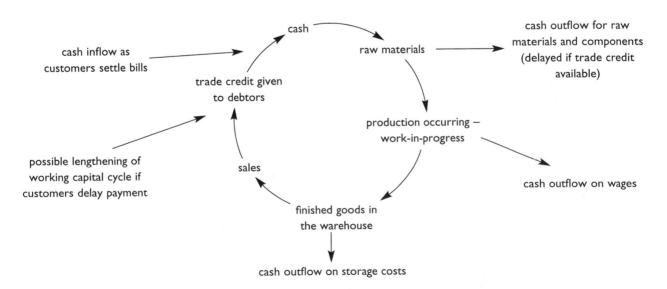

Figure 3.11 *The working capital cycle*

Causes of working capital problems

Difficulties with working capital are a very common cause of business failure, even amongst firms that have the potential to generate a profit. The fundamental cause of problems in relation to working capital is poor financial management. Managers who plan ahead, forecasting their expected need for working capital against the likely inflow of cash, are less likely to encounter problems with working capital. If periods of potential difficulty can be identified, appropriate action can be taken.

Key terms

Creditors *are individuals or businesses to whom an organisation owes money.*
Trade credit *is a period of time offered by suppliers before payment for goods or services is due.*

Business in Focus

The UK's pig farmers are in crisis. The industry is facing severe liquidity problems as a result of overproduction of pork and bacon products and a glut on the world market. Overproduction has resulted in prices tumbling and pig farmers suffering declining revenues and experiencing difficulties in paying their own bills.

Analysts estimate that the pig farming industry is losing £4m each week and expect a further 24 000 job losses in an industry which has shed large amounts of surplus labour already. The industry is experiencing difficulty in competing with a flood of imports from countries which operate less strict controls on meat production and can therefore produce more cheaply.

I To what extent might careful management of working capital help the UK's pig farmers deal with the situation described?

A number of other causes of working capital problems can be identified:

- **external changes.** A number of changes in the economy can place pressure on a business's working capital. A sudden increase in interest rates will increase a firm's interest payments, and thereby drain cash from the business. The economy moving into a recession may restrict demand (especially for income elastic goods such as foreign holidays and designer clothing) meaning a business's receipts from sales decline dramatically whilst expenditure is temporarily unchanged

- **poor credit control.** In a well-managed business emphasis is given to monitoring debtors to ensure that they settle their accounts and that they do so punctually. If a business fails to operate an effective system of credit control, then the incidence of bad debts may increase resulting in a loss of revenue for the business. Furthermore, other customers may delay their payments, resulting in a lengthening of the working capital cycle

- **internal problems.** A business can suffer a variety of difficulties resulting in liquidity problems, as working capital proves insufficient to meet the needs of the business. Production problems can lead to a business incurring extra costs whilst suffering a decline in sales revenue. Similarly, misjudging likely sales can damage a business's working capital position. Production takes place and costs are incurred, including storage, whilst revenue is not received from sales

- **financial mismanagement.** Working capital or liquidity problems may arise simply because managers misread a situation by, for example, underestimating costs of production. Alternatively, they may invest too much in fixed assets as a consequence of overestimating the production capacity the firm requires. A business that borrows too much may not, in fact, improve its working capital position. The high and unavoidable costs of servicing the debts may place a strain on the liquidity position of the organisation.

POINTS TO PONDER

In 1999 Coca-Cola admitted that some of the Belgian production had become 'contaminated'. The company spent over £60m to overcome the crisis including the withdrawal of 14m cases of the world's most famous soft drink. The impact on the company's liquidity position was immense.

Implications of poor management of working capital

Poor management of working capital can have an adverse effect on a number of aspects of a business's performance:

- **weakened market position**. A firm that experiences liquidity problems may decide to require its customers to settle their accounts more quickly. By reducing the interest-free period a company may lose sales, particularly in a highly competitive market, where products and prices are similar and differentiation is achieved through aspects of service such as trade credit. Difficulties with working capital may also prevent a firm taking advantage of market opportunities requiring an expansion of output
- **difficulties with creditors**. A business experiencing liquidity problems may be unable to pay its own debts as they fall due. If this situation cannot be resolved a business may become insolvent and be forced to cease trading. Alternatively, suppliers may refuse to provide trade credit, demanding immediate payment for raw materials and components, thereby placing greater pressure on the business's working capital
- **damage to corporate image**. A firm that is experiencing liquidity problems may experience difficulty in negotiating loans, customers may refuse to place orders because they fear the business will be unable to fulfil them, and suppliers and other firms, sensing non-payment is a possibility, might be unwilling to enter into commercial agreements

- **financial collapse**. In the most serious cases, liquidity problems can result in a firm becoming insolvent as it becomes unable to pay its liabilities as they fall due. In these circumstances it is illegal for a business to continue trading.

Business in Focus

In May 2000 Boo.com, the internet-based fashion retailer, announced that it was ceasing trading and calling in the liquidators. The company had traded for a little over two years and in that time had achieved a high profile as a result of spending large sums of money on marketing. In 18 months the company spent £80m, much of it on marketing activities.

Accountants KPMG, the company's liquidators, announced that 225 jobs (out of 250) were redundant. Boo.com expanded rapidly opening six offices around the world and announcing its intention to supply fashion clothing in 18 countries almost immediately. The management team did not appear to realise that an internet-based operation could serve an international market from a small number of locations. As part of the company's rapid development of a global strategy staffing numbers rose to 450. This represented excessive spending for a business that only achieved £460 000 in sales during its first three months of trading. Sales had risen in the weeks immediately before the company collapsed, but the injection of working capital came too late.

Accountants KPMG said that there was no clear indication of the weekly losses incurred by the firm, or of the assets remaining within the company. In spite of this statement the liquidators had received 27 potential offers for the business within 24 hours.

Adapted from the Electronic Telegraph

1 Boo.com's liquidators received 27 expressions of interest from potential purchasers within 24 hours. Discuss the reasons why a business might want to take over an enterprise with such a troubled history.

Solving working capital problems

A number of techniques are available to businesses experiencing problems with their working capital. The effectiveness of these techniques depends upon the type and size of firm, the nature of its product(s) and its strength relative to its competitors.

*P*OINTS TO PONDER

British Telecom and One2One have claimed £85m in damages from the UK government following the award of licences to operate mobile telephone services. The companies claimed that they were forced to pay immediately whilst rivals Vodafone and Orange were given four month's grace. The damages are in respect of interest payments on their licences.

How important is working capital?

Working capital is important to all businesses. It has been described as the 'lifeblood' of a successful enterprise. If any business is unable to pay its bills promptly, then it may be forced to close down as a consequence of insolvency. However, working capital is of particular importance to certain types of

technique	advantages	disadvantages	suitable for...
reduce trade credit	■ quick and simple to implement ■ under the control of the business	■ may damage firm's image with customers ■ may result in loss of sales	small firms with few other options
negotiate extra credit with suppliers	■ a 'free' source of finance ■ may be able to implement quickly	■ may lose out on price reductions available for prompt payment	larger businesses with secure financial reputation
negotiate additional short-term loans	■ can provide immediate inflow of cash ■ minimal long-term impact	■ can be very costly ■ may be difficult to arrange in times of financial crisis	firms experiencing short-term liquidity problems
cut production costs	■ can improve profitability as well as liquidity ■ may enhance competitive position	■ may lead to additional short-term costs, eg redundancy payments ■ may reduce quality if cheaper components used	businesses with potential to reduce expenditure without harming competitive position
careful financial planning	■ minimal costs ■ improve business's competitive position	■ may take time to have any impact ■ only eliminates problems relating to mismanagement	firms that do not normally experience liquidity problems
sale and leaseback	■ can provide major injection of cash ■ all assets retained by business	■ outflow of cash is necessary to retain use of asset ■ difficult to obtain the best price for an asset when selling under pressure	relatively large firms with valuable fixed assets, or those with surplus assets (in which case they may not be leased back)

Table 3.12 *Techniques for solving working capital problems*

businesses, requiring effective management of this important asset:

1 **new businesses**. Any business new to a market is under threat of liquidity problems. They are likely to be committed to substantial levels of expenditure (rent, rates, wages and other costs) whilst sales may be uncertain. Newly created businesses often have to offer reduced prices, extended periods of trade credit and engage in extended marketing campaigns just to establish themselves in the marketplace. All of these actions are likely to place a great stress on the business's liquidity position.

2 **small businesses**. This category of business can be especially vulnerable to problems with working capital for a number of reasons. Large firms often deliberately delay payments to small suppliers to improve their own liquidity position. They know that the smaller firm will not complain too much as they cannot afford to lose large orders. Secondly small businesses often do not have access to sufficient funds to be able to improve their liquidity position easily. For example, banks may be unwilling to make loans to small businesses with few assets and experiencing liquidity problems.

3 **expanding businesses**. A growing business is likely to find its position with regard to working capital under pressure as it increases its expenditure on raw materials and components before it receives the revenue from its increased output. Even large firms can experience liquidity problems at this time.

4 **businesses with a long working capital cycle**. Many manufacturing businesses have substantial working capital requirements, simply because of the nature of their production. Firms engaged in shipbuilding may incur costs up to three years before they receive complete payment for their products. Clearly a firm that needs to generate large amounts of working capital as a part of its normal trading activity is especially vulnerable to changes such as slumps in demand.

Progress questions

1 Distinguish between current assets and current liabilities. *(4 marks)*

2 Explain the possible consequences of a business having too much working capital. *(6 marks)*

3 Outline **three** factors that might influence the amount of working capital held by a firm. *(9 marks)*

4 Explain **two** external factors that might affect the amount of working capital generated by a manufacturing business. *(6 marks)*

5 Outline **two** solutions for a firm experiencing liquidity problems, if they are not expected to persist. *(6 marks)*

6 Analyse why a firm experiencing rapid growth might be vulnerable to problems with working capital. *(8 marks)*

Analysis and evaluation questions

1 'The major cause of liquidity problems is poor management of working capital.' To what extent do you agree with this statement? *(15 marks)*

2 Examine whether firms engaged in manufacturing are more vulnerable to problems with working capital. *(12 marks)*

3 Discuss whether large firms are relatively immune from liquidity problems. *(15 marks)*

DEPRECIATION

Depreciation was not a topic at AS level and therefore this section of the current unit can be read in isolation.

Key terms

Amortisation is the reduction in value of intangible assets such as goodwill and brands over time.
Capital expenditure is the spending by a business on fixed assets such as premises, production equipment and vehicles.
Depreciation is the loss in value of a business asset over a period of time.
Revenue expenditure refers to the purchase of items such as fuel and raw materials that will be used up within a short space of time.

POINTS TO PONDER

The UK's image as a nation of shopkeepers has been strengthened by recent data on capital expenditure in the UK. The retail sector accounted for nearly 9% of the £75bn total capital expenditure in 1999, compared with just 8% for engineering. UK-based shops are spending far more than international competitors.

Nature of depreciation

A business may spend its capital in two broad ways as illustrated in table 3.13. Both types of expenditure are essential for a business's success, but only capital expenditure has any relevance to the process of depreciation.

Depreciation is the reduction of the value of an asset over a period of time. Thus, a brewery may purchase equipment for the brewing of beer at a cost of £80,000 and reduce its value as shown in table 3.13.

year	value of asset on balance sheet at end of year	amount depreciated annually
2001	60 000	20 000
2002	40 000	20 000
2003	20 000	20 000
2004	0	20 000

Table 3.14 *The Norfolk Ale Company*

	revenue expenditure	capital expenditure
Explanation	This is spending on assets that are used up in a relatively short period of time	This is spending on fixed assets that will be used by the business for a prolonged period of time
Examples	Spending on fuel, components and raw materials	Expenditure to purchase property, vehicles and production equipment
Effects on financial statements	This type of expenditure is recorded on the profit and loss account under headings such as 'cost of sales' and 'administrative expenses'. It will only affect the accounts in the financial year in which the expenditure occurs	The value of fixed assets purchased through capital expenditure is shown on the balance sheet. The reduction in value of these assets over time is listed on the profit and loss account. This type of expenditure affects the balance sheet and profit and loss accounts for a number of years
Possible effects on profits	Revenue expenditure is essential to production, but if not controlled, can have an immediate and damaging effect on a business's profits.	This type of spending has no immediate effect on profits. However, capital expenditure is essential if a firm is to generate long-term profits

Table 3.13 *Capital and revenue expenditure*

Table 3.14 illustrates the effects of depreciation on the balance sheet and the profit and loss account of the Norfolk Ale Company. The initial cost of the brewing equipment in 2000 was £80 000. The company expects that this equipment will last for four years and have no resale value. The value of the asset falls by £20 000 each year reflecting its decline in value. The amount of the decline in value (ie depreciation) is shown as an expense on the Norfolk Ale Company's profit and loss account.

Firms have to depreciate their fixed assets for a number of reasons.

1 To spread the cost of an asset over its useful life. In the case of the Norfolk Ale Company it would have been incorrect to show the value of the brewing equipment as £80 000 throughout its life. Its resale value would decline for a number of reasons:
   - the equipment would lose value as a result of wear and tear
   - the production of more modern equipment would mean that the value of this 'older' style equipment declined
   - poor or inadequate maintenance of the equipment may mean expensive repairs are necessary, further reducing the brewing equipment's value.

   Thus, reducing the value of an asset in line with these factors ensures that the value of the business recorded on the balance sheet is a relatively accurate indication of the true worth of the business.
2 Depreciation also allows firms to calculate the true cost of production during any financial year. The Norfolk Brewery would have overstated its costs in 2000 if it had allocated the entire cost of

its new brewing equipment to that particular financial year. By depreciating the equipment by £20 000 each year for four years, one quarter of the cost of the equipment is recorded each year on the Norfolk Ale Company's profit and loss account. This helps to gain an accurate view of the profitability (or otherwise) of the business over the lifetime of the equipment.

Depreciation: a non-cash expense

Depreciation is an expense or a cost to a firm that is recorded on the profit and loss account. However, depreciation is unusual in that it is a non-cash expense. Depreciation does not require a business to make any payment. It is recognition of the cost of providing a particular expense normally made at the time the asset was purchased. Depreciation is **not** a method of providing the cash necessary to replace the asset at the end of its useful life.

*P*OINTS TO PONDER

According to the NHS executive, depreciation in the health service as a whole currently amounts to some £900m on an asset value of £21bn, or 5%.

Methods of depreciation

There are a number of methods by which a UK business can calculate the decline in value of its fixed assets over a period of time. Of these, two are relevant to students of A level business studies.

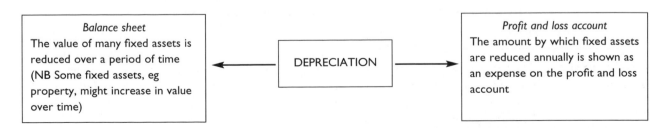

Figure 3.12 *Depreciation – a link between the balance sheet and profit and loss account*

Straight-line method

This is a simple method of depreciation that reduces the value of a fixed asset by the same amount each year until the asset is of no further use and is sold or scrapped. This method of depreciation can be calculated through the use of the following formula.

Straight-line depreciation $=$
$$\frac{\text{cost of machine} - \text{residual value}}{\text{working life in years}}$$

The residual value of a fixed asset is the amount received when the asset is no longer required and is sold.

Business in Focus: an example of straight-line depreciation

Alan Cork, managing director of *Frenzy*, a nightclub in Portsmouth, has just authorised the purchase of a new sound system. The new system cost £18 000 and Alan estimates that in a rapidly changing world he will need to replace it at the end of three years. The company supplying the sound system have advised Alan that the resale value after three years would be £3000.

Straight line depreciation $=$
$$\frac{18\ 000 - 3\ 000}{3\ \text{years}} = \frac{15\ 000}{3} = £5000$$

Thus the value of the new sound system on the balance sheet of South Coast Leisure (the company that owns the nightclub) would be reduced by £5000 annually. At the same time the amount of depreciation entered as a cost on the profit and loss account would also be £5000. Thus this method of depreciation spreads the £15 000 cost of the sound system evenly over the three years of its working life.

Straight-line depreciation is simple to calculate, but this simplicity is also its principal weakness. Few assets lose their value steadily over a period of time. It is much more common for an asset to lose value more heavily in the early years of its life.

Reducing balance method

The reducing balance method of depreciation lowers the value of a fixed asset by a given percentage each year. Because the value of the asset is declining over time, this means that the value by which the asset is reduced declines throughout its life. The key factor determining the reduction in value of an asset using this approach is the expected life of the asset. Thus, if an asset is expected to have a useful working life of ten years and no resale value, it should be depreciated by 10% on the balance sheet each year.

The use of the reducing balance method of depreciation means that fixed assets are depreciated by larger amounts during the early years of their lives. It is argued that this is perhaps more realistic because assets do tend to lose larger amounts of value in the earlier years.

POINTS TO PONDER

Many consumers encounter depreciation when they purchase cars. The depreciation on some vehicles can be considerable. A two-year-old Ford Focus is estimated to depreciate at a rate of £50 per week.

Straight-line and reducing depreciation: a comparison

The choice of method of depreciation has an impact on the value of the business as recorded on the balance sheet as well as the level of net profits generated in any particular year. Table 3.15 illustrates the two methods of depreciation in relation to the purchase of the sound system for a Portsmouth nightclub that we used earlier.

Business in Focus: an example of reducing balance depreciation

Assume that South Coast Leisure decided to use the alternative reducing balance method of depreciation to calculate the value of its new sound system. The value of the asset recently purchased at a cost of £18 000 and installed at *Frenzy* in Portsmouth would still be £3000 after five years of use. However, the firm's accountants have advised the company that they will need to depreciate their system by 45% each year for the five years. This would result in the situation shown as follows.

Original cost	£18 000
Year one depreciation £18 000 × 45% =	(£8100)
Value at end of year one =	£9900
Year two depreciation £9900 × 45% =	(£4455)
Value at end of year two =	£5445
Year three depreciation £5 445 × 45% =	(£2450)
Value at end of year three =	£2995*

* value does not exactly equal £3000 due to rounding of percentages for simplicity in calculation.

Which method of depreciation should be used?

A major argument for using the reducing balance method to depreciate fixed assets is that this approach will, in many circumstances, give a more accurate value to the assets in question, and therefore to the business. The worth of many assets such as vehicles and production equipment falls most quickly in the early years and therefore this provides a more accurate calculation of the cost of using the asset.

A further argument for the reducing balance method is that most firms believe that the cost of using an asset is fairly stable over a period of time. When maintenance costs (repairing breakdowns, and replacing worn out parts) are included in the overall cost of operating the asset, a fairly stable cost pattern emerges. As the charge of annual depreciation declines as the asset ages, maintenance costs inevitably rise keeping the overall expenses of operation roughly constant. This strengthens the case for using a reducing balance method.

The straight-line method is often used because it is simple to apply and to understand. The use of this method is encouraged by the general acceptance that certain assets are depreciated over an agreed number of years. For example, all vehicles are subject to straight-line depreciation over a period of four years (at 25% per annum) and computer equipment over five years (at 20% annually).

In theory the method of depreciation used should be most appropriate to the circumstances and the nature of the assets. Thus it might be more appropriate to use reducing balance to depreciate vehicles, which lose large proportions of their value in the early years. However, the fact that straight line is simpler and approved by the Inland Revenue means that this is more likely to be used in many circumstances.

	straight-line method		reducing balance method	
year	value at end of financial year	annual depreciation	value at end of financial year	annual depreciation
1	13 000	5 000	9 900	8 100
2	8 000	5 000	5 445	4 455
3	3 000	5 000	2 995	2 450

Table 3.15 *Frenzy's new sound system: a comparison of straight-line and reducing balance methods of depreciation.*

Why is depreciation important?

Depreciation is an important matter to businesses for a number of reasons.

- Depreciation provides an accurate value of a business's assets throughout the life of those assets. This allows for a 'true and fair' assessment of the overall worth of the business at any time. Having an accurate figure for the overall value of the business is important for stakeholders such as investors and creditors.
- The amount of annual depreciation affects the overall value and profits of a business as shown in table 3.16.

	too much depreciation	too little depreciation
Effects on balance sheet	fixed assets are valued at less than their true worth – value of business understated	fixed assets are overvalued giving a false impression of the company's worth
Effects on profit and loss account	depreciation expenses are overestimated, reducing level of profits	low rates of depreciation will reduce the expenses incurred by a business. This will result in a business's profits being higher than they would otherwise be
Wider effects	business may look unattractive to prospective investors. Tax liability on profits may be reduced, but Inland Revenue might investigate! Business may record surplus when asset finally sold	this may make the company more attractive to investors but will also increase its tax liability

Table 3.16

Progress questions

1 Outline why a successful firm needs to engage in capital expenditure as well as revenue expenditure. *(8 marks)*

2 Why does a firm need to depreciate its fixed assets over time? *(7 marks)*

3 Explain the difference between the straight-line and reducing balance methods of depreciation. *(6 marks)*

4 Outline why it is important to value fixed assets as accurately as possible. *(7 marks)*

Analysis and evaluation questions

1 'A well-managed firm should value its assets as accurately as possible.' Discuss this view. *(15 marks)*

2 'It doesn't matter what method of depreciation a firm uses as businesses frequently pay for the assets at the time of purchase.' Critically evaluate this statement. *(15 marks)*

TRADING, PROFIT AND LOSS ACCOUNTS

Starting points

Company accounts, including the trading, profit and loss account, were not covered in the AS business studies textbook and will be examined fully and in detail in this unit. This account is usually referred to as simply the profit and loss account. However, before we consider this account in detail it is important to note that some key AS principles underpin the study of this financial statement.

■ Revenue is the income received by a business as the result of its activities. In its simplest form it is calculated by multiplying sales volume (the number of units sold) by the average selling price.

■ Firms may generate revenue from trading activities – i.e. selling their products, but also from non-trading activities, eg the sale of surplus fixed assets.

■ A business incurs different types of costs. Overheads are those expenses that are not related to a particular product or aspect of the business's activities. In many senses these are similar to fixed costs, which do not vary with the level of a business's output.

*P*OINTS TO PONDER

Britain Airways would have recorded a loss on a full year's trading in 2000, for the first time ever, had the company not raised £249m through the sale of assets. The UK's 'favourite airline' sold its stakes in Equant telecommunications service and in the Galileo ticketing system to spare its blushes.

What is profit?

At its simplest, profit is what remains from revenue once costs have been deducted. However, in the

construction of the profit and loss account there are two main types of profit identified:

1 **gross profit.** This form of profit is calculated by deducting direct costs (such as materials and shop-floor labour) from a business's sales revenue. This gives a broad indication of the financial performance of the business without taking into account other costs such as overheads.

2 **net profit.** This is a further refinement of the concept of profit and is revenue less direct costs and indirect costs or overheads such as rent and rates as well as interest payments and depreciation. This is a better indication of the performance of a business over a period of time as it takes into account all costs incurred by a firm over a trading period. Net profit can take a number of forms:

■ **trading or operating profit**. This type of profit takes into account all earnings from regular trading activities and all the costs associated with those activities. However, this form of profit excludes any income received from, or costs incurred by, activities that are unlikely to be repeated in future financial years

■ **net profit before tax** is a business's trading or operating profit plus any profits from one-off activities. For example, in October 2000 Abbey National, the building society that has become a bank sold all of its high-street properties for £457m. The Abbey National expected to make £70m profit from the deal after allowing for the cost of leasing the properties back again from the new owner. This £70m would appear as a one-off item as

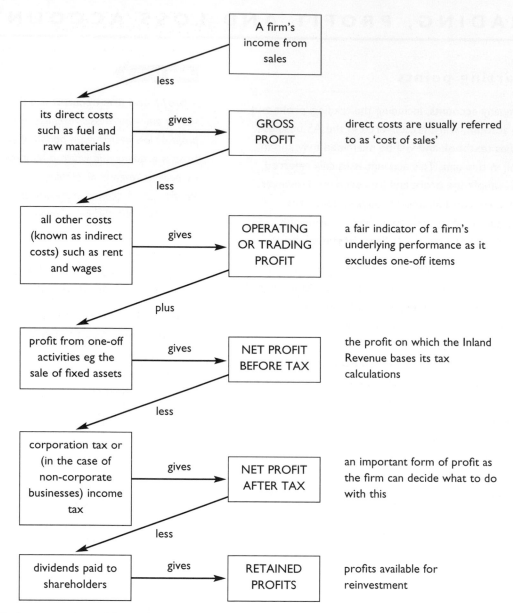

Figure 3.14 *The basic structure of the profit and loss account*

this is not an action that Abbey National could repeat

■ **net profit after tax** is the amount left to the business once corporation tax (or income tax in the case of a sole trader or partnership) has been deducted. This is an important form of profit. There are no more charges on this profit and the managers of the business can decide what to do with it

■ **retained profit** is the profit that the managers decide to keep within the business. It is thus profit after tax less any dividends paid to the shareholders of a company. Retained profit is used to provide capital for the business, and is often used to purchase further fixed assets.

Key issues

Profit is one of the most commonly used words in business. Clearly it is important for a number of reasons. It acts as a signal to attract new businesses into a market and to encourage an existing business to grow. The pursuit of profit is an important business motive.

But profit is not always so important. Some businesses (eg charities and mutual organisations) do not aim to make profits. And profits that impose high social costs on others may not be highly valued. Businesses that generate high profits through polluting the environment or hiring sweat-shop labour in the Third World, may attract criticism and lose sales in the long run.

Because of increased public awareness of ethical and environmental issues many businesses are taking a long-term view of profit. They may be prepared to incur higher costs in the short term (through using more expensive materials from sustainable sources, for example) to maintain a positive corporate image and higher profits in the long term.

Quality of profit

It may seem strange, but some profits are better than others. Firms regard profit that is likely to continue into the future as high-quality profit. Thus, if a business introduces a new product onto the market and it immediately begins to generate a surplus and looks to have a promising future, then this will be high-quality profit. Alternatively, the £70m profits generated by Abbey National Bank in 2000 through negotiating a sale and leaseback deal on their high-street properties would be regarded as low-quality profit. This form of profit will not continue into the future.

POINTS TO PONDER

In its last few months of trading the much-criticised Millennium Dome sold surplus equipment to provide income to keep going until 31 December 2000. By selling surplus stock such as hand-held computers, the dome reduced its expected loss over the year.

The amount of trading or operating profit earned by a firm is more likely to represent high-quality profit as it excludes any one-off items. This level of profit might reasonably be expected to continue into the future, depending upon market conditions. Shareholders are interested in profit quality as it gives some indication of the company's potential to pay dividends in the future.

EXAMINER'S ADVICE

Considering the quality of profit generated by a particular activity can be a powerful evaluative theme. Most students do not remember that some types of profit are 'better' than others and use this in their answers. Considering the quality of profit helps to bring a more strategic aspect into examination answers.

Structure of the profit and loss account

Figure 3.14 provides an initial guide to the structure of the trading, profit and loss account, to give the statement its full name. The profit and loss account is divided into three sections:

1 the trading account – calculates the business's gross profit.
2 the profit and loss account – sets out other costs and one-off revenues to provide net profit after tax.
3 the appropriation account – records the uses of net profit after tax.

This is illustrated in figure 3.15.

HOLLINGWORTH PHARMACEUTICALS plc
Profit and loss account for the period ending 31 July 2001

£m

THE TRADING ACCOUNT	Sales revenue	5000
	Cost of sales	3250
	GROSS PROFIT	1750

PROFIT AND LOSS ACCOUNT	*Less expenses*		
	Sales and distribution	460	
	Administration	320	
	Rent and rates	510	
			1290
	OPERATING PROFIT		460
	plus one-off items		140
	NET PROFIT BEFORE TAX		600
	less corporation tax		150
	NET PROFIT AFTER TAX		450

APPROPRIATION ACCOUNT	*less* Dividends	200
	RETAINED PROFITS	250

Figure 3.15 *Structure of the profit and loss account*

The overall profit and loss account details a business's income (or turnover) and all of its costs for a period of time, normally one year. This is a major distinction between the balance sheet and the profit and loss account; the former is a snapshot at a particular point in time, whereas the latter relates to a trading period, normally one year.

EXAMINER'S ADVICE

The profit and loss accounts provided as part of examination questions usually only contain key items such as the one illustrated in figure 3.15. Prior to examinations ensure you are familiar with and understand fully this format of the account.

Key terms

Cost of sales is the direct costs generated through a firm's sales over a trading period.
Stock is raw materials and other items necessary for production to take place which are ordered in advance and stockpiled.

Trading account

This section of the profit and loss account states the income earned by a business over the trading period. Immediately following is recorded the direct costs associated with this trading activity – the cost of sales. By deducting the cost of sales from the sales income or turnover of the business, we arrive at gross profit.

The sales revenue figure should only include sales once the goods are delivered to the customer. Goods that are produced, but not sold (perhaps because they are added to stock) should only be a part of sales revenue when a customer receives them. This may occur in a different trading period. The figure for sales revenue (or sales income or turnover) may be subject to a number of adjustments before the final figure is calculated.

■ Taxes on spending, eg VAT (Value Added Tax) are excluded because the business is just a collector of taxes on behalf of the government. The business charges its customers VAT and then passes the money received to the Customs and Excise. To include VAT in the profit and loss account would inflate a business's turnover and not be a true record of its trading history.

■ Errors occur in the process of trading. Incorrect invoices are sent out and customers return goods for a variety of reasons. The turnover of a business must be adjusted to reflect these happenings.

Companies are legally obliged to state the turnover of the business separately from that of any other businesses they have purchased during the trading year. These are referred to as acquisitions. Similarly, companies are obliged to identify any sales revenue from trading activities that are to be discontinued.

The other major entry in the trading account is the total of direct costs incurred by the business. This figure is termed 'cost of sales'. The main costs making up cost of sales include

■ raw materials
■ components
■ fuel
■ wages of shop-floor labour.

Only expenditure on goods intended for resale is included in the cost of sales figure. Thus components and raw materials are included as they are resold as part of the final product. Expenditure on sales brochures and advertisements would not be included under this heading. They form part of expenses listed within the profit and loss section of the account. We shall consider this in more detail shortly.

It is important that the cost of sales figure is adjusted to make allowance for any changes in stock. Only purchases of raw materials and components used during the financial year in question should be included in the calculation. This is illustrated in table 3.17 in the example of Solent Stores, a company selling boating equipment and clothes to sailing enthusiasts.

During the financial year ending 31 July 2001 Solent Stores purchased more stock than it sold. This can be seen in that the amount of stock held by the company rose by £180 000 during the year. The purchase of this stock is excluded from the cost of sales figure, as it was not sold during the year in question. It was not therefore, a cost incurred to achieve the sales that did take place.

	£000s	£000s
Turnover		7 860
Less cost of sales:		
Opening stock 1 August 2000	1 250	
Purchases during year	5 982	
	7 232	
Closing stock 31 July 2001	1 430	
Cost of sales		5 802
Gross profit		**2 058**

Table 3.17 *Solent Stores Ltd – trading account for the period ending 31 July 2001*

Profit and loss account

The middle section of the profit and loss account is, confusingly, called the profit and loss account. This apparent contradiction occurs because of the tradition of shortening the name of this financial statement. It is perhaps appropriate in that most of the detail of the profit and loss account is included within this section.

The profit and loss section of the overall account starts with the figure for gross profit. Thereafter a series of minor calculations take place until the figure for net profit after taxation is revealed.

The first element of the profit and loss account is expenses. This records the indirect costs or overheads paid by the firm as part of its trading. These costs do not vary directly with the level of production and sales achieved by the firm and include items such as the wages of administrative staff and marketing costs. This section of the account also states interest paid by the business on loans, eg debentures and also the depreciation arising as a result of writing down the value of fixed assets.

To ensure that the accounts are a true and fair reflection of the business's activities any costs incurred during the trading period are included. Thus if a business does not actually pay all its rent until the next financial year, it will still form part of this year's profit and loss account, because this is when the cost was incurred.

POINTS TO PONDER

Advertising group Saatchi and Saatchi suffered in 2000 at the hands of the National Lottery. The group lost the contract to promote the lottery and saw its operating profit in the UK fall as a consequence.

By subtracting all operating expenses from gross profit the company can state its operating profit. Thus

operating profit = gross profit − expenses

It is normal for a company to add non-operating income to its operating profit at this point in the account. Assuming the company has generated non-operating income, this could be from a number of sources:

- interest received on money held in bank accounts
- dividends from shares held in other companies
- rent received from leasing surplus property.

In our continuing example of Solent Stores we can see the profit and loss section of the overall profit and loss account in table 3.18. We have carried down the gross profit figure from the trading section of the account for continuity. Solent Stores

	£000s	£000s
Gross profit (from the trading account)		*2 058*
(less) Expenses:		
Administration expenses	115	
Advertising	57	
Heat and light	124	
Rent and rates	350	
Insurance	42	
Telephone	38	
Depreciation	110	
		836
Operating profit		**1 222**
(plus) non-operating income		92
Net profit before taxation		**1 314**
(less) taxation		325
Net profit after taxation		**989**

Table 3.18 *Solent Stores Ltd – profit and loss for the period ending 31 July 2001*

generated an operating profit of £1 220 000 for the year and non-operating income amounting to £92 000. The firm's non-operating income might have arisen from the dividends paid on shares held by the company in another company or as a result of interest received on its bank accounts. This is income not arising from Solent Stores' ordinary trading activities.

POINTS TO PONDER

The computer company run by the UK's highest-paid woman enjoyed a 59% rise in pre-tax profits in 2000. Hilary Cropper, executive chairman of FI Group was paid £17m during the financial year in which the company increased profits to £27m and reduced the wage bill by £3.9m.

The addition of non-operating income provides the net profit before tax for a company. This figure is frequently referred to as simply 'net profit'. The Inland Revenue uses this figure as a basis for its computation of the tax liability of the company. All companies earning a certain level of profits are liable for corporation tax. In our example, Solent Stores pays £325 000 in corporation tax. This is deducted from net profit before taxation to give net profit after taxation.

Appropriation account

This is the final section of the profit and loss account. The appropriation account records the uses made of the net profit after taxation. Net profit after taxation is important because the directors of the business can decide how to use this money. Essentially they have two options.

1 Pay some of the profit to shareholders in the form of dividends.
2 Retain a proportion of the profit within the company for reinvestment.

Almost certainly a business will split the net profit after taxation between these two uses. The company is not obliged to provide shareholders with a dividend, but they are likely to face strong

Business in Focus

Proposed changes to accounting rules mean that many companies may record lower figures for net profit before taxation. The ruling body, the Accounting Standards Board, has said that firms should include the cost of granting employees share options as a cost in the profit and loss account, thereby reducing profits.

Under share option schemes employees are offered the opportunity to purchase shares in the company at some point in the future at an agreed price. Employees only take up the option if the actual share price is higher than the agreed price. (For example, an employee offered the chance to buy shares at a price of £2 each in two years' time would take up the option if the market price at that time was higher than £2. An immediate profit would be available.)

However, firms bear the cost of providing share options as the capital raised from the sale of shares is less than would be realised on the free market. Thus the ASB has proposed to include them as a cost. Analysts suggest that firms giving share options would see their pre-tax profits fall by an average of 5.65%.

Adapted from an article in Guardian Unlimited, *18 October 2000*

1 Discuss the disadvantages for a UK company trading in international markets if this proposal is adopted. Would any stakeholders in a business benefit from the change?

opposition from shareholders if no dividend is paid. However, paying all the profit to shareholders and not retaining any for reinvestment may be equally unwise. Retained profit is a relatively cheap and important source of capital for investment.

	£000s
Net profit after taxation	989
Dividends	445
Retained profit for the period	**544**

Table 3.19 *Solent Stores – appropriation account for the period ending 31 July 2001*

Putting the three elements together

We separated the components of the profit and loss account to explain how it is constructed and from where each figure is drawn. In reality the profit and loss account is presented as a single statement and will contain less detail than in table 3.19. The overall trading, profit and loss account for Solent Stores is shown in table 3.20.

	£000s
Turnover	7 860
less cost of sales	5 802
Gross profit	**2 058**
(less) Expenses:	836
Operating profit	**1 222**
(plus) non-operating income	92
Net profit before taxation	**1 314**
(less) taxation	325
Net profit after taxation	**989**
Dividends	445
Retained profit for the period	**544**

Table 3.20 *Solent Stores – trading, profit and loss account for the period ending 31 July 2001*

Variations in profit and loss accounts

There is no single format for a limited company's profit and loss account. The Companies Act of 1985 provided a choice of four formats, though some modification can be made to ensure a 'true and fair view' of the business's performance.

Some minor differences exist in the presentations of profit and loss accounts according to the legal definition of the business. Solent Stores, our example in the previous section, is a private limited company. Thus, the profit and loss account we constructed would be a little different for a public limited company trading its shares on the Stock Exchange, or for a sole trader.

Public limited companies' profit and loss accounts

The profit and loss account in table 3.21 is for Dorling Kindersley, an educational publisher.

	Notes*	£000s 1999	£000s 1998
Turnover	I	**197 541**	**181 556**
Cost of sales		(133 804)	(127 196)
Gross profit		**63 737**	**54 360**
Expenses		(52 235)	(44 969)
Operating profit	2	11 502	9 391
Share of operating profit in joint ventures		570	750
Total operating profit		**12 072**	**10 141**
Extraordinary item†	3	(837)	–
Profit before tax and interest		**11 235**	**10 141**
Interest		(584)	(1 136)
Taxation		(4 006)	(3 242)
Profit after taxation		6 645	5 763
Dividends		(3 446)	(3 332)
Retained profit for the year		**3 199**	**2 431**
Earnings per ordinary share		9.3p	8.1p
Dividend per ordinary share‡		3.8p	3.6p

Dorling Kindersley Annual Report and Accounts, 1999

Table 3.21 *Dorling Kindersley's profit and loss account*
*Provide more detail regarding individual items in the accounts.
†The result of a one-off transaction having a significant effect on the account.
‡Included to provide shareholders with essential information on the returns earned on their investments.

The accounts of a public limited company may include 'one-off' transactions. These can fall into two categories:

1 **extraordinary items**. These are the results of financial transactions that are not a part of the normal trading activities of the company and are therefore extremely rare. In the case of Dorling Kindersley, the 1999 profit and loss account includes an extraordinary item listing the costs association with the closure of one of the company's divisions. Accounting regulations stipulate that such transactions should be included within the accounts.

2 exceptional items. These are more unusual. They arise as a consequence of normal trading activities but are of a sufficient scale to have the potential to distort a company's accounts. A company generating unexpected surpluses on its pension fund might include these in the accounts as an exceptional item. By presenting it as an exceptional item it is possible for stakeholders to interpret the accounts accurately.

POINTS TO PONDER

Eidos, the company responsible for Lara Croft and the Tomb Raider computer games, has attracted criticism for its accounting practices. The company has suffered lower sales for its products due to delays by Sony in supplying Playstation2 consoles. The company has accounted for this as an exceptional item, provoking a cynical reaction from financial analysts.

A public limited company's profit and loss account will also show details of the income paid to shareholders. This will not simply be recorded as a global figure for dividends in the appropriation account. This account normally provides greater detail for shareholders. As in the case of Dorling Kindersley, two additional pieces of information may be given:

1 earnings per share. This is the profit after tax generated by the company divided by the number of shares the company has issued. In 1999 Dorling Kindersley's net profit after taxation was £6 645 000, representing an earning of 9.3 pence for each of the company's 714 51 612 shares.
2 dividend per share. This figure is perhaps more meaningful for shareholders as it indicates the income they can expect on each of their shares. It is calculated by dividing the total dividend announced by the number of shares. Dorling Kindersley paid a total dividend of £3 446 000 giving its shareholders a dividend of 3.8 pence for each share held.

The accounts of public limited companies also contain notes giving further details of the figures

included in the profit and loss account. Thus, in the case of Dorling Kindersley, note 3 explains the nature of the extraordinary item included within the accounts. This depth of information is important to allow shareholders and other interested parties to make an accurate assessment of the financial performance of the business.

Sole traders' profit and loss accounts

The profit and loss accounts of sole traders are very similar to those of companies. Two principal differences exist.

- Sole traders normally give more information on the business's expenses. This is possible due to the business's financial affairs being less complex and assists in managing the business from year to year.
- Sole traders do not have an appropriation account as all the profits belong to the single owner of the business.

Interpreting profit and loss accounts

A number of groups are likely to have an interest in a business's profit and loss account. These stakeholders are illustrated in figure 3.16.

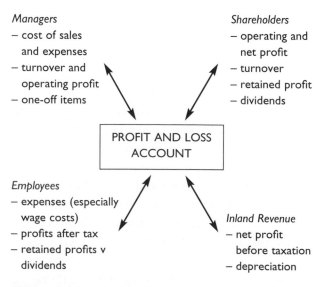

Figure 3.16 *Some groups with an interest in profit and loss accounts*

- **Shareholders** are perhaps the most obvious group with an interest in the profit and loss account. Shareholders will be interested in a business's turnover and operating/net profit. This will provide some guidance as to the performance of the enterprise, especially when compared to previous years. They will also be likely to examine the appropriation account closely to see how profits have been utilised. Some shareholders may seek the maximum dividend possible. Others may be interested in a longer-term return and welcome substantial reinvestment in the expectation of future profits.

- **Managers** use the profit and loss account as an important source of information regarding the performance of the business. Managers are, of course, able to see the profit and loss account in much more detail than that provided in the annual report and accounts. Published accounts contain the minimum amount of information required under law to avoid giving competitors any advantage. Managers will monitor sales performance through turnover figures and judge costs against sales revenue. If expenses and cost of sales rise by a greater amount than turnover, action may be necessary. Managers will also consider carefully the effects of one-off items on the account.

- **Employees** may be interested in profits after tax if their pay is related to company performance through a profit-related pay scheme. They may also be interested in the level of dividends if they are shareholders. The level of profits after taxation may also be an indication of the company's ability to fund a pay increase or, alternatively, of the security of their employment.

- **Inland Revenue** is the organisation responsible for collecting corporation tax from companies on the government's behalf. The Inland Revenue will therefore scrutinise company accounts and use net profit before tax as the basis for their calculation of tax liability (the amount of tax to be paid). They may also check that the profit and loss account meets all necessary standards, eg the basis upon which fixed assets have been depreciated.

A number of key aspects of a business's profit and loss account can be considered as part of the evaluation of a business's performance:

1 **trends**. A better judgement can be made concerning a business if its performance in one year is measured against that of previous years. As in the case of Dorling Kindersley, it is normal for businesses to present two years' figures alongside one another. Many companies also offer five-year summaries of financial performance. Using this sort of evidence it is possible to see what has happened to turnover, costs and expenses and profits over a period of time.

POINTS TO PONDER

The UK's farmers are experiencing hard times on a scale unknown before. A recent survey showed that farm incomes have fallen by 90% in five years. As a result earnings from a typical 500-acre farm have fallen from £80 000 in 1995 to £8000 in 2000. The government is promising financial support.

2 **the period to which the statement relates.** It is normal for a profit and loss account to cover a period of one year. However, this statement can relate to a longer or shorter period. Such changes occur when, for example, the business changes the dates of its financial year. This either prolongs or shortens the year in which the change is made. A 20% increase in profits may not appear so exceptional if the profit and loss account covers a period of 15 months.

3 **comparing gross and net profit.** The calculation of gross profit only includes direct costs (labelled as cost of sales). Operating profit, on the other hand, takes into account all costs – direct and indirect. A rise in gross profit, but a fall in operating profit may indicate that managers are not controlling indirect costs effectively.

4 **the business(es) to which the profit and loss account relate(s).** Many companies trade as part of a group of businesses. In these circumstances the enterprise will produce a profit and loss account (and a balance sheet) for the individual company and also one for the entire group. These latter accounts are referred to as consolidated accounts. These are an aggregation of the accounts of the individual companies that make up the group.

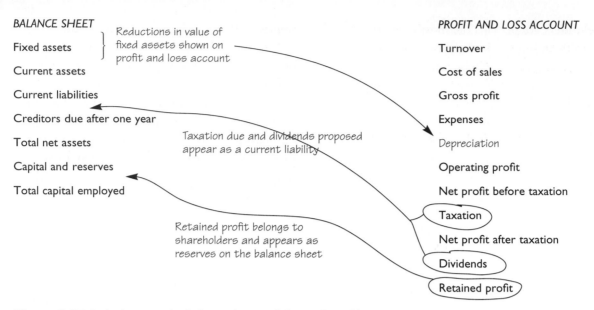

Figure 3.17 *Links between the balance sheet and the profit and loss account*

Value of the profit and loss account

Unquestionably the profit and loss account offers valuable information to a business's stakeholders. This financial statement gives details on a company's turnover, indicating whether or not it has grown. It also provides details about the costs incurred and how successful managers have been in controlling these. Finally, the level of net profit is of value to interested parties as are the uses to which the profit has been put. This latter information might suggest how successful the venture may be in the future. If large amounts of profit are retained for reinvestment, the company may be expected to grow in the future and generate larger profits.

However, caution has to be exercised when interpreting a profit and loss account. Inflation can distort accounts, exaggerating any increase in turnover that may have taken place. Firms attempt to window dress the profit and loss account by bringing forward sales from the next trading period to increase turnover and profit. Profits can be altered by adjusting depreciation policies or by including one-off items as part of ordinary activities.

A profit and loss account alone is not a good indicator of a business's financial performance. It should be read in conjunction with the balance sheet. However, evaluating the performance of any

Business in Focus

SkyPharma, a company involved in developing systems to make it easier for patients to take drugs, have announced that they are unlikely to record a profit until the end of the next financial year. The company has seen sales rise substantially in recent months (25% in the last six months), but has increased expenditure on research and development significantly. As a result pre-tax losses have risen to £11.4m from £6.2m in the previous year.

1 What additional information would a potential shareholder require before being able to reach a proper judgement on whether to invest in SkyPharma?

business requires more than the current year's accounts. Analysts should consider the financial performance of a business over an extended period, perhaps five years. This allows trends in key variables such as turnover and profit to be identified. Furthermore, non-financial factors should be considered. The strength and actions of competitors, the growth (if any) in the market for the firm's products and the quality of a business's labour force are also factors that should be taken into account.

Progress questions

1 Explain the difference between net profit and gross profit. *(4 marks)*

2 Explain what is meant by the term high-quality profit. *(3 marks)*

3 Outline the importance of retained profit to a newly established business operating in an expanding market. *(7 marks)*

4 Explain why the figure for cost of sales should exclude any increases in holdings of stock. *(6 marks)*

5 Outline **two** reasons why a company may try to maintain its dividend payments, even following a poor trading year. *(7 marks)*

6 Explain **two** differences between the profit and loss account of a public limited company and that of a sole trader. *(6 marks)*

7 Explain why an extraordinary item should be listed separately in a company's profit and loss account. *(7 marks)*

8 Outline **two** aspects of a company's profit and loss account that might be of particular interest to a shareholder considering making an investment in the company. *(6 marks)*

9 Explain why employees might take an interest in a business's profit and loss account. *(7 marks)*

10 Outline **two** reasons why it is important to assess a business's profit and loss accounts over a number of years. *(8 marks)*

Analysis and evaluation questions

1 Discuss whether the level of profit earned is a good indicator of the success of the business. *(15 marks)*

2 'A company's profit and loss account is of little value without considering the balance sheet.' Critically evaluate this statement. *(15 marks)*

3 'The annual report and accounts of many businesses are a public relations document, rather than a serious attempt to provide financial information.' To what extent do you agree with this view? *(15 marks)*

4 Dorling Kindersley's profit and loss account was reproduced earlier in this unit. Analyse the additional information that you would require to make a judgement concerning the financial performance of the company. *(12 marks)*

5 Discuss whether a typical profit and loss account is a useful document for the directors of the company in planning future strategy. *(15 marks)*

RATIO ANALYSIS

Starting points

Ratio analysis is based on the interpretation of a business's profit and loss account and balance sheet. Ratio analysis was not covered at AS level and therefore the material introduced in this unit is entirely new.

Key terms

Ratio analysis is a technique for analysing a business's financial performance by comparing one piece of accounting information with another.
A *stakeholder* is any group or individual having an interest in the activities of a business.

Introduction

Accounting information

There are a number of groups who are interested in the financial information provided by businesses and especially by public limited companies. Collectively these groups can be referred to as stakeholders and they may take an interest in the published accounts of a business for a variety of reasons. For example, suppliers may want to judge the financial position of a business to evaluate whether they should offer the firm credit. Similarly, individuals contemplating buying shares in the business may try to assess the business's potential to make profits in the future. Figure 3.18 summarises stakeholder groups and their interest in a company's financial performance.

What is a ratio?

Ratio analysis allows stakeholders to evaluate a business's performance through the investigation of key financial statements such as the balance sheet and the profit and loss account. The key feature of ratio analysis is that it compares two pieces of financial information. By comparing two pieces of data in this way it is possible to make more informed judgements about a business's performance.

A comparison of the financial performance of two companies in 1999–2000 can illustrate the advantages from comparing two pieces of data to make more informed judgements. Monsoon, the

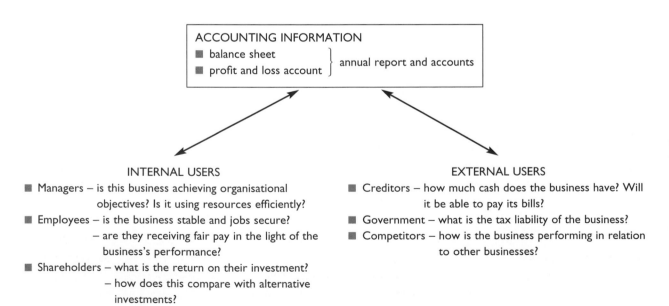

ACCOUNTING INFORMATION
- balance sheet
- profit and loss account
} annual report and accounts

INTERNAL USERS
- Managers – is this business achieving organisational objectives? Is it using resources efficiently?
- Employees – is the business stable and jobs secure?
  – are they receiving fair pay in the light of the business's performance?
- Shareholders – what is the return on their investment?
  – how does this compare with alternative investments?

EXTERNAL USERS
- Creditors – how much cash does the business have? Will it be able to pay its bills?
- Government – what is the tax liability of the business?
- Competitors – how is the business performing in relation to other businesses?

Figure 3.18 *Stakeholders and financial information*

high street clothes retailer recorded a net profit after taxation of £20.42m over the trading year. In comparison, J D Wetherspoon, a company that operates a nationwide chain of pubs, turned in a profit of £26.21m for the year. A simple judgement would therefore suggest that J D Wetherspoon has performed more successfully. However, if we took into account the volume of sales achieved by the two companies, a more meaningful judgement could be made.

company	net profit before tax (£m)	turnover (sales) (£m)	net profit as a percentage of sales
Monsoon	20 426	132 030	15.47
J D Wetherspoon	26 214	269 699	9.72

Table 3.22 *Comparing the financial performance of two companies by using a simple ratio*

Table 3.22 shows that when we compare net profit to turnover Monsoon's performance could be judged superior to that of J D Wetherspoon. Monsoon earned over 15 pence profit from each £1

of sales, whilst Wetherspoon failed to make 10 pence of profit on each pound of sales. Using this ratio (which is called the net profit margin) it is possible to make a more accurate judgement than simply comparing level of profit. We shall consider the net profit margin in more detail later in this unit.

Ratio analysis allows managers, directors, shareholders and other interested parties to place key figures such as profits and turnover in context. Ratio analysis does not guarantee that a manager or shareholder will take a correct decision. The results of ratio analysis do, however, give decision makers more information and makes a good quality decision more likely.

Types of ratio

There are a number of ways of classifying ratios. One approach is to identify five main categories of ratio:

1 **liquidity ratios** also known as solvency ratios measure the ability of the business to settle its debts in the short term.

type of ratio	liquidity ratios	efficiency ratios	profitability ratios	gearing	shareholders' ratios
Ratios used	■ current ratio ■ acid test (or quick) ratio	■ asset turnover ratio ■ stock turnover ratio ■ debtor days	■ net profit margin ■ gross profit margin ■ return on capital employed	■ gearing – loans: capital	■ dividend per share ■ dividend yield ■ price–earnings ratio
Purpose of ratios	to assess the ability of the business to pay its immediate debts	these provide evidence on how well the managers have controlled the business	provide a fundamental measure of the success of the business	assess the extent to which the business is based on borrowed money	give investors information on returns on their investment
Interested stakeholders	■ creditors ■ suppliers ■ managers	■ shareholders ■ managers ■ employees ■ competitors	■ shareholders ■ creditors ■ managers ■ competitors ■ employees	■ shareholders ■ managers ■ creditors	■ shareholders ■ managers

Table 3.23 *Types of ratios*

2 **efficiency ratios** measure the effectiveness with which an enterprise uses the resources available to it. These are also termed internal control ratios.

3 **profitability ratios** assess the amount of gross or net profit made by the business in relation to the business's turnover or the assets or capital available to it.

4 **gearing** examines the relationship between internal sources and external sources of finance. It is therefore concerned with the long-term financial position of the company.

5 **shareholders' ratios** measure the returns received by the owners of the company allowing comparison with alternative investments. For obvious reasons they are also called investment ratios.

Sources of information for ratio analysis

The most obvious sources are the published accounts of the business or businesses concerned. In particular, ratio analysis requires access to a business's balance sheet and trading, profit and loss account. However, although this might be essential information, it is not all that is required to conduct an in-depth ratio analysis of a business. Other possible sources of information include the following:

■ **the performance of the business over recent years**. Having an understanding of the trends of ratios over time can assist in making judgements. Thus a profitability ratio might appear fairly low, but if it represents a continuation of a steadily rising trend then the figure may be more acceptable to stakeholders

■ **norms or benchmarks for the industry**. The results of ratio calculations should be judged against what is normal for the industry. Thus an investor might calculate that a company's debtor day ratio is 35 days (the number of days, on average, that customers take to settle their bills). This might be acceptable for a manufacturing business, but not for a fast food business

■ **the economic environment.** A decline in profit ratios might appear to reflect an unsuccessful business. However, this might be more

acceptable in the context of a severe economic recession whereby sales and prices have declined.

Liquidity ratios

These ratios allow managers and other interested parties to monitor a business's cash position. Even profitable businesses can experience problems with liquidity and may be unable to pay their bills as they fall due. Liquidity ratios measure the liquid assets held by a firm (cash and other assets such as debtors that are easily convertible into cash). The value of these assets is then compared with the short-term debts or liabilities the business will incur. In this way stakeholders may evaluate whether the business's performance may be harmed as a result of liquidity problems.

1. Current ratio

This measures the ability of a business to meet its liabilities or debts over the next year or so. The formula to calculate this ratio is

$$\text{current ratio} = \frac{\text{current assets}}{\text{current liabilities}}$$

The current ratio is expressed in the form of a ratio, for example 2:1. This would mean that the firm in question possessed £2 of current assets (cash, debtors and stock) for each £1 of current liability (creditors, taxation and proposed dividends, for example). In these circumstances it is probable that the business would be able to meet its current liabilities without needing to sell fixed assets or raise long-term finance.

Using this ratio

- For years holding current assets twice the value of current liabilities was recommended. This is no longer accepted partly due to the use of computers in stock control and the widespread use of just-in-time systems of production. A more typical figure might now be 1.6:1.
- In spite of this, the 'normal' figure for this ratio varies according to the type of business and the state of the market. Fast food outlets and banks typically operate with lower ratios, whereas some manufacturing firms may have higher ratios.
- Firms with high current ratio values (say, 3:1) are not necessarily managing their finances effectively. It may be that they are holding too much cash and not investing in fixed assets to generate income. Alternatively, they may have large holdings of stock, some of which might be obsolete.
- Firms can improve the current ratio by raising more cash through the sale of fixed assets or the negotiation of long-term loans. (NB: note that raising more cash through short-term borrowing will increase current liabilities, having little effect on the current ratio.)

Expressing ratios

Ratios are normally expressed in one of three forms:

1 as a proper ratio – eg the current ratio is 1.6:1.
2 as a percentage – ROCE expresses operating profit as a percentage of capital employed by the business.
3 as a multiple – stock is turned over (or sold) five times a year.

2. Acid test (or quick) ratio

This ratio measures the very short-term liquidity of a business. The acid test ratio compares a business's current liabilities with its liquid assets (ie current assets less stock). This can provide a more accurate indicator of liquidity than the current ratio as stock can take time to sell. The acid test ratio measures the ability of a firm to pay its bills over a period of two or three months without requiring the sale of stock.

The formula for the acid test ratio is

$$\text{acid test ratio} = \frac{\text{liquid assets}}{\text{current liabilities}}$$

The acid test ratio is also expressed in the form of a ratio, eg 2:1.

Using this ratio

- Conventionally a 'normal figure for the acid test ratio was thought to be 1:1, giving a balance of liquid assets and current liabilities. However, by the Millennium, a number of businesses were operating successfully with acid test figures nearer to 0.7:1.
- The value of the acid test ratio considered acceptable will vary according to the type of business. Retailers might operate with a figure of 0.4:1, because they trade mainly in cash, and have close relationships with suppliers. A manufacturing business might operate with a ratio nearer to the standard 1:1.
- Firms should not operate over long periods with high acid test ratios as holding assets in the form of cash is not profitable and does not represent an effective use of resources.
- As with the current ratio the acid test ratio can be improved by selling fixed assets or agreeing long-term borrowing.

*P*OINTS TO PONDER

Internet auctioneer QXL is hunting for an investor to supply a much-needed £35m to cover its losses. The company, which recently floated on the Stock Exchange, is not expected to make a profit for three years. The company lost £15m in cash over the final three months of 2000.

Liquidity ratios are based on figures drawn from the balance sheet relating to a particular moment in time. Because of this some caution should be exercised when drawing conclusions from this type of ratio. The actual figures on the balance sheet may be unrepresentative of the firm's normal position due to factors such as window dressing or a sudden change in trading conditions.

company	date of balance sheet	current assets £m	stock £m	current liabilities £m	current ratio	acid test ratio
J Sainsbury	01/04/2000	3 575	986	4 720	0.76	0.55
Rolls Royce	31/12/1999	3 951	1 274	2 467	1.60	1.09
Unilever	31/12/1999	11 364	3 185	6 326	1.80	1.29

Table 3.24 *The liquidity ratios of three public limited companies*
Notes: Sainsbury, a retailer is able to operate successfully with lower levels of liquidity than Rolls Royce and Unilever, who are both manufacturers. However, both manufacturing firms show the recent trend towards trading with less liquid assets.

Key terms

Debenture: a long-term loan to a business carrying a fixed rate of interest and a specified repayment date.
Ordinary shares: a financial security representing part ownership of a business that does not entitle the holder to a fixed payment from profits, but does confer voting rights.
Preference shares: a financial security representing part ownership of a business that entitles the holder to a fixed payment from profits.
Stock: the amount of raw materials, components and finished goods held by a business at a given time.

Gearing

Gearing measures the long-term liquidity of a business. Under some classifications gearing is included as a liquidity ratio. There are a number of methods of measuring gearing; we shall consider the simplest form of the ratio. This ratio analyses how firms have raised their long-term capital. The result of this calculation is expressed as a percentage.

There are two main forms of long-term finance available to businesses:

1 debt including long-term borrowing, preference shares and debentures (all have fixed interest payments).
2 equity capital from selling ordinary shares.

Gearing =

$$\frac{\text{fixed return capital (loans, debentures and preference shares)}}{\text{equity capital plus reserves}}$$

This measure of a business's performance is important because by raising too high a proportion of capital through fixed interest capital firms become vulnerable to increases in interest rates. Shareholders are also unlikely to be attracted to a business with a high gearing ratio as their returns might be lower because of the high level of interest payments to which the enterprise is already committed.

- A **highly geared business** has more fixed interest capital than equity capital and reserves, meaning the result of the calculation is **greater than 100%.**
- A **low geared business** has less fixed interest than equity capital and reserves giving a calculation of **less than 100%.**

Much attention tends to be given to businesses that have high gearing and are vulnerable to increases in interest rates. However, this may be considered acceptable in a business that is growing quickly and generating high profits. Furthermore, a low-geared business may be considered too cautious and not expanding as quickly as possible. In 1999 BOC, the industrial gases group announced its intention to raise £500–£600m through borrowing as its gearing ratio was only 50%. The company's managers felt that they had the financial capacity to grow more quickly and to provide better-quality products.

Using this ratio

- The key yardstick is whether a business's fixed interest capital is greater than non-fixed interest capital. A 100% figure is the normal maximum.
- Companies with secure cash flows may raise more fixed interest capital because they are

company	date of balance sheet	fixed interest capital (£m)	equity capital and reserves (£m)	gearing ratio
British Airways	31 March 2000	6 728	3 147	213.8%
British Telecom	31 March 2000	6 410	15 795	40.6%
Cable & Wireless	31 March 2000	5 858	8 096	72.4%

Table 3.25 *Gearing ratios of some leading companies*
Notes: British Airways has borrowed heavily and is clearly highly geared. The company is negotiating the sale of its low cost subsidiary Go, which would allow it to reduce its long-term debt. British Telecom appears cautious in its use of resources, possibly reflecting the uncertainties of trading in a highly competitive market.

confident of being able to meet interest payments. Equally a business with well-known brands may be able to borrow heavily against these brands to increase fixed interest capital.

■ Firms can improve their gearing by repaying long-term loans, issuing more ordinary shares or redeeming debentures.

Business in Focus

Even before it opened the Millennium Dome was experiencing financial problems. By November 1999 (one month before it commenced trading) the dome had used up its £399m grant and £43m of a £50m loan. The company had sold only £3.9m of tickets, rather than the £18.9m included in the budget. By April 2000 the Dome called for a further £38m, claiming it would cost over £200m to close the project.

l The Millennium Dome was financed mainly through public grants. To what extent did the way in which the project was financed contribute to its problems?

Efficiency ratios

This group of ratios measures the effectiveness with which management controls the internal operation of the business. They consider the following aspects of the management of an enterprise:

■ the extent to which assets are used to generate profits
■ how well stock is managed

■ the efficiency of creditor control – ie how long before customers settle their accounts.

There are a large number of ratios that fall under this heading, but we shall concentrate on just three.

1. Asset turnover ratio

This ratio measures a business's sales in relation to the assets used to generate these sales. The formula to calculate this ratio is

$$\text{asset turnover} = \frac{\text{sales (turnover)}}{\text{net assets}}$$

Net assets are defined as total assets less current liabilities.

This formula measures the efficiency with which businesses use their assets. An increasing ratio over time generally indicates that the firm is operating with greater efficiency. Conversely, a fall in the ratio can be caused by a decline in sales or an increase in assets employed.

Using this ratio

■ It is difficult to give a standard figure for this ratio as it varies significantly according to the type of business.
■ A business with high sales and relatively few assets (a supermarket, for example) might have a high asset turnover ratio and earn low profits on each sale.
■ Conversely other businesses may have a high value of assets, but achieve few sales so having a low asset turnover ratio. A high-class jeweller is an example of this category of business. The compensation for such a firm is that it normally

	Data for financial year ending 31/12/1998			Data for financial year ending 31/12/1999		
	turnover £m	net assets £m	result	turnover £m	net assets £m	result
Rolls Royce	4 496	2 643	1.70 times	4 744	3 884	1.22 times

	Data for financial year ending 31/03/1999			Data for financial year ending 31/03/2000		
	turnover £m	net assets £m	result	turnover £m	net assets £m	result
J Sainsbury	16 433	5 501	2.99 times	16 271	5 832	2.79 times

Table 3.26 *Comparing asset turnover ratios*

Notes: These results highlight the differences in asset turnover between different types of business. Rolls Royce does not achieve particularly high sales in relation to its assets. However, the company earns a substantial profit margin on each sale. During 1999 the company took over a number of smaller businesses, increasing its assets. This may explain the decline in the ratio.

Sainsbury is a very different company achieving high sales from a relatively small asset base. The proportion of profit received from each sale is significantly smaller. The decline in performance shown by this ratio between 1999 and 2000 may reflect the increasing competitiveness of the groceries market.

earns a high level of profit on each sale.

■ A business can improve its asset turnover ratio by improving its sales performance and/or disposing of any surplus or underutilised assets.

2. Stock turnover ratio

This ratio measures a company's success in converting stock into sales. The ratio compares the value of stock with sales achieved valued at cost. This permits an effective comparison with stock, which is always valued at cost. If the company makes a profit on each sale, then the faster it sells its stock, the greater the profits it earns. This ratio is only of relevance to manufacturing businesses, as firms providing services do not hold significant quantities of stock.

$$\text{Stock turnover ratio} = \frac{\text{cost of sales}}{\text{stock}}$$

In this form the results of calculating this ratio are expressed as a number of times a year. On 31 March 2000 Sainsbury held stock valued at £986m. During the company's financial year which ended on that day the company had achieved sales (at cost) of £15 201m. The company's stock turnover ratio was therefore 15.4 times.

The stock turnover formula can be reorganised to express the number of days taken on average to sell the business's stock.

$$\text{Stock turnover ratio} = \frac{\text{stock} \times 365}{\text{cost of sales}}$$

Our Sainsbury calculation would then become £986m × 365 divided by £15 201m giving an answer of 23.68 days. Thus, if Sainsbury sell their entire stock every 23 days, they will sell this stock approximately 15 times during a year.

Using this ratio

■ The standard figure for this ratio varies hugely according to the type of business. A market trader selling fruit and vegetables might expect to sell his entire stock every two or three days – about 100 times a year. At the other extreme an antiques shop might only sell its stock every six months – or twice a year.

■ A low figure for stock turnover could be due to obsolete stock. A high figure can indicate an efficient business, although selling out of stock results in customer dissatisfaction.

■ Improving the stock turnover ratio requires a business to hold lower levels of stock or to achieve higher sales without increasing stock levels.

P OINTS TO PONDER

Some business analysts have argued that recent changes have meant that stock turnover is of less importance in a modern economy. The use of JIT techniques and the increasing importance of service industries mean that much less stock is held by a modern business. To what extent do you agree with this view?

3. Debtors' collection period

This ratio (also referred to as debtor days) calculates the time typically taken by a business to collect the money that it is owed. This is an important ratio, as granting customers lengthy periods of credit may result in a business experiencing liquidity problems. If a company has substantial cash sales these should be excluded from the calculation.

$$\text{Debtors' collection period} = \frac{\text{debtors} \times 365}{\text{turnover}}$$

Using this ratio

- There is no standard figure for this ratio. In general a shorter figure is preferred as the business in question receives the inflow of cash more quickly. However, it can be an important part of a business's marketing strategy to offer customers a period of trade credit of perhaps 30 or 60 days.
- A rise in this ratio may be due to a number of causes. A period of expansion may mean that a business has to offer improved credit terms to attract new customers or a 'buy now pay later' offer may have been introduced.
- This ratio may be improved by reducing the credit period on offer to customers or by insisting on cash payment. A more focused approach is to conduct an aged debtors' analysis. This technique ranks a business's debtors according to the period of credit taken. This allows managers to concentrate on persuading the slowest payers to settle their accounts.

*P*OINTS TO PONDER

In spite of the passing of the Late Payment Act in 1998, firms are still slow to settle their debts. In the 15 months following the passing of the Act, the average time taken by firms to pay bills has risen by two days to 74 days.

Key terms

Capital employed is the total funds invested in a business, including that provided by shareholders and through long-term loans.
Credit: an arrangement under which a purchaser is given a specific amount of time (normally 30 or 60 days) before an account has to be paid.

Profitability ratios

These ratios compare the profits earned by a business with other key variables such as the level of sales achieved or the capital available to the managers of the business.

1. Gross profit margin

This ratio compares the gross profit achieved by a business with its sales turnover. Gross profit is earned before direct costs such as administration expenses are deducted. The ratio calculates the percentage of the selling price of a product that constitutes gross profit. The answer is expressed as a percentage.

$$\text{Gross profit margin} = \frac{\text{gross profit} \times 100}{\text{turnover}}$$

For example, in 1999 Sony's gross profit was $17\,846\,925$m. This was achieved on a turnover of $56\,621\,825$m.

$$\text{Gross profit margin} = \frac{17\,846\,925 \times 100}{56\,621\,825} = 31.25\%$$

This may appear a fairly high profit margin, but direct costs have not been deducted.

Using this ratio

- The figure for gross profit margin varies depending upon the type of industry. Firms that turn over their stock rapidly and then can trade with relatively few assets may operate with low gross profit margins. Greengrocers and bakers may fall into this category. Firms with slower turnover of stock and requiring substantial fixed assets may have a higher figure. House builders may fall into this category.

■ The sales mix can have a major influence on this ratio. A farmer selling eggs at a 10% gross profit margin and renting out holiday cottages at a 40% margin could improve the business's overall profit margin (but reduce its turnover) by discontinuing egg production.

■ This ratio can be improved by increasing prices although this may result in lower turnover. Alternatively, reducing direct costs (raw material costs and wages, for example) will also improve the figure.

2. Net profit margin

This ratio calculates the percentage of a product's selling price that is net profit (ie after all costs have been deducted). Because this ratio includes all of a business's operating expenses, it may be regarded as a better indication of performance than gross profit margin. Once again the answer to this ratio is written as a percentage.

$$\text{Net profit margin} = \frac{\text{net profit} \times 100}{\text{turnover}}$$

Continuing our example of Sony, the company's net profit margin for the trading year ending in December 1999 was $2 822 075. The company's net profit margin is shown as follows:

$$\text{Net profit margin} = \frac{2\,822\,075 \times 100}{56\,621\,825} = 3.98\%$$

Using this ratio

■ Results of this ratio can vary according to the type of business, though a higher net profit margin is preferable.

■ A comparison of gross and net profit margins can be informative. A business enjoying a stable gross profit margin and a declining net profit margin may be failing to control indirect costs effectively. This may be due to the purchase of new premises, for example.

■ Improvements in the net profit margin may be achieved through higher selling prices or tighter control of costs, particularly indirect costs.

*P*OINTS TO PONDER

Profits amongst manufacturing companies are much higher than expected according to a report carried out in 2000. The report highlights that profits have risen following an increase in investment, much of it from overseas.

3. Return on capital employed

This is a vital ratio comparing the operating profit earned with the amount of capital employed by the business. Its importance is reflected in the fact that it is also termed 'the primary efficiency ratio'. The result of this ratio, which is expressed as a percentage, allows an assessment to be made of the overall financial performance of the business. A fundamental comparison can be made between the prevailing rate of interest and the ROCE generated by a business.

$$\text{Return on capital employed} = \frac{\text{operating profit} \times 100}{\text{capital employed}}$$

Using this ratio

■ A typical ROCE may be expected to be in the range of 20–30%. It is particularly important to compare the results from calculating this ratio with the business's ROCE in previous years and also those achieved by competitors.

■ A business may improve its ROCE by increasing its operating profit without raising further capital or by reducing the amount of capital employed, perhaps by repaying some long-term debt.

Shareholders' ratios

The results of this group of ratios are of particular interest to the shareholders of a company or to anyone considering purchasing shares in a particular company. They are also known as investment ratios. Shareholders can receive a return on their purchase of shares in two ways:

1 through dividends paid from the company's profits over the financial year.

company name	description of company's activities	date of accounts	operating profit £m	capital employed £m	ROCE %
Allied Domecq	retailer of wines and spirits in international markets. Restaurant operator	31/01/2000	420.0	1312.0	32.01
Carlton Communications	media interests operating terrestrial and satellite TV and DVD manufacture	31/09/2000	231.9	1099.2	21.10
Scottish Power	supplier of gas and electricity principally to Scottish customers	31/10/2000	807.8	12093.3	6.68
British Airways	airline operator across the globe	31/03/2000	159.0	10149.0	1.57

Table 3.27 *ROCE data for a selection of companies*

Notes – a substantial range of ROCE figures for businesses engaged in very different markets. A more realistic assessment requires a comparison with other firms in the same industry and over a period of several years. British Airways experienced falling sales in the period to which the accounts relate, depressing profit figures.

2 as a result of a rise in the price of the shares – called a capital gain.

Dividends offer a short-term return on an investment and may be of interest to shareholders seeking a quick return. However, other shareholders may seek a long-term return on their investment. They may be prepared to forego high levels of dividends in the short run to allow profits to be invested. They hope that the business will grow, increasing the price of shares and providing a capital gain for shareholders.

There are a number of ratios that may be used by shareholders. However, we shall concentrate on ratios that compare the dividends received against the capital investment made by shareholders when purchasing shares.

1. Dividend per share

This is an important shareholders' ratio. It is simply the total dividend declared by a company divided by the number of shares the business has issued.

$$\text{Dividend per share} = \frac{\text{total dividends}}{\text{number of issued shares}}$$

Results of this ratio are expressed as a number of pence per share.

In 1999 Kingfisher, a UK-based retailing group (it owns B&Q and Woolworth's and other businesses), announced dividends totalling £175.3m. The dividend per share for the company was calculated as follows.

$$\text{Kingfisher's dividend per share} = \frac{£175.3m}{1348.5m \text{ shares}}$$

$$= 13.0 \text{ pence per share}$$

It is normal for dividends to be paid in two parts: an interim dividend halfway through the financial year and a final dividend at the end of the year.

Using this ratio

- A higher figure is generally preferable to a lower one as this provides the shareholder with a larger return on his or her investment. However, some shareholders are looking for long-term investments and may prefer to have a lower DPS now in the hope of greater returns in the future and a rising share price.
- It is wise to compare the dividend per share with that offered by alternative companies. However, it is also important to bear in mind how much has to be invested to buy each share. A low dividend per share may be perfectly acceptable if the company has a low share price.
- A business can improve this figure by announcing higher dividends (and therefore reducing the amount of profit retained within the business). This may prove attractive to some

shareholders, but may not be in the long-term interests of the business, particularly if profits are not rising.

Business in Focus

BP announced record profits in November 2000, just a few weeks after widespread protests about the price of petrol in the UK. During 2000 BP made profits in excess of £2.7bn from its trading activities in the UK alone. A company spokesperson was quick to point out that it had also invested £2bn in the UK over the same period.

BP's record rise in profits resulted from the rapid increase in oil prices during 2000 and an increase in the value of its stocks. The company claimed that the cost of petrol in the UK before taxes is the lowest in Europe. The company's explanations fell on deaf ears. Various groups, including trade unions called for a windfall tax on the profits of oil companies. John Edmonds, the general secretary of the GMB (general workers' union) claimed that the Chancellor could use the proceeds from a windfall tax to fund a price cut of 125 pence a gallon.

BP confirmed that their profits were broadly in line with expectations, although they had spent an extra £15m on marketing in the UK during the fuel crisis.

Adapted from the Electronic Telegraph

1 Explain the conflict between stakeholder interests that can be seen within this case study. *(15 marks)*
2 Discuss ways in which BP might have protected their public image in these circumstances. *(15 marks)*
3 To what extent does this case confirm the need for stricter controls over the behaviour of large businesses? *(20 marks)*

---

dividend received on a single share with the current market price of that share. This provides shareholders with a better guide to a business's performance as it compares the return with the amount that would need to be invested to purchase a share. The result of calculating this ratio is given as a percentage.

$$\text{Dividend yield} = \frac{\text{dividend per share} \times 100}{\text{market price of share}}$$

Imagine a shareholder was considering investing in the Kingfisher group and noted that the share price on one particular day was 220 pence, and that the dividend per share for the company was 13 pence. He or she could calculate the dividend yield as follows.

$$\text{Dividend yield} = \frac{13.0 \times 100}{220} = 5.91\%$$

Using this ratio

- A higher return will be regarded as preferable by shareholders seeking a quick return. Longer-term investors might settle for a lower figure, allowing the firm to reinvest profits and offering the possibility of higher profits and dividends in the future.
- Results for this ratio can vary dramatically according to fluctuations in the company's share price.
- This ratio can be improved by increasing the proportion of profits distributed to shareholders in the form of dividends.

*P*OINTS TO PONDER

Durlacher is a company that invests in internet companies and makes modest profits but does not pay dividends. However, the Stock Exchange recognises that the company has potential. Its shares have risen from around 71p in early 1999 to more than £32 in summer 2000.

---

2. Dividend yield

This ratio is really a development of the previous ratio and provides shareholders with more information. The dividend yield compares the

Limitations of ratio analysis

Ratio analysis provides stakeholders with an insight into the performance of a business. However, to offer the maximum amount of information, the details gained from ratio analysis need to be compared with other data, such as that outlined below:

- **the results for the same business over previous years**. This allows stakeholders to appreciate the trend of the data. Thus a low, but steadily increasing figure for ROCE might be reassuring to investors
- **the results of ratio analysis for other firms in the same industry**. We have seen that results expected from various ratios vary according to the type of firm under investigation. Thus, the stock turnover ratio will be much higher for a retailer selling perishable products, than for a manufacturer. By comparing like-with-like a more informed judgement may be made
- **the results of ratios from firms in other industries**. Stakeholders can compare the ratios of a particular business with those from a wide range of firms. This might allow, for example, a comparison between two firms experiencing rapid growth. The Centre for Inter-Firm Comparisons offers anonymous data on the financial ratios of many UK firms.

A significant weakness of ratio analysis is that it only considers the financial aspects of a business's performance. Whilst this is undeniably important other elements of a business should be taken into account when evaluating performance:

- **the market in which the business is trading**. A business that is operating in a highly competitive market might experience relatively low profits, depressing ratios such as the return on capital employed
- **the position of the firm within the market**. A market leader might be expected to provide better returns than a small firm struggling to establish itself. However, the small struggling firm may be investing heavily in developing new products and establishing a brand identity. The struggling firm may generate large profits in the future
- **the quality of the workforce and management team**. These are important factors in assessing a business, but not ones that will be revealed directly through ratio analysis. Indeed a business that invests heavily in its human resources may appear to be performing relatively poorly through the use of ratio analysis
- **the economic environment.** In general businesses might be expected to perform better during periods of prosperity and to produce better results from ratio analysis.

Progress questions

1 Explain, with the aid of an example, why a ratio might provide more detail on a firm's performance, than a single piece of financial information. (7 marks)

2 Distinguish between efficiency ratios and profitability ratios. (6 marks)

3 Outline **two** sources of information that might be important when conducting ratio analysis. (6 marks)

4 Marsham Trading has current liabilities amounting to £2.8m. Its current assets are: debtors £1.1m, stock £2.0m and cash £0.9m. Calculate the business's current and acid test ratios. (8 marks)

5 Explain **two** reasons why the results of liquidity ratios might be treated with caution. (6 marks)

6 Pelennor Products is a rapidly growing business providing IT services. The company's debtor collection ratio has increased from 33.2 days to 41.7 days over the past year. Outline the possible implications of this for the business. (9 marks)

7 Fangorn plc has seen an improvement in its gross profit margin over the financial year. At the same time its net profit margin has deteriorated. Explain the implications of this for the business and outline possible actions that the management team might take. (10 marks)

8 Explain why the return on capital employed (ROCE) is such an important ratio for stakeholders. (6 marks)

9 Why might the dividend yield ratio provide a better indication of a company's performance than the dividend per share ratio? (5 marks)

10 Outline **two** external factors that need to be taken into account when conducting ratio analysis. (6 marks)

Analysis and evaluation questions

1 'Any ratio analysis that uses data from the balance sheet is suspect, because the data on this statement relate to a particular moment in time.' Critically assess this view.   *(15 marks)*

2 Analyse whether ratio analysis is worthwhile without considering the market position of the firms concerned.   *(12 marks)*

3 'Standard or normal figures for ratios are of little value because results vary so much between firms in different industries.' To what extent do you agree with this statement?   *(15 marks)*

4 Ratio analysis gives stakeholders historical information about a business. Discuss whether this means that it is of little value in predicting a company's future performance.   *(15 marks)*

5 An investor is considering purchasing shares in Manchester United plc. Examine the information that the potential shareholder should consider before taking a decision.   *(12 marks)*

Case study

Retailing group Rohan are reported to have made a £229m bid for the East Anglian based supermarket chain Breckland Stores. A spokesperson for Rohan commented that Breckland represented a valuable addition and would enable the group to have a real presence throughout the UK. 'We have over 7m customers in other parts of the UK, but East Anglia has been a black spot for us until now. This is the start of a period of rapid growth for us. We intend to increase our share of the European groceries market over the next year or two.'

City analysts were cautious about the takeover. One senior trader commented that Rohan had already expanded very rapidly and that the price paid for Breckland did not represent a bargain. 'The groceries market is global and the degree of competition is increasing rapidly. Rohan is still small in comparison with other supermarkets in the UK.'

Rohan's share price fell by 73 pence to 473 pence on the news of the takeover.

	2001 £m	2000 £m
Turnover	6 252	4 944
Cost of sales	5 413	4 375
Gross profit	839	569
Expenses	527	399
Operating profit	312	170
Dividends	162	88

Table 3.29 *Rohan group – extracts from profit and loss accounts*

	2001 £m	2000 £m
Fixed assets	1 182	842
Current Assets		
Stock	298	202
Debtors and cash	206	104
Less current liabilities	(662)	(577)
Creditors: amounts due within one year	(715)	(376)
Net assets employed	309	195
Share capital	225	105
Reserves	84	90
Capital employed	309	195

Table 3.28 *Rohan group – balance sheet as at 31 September*

1 Outline **two** possible sources of finance available to the Rohan group for its proposed takeover of Breckland Stores.   *(6 marks)*

2 Rohan's share price fell by 73 pence following the announcement of the proposed takeover. Examine the possible implications of this for the company.   *(10 marks)*

3 Consider the case for and against the Rohan group spending £229m on a takeover of Breckland Stores.   *(18 marks)*

4 Discuss the value of ratio analysis in assessing the financial performance of a business such as the Rohan group.   *(16 marks)*

INVESTMENT DECISION MAKING

Starting points

This topic was not covered at AS level and is therefore developed fully in this unit.

Key terms

Capital expenditure is spending by a business to purchase fixed assets such as property, machinery and vehicles.

Investment involves the risk of resources in pursuit of some goal – in the context of this chapter it means investing in fixed assets in the hope of earning a profit.

Interest rates: the price of borrowed money.

Investment is an important term within business studies and often entails managers taking major decisions. Investment can mean a decision to purchase part or all of another business, perhaps as a result of a takeover bid. However, it is perhaps more common to use the term in relation to the purchase of a fixed asset or some other major expenditure. What is common is that all such actions involve a degree of risk. This must be judged against the likely return. The final decision will depend upon managers' assessment of these two factors.

EXAMINER'S ADVICE

Students frequently only consider numerical aspects of investment decisions. However, it is common for non-financial factors to be a significant part of the decision. For example, investment in new fixed assets may result in less job security for employees (as they fear being replaced by the new assets). This could damage the performance of the workforce and possibly the business's corporate image. A well-balanced answer would take into account financial and non-financial information.

Businesses take decisions regarding investment in a variety of circumstances:

- when contemplating introducing new products.

A business may assess the likely costs and returns from investing in one or more new products

- expansion. Evaluating whether or not to invest in new fixed assets as part of a planned programme of growth. Liverpool Football club is set to invest over £80m in a new stadium, just a few hundred yards from its existing ground – Anfield. The Club hopes to increase its sales revenue by attracting larger crowds into the new stadium

- investing in new technology. This is often undertaken to reduce costs and improve productivity. Brainspark, the venture capital company, has announced a £1m investment in a commercial property website. The site, to be called Propex, will be a showcase for the property industry, allowing agents, buyers and sellers to advertise requirements to the marketplace

- businesses may also use techniques of investment appraisal before spending heavily on promotional campaigns, developing new brands or products or retraining the workforce.

In each circumstance, however, the business must adopt an appropriate appraisal technique to decide whether the returns received from an investment are sufficient to justify the initial capital expenditure.

Financial techniques of investment appraisal

A number of techniques are available to managers to assist them in taking decisions on whether to go ahead with investments, or to help in making a judgement between two or more possible investment opportunities. This section will look at three of the most important of these techniques: payback, the average rate of return and discounted cash flow.

These financial techniques are valuable but do depend upon a number of assumptions:

- all costs and revenues can be easily and accurately forecast for some years into the future;
- that key variables (eg interest rates) will not change
- that the business in question is seeking maximum profits.

Business in Focus

Beazer Group, the house building company, is waging war on costly and unreliable building site workers by shifting its operations away from building sites and into factories.

The company has said it plans to open a new £2m factory in the south of England, which will produce timber frames, panels and doors, reducing the need for costly on-site labour. John Low, chief executive, said 'The demand for labour is pushing up costs but by moving the process and technology of house building to factories, we should be able to economise on time and expense.'

1 Develop arguments in favour of and against Beazer's decision to transfer some of its construction work into a factory. In what ways do you think financial and non-financial factors contributed to the overall decision?

There are two major considerations for managers when deciding whether or not to invest in a fixed asset or another business:

1 the total profits earned by the investment over the foreseeable future.
2 how quickly the investment will recover its cost. This occurs when the earnings from the investment exceed the cost of the investment.

The process of assessing these factors is called investment appraisal and refers to the process of assessing one or more potential investments. Forecasting future costs and revenues can be a very difficult and at times expensive exercise to undertake. Forecasts about future revenues could prove to be inaccurate for a number of reasons.

- Competitors may introduce new products or reduce their prices, reducing forecast sales and revenues.
- Tastes and fashions may change resulting in an unexpected slump in demand. The company managing the Millennium Dome forecast visitor numbers considerably in excess of those actually attending.

- The economy may move into recession or slump (or alternatively into an upswing) resulting in sales figures radically different from those forecast.

Costs can be equally tricky to forecast. Unexpected periods of inflation, or rising import prices might result in inaccurate forecasts of expenditures. This can lead to a significant reduction in actual profits when compared with forecasts.

Companies that operate in a stable economic environment are much more easily able to forecast into the future as they have confidence that their predictions on the rate of inflation, likely rate of interest, level of unemployment and hence demand are as accurate as they can make them. A stable economic environment should lead to more accurate forecasts of both costs and revenues associated with investment projects.

Investment appraisal and related topics

It is easy to regard investment appraisal as simply a technique to be used when a business is contemplating purchasing fixed assets. However, investment appraisal can be used in relation to a number of a business's activities, all of which involve significant expenditure. These might include

- investing in a major new advertising campaign
- expanding into new markets, perhaps overseas
- attempting to adjust management styles and corporate cultures, possibly entailing reorganisation and retraining
- adopting new techniques of production including JIT and kaizen
- researching and developing new products.

Investment appraisal is an important element of most aspects of business activity. It can help to quantify proposed actions by managers and provide important information assisting managers to take good-quality decisions.

1. Payback

Payback is a simple technique that measures the time period required for the earnings from an investment to recoup its original cost. Quite simply it finds out the number of years it takes to recover the cost of an investment from its earnings. In spite of the obvious simplicity of the payback technique, it remains the most common method of investment appraisal in the UK.

An example of payback:

Year	Cash outflow (£)	Cash inflow (£)
1	500 000	100 000
2		200 000
3		200 000
4		150 000

In this case the calculation is simple: payback is achieved at the end of year three when the initial investment of £500 000 is recovered from earnings – £100 000 in year one plus £200 000 in each of years two and three.

Calculations can be a little more complex, however, as shown in the following example.

Year	Cash outflow (£)	Cash inflow (£)
1	500 000	100 000
2		100 000
3		200 000
4		300 000

In this case payback is achieved during the fourth year. The formula used to calculate the point during the year at which payback is achieved is as follows. Number of full years + (amount of investment not recovered/revenue generated in next year).

In the second example the investment has recovered £400 000 after three years. Therefore £100 000 remains to be recovered in year four before payback point is reached. During year four the investment will generate £300 000.

Thus payback = 3 years + 100 000/300 000 = $3\frac{1}{3}$ years or three years and four months. Figure 3.19 illustrates the concept of payback in the form of a graph.

*P*OINTS TO PONDER

The government has announced that from 2003 public sector investment projects will be appraised and managed in much the same way as in the private sector. This decision was taken in the light of a government commitment to reassure the public that money would not be wasted.

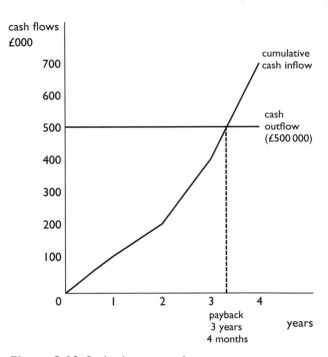

Figure 3.19 *Payback on a graph*

Payback has the advantage of being quick and simple and this probably explains its popularity, especially with small businesses. However, it does have disadvantages. It ignores the level of profits that may be ultimately generated by the investment. For profit maximising businesses this may represent an important omission. Furthermore, payback ignores the timing of any receipts. The following example highlights this weakness.

Two investment projects A and B each require an investment of £1m. Their expected earnings are as follows.

Year	Project A cash inflow (£)	Project B cash inflow (£)
1	500 000	100 000
2	300 000	200 000
3	200 000	300 000
4	100 000	500 000

Both investment projects achieve payback at the end of year four. However, A is obviously more attractive because it yields greater returns in the early years. Payback does not take into account the timing of any income received.

2. Average rate of return

The average rate of return (or ARR) is a more complex

Business in Focus: money down the tube?

London's Underground system is in desperate need of refurbishment. Stations are in a state of disrepair and many of the trains urgently need replacing. Much of the system has had little money spent on it in a quarter of a century. Because this refurbishment requires a huge investment programme (estimated at £13bn), the government is considering offering private firms the chance to invest in improving and maintaining the Underground. This investment would take place as part of a public–private partnership (PPP). If private funding were used firms would be invited to invest funds and receive returns from ticket sales over a period of 30 years.

I   Discuss the financial and non-financial information a business would require before taking a decision on whether to invest in London's Underground system.

and meaningful method of investment appraisal. This technique calculates the percentage rate of return on each possible investment. The resulting percentage figure allows a simple comparison with other investment opportunities, including investing in banks and building societies. It is important to remember, however, that a commercial investment (such as purchasing CAD/CAM equipment for a production line) involves a degree of risk. The returns may not be as forecast. Therefore it is important that such an investment earns significantly more than the rate of interest available in the local building society. If the percentage return on purchasing the CAD/CAM equipment was identical to that on a high-interest account in a building society, the latter would represent the better investment, as it carries little risk.

The formula for calculating ARR is

average profit/asset's initial cost $\times$ 100%

Average profit = total net profit before tax over the asset's lifetime/useful life of the asset

The average rate of return is considered to be more useful than Payback because it considers the level of profits earned from an investment rather

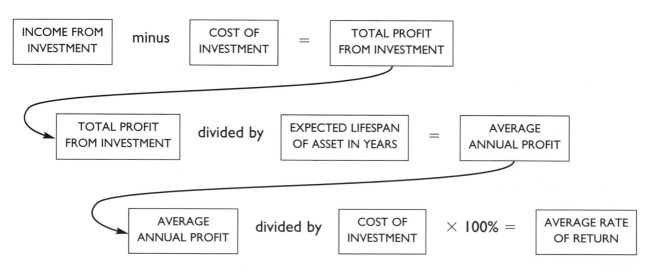

Figure 3.20 *How to calculate average rate of return*

total income from IT investment	cost of investment	net profit from investment	annual average profit	ARR (annual average profit/ initial cost $\times$ 100)
£220 000	£120 000	£100 000	£20 000	20%

Table 3.30 *Presenting the calculation of average rate of return on a table. This figure illustrates the decision facing Miller Reprographics outlined overleaf.*

Business in Focus: Miller Reprographics

Purchasing new IT equipment for Miller Reprographics is estimated to cost £120 000 and a return of £220 000 over five years is anticipated.

The total profit from investing in IT over five years = £220 000 − £120 000 = £100 000

On an annual basis this is £100 000/5 = £20 000

Average rate of return = $\dfrac{£20\,000}{£120\,000} \times 100\% = 16.67\%$

Miller Reprographics may consider this to be an attractive investment as a rate of 20% is considerably higher than that available on any interest-bearing account at a bank or building society, even allowing a premium for risk. However, the business may have an alternative investment offering a higher rate of return.

than simply the time taken to recover cost. It also offers easier comparison with returns on other investments, notably financial investments in banks and building societies. However, this technique also fails to differentiate between investments that generate high returns in the early years and those that offer greater rewards later on.

Integrated Business: Prescott Engineering

Prescott Engineering continues the tradition of engineering for which Birmingham was world famous during the nineteenth and early twentieth centuries. However, the company has reached a crossroads. It is experiencing increasing difficulty in competing with other firms (mainly located elsewhere in the European Union) partly due to a lack of scale and because labour and capital productivity remain substantially below levels achieved by competitors.

The European market is very important to the company, although it has struggled to be price competitive with major European producers. The directors and managers of Prescott Engineering have lobbied extensively for the full entry of the UK into the European Monetary Union, believing that the company will benefit significantly from this action.

The company is contemplating two alternative investments as part of a process to improve international competitiveness. Some directors favour investment in computer-aided manufacturing equipment to improve the performance of the company's production line. Although opposed by the Allied Union of Engineering Workers, the managing director supports this move arguing that it will 'bring the company into the twenty-first century'. An alternative view is that the company should invest heavily in staff training allowing the adoption of new methods of production including just-in-time production and a widespread adoption of teamworking. It is expected that this approach would allow empowerment of the workforce with the intention of improving labour productivity levels.

The director of finance has estimated the expected costs and returns associated with the two approaches. All figures are in £m.

	CAM equipment	Retraining and empowerment
Initial investment	25.5	18.7
Income year one	7.2	1.9
Income year two	7.4	5.1
Income year three	7.7	8.5
Income year four	7.9	11.4
Income year five	8.3	13.6

1 Using a financial technique of your choice assess the merits of the two alternative investment projects. *(10 marks)*
2 The director of human resources is reported to have commented 'the human issue should be a vital issue in this decision.' To what extent do you agree with her view? How might the human aspect of the decision affect the final outcome? *(20 marks)*
3 Prescott Engineering has lobbied in support of the UK's entry to the European Monetary Union. Discuss the reasons why the board of directors might have taken this view. *(20 marks)*

3. Discounted cash flow

Key terms

Discounting is the reducing of the value of future earnings to reflect the opportunity cost of an investment.
Present value is the value of a future stream of income from an investment, converted into its current worth.

The technique of discounted cash flow takes into account what is termed the 'time value' of money. The time value of money is based on the principle that money at the present time is worth more than money at some point in the future. Thus, according to this principle £1000 today is of greater value than £1000 in one or two years' time. There are two major reasons why this time value principle exists:

1 **risk**. Having £1000 now is a certainty; receiving the same amount at some point in the future may not occur. The full £1000 payment may not be made; indeed no payment at all may be made. An investment project may fail to provide the expected returns because of a competitor's actions, because of a change in tastes and fashions or as a result of the consequence of technological change.
2 **opportunity cost**. This is the foregone alternative. Even if no risk existed, the time value of money would still exist. This is because the money could be placed into an interest-bearing account generating a return. Thus, if we assume that a rate of 5% is available on an interest-bearing account, £1000 in one year's time is worth the same as £953 today. The reason for this is that by investing £953 at an interest rate of 5%, we would have £1000 after one year.

This time-value principle means that the longer the delay before money is received, the lower its value in present-day terms. This is called present value. Table 3.31 shows two investments requiring identical outlays. Both projects also receive the same cash inflow over a four-year period and would generate the same average rate of return (10%). However, the majority of the cash inflow for project

A occurs in year one, whilst in project B this is delayed until year 3. The time-value principle would suggest that project A is preferable to project B. To show the effect of the time principle we need to calculate the present value of cash inflows and outflows through the use of discounting.

year	investment project A £000s	investment project B £000s
0 (now)	(500)	(500)
1	400	100
2	100	100
3	100	100
4	100	400

Table 3.31 *Two similar investment projects with different time patterns for cash inflows*

℘ OINTS TO PONDER

The UK remains the most popular country in Europe for inward investment – ie investment from individuals and businesses overseas. In 1999/2000 foreign investment in the UK exceeded £82bn. This is in spite of the UK's decision not to adopt the euro.

Discounting

Discounting is the process of adjusting the value of money received at some future date to its present value – ie its worth today. Discounting is, in effect, the reverse of adding interest. Discounting tables are available to illustrate the effect of converting future streams of income to their present values. The rate of interest plays a central role in discounting – in the same way as it does in predicting the future value of savings. Table 3.32 shows the discounting figures and the value in present day terms of £1000 over a period of five years into the future. If the business anticipates relatively high interest rates over the period of the investment then future earnings are discounted heavily to provide present values for

year	discounting factor used to convert to present value assuming 10% rate of interest	present value of £1000 at a discount rate of 10% £	discounting factor used to convert to present value assuming 5% rate of interest	present value of £1000 at a discount rate of 5% £
0 (now)	1	1000	1	1000
1	0.909	909	0.952	952
2	0.826	826	0.907	907
3	0.751	751	0.864	864
4	0.683	683	0.822	822

Table 3.32 *The process of discounting*

the investment. Lower rates result in discounting having a lesser effect in converting future earnings into present values.

The basic calculation is that the appropriate discounting factor is multiplied by the amount of money to be received in the future to convert it to its present value. Thus, at a rate of interest of 10% the present value of £1000 in two years' time is £826 (£1000 × 0.826). The present value of £1000 received in fours years' time is £683. This figure is lower because the time interval is greater and the effect of the time-value principle more pronounced.

From this example we can see that the rate of interest has a significant effect on the present value of future earnings. The higher the rate of interest, the greater the discount. Thus, the present value of £1000 in three years' time is £751 if the rate of interest is assumed to be 10%. However, if the rate of interest is estimated to be 5% the present value is greater: £863.

The choice of interest rate to be used as the basis for discounting is an important decision by a business undertaking investment appraisal. The discounting rate selected normally reflects the interest rates that are expected for the duration of the project. However, as we shall see later another approach is to choose the rate the firm would like to earn on the project and to use this as the basis of the calculation.

*P*OINTS TO PONDER

EMAP the publisher of 'lad's' magazine FHM is cutting its planned investment in putting its titles on the internet due to advertising revenue declining since the original decision was taken. The company said they had decided to cut their investment in on-line publishing from £250m to £120m as a result of investment appraisal techniques.

Key *issues*

Risk is an important factor within investment decision making. Risk can be defined as uncertainty that is quantifiable or that can be measured. There are two major types of risk.

1 Systematic risk relates to the environment in which a project will operate. Thus this type of risk could include a loss of sales and cash inflow due to, say, an adverse movement in the exchange rate.

2 Specific risk is associated with a particular project, eg launching a new product which is entirely new and of which the firm has little experience.

Techniques of investment appraisal can incorporate an allowance for risk perhaps, by reducing cash inflows or increasing costs. More sophisticated techniques use the theory of provability to attempt to arrive at more accurate predictions.

Risk should be distinguished from uncertainty. Uncertainty is not measurable and cannot be included in numerical techniques of investment appraisal. An investment project which appears to have a high degree of uncertainty attached to it may not be undertaken because the firm in question may be unable to assess its likely costs and benefits.

Net present value

Discounting expected future cash flows is the basis of calculating net present value. This method of investment appraisal forecasts expected outflows and inflows of cash and discounts the inflows and outflows. To calculate net present value we need to know

- the initial cost of the investment
- the chosen rate of discount
- any expected inflows and outflows of cash
- the duration of the investment project
- any remaining or residual value of the project at the end of the investment (if the investment is to purchase production equipment this may have scrap value once it is obsolete, for example).

The outflows of cash are subtracted from the inflows to provide a net figure: the net present value. This figure is important for two reasons.

1 If the net present value figure is negative, the investment is not worth undertaking. This is because the present value of the stream of

earnings is less than the cost of the investment. A more profitable approach would be to invest the capital in an interest-bearing account.

2 When an enterprise is considering a number of possible investment projects it can use the present value figure to rank them. The project generating the highest net present value figure is the most worthwhile in financial terms. In these circumstances a business may select the project – or projects – with the highest net present values.

An example of calculating net present value

Do It yourself is one of the UK's most popular DIY magazines. The owners of the magazine, Bure Publishing, are investigating the production of an on-line edition and have conducted negotiations with two software houses regarding the development of a website for their new product *e-DIY*. The two software houses offered very different ideas: one (proposal A) suggesting a basic product allowing Bure Publishing to offer access to the new website at a bargain price. The other software house proposed a more sophisticated product, to a higher technical standard offering the opportunity for premium pricing (proposal B).

The cash flows associated with these proposals over a five-year period are set out in table 3.33. These show the cost of developing the website and the expected revenues less operating costs for the site each year. Bure Publishing estimates that a 10% discount rate would reflect likely market rates of interest.

year	Proposal A annual cash flows £s	Proposal A discounting factors at 10%	Proposal A present value £s	Proposal B annual cash flows £s	Proposal B discounting factors at 10%	Proposal B present value £s
0	(212 000)	1	(212 000)	(451 000)	1	(451 000)
1	46 000	0.909	41 814	89 400	0.909	81 265
2	57 500	0.826	47 495	115 000	0.826	94 990
3	63 250	0.751	47 501	122 500	0.751	91 998
4	69 000	0.683	47 127	144 275	0.683	98 540
5	71 000	0.621	44 091	140 000	0.621	86 940
		net present value	£16 28		net present value	2 733

Table 3.33 *Comparing investment projects using discounted cash flow.*

Bure Publishing would opt for proposal A on the basis of this financial information, as the net present value for proposal A (the cheaper option) is higher than that for proposal B. The net cash flow for proposal A is also positive as cash inflows exceed outflows. Therefore the investment is viable. However, non-financial information may affect this investment decision.

Internal rate of return (IRR)

This is another way in which discounting and the concept of present value can be used in the process of investment appraisal. The internal rate of return does not choose a particular discounting rate. Instead a series of calculations are carried out using computers until a rate of discount is discovered which results in the net present value of the project equalling zero. That is, the cash outflows and inflows when discounted at this particular rate exactly equal one another.

This rate of discount can be compared with

- a target rate of return for which the business aims or
- the expected rate of interest.

If the internal rate of return is higher the project should be considered viable. Although this appears to require complex calculations, computers can work out the IRR for any investment project almost instantaneously.

A comparison of investment appraisal methods

The method of investment appraisal chosen will depend upon the type of firm, the market in which it is trading and its corporate objectives. A small firm may be more likely to use payback because managers may be unfamiliar with more complex methods of investment appraisal. Small businesses also often focus on survival and an important aspect of any investment will be how long it takes to cover the cost of the investment from additional revenues. Payback is therefore valuable for firms who wish to minimise risk.

Larger firms having access to more sophisticated financial techniques may use the average rate of return or discounted cash flow methods. These methods highlight the overall profitability of investment projects and may be more appropriate for businesses where profit maximisation is important.

method of investment appraisal	advantages	disadvantages
payback	■ easy to calculate ■ simple to understand ■ relevant to firms with limited funds who want a quick return	■ ignores timing of payments ■ excludes income received after payback ■ does not calculate profit
average rate of return	■ measures the profit achieved on projects ■ allows easy comparison with returns on financial investments (bank accounts, for example)	■ ignores the timing of the payments ■ calculates average profits – they may fluctuate wildly during the project
discounted cash flow	■ makes an allowance for the opportunity cost of investing. ■ takes into account cash inflows and outflows for the duration of the investment	■ choosing the discount rate is difficult – especially for long-term projects ■ a complex method to calculate and easily misunderstood

Table 3.34 *A comparison of techniques of investment appraisal*

Is it worth using techniques of investment appraisal?

The results of investment appraisal calculations are only as good as the data on which they are based. Firms experience difficulty in accurately forecasting the cost of many major projects. It is even more difficult to estimate the likely revenues from investment projects, particularly long-term ones. It is perhaps possible to make an allowance to represent risk – for example, the possibility of a competitor taking actions that result in sales being lower than forecast. However, uncertainty – which cannot be measured – may make any investment appraisal worthless.

In assessing the value of numerical techniques of investment appraisal, some thought has to be given to the alternative. Without the use of payback and the like, managers would operate on the bases of hunches and guesswork. Some managers may have a good instinct for these matters whereas others may not. As markets become more complex and global the need for some technique to appraise investments becomes greater. It is more difficult for an individual or a group to have an accurate overview of a large international market comprising many competitors and millions of diverse individuals. Detailed market research to forecast possible revenues and the use of appropriate techniques of investment appraisal may become even more important in the future.

Qualitative techniques of investment appraisal

The financial aspects of any proposed investment will clearly have an important influence upon whether a business goes ahead with the plan. However, a number of other issues may affect the decision:

- **corporate image**. A firm may reject a potentially profitable investment project, or choose a less profitable alternative, because to do otherwise might reflect badly on the business. Having a positive corporate image is important in terms of long-term sales and profits and may be considered more important than gaining short-term advantage from profitable investments. In the UK the National Westminster Bank has invested heavily in internet banking and had planned to close many high street branches as part of this investment programme. However, the bad publicity given to branch closures by all banks led the National Westminster to reverse the closure decision. The firm's investment in internet banking may prove less profitable as a consequence

- **corporate objectives**. Most businesses will only undertake an investment if they consider that it will assist in the achievement of corporate objectives. For example, Rolls Royce engineering, a company that publicly states its aim to produce high-quality products may invest heavily in training for its staff and in research and

---

Business in Focus

Royal Dutch Shell, the oil company, has recognised the increasing importance of the environment in business decisions by incorporating the cost of greenhouse-gas emissions in its investment appraisals. Increasing public and governmental concern over the implications of global warming has brought about this initiative.

International agreements to reduce carbon dioxide emissions (caused by burning fuels such as oil, for example) are expected to have a substantial impact on oil consumption and production. The company expects that governments in many countries will tax oil production and consumption heavily to reflect the carbon emissions made as a by-product of using the product. In many markets Shell will not be able to pass on the taxes associated with the production of oil and gas. This may make certain investments (in extracting oil and gas in certain countries, for example) produce returns that are unacceptable to the company. Without the so-called carbon taxes, the investment may have been deemed viable.

The Financial Times

development. This will assist in the manufacture of world-class aero engines and vehicles

■ **environmental and ethical issues**. These can be important influences on investment decisions. Some firms have a genuine commitment to trading ethically and to inflicting minimal damage on the environment. This is a core part of the business philosophy of some firms. As a consequence they would not exploit cheap Third World labour or use non-sustainable resources.

Other firms may have a less deep commitment to ethical and environmental trading but may avoid some investments for fear of damaging publicity

■ **industrial relations**. Some potentially profitable investments may be turned down because they would result in a substantial loss of jobs. Taking decisions that lead to large-scale redundancies can be costly in terms of decreased morale, redundancy payments and harm to the business's corporate image.

Progress questions

1 Outline **three** business decisions that may require the application of investment appraisal techniques.
(9 marks)

2 Explain why forecasts of sales revenues arising from an investment may prove to be inaccurate.
(7 marks)

3 Why might investment appraisal be easier to conduct in a stable economic environment?
(7 marks)

4 Thames Radio is considering investing in new broadcasting equipment. The cost of the investment is forecast to be £150 000. The expected additional revenue from being able to broadcast to a larger area is £40 000 per annum. What is the payback period of this investment?
(5 marks)

5 Explain **one** disadvantage of using payback in the circumstances in question 3. *(4 marks)*

6 Outline the stages that have to be completed to carry out an average rate of return calculation.
(6 marks)

7 Wessex Leisure is considering the purchase of a pleasure cruiser for use in the Solent. The Meriden is available at a cost of £900 000 and would cost £100 000 each year to operate. Over its ten-year life the cruiser would generate £280 000 in revenue each year. Calculate the average rate of return on this investment. *(7 marks)*

8 Explain what is meant by the 'present value' of a stream of earnings from an investment. *(5 marks)*

9 Chedgrave Printers are appraising the costs and benefits from a new piece of machinery. The equipment costs £300 000 and has a working life of four years. The company expects to generate revenue of £120 000 each year if they purchase the machine. Calculate the net present value of this project assuming an interest rate of 10%.
(7 marks)

10 Outline **two** qualitative factors that an oil company may consider as part of the appraisal of a proposed investment to extract oil from the sea bed under the English Channel. *(6 marks)*

Analysis and evaluation questions

1 'Techniques of investment appraisal that ignore the timing of cash flows are of little value.' Critically evaluate this statement. *(15 marks)*

2. Analyse whether the method of investment appraisal selected should depend upon the type of business and its corporate objectives. *(12 marks)*

3. 'For businesses in the primary sector, qualitative factors are more important than financial factors when taking an investment decision.' To what extent do you agree with this statement?
(15 marks)

3. Discuss whether the existence of uncertainty means that all techniques of investment appraisal are a waste of time.
(15 marks)

5. In spite of the benefits of carrying out an appraisal, many investment decisions are still made on the basis of instinct and hunch. Examine the factors that may cause this to happen.
(12 marks)

Case study

Transit was in the doldrums. The company is one of the UK's best-known train and coach operators. The company enjoyed considerable success following the privatisation of rail services in the early 1990s. Transit won the franchise to operate trains in the north of England and southern Scotland. Its trains were instantly recognisable because of their blue and gold livery. Unusually they also won a reputation for arriving on time and for providing a comfortable and speedy service. Transit was a rising star.

The media eagerly sought interviews with Transit's managing director Craig Prescott and enjoyed his quick wit and public relations skills. Craig had worked in transport companies in Singapore and the USA before coming back to the UK to head up the company bidding for the franchises to operate trains on a number of routes. Transit had run coach services for many years, but was looking to expand its business into related areas. Running trains on some lines in the UK meant that the company could use the skills already available.

Five years ago Transit was a star performer on the Stock Exchange offering investors excellent returns and promising substantial growth in the years ahead. Since then the company's fortunes have foundered. A number of factors were responsible for the change in fortune. The company's decision to purchase hotels throughout Ireland seemed a risky decision at the time and events appear to have proved the critics to be correct. Some analysts argued that the company should concentrate on investing in its core business – transport. Concerns were also expressed about the way in which the company financed its growth which had made Transit vulnerable to interest rate rises. The company's shareholders began to wonder whether they had been seduced by the abundant charm of the managing director, rather than the true potential of the business.

By 2001 Craig Prescott and Transit were under pressure. The company's sales had stagnated, profits were down and the quality of service seemed to have declined. Passenger groups were complaining about late trains, poor catering facilities and dirty carriages. Transit appeared to have lost its sense of purpose. At a board meeting towards the end of the year, Craig put forward a number of plans to his fellow directors.

He explained that a holiday company, Celtic Tours, had asked Transit to provide transport for their European coach tour holidays. Craig noted that this would make more effective use of Transit's fleet of coaches, but commented that the daily rate on offer was not attractive. 'We normally receive £400 a day for a coach and driver. Celtic is only offering £325. However, this is a large contract – it could amount to over 2000 days' work each year.' He concluded that the costs (set out in Appendix C) were difficult to estimate. 'Fuel costs might vary and the transport market is very changeable: it is equally difficult to predict prices and costs.'

However, Craig was much more excited by another item on the agenda of the meeting. 'I believe that we need to expand and to use our expertise in passenger transport. We have to generate increased profits and to capture the attention of investors in the City once again. There are two exciting possibilities open to us. The franchise for West Coast trains is up for grabs and I think we should bid for it. I have outlined likely expenditure and returns over the next five years for this investment (Appendix A). This would allow us to build upon the success we have achieved in running our existing franchises. The alternative is to invest in the rail network in Hong Kong. H K Transport operates the system out there and is looking for a partner to put in money and expertise. I have a number of contacts out there and the projections of income from an investment look good.'

Craig explained that he didn't think the company could make both investments, so a choice would have to be made. 'We have to project a more exciting image and we have to begin to grow again. Both of these investments will make us money. Marketing is a critical factor in our future success – all our financial forecasts depend upon the anticipated level of sales. If we get our marketing correct, we will have few financial problems. We just need to make a choice between the two.'

Craig didn't receive the response he had expected. Several directors didn't believe there was a choice to be made. One remarked 'Investing overseas is foolish, and I'm uncertain about the wisdom of expansion at the moment. We should concentrate on improving our existing businesses and making them more profitable. And, anyway, I am not sure we should be investing these amounts of money.'

cost	daily rate £
drivers' wages (including overtime)	112
average fuel costs	95
parking, drivers' accommodation and other costs (average figure)	85

Table 3.37 *APPENDIX C – costs of supplying coach services*

year	West Coast trains net cash flows (£m)	H K Transport net cash flows (£m)
2002	(240)	(250)
2003	69	90
2004	101	95
2005	106	95
2006	108	150

Table 3.35 *APPENDIX A – forecast cash flows for the two alternative investments.*

1 a) Assume the fixed costs of operating the coaches on behalf of Celtic Tours is £160 000. Should Transit take up the offer from Celtic Tours? *(7 marks)*

b) Discuss whether the changing nature of the transport market means that break-even analysis has little value to Transit. *(13 marks)*

2 a) Calculate the following ratios for Transit:
   ■ gearing ratio
   ■ acid test
   ■ return on capital employed. *(9 marks)*

b) In the light of your ratio calculations and the other evidence in the case, discuss how Transit might finance its expansion plans. *(11 marks)*

3 a) Calculate the average rate of return for the two expansion projects and state which the managers of Transit should adopt on the basis of your calculations. *(8 marks)*

b) Assess whether investment appraisal techniques might be of value in deciding Transit's future strategy. *(12 marks)*

profit and loss account year to 31 March 2002		balance sheet as at 31 March 2002	
	£m		**£m**
turnover	**402.6**	**fixed assets**	**606.4**
cost of sales	163.4	stock	23.7
gross profit	**239.2**	debtors	23.3
overheads	135.7	cash	23.9
depreciation	11.2	creditors	78.1
operating profit	**92.3**	**net current assets**	**(6.2)**
one-off item	5.9	**net assets employed**	**600.2**
pre-tax profit	86.4	long-term loans	296.6
		share capital	193.5
		reserves	109.1
		capital employed	**600.2**

Table 3.36 *APPENDIX B – accounts for Transit plc (year to March 2002)*

4 a) How might window dressing be used to improve the look of Transit's end-of-year accounts? *(6 marks)*

b) Craig Prescott argues that 'Marketing is a critical factor in our future success – all our financial forecasts depend upon the anticipated level of sales. If we get our marketing correct, we will have few financial problems.' To what extent do you agree with him? *(14 marks)*

People and Organisations

Introduction

The subject matter that comprises people and organisations within A level business studies is divided between the AS and A2 elements of the specification. The major parts of your AS programme will have included the following topics:

- the structure of the organisation
- management by objectives
- delegation and consultation
- motivation – in theory and practice
- leadership and management styles
- human resource management – part of this important topic only if you are following the AQA specification.

The A2 specification for business studies builds upon the subject knowledge and skills acquired during the AS programme. It is worthwhile looking back over your AS materials before starting to study A2 people and organisations. More specific advice is given on any prior knowledge required at the outset of each unit.

During your A2 programme you will study the following:

- communications
- types of employer–employee bargaining and different types of contracts of employment
- ways in which employees can participate in decision making within the business
- the roles of trade unions and bodies such as ACAS in employer–employee relationships
- the basic principles of employment law
- human resource management and workforce planning – on some specifications this topic is split between AS and A2 study, and revision before commencing A2 work is essential
- methods of measuring the performance of the workforce, such as productivity.

COMMUNICATIONS

Starting points

Much of the material covered during the AS course provides a basis for a thorough understanding of communication within businesses. In particular three elements of the people and organisations specification at AS level relate to communications.

1 **The leadership style or management** adopted by the organisation will have a significant impact on the amount and effectiveness of communication taking place. A democratic style of leadership involves junior people in the organisation in decision making to varying

degrees. This requires two-way communication to be effective. Senior employees need to communicate with their subordinates on a range of issues and listen to their ideas. Organisations with autocratic and paternalistic leaders are likely to have less communication and much of it will be downwards from manager to subordinate.

2 **Organisational structures** also play an important role in shaping the amount and direction of communication within a business. Traditional organisations with many layers of hierarchy frequently rely upon downward communication and place relatively little value upon the opinions and views of junior employees. The modern trend towards 'flatter' organisational structures, achieved through delayering, has meant that businesses have had

to encourage more effective two-way communication. The removal of many middle managers and the delegation of greater responsibility to junior employees have made it essential that good-quality communication takes place.

3 **Motivational techniques** have changed over recent years. In the past many firms used pay systems to motivate employees, eg piece-rate pay. Although money is still perceived as a motivator, more sophisticated options are used, such as performance-related pay and share options. Non-financial methods of motivation – mainly related to the design of jobs have become more widely used. For example, teamworking has become much more popular and this style of working can only succeed if good communication occurs between employees at all levels within the organisation.

Key terms

Delegation *means passing authority down the hierarchy. This is only genuine if the manager relinquishes some control to the subordinate.*

Feedback *is a response to communication that may confirm receipt and comprehension.*

Leadership *is influencing others to achieve certain aims or objectives. Effective leadership skills can help a manager to carry out their duties.*

Motivation *can be defined as the will to work due to enjoyment of the work itself. This implies that motivation comes from within the individual. Other writers regard motivation as the will or desire to achieve a given target or goal.*

Organisational structure *is the particular way in which a firm is arranged in order to carry out its activities.*

Theory of communication

Communication is the transfer of information between people. A transmission mechanism is simply the means by which one person communicates with another – letters and e-mail are examples.

Communication involves a number of elements as shown in figure 4.1.

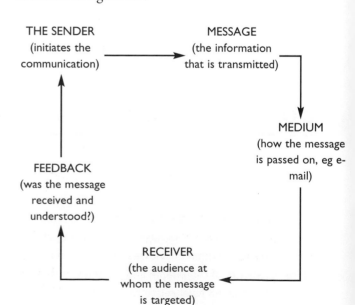

THE SENDER
(initiates the communication)

MESSAGE
(the information that is transmitted)

MEDIUM
(how the message is passed on, eg e-mail)

RECEIVER
(the audience at whom the message is targeted)

FEEDBACK
(was the message received and understood?)

Figure 4.1 *The process of communication*

Who Says Dreams Don't Come True?

Now the dream holiday you've always promised your family is even more affordable. All the magical, sun drenched attractions of the *Walt Disney World* Resort in Florida are yours to experience from as little as £790 per adult and only £246 for kids. Plus, book with us before January 31st 2001 and we'll give you $200 free Disney Dollars* that you can spend anywhere in the parks. Nobody knows more than the *Walt Disney Travel Company* about all there is to do and can offer such valuable insider advice on how to make the most of it all. Call for a brochure, or see your local travel agent.

Summer 2001 prices start from only £790 per adult and just £246 per child, and include:

- Return flights from Gatwick.
- Seven nights hotel.
- Disney Five Day Park Hopper Plus Ticket.
- Rental car.
- $200 free Disney Dollars.*

Flights are also available from sixteen other regional airports.

MULTI-DAY PARK TICKET INCLUDED
Prices from only
£790

TO BOOK CALL 0870 24 24 936
OR SEE YOUR LOCAL TRAVEL AGENT

Walt Disney Travel Company

Figure 4.2 *Advertising, an example of business communication*

Observer, 7 January 2001

Advertising, see Walt Disney's Travel Company in figure 4.2, provides an example of business communication.

- The sender is the company who commences the process of communication.
- The message is the information that the business wishes to send to its audience. In the case of Walt Disney they wish to convey information concerning holidays in Florida.
- The medium is the way in which the message is communicated. Walt Disney chose to use a newspaper to transmit their message – in this case the *Observer*.
- The audience is the target group at whom Walt Disney aimed this message – the parents of school-age children, and relatively well-off parents, given the prices of the holidays. Perhaps this explains the choice of medium.
- Feedback in this case could take the form of the company asking customers where they heard about the holiday when making a booking. This allows Walt Disney to assess which of its advertising communications is most effective in getting the message across.

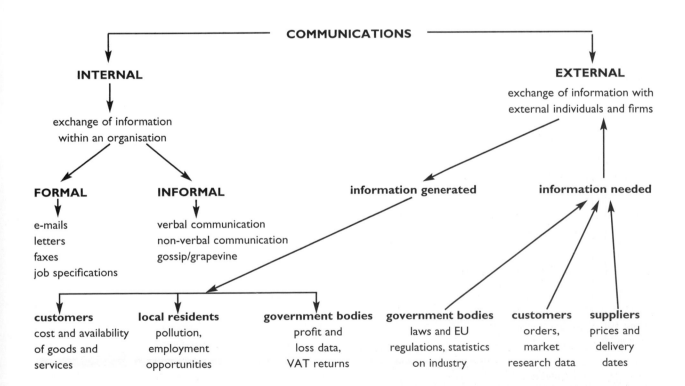

Figure 4.3 *Internal and external communication*

Businesses engage in communication for a variety of purposes as illustrated in figure 4.3. This communication can be internal, ie with other individuals or groups within the business. Thus, a memo sent from the director of human resources to team leaders concerning overtime rates would be an example of internal communication. External communication takes place between a business and other organisations or individuals. For example, a business providing details of job vacancies as part of the process of external recruitment would be communicating externally.

Communication can also be classified in other ways.

■ **Formal communication** is the exchanging of information and ideas within and outside a business using official channels. Examples of formal communication include board meetings or team briefings, through e-mail, memos and letters.

■ **Informal communication** takes place outside the official channels of an organisation – gossip is an obvious example.

Figure 4.4 illustrates the range of methods of communication available to a business. It also shows that there exists a trade-off between cost of communication and the speed at which it takes place. Modern methods of communication such as video conferencing and intranets are generally quick, but costly.

Effective communication

Effective communication is an essential element of business success. A recent survey by the Institute of

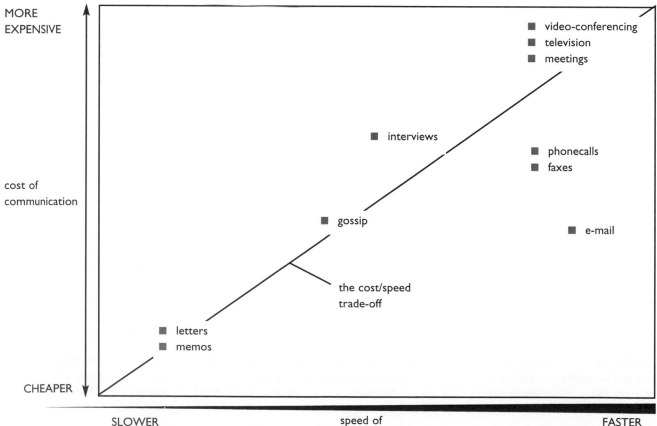

Figure 4.4 *Methods of communication*

Management and UMIST stressed the importance of good quality communications within businesses. The survey reported that good communication could assist employees of all types within a business.

- Good communication makes it easier to implement change – an important issue in a business environment subject to rapid and continual change.
- Good communication encourages and develops commitment to the business from employees at all levels within the organisation.
- Effective communication helps to ensure that the business is coordinated and that all employees pursue the same corporate objectives.

The role of a manager in a modern organisation is to communicate with everyone – shareholders, the media, superiors, customers and suppliers. The measure of today's manager is how well they communicate and not so much what they communicate. Good-quality communication by

managers with the business's stakeholders offers many benefits.

Successful decision making requires that managers have access to as much relevant information as possible. The key management roles of planning, prioritising, coordinating and controlling depend upon access to information. This emphasises the importance of good communication to businesses.

For example, modern techniques such as just-in-time production place great emphasis on effective communication systems. If supplies of components or raw materials are not available when required businesses are likely to incur substantial – and unnecessary – costs as well as being unable to provide high quality customer service. Similarly, techniques such as kaizen (continuous improvement) rely heavily upon effective two-way internal communication.

Good communication can have a positive impact upon employee motivation and performance. Praise

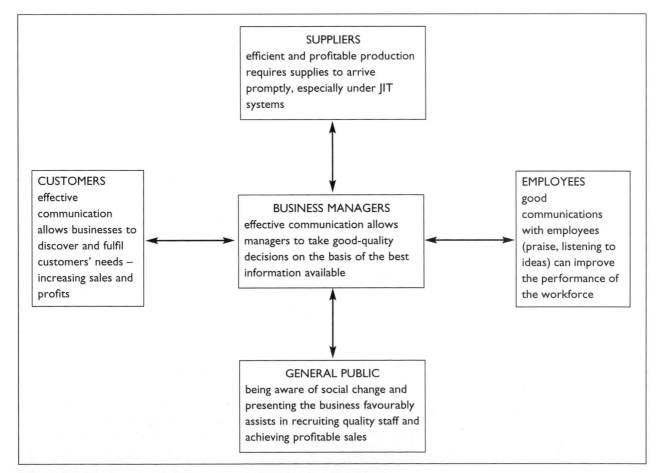

Figure 4.5 *The benefits of effective communication with stakeholders*

and recognition are widely seen as motivators, but rely upon communication. Communication can also give employees important feedback about their performance and help to improve it in the future. In this respect appraisal systems (and especially developmental appraisal systems) have been of considerable value.

Communication is the cornerstone of coordination. In large businesses it is easy for different departments or parts of the organisation to pursue differing objectives. Regular and effective communication can help to ensure that all employees remain closely focused on agreed corporate objectives.

Effective communication with customers is essential for businesses. The pursuit of quality means that businesses have to satisfy customers' needs. A key element here is to establish exactly what the customer requires – perhaps through market research. It is also important to make sure that these needs are being satisfied on an ongoing basis.

⫶ OINTS TO PONDER

Is it more important for a business to have effective communications during a period of rapid change?

Causes of ineffective communication

A principle cause of poor communication is that managers do not recognise the problem. Symptoms of poor communication (such as poor industrial relations and low levels of motivation) may be thought to have other causes. Because senior managers have access to all the information they require and can communicate easily with all in the organisation they may be unaware that others in the business do not receive information essential to their jobs.

Some managers use leadership styles that discourage effective two-way communication within the business. Some prefer to operate an autocratic

leadership style and a traditional organisational structure. This encourages downward communication only.

EXAMINER'S ADVICE

The importance of communication to a business cannot be underestimated. When dealing with case studies it is often an important argument to say that a business's performance can be improved in many ways through better communication.

Mergers and takeovers create larger and more complex business. In 2000 Glaxo Wellcome and SmithKline Beecham announced they were merging to form an enterprise valued at £114bn and employing over 60 000 people across the globe. Because of this the new company's need for information has increased dramatically; at the same time it has become more difficult to meet these needs. Mergers result in new systems and procedures making effective communication more difficult at a time when it is particularly important. The newly merged GlaxoSmithKline has experienced problems similar to those encountered by most merged organisations.

⫶ OINTS TO PONDER

In 2000 AOL (America On Line) and TimeWarner concluded the largest merger in history. The deal created a new business worth £220bn, but investors were unsure about the new company and the shares in both companies fell. The fall wiped £10bn off the worth of the two companies – approximately equal to the value of BSkyB in the UK!

The increasing need for information (and thus communication) has been further increased by developments such as delegation, empowerment, decentralisation, just-in-time and kaizen groups. Extending the roles and authority of employees creates a greater need for, as well as new, channels of communication. In view of this it is, perhaps, not surprising that many businesses have been unable to keep up! The use of consultants and contract workers and the rise in teleworking have increased the diversity of communication required. Through the involvement of so many groups communication has become more difficult to carry out efficiently.

Some businesses have recognised the imperfections in their communications systems. However, many have relied upon IT to overcome these problems and have created further problems. If IT is to be effective it requires that employees be trained and that systems suit the precise needs. Simply throwing IT at the problem creates more, rather than better, communications.

Business in Focus: internet company fails to communicate

Altavista, the internet service provider, announced that managing director Andy Mitchell was resigning following a string of mistakes over recent months.

Altavista had planned to charge a £60 a year fee to 270 000 customers who registered for its unmetered internet service. This would save users from paying telephone call charges, allowing unrestricted access to the net.

However, Altavista customers were unable to get on-line once the company realised that the service would not be profitable as British Telecom insisted on charging ISPs for telephone use by the minute. This exposed Altavista to enormous losses if it carried its plans through. Mitchell compounded his error by failing to tell Altavista customers of the scrapping of the new service until the farce was exposed through a campaign in the media.

Adapted from the Electronic Telegraph, *31 August 2000*

I Altavista has a major public relations problem. Discuss the actions the company might take to improve its public image.

Improving communication

Good quality communication is essential for successful management. Globalisation is resulting in businesses becoming larger and more diverse,

meaning that to operate successfully, good communications are even more important than ever. To adapt to the changing demands of the global marketplace a business can take a number of actions to improve its communications:

- **train employees in communication skills**. Modern business communication is a complicated activity often requiring competence in a range of activities: listening, speaking, writing and reading skills, to say nothing of technological skills. To carry out all these activities satisfactorily employees will require training at regular intervals – it is not a one-off action. In spite of this, training in communication skills is a priority with a relatively small number of businesses and training budgets are often cut during less prosperous periods
- **avoid the danger of generating too much information**. Modern technology has substantially increased the risk of this occurring and many firms simply invest in technology when facing communications problems. By evaluating communications needs before taking any action a business increases the probability of implementing an effective solution. In 2000 a survey showed that nearly 50% of voicemail systems are switched off within a year of installation, indicating that many managers do not spend time evaluating the position before taking decisions
- **recognise that cultural and linguistic differences exist**. These are common within a large multinational and can inhibit effective communication. Honeywell, the computer manufacturer, operates in 11 countries, and encourages employees to be sensitive to cultural differences when communicating. The company stresses that it is important to respect and value cultural differences, to be aware of prejudice and to ensure that employees have the full picture when communicating before making judgements. Multicultural communication is set to become a common feature in the lives of more employees as business becomes increasingly global.

Integrated Business: Oxfam's retail crisis

The Oxfam shop is a familiar and reassuring feature of the UK's high streets and has been a steady source of income for one of the country's best-known charities. However, fierce competition amongst retailers, along with the apparent failure of the charity's retail strategy, have left the shops facing a financial crisis.

Oxfam's retail business is losing money, mainly due to higher costs. Two years ago the charity hired 500 professional managers for its busiest shops, dispensing with the services of many voluntary workers at the same time. Unfortunately at this time, the retail business entered a slump with even major players such as Marks and Spencer suffering. As a result the surplus from the shops declined from £16.5m in 1998 to £7.6m in 2000 and was expected to fall to £3.7m by 2004 if no action was taken.

The charity's turnover in the shops remained unchanged, with the professional managers unable to improve the position. Partly this was due to falling prices for clothes, caused by companies such as Matalan offering low-price products. At the same time the number of charity shops has doubled over the past decade. Oxfam's retail strategy did not allow for such changes in the external environment. In spite of this the charity has maintained its revenue at approximately £60m annually, but has been unable to cope with higher costs.

The increase in Oxfam's costs is entirely responsible for the decrease in the surplus generated. Oxfam received bad publicity for awarding director David Bryer a pay increase of £25 000 per annum giving him a salary in the region of £75 000. At the same time an Oxfam volunteer claimed that Bryer had presided over a culture of rising costs with less than 20 pence of every £1 earned in Oxfam shops going to aid projects. An Oxfam spokesperson said that part of the reason for reduced surpluses was the charity's commitment to selling 'Fair Trade' products, which have a small profit margin.

The charity plans to make redundancies to cut costs. The job losses are expected to come from middle managers involved in supporting the shops, as the plan is for shop managers to be given more autonomy over how their enterprises are run. Oxfam is not prepared to reverse its decision to use professional managers – even though they cost £3m each year.

The Guardian

1 Calculate how much revenue Oxfam would have needed to raise in its shops to allow it to spend £87m on aid projects.   *(5 marks)*
2 To what extent do you think poor internal and external communication contributed to the problems faced by Oxfam?   *(15 marks)*
3 Examine the benefits Oxfam might expect from giving its shop managers more autonomy in operating their outlets.   *(10 marks)*
4 Discuss the case for and against Oxfam being described as an ethical business.   *(20 marks)*

Communication and motivation

To be successful managers have to be able to communicate effectively. This is particularly important during times of change, such as during a takeover or introducing a new production system. If change is to be implemented successfully managers will require the co-operation and support of the workforce. Good communication can help in implementing change by enhancing levels of employee motivation. It is also true that high levels of motivation in the workplace tend to result in good quality two-way communication.

Quality communication within a business may improve motivation for a number of reasons. The writings of Elton Mayo (eg the Hawthorne experiment) provide evidence that employees respond positively to receiving attention from managers. Later research has strengthened this link. Abraham Maslow developed his hierarchy of needs, and good communication underpins some of the higher-level needs identified in his theory. The need for recognition, for example, relies heavily upon managers communicating with subordinates.

Similarly, Frederick Herzberg wrote that direct communication (rather than through unnecessary layers of hierarchy) was an important means of improving employee motivation.

Recent developments in business practice draw strongly upon the interrelationship between motivation and communication. The operation of kaizen groups, the increasing use of delegation and the empowering of junior employees all have the potential to improve motivation, but depend on good-quality communication.

Empowering employees, perhaps through the use of teamworking, is unlikely to improve a business's performance unless the team members understand precisely what is required of them. Senior managers will need to make clear the new responsibilities of the teams and the limitations upon their authority. Teams will need to communicate amongst themselves, and with other teams. Teams cannot, for example, decide upon production priorities without knowledge of patterns of demand and availability of components and other resources. Wise managers will also ensure arrangements are in place to allow them to monitor the performance of teams, especially in the period immediately following the implementation of teamworking. Thus empowerment through teamworking should improve motivation as employees carry out more fulfilling and responsible roles, but will flounder without effective communication.

POINTS TO PONDER

A report by the Industrial Society in December 2000 concluded that office gossip about secret liaisons, inept managers or Christmas bonuses should be encouraged, to build a more harmonious and sociable environment at work. The report suggest that firms should create more communal areas to help the process.

High levels of motivation can have a positive influence upon communication. Motivated confident employees will have the assurance to communicate with more senior employees. This may result in suggestions on how to improve products or processes. Motivated employees are more likely to be members of quality circles or kaizen groups and to assist in improving the organisation's performance. Motivated employees are more likely to have an interest in the affairs of the organisation in which they work. They may volunteer for working parties and take actions and decisions in the best interests of the business.

Communication and motivation are interrelated. If managers take actions to improve communications they are likely to have a positive effect on motivation. Similarly, techniques to improve motivation rely heavily upon improving communication. This is an important interrelationship within businesses and can be a powerful force for improving workforce performance.

POINTS TO PONDER

The international corporation Iridium went into liquidation in March 2000 having invested $4.5bn in a satellite system to operate mobile telephones. Instead of the 5m users forecast, the company sold just 55 000 phones and collapsed with debts of $4.5bn.

Information technology and communication

Key terms

Intranets link computers within an individual business allowing employees to use e-mail and to have access to a range of on-line services.
Internet links computers across the world allowing communication and commercial activity between an estimated 75m users.

Many observers believe that IT can solve the communication problems that many businesses face. They point out the benefits provided by databases, e-mail, intranets and the internet. However, some firms have found that IT worsens communication problems faced by many businesses. Table 4.1

the case for ...	... and the case against
■ Technology can provide managers with vast amounts of data on which to base decisions. Through the use of management information systems, firms can bring together data relating to sales, costs, production, stocks and orders and make better-quality decisions.	■ Many firms introduce communications technology without adequate preparation. Success depends upon an analysis of the communications problem to ensure the appropriate solution. It also requires training of employees to ensure they understand how to use the equipment.
■ Technology offers opportunities to improve performance by providing better communications. Thus automated switchboards can deal with higher volumes of calls than those operated by receptionists. This technology can reduce costs too, enhancing a business's competitiveness.	■ Technology to improve communications can be expensive especially if it is tailor-made to suit particular circumstances. Also such equipment may need replacing frequently because of the pace of technological change. These funds may prove more profitable if used to purchase production-line technology.
■ Technology can be used to improve communications in marketing. Supermarkets use electronic loyalty cards to collect huge amounts of valuable data on their customers. Even small businesses are able to market and sell their products internationally through a web site on the internet.	■ Many customers do not like dealing with communications technology and prefers to speak to employees. A survey by BT showed that 70% of callers hang up without speaking when confronted by an automated answering system. Firms may cut costs, but lose sales through the use of communications technology.

Table 4.1 *The case for and against using technology to improve communication*

considers the arguments for and against using IT to improve communication.

It is worth distinguishing between the effects of communications technology in the short and long run. Employee resistance and inadequate training may mean that communication initially becomes worse following the introduction of technology. This may result in some confusion internally and a lowering of customer service. Over time, however, employees may become more familiar with the new

technology, initial problems may be resolved and the effectiveness of communication improve.

*P*OINTS TO PONDER

Accountants KPMG have revealed that company directors in the UK spend an estimated 11% of their working time sending and responding to e-mails.

Progress questions

1 Describe the process of communication. *(5 marks)*

2 Distinguish, with the aid of examples, between internal and external communication. *(6 marks)*

3 Explain **two** reasons why high levels of informal communication might be harmful to a business. *(6 marks)*

4 Outline **two** ways in which effective communication might assist managers in implementing a major programme of change successfully. *(8 marks)*

5 Explain how changes in working practices have affected the importance of good communication within the organisation. *(7 marks)*

6 What benefits might a firm expect as a result of having effective communication with customers and suppliers? *(8 marks)*

7 Outline **two** reasons why a large, multinational business might experience communication problems. *(6 marks)*

8 Explain how a traditional retail business with many branches throughout the UK might improve its communications. *(8 marks)*

9 Examine **two** ways in which improved communication might improve the motivation of a workforce. *(6 marks)*

10 Outline **two** reasons why the introduction of communications technology within a workforce might lead to less effective communication. *(6 marks)*

Analysis and evaluation questions

1 'The ability to communicate effectively is the most important skill a manager of a modern business can have. Critically evaluate this statement. *(15 marks)*

2 Venables Ltd is a traditional producer of biscuits. The firm has 2000 employees, low labour turnover and four locations. The company is contemplating introducing a JIT system of production and making more use of teams. Examine the case for and against the company investing £125 000 in technology to improve all aspects of its communications. *(12 marks)*

3 Discuss whether globalisation has increased the importance of effective communication within modern businesses. *(15 marks)*

4 'Most poor communication within businesses is a deliberate policy on the part of senior managers. To what extent do you agree with this statement? *(15 marks)*

5 Analyse whether the most important argument for improving communication is that it has a positive effect on the motivation of the workforce. *(12 marks)*

Case study

Dilip Singh is one of West Yorkshire's best-known entrepreneurs. He is the chief executive of Three Ridings Leisure, the operator of pubs and clubs throughout Yorkshire. His company has enjoyed a prolonged period of financial success despite being in competition with larger companies with much larger resources. Dilip is noted for a strong and individualistic leadership style.

A former employee commented 'I liked working there in many ways but I never knew what was happening. There is little formal communication within Three Ridings Leisure – I found out most things as a result of gossip. It's lucky most employees knew one another. Dilip likes to keep things to himself, but he does have a Midas touch. The business was certainly successful.'

However, Dilip and Three Ridings Leisure seem to be bowing to the inevitable. He has announced a merger with White Rose Enterprises who operate licensed premises throughout the Midlands and the north of England. Three Ridings Leisure will be much the junior partner as its turnover last year was £12.4m, compared with £39.7m for its new partner. Analysts foresee problems for the newly merged business, as it will contain two strong characters in Dilip and Roger Knight. Communication between the two elements might be patchy was the comment of another former employee. Dilip has admitted that problems might exist but revealed that the new company (whose name is yet to be decided) would invest in information technology to overcome any problems.

1 a) Explain the difference between formal and informal communication.   *(4 marks)*

   b) Why might a relatively small business such as Three Ridings Leisure have communication problems?   *(10 marks)*

2 Discuss the communication problems that the new organisation might face if the proposed merger with White Rose Enterprises goes ahead.   *(16 marks)*

3 Dilip has proposed investing in information technology to overcome any communication problems the new business may encounter. Evaluate the actions the management of the new company might take to increase the possibility of this strategy proving successful.   *(20 marks)*

EMPLOYER–EMPLOYEE RELATIONS

Starting points

Employer–employee relations are closely related to the leadership style of the organisation and the techniques adopted to motivate employees.

■ The leadership style is likely to have a significant impact upon the style of employer–employee relations that are occurring. Leaders who favour a democratic approach will be more likely to adopt an approach that encourages discussion between employers and employees. This may take a number of forms: negotiations on pay and conditions, consultation groups, eg works councils and quality circles. More autocratic styles of leadership will probably prefer an environment with less communication between employers and employees and may not accept trade unions within the workplace. Negotiations between the employer and the employee may take place on a more individual basis.

■ Democratic styles of leadership are likely to give employees substantial amounts of authority. This is likely (but not certain) to take place against a background of close relationships between employers and employees, suggesting open and friendly working relations in the workplace.

■ Communications, which we considered in the previous unit, also play a fundamental part in employer–employee relations. Effective two-way communication is an important element of an open and understanding relationship between employers and employees.

Key terms

Communication is the transfer of information between people.

Employer–employee relations describe the attitudes of management and employee representatives towards each other. This relationship is also shown in their behaviour within the workplace.

Leadership is influencing others to achieve certain aims or objectives. Effective leadership skills can help a manager to carry out their duties.

EXAMINER'S ADVICE

Before reading this unit, it is worthwhile revisiting the units in your AS business studies textbook on leadership, organisational structures and motivation. These will provide you with a good foundation for studying employer–employee relations.

Introduction

Employer–employee relations is a wide-ranging term covering a number of aspects of the relationship between workers and management. Key elements of this relationship include the following:

■ negotiations about pay and working conditions
■ communication between management and employees
■ employee participation in management decisions
■ policies for improving co-operation between management and employees
■ a general approach designed to minimise conflict between the two parties.

Individual and collective bargaining

Collective bargaining is a tradition for which businesses in the UK are noted. Collective bargaining entails negotiations between management and employees' representatives, usually trade unions, over pay and other conditions of employment. Collective bargaining can only occur if the employer recognises the right of a trade union to act on behalf of the workforce. Under a collective agreement the terms negotiated by the employees'

Key terms

Collective bargaining is negotiation between employers and the representatives of the workforce, usually trade union officials.

Individual bargaining takes place when a single employee negotiates his or her own pay and working conditions with management representatives.

Trade unions are organisations of workers established to protect and improve the economic position and working conditions of their members.

Union recognition: circumstances whereby the managers of a business accept the right of a particular trade union to negotiate on behalf of its members.

The European Union may help the reintroduction of collective bargaining into the workplace. In 2000 the EU announced that it was planning to make consultation with employees on a range of items compulsory for companies with over 50 employees.

The use of collective bargaining in the UK declined for a number of reasons.

■ During the 1980s and 1990s trade union membership in the UK declined. As a consequence the influence of unions waned allowing businesses to move away from collective bargaining more easily.

■ Government have passed legislation designed to restrict the power of trade unions (and their usefulness in collective bargaining) and to allow labour markets to operate more freely, thereby discouraging collective agreements.

■ Over the last 40 years governments have introduced legislation granting basic protection to employees (from unfair dismissal, from sexual and racial discrimination in employment, and the provisions of redundancy payments, for example). Individuals can seek to protect their position by taking their cases to industrial tribunals rather than relying upon support from their trade union.

■ Employers have introduced strategies that emphasise and reward individuals and teams. This represents a change of approach from collective employer–employee relationships conducted through trade union officials.

representatives are binding upon the entire workforce – this is the 'collective' aspect of this form of negotiation.

In spite of the tradition of collective bargaining in the UK, for many years it became less common as shown in table 4.2. Simultaneously, the proportion of firms recognising trade unions for the purposes of collective bargaining declined. However, the situation was reversed to some degree by the passing of the Employment Relations Act, which came into force in 2000. Under this Act a trade union with a membership exceeding 50% of the employees in any particular business (or part of a business where negotiations take place) can demand union recognition and thereby the right to reintroduce collective bargaining. If a union has more than 10% of the workforce as members it can call for a ballot and needs the support of 40% of the employees to be successful. The newly formed Central Arbitration Committee may settle disputes about union recognition.

	1984	1990	1998
percentage of businesses operating collective bargaining	70	54	40
percentage of businesses where trade unions are recognised for the purposes of collective bargaining	90	81	69

1998 Workplace Employee Relations Survey

Table 4.2 *The decline of collective bargaining and trade union recognition in the UK 1984–1998. However, recent changes in legislation are likely to reverse these trends to some extent.*

Business in Focus

Air 2000, the British Charter Airline, is to derecognise the Transport & General (TGWU) as the body representing its staff in collective bargaining. The company argues that only 10% of its 1600 staff are members of the union and that these were former members of staff of Leisure International, which Air 2000 bought in 1998. The company explained that some employees had complained that the union did not accurately represent their views.

A TGWU spokesperson was 'extremely disappointed' at the decision. The union accepted that it had no more than 10% of staff as its members. The spokesperson acknowledged that the company was not anti-union, but that no other union had approached the company to take the place of TGWU.

The Financial Times

1 Assess the case for and against Air 2000 going ahead with its decision to derecognise the TGWU.

Individual bargaining

The move away from collective bargaining has been driven by a change in philosophy within many modern businesses. The adoption of the principles of human resource management has resulted in many enterprises seeking to make the most effective use of each and every member of the workforce. This has had two main consequences.

1 Instead of paying a standard wage or salary to every worker carrying out a particular role (as would have been likely under collective bargaining) individual bargaining means that workers may be paid according to their contribution. This may reduce the labour costs of a business and has the potential to provide financial motivation for employees.

2 The other side to individual bargaining is that some businesses seek to develop their employees to encourage them to make the maximum possible contribution to the performance of the business.

Other firms have simply chosen not to recognise trade unions in the hope of being able to keep wage increases and costs to a minimum without the upward pressure of collective bargaining.

POINTS TO PONDER

Collective bargaining can result in employees receiving wages over 30% higher than in non-unionised workplaces. A survey conducted by the London School of Economics showed that wages set under collective bargaining for black and Asian workers averaged £8.95 an hour, compared with £6.77 hourly in companies that do not recognise unions.

In spite of the move away from collective bargaining during the 1990s, individual bargaining is most commonly used when employees have substantial skill levels and the ability to negotiate their own packages of pay and conditions.

Many employees in the UK have their pay determined by one of two systems outlined as follows:

1 pay reviews. These are frequently used in the public sector to settle the pay levels for groups such as teachers and nurses. A committee of 'experts' considers all the relevant information before arriving at a decision.

2 management determines pay unilaterally. It is used in some workplaces, often as part of a decentralised arrangement. Management decisions commonly reflect the current rate of inflation.

Flexible workforces

Changing patterns of employment

In recent years a number of trends have emerged in the UK's workforce:

- **rising numbers of temporary workers.** The number (and proportion) of workers within the UK on temporary contracts (for a fixed-time period) has risen steadily since the early 1980s,

Flexible workforces exist when businesses place less reliance upon permanent full-time employees and make greater use of part-time and temporary workers.

Temporary workers have contracts of employment that only exist for a specific period of time – perhaps six months.

Annualised hours operate when an employer states the number of hours employees must complete over a year. Weekly working hours can be varied to suit the circumstances.

though it does appear to have levelled out in the last year or so. In 2000 nearly 2m UK workers were on temporary contracts.

■ **part-time working**. The number of employees within the UK who work part-time has also increased year-on-year. By 2000 over a quarter of all employees worked part-time – approximately 7m people.

■ **self-employment**. This form of employment has generally been in decline over recent years. However, 2.5m people still work for themselves

■ **contractors and consultants.** Many businesses have replaced full-time employees with consultants or have contracted out duties to other organisations. For example, it is common for firms to employ contract staff to design and manage IT systems rather than use permanent full-time employees in these roles

■ **full-time permanent employees**. Firms use fewer full-time employees than was the case in the 1980s. Such employees are relatively

expensive as the firm incurs all the costs of employment such as making pension contributions and providing training. Using consultants and contractors avoids these costs and ensures employees are only hired when needed. Full-time employees tend to be highly skilled and perform central roles within an organisation.

The data in table 4.3 show that UK businesses have opted for workforces containing increasing numbers of part-time and temporary employees. Labour forces with high proportions of these types of employees are called flexible workforces.

The balance between advantages and disadvantages from employing flexible workforces depends upon the circumstances. Flexible workforces arguably offer the greatest potential to businesses when the employees in question are either highly skilled or have few skills. Highly skilled employees are expensive to hire and may require constant retraining to ensure their skills remain up to date. Employing such people through temporary contracts, or as self-employed workers, may provide benefits without incurring heavy long-term expenditure.

Equally employees with few skills may be hired on a part-time, flexible hours or temporary basis. This allows firms to have the appropriate amount of labour available to meet varying levels of demand. High levels of turnover of staff may not be a problem in such circumstances as training is likely to be minimal.

	total employment (m)	full-time employees (% of total)	part-time employees (% of total)	temporary employees (% of total)	self-employed (% of total)
1992	24.17	64.37	21.94	4.6	10.26
1995	26.25	64.56	24.43	7.1	10.38
2000	27.98	64.75	24.05	7.0	8.8

Table 4.3 *Trends in employment in the UK 1992–2000*

Office for National Statistics, www.statistics.gov.uk

the case for ...	... and the case against
■ Flexible employees are cheaper because firms avoid many of the costs of full-time employment (such as pension contributions). Wages are also generally lower. This makes the firm more price competitive, which may be important in an increasingly global market.	■ Communication is tricky with flexible workforces. More employees, unfamiliar to one another, with different patterns of attendance make it difficult to pass on information. Formal and informal communication is poorer causing lower-quality customer service damaging the firm's image.
■ Flexible workforces assist businesses in dealing with fluctuations in demand. Being able to call on part-time or self-employed workers at a busy time avoids the problems associated with unfulfilled orders. At quiet times firms do not have expensive workers with little to do, or have to pay to make employees redundant.	■ The turnover of staff is higher with flexible workforces. Lack of job security leads people to move to permanent employment when possible. High rates of labour turnover mean workers are unfamiliar with their duties and firms incur greater recruitment.
■ Firms can reduce training costs by subcontracting work to other organisations or by hiring self-employed workers. Businesses acquire staff with up-to-date skills without having to pay for their training. This is particularly useful in industries subject to rapid change such as the microelectronics industry.	■ Morale can be lower with flexible workforces. Security needs may not be met through these forms of employment and employee performance may be hampered by this factor. The failure to form groups at work – or the regular breaking up of these groups – may mean that social needs also remain unfulfilled, leading to lower levels of motivation.
■ Flexible patterns of employment allow businesses to have access to highly specialised skills without bearing the costs of permanently employing what can be hugely expensive workers. Thus, even relatively small businesses may hire self-employed systems analysts to carry out highly technical work with their computer systems.	

Table 4.4 *The case for and against flexible workforces*

Employee participation and industrial democracy

> **Key terms**
>
> *Employee participation relates to the involvement of employees in the process of decision making within a business. This might be achieved through the use of quality circles.*
> *Industrial democracy has a similar meaning referring to ways in which employees can influence the decisions taken within the business. The use of worker directors is an example.*

The writing of notable theorists such as Elton Mayo, Abraham Maslow and Frederick Herzberg in the middle of the twentieth century drew attention to the capacity of the workforce, if used effectively, to contribute to the achievement of an organisation's objectives. In the period prior to this the views of the 'scientific' school of management held sway with workers portrayed as uninterested in working and unable to contribute to organisational decision making. The scientific school encouraged the restriction of the role of workers within the organisation to carrying out simple repetitive tasks and without questioning their roles or proposing improvements.

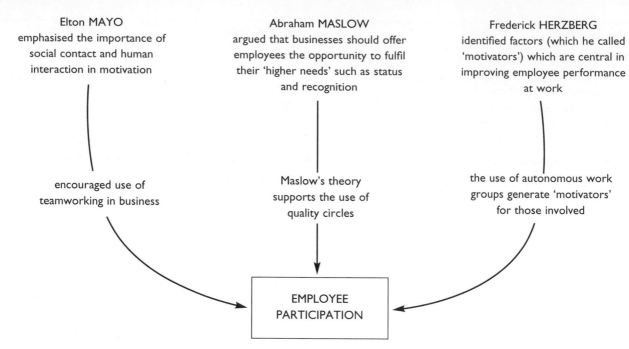

Figure 4.6 *The origins of employee participation and industrial democracy*

Since the 1950s, businesses have recognised the benefit of greater involvement of all employees in problem solving and decision making within the organisation. A number of techniques have evolved to allow employees a more significant role in the enterprise.

Trade unions are often opposed to the use of employee participation because approaches such as quality circles and particularly works councils can replace unions within the workplace. If employers effectively and successfully deal with employee concerns through works councils, for example, then it is less likely that employees will turn to a union for assistance. Trade unions view industrial democracy more favourably. For some unions, industrial democracy indicates sharing of power and increased rights for their members whilst maintaining the role of unions in the workplace.

1. Quality circles

Quality circles are groups of workers who meet regularly to identify methods of improving all aspects of the quality of their products. Quality circles developed in Japan and consider issues relating to working methods as well as the products themselves. They normally comprise three to ten employees from all levels within the organisation who assemble to discuss company problems and possible solutions. Quality circles meet for one or two hours, two or three times a month, usually in working time and can provide businesses with imaginative solutions to production problems. Quality circles have been used in the UK by numerous firms including Wedgwood, Philips, Rolls Royce and Marks and Spencer.

2. Works councils

A works council is a forum within a business where workers and management meet to discuss issues such as working conditions, pay and training. Employee representatives on a works council are normally elected. It is common for works councils to be used in workplaces where no trade union representation exists. However, in businesses where works councils and trade unions co-exist, the former is normally excluded from discussing pay and working conditions.

Key *issues*

European works councils bring together employee representatives in a multinational company from across Europe, to inform and consult them on the group's performance and prospects. European works councils can help trade unionists and employee representatives to respond to the decisions that employers increasingly take on a European and global basis. European works councils affect any business with at least 1000 employees and at least 150 employees located in two or more Member States of the European Union.

A European works council is made up of at least one elected employee from each country in which the multinational is based and representatives from senior management. They normally meet annually and discuss issues affecting employees throughout the organisation. These include health and safety, merger proposals, the closure of plants and the implementation of new working practices such as teamworking.

Although European works councils have been operating for several years, it is only since January 2000, when new regulations came into force, that multinational firms in the UK have been obliged legally to have this type of works council. These regulations mean that more UK companies have to implement European works councils and UK employees have gained new rights.

POINTS TO PONDER

Vauxhall's decision to close its Luton factory in 2002, threatening 2250 jobs, attracted much criticism from the company's employees. In particular workers protested that the issue should have been discussed in the firm's European works council.

3. Employee shareholders

Firms in the UK operate a number of schemes whereby their employees are able to purchase shares in the business. Companies can gain a number of benefits from encouraging employees to buy shares in the business. If the company operates a share ownership scheme approved by the Inland Revenue it can gain tax advantages. Primarily, of course, share ownership schemes are intended to improve

employee motivation and performance. Because employees have a stake in the financial performance of the company, it is anticipated that they will work harder in the mutual interests of themselves and the company.

Companies normally regard share ownership schemes as a tax-efficient means of rewarding employees, rather than an extension of industrial democracy. Because the number of shares involved is relatively small they do not allow employees to influence companies' policies through voting at annual general meetings. ASDA is noted for its commitment to employee shareholders.

4. Autonomous work groups

These are teams of employees who are given a high level of control over their working lives. Senior managers delegate considerable authority to those further down the hierarchy allowing them to decide what tasks to complete at what times and giving some control over the resources available to the group. In some cases autonomous working groups elect their own leader and appoint new staff. The intention behind the creation of such groups is improved motivation and productivity. Such an approach is unlikely to succeed without careful preparation and significant amounts of training.

4. Teamworking

There has been a major trend in businesses towards teamworking over recent years. Teamworking is a major part of the so-called Japanese approach to production and its benefits have been extolled by major companies such as Honda, John Lewis, Toshiba and Vauxhall Motors.

POINTS TO PONDER

A survey of 700 employers throughout the country by the Industrial Society has revealed that 86% of employers have increased the amount of teamworking occurring within their organisation over the last three years.

Teamworking occurs when a business breaks down its production processes into large units instead of relying upon the use of the division of labour. Introducing a production system based on teams is likely to represent major change for any business. This requires businesses to prepare thoroughly.

*P*OINTS TO PONDER

Teamworking represents a major change in the way employees are used within a business. Discuss the preparations that a large-scale manufacturer may need to make before introducing teamworking.

Many managers are enthusiastic supporters of teamworking. However, others are more sceptical. They argue that teamworking may prove to be a fad, abandoned as businesses implement newer philosophies and techniques. Critics also contend that it is not applicable in all circumstances and that wise managers would carefully compare the costs against the expected benefits.

Teams may not be the answer to improving organisational performance. Businesses need to analyse the actual work to be completed before they take the decision to form a team or teams. It may be that the work in question is creative or simplistic and would be best completed by an individual. Table 4.5 summarises the arguments against and in favour of teamworking.

Business in Focus: teamworking at Honda

Honda is one of the success stories of car manufacturing in the UK. The Swindon-based manufacturer announced in 2000 that it intended to increase its production of cars within the UK from 100 000 to 250 000 in 2002. The company confirmed that some cars manufactured in the UK would be exported to Japan. In September 2000 Honda reduced its prices by 9%.

The company plans to build a new factory at Swindon to produce the additional vehicles. The company is unusual in that it takes pride in not accepting state aid. This is a stark contrast to Nissan, still lobbying for a £40m aid package for its Sunderland plant.

Honda's success is partly due to its 'New Manufacturing System' which allows it to switch production from one model to another in only eight weeks. Honda relies heavily on its workforce for its hard working and flexible approach to production. The basis of the Honda approach to manufacturing is the use of flexible teams throughout the production process. The teams are given considerable authority and encouraged to propose solutions to problems in the workplace.

1 Discuss the ways in which the use of teamworking in the Swindon factory might have contributed to Honda's success.

The use of teamworking offers firms advantages and disadvantages as illustrated in table 4.5.

Teamworking can have a positive impact upon the motivation of employees at all levels within the organisation. However, this will not happen automatically. Firms need to prepare thoroughly for what is a major change in production techniques. Training is an essential element of this preparation to give employees the necessary skills and confidence to enjoy their new roles. In this way the positive effects on motivation can be maximised.

Equally important is to create the right type of organisation. Teamworking can be best established and encouraged by a democratic form of leadership, and effective two-way communication.

EXAMINER'S ADVICE

When discussing the benefits of good employer–employee relationships or of employee participation it is useful to focus on the overall benefits to the business. These can usually be expressed in terms of enhanced international competitiveness or increased profitability.

advantages of teamworking	disadvantages of teamworking
■ Teamworking offers shop-floor employees the opportunity to meet Maslow's higher needs, thereby improving quality and productivity. Because employees are better motivated they are less likely to leave the company and recruitment and retraining costs are likely to be reduced. As a consequence costs should be reduced, enhancing the business's profitability.	■ Teamworking often results in early retirement or redundancy of middle managers, who have considerable experience of the business. Firms recognise that this has drawbacks. The loss of large numbers of experienced employees can mean that the organisation does not possess the necessary knowledge or skills to perform its functions effectively. Knowledge management has become an important part of implementing teams.
■ Teamworking makes fuller use of the talents of the entire workforce, eg allowing those closest to problems to suggest and implement solutions. It allows individuals to complement each others' strengths and weaknesses creating a more effective and productive unit as well as a more positive working environment.	■ The introduction of teamworking will involve businesses in considerable expenditure. Firms may incur redundancy costs if some employees are laid off, and the introduction of teamworking may cause disruption to production, increasing costs. Finally, training is an essential component of the successful introduction of teamworking.
■ Teamworking can reduce management costs as it is often accompanied by delayering of the organisation. The removal of a number of middle managers is likely to cut the corporate wage bill substantially.	

Table 4.5 *The advantages and disadvantages of teamworking*

Employer–employee relations and related topics

This unit has illustrated that employer–employee relations have links with many other topics within people and organisations. However, employer–employee relations also have connections with other important aspects of business studies. Some examples of these include

- production techniques. The use of methods such as kaizen groups is likely to be much more effective when industrial relations are conducted with trust and co-operation

- implementing change. Any type of change (expansion or rationalisation, for example) is likely to be more straightforward to implement within an atmosphere of harmonious employer–employee relations

- corporate image. A reputation for good industrial relations will improve society's view of the business. This may enhance sales and particularly assist in the recruitment of good-quality employees.

Progress questions

1 Distinguish between individual and collective bargaining. *(5 marks)*

2 Outline **two** benefits to employees that may result from the process of collective bargaining. *(6 marks)*

3 Explain the advantages to employers that might arise from derecognition of the only trade union within a business. *(7 marks)*

4 Examine why the use of collective bargaining in the UK declined in the 1980s and 1990s. *(9 marks)*

5 Outline the principal legal changes that have led to an increase in union recognition by employers since 2000. *(6 marks)*

6 Explain the term flexible workforce. *(3 marks)*

7 Outline **two** ways in which a manufacturing firm might increase the flexibility of its workforce. *(6 marks)*

8 Examine the ways in which a business might increase the degree of employee participation in decision making. *(9 marks)*

9 Explain **two** reasons why a business may decide **not** to introduce teamworking onto its production line. *(6 marks)*

10 Outline the ways in which the implementation of teamworking might improve the motivation of a workforce. *(7 marks)*

Analysis and evaluation questions

1 'Employers do not really want to engage in collective bargaining, they only do so because the law forces them to.' Discuss this statement. *(15 marks)*

2 Analyse the circumstances under which employees might benefit from individual bargaining. *(12 marks)*

3 'Businesses only benefit from the use of flexible workforces if they employ mainly unskilled labour.' To what extent do you agree with this view? *(15 marks)*

4 Charles Fik Ltd manufactures components for the motor industry on a traditional production line. The company is run on a traditional basis with employees having little control over their working lives. Examine the problems the company might encounter when introducing teamworking. *(12 marks)*

5 Many UK businesses operate a number of techniques allegedly intended to promote industrial democracy for example, employee share ownership schemes. Evaluate whether these techniques are really introduced for public relations reasons rather then because of a genuine desire to involve the workforce in decision making. *(15 marks)*

Case study

The banking group HSBC is a high profile target for union recognition under new employment legislation. The company withdrew the right of representation from 9000 middle managers in 1996 and has refused to reinstate it. An HSBC spokeswoman said the original decision was because union membership had been declining.

Under the Employment Relations Act, trade unions can claim 'automatic' recognition if they have more than half the relevant workforce as members. If a union has more than 10% of the workforce as members it can call for a ballot, in which 40% of the constituency have to vote 'Yes'.

Some employers have criticised the legislation as unnecessary and an example of 'turning the clock back'. They fear that this will result in higher costs of production and an increase in damaging industrial disputes. A union spokesperson disagreed. 'This will result in a more harmonious workplace, which will benefit all the stakeholders of a business.'

Adapted from *The Independent*

1 Outline the reasons why HSBC might have withdrawn union recognition in 1996. *(7 marks)*

2 Analyse the benefits a middle manager with HSBC might expect from the introduction of collective bargaining. *(10 marks)*

3 Discuss the case for and against HSBC reintroducing union recognition following the introduction of the new legislation. *(15 marks)*

4 The Employment Relations Act, 2000 represents a major intervention by the government in employer–employee relations. Critically evaluate whether the government should intervene in this way. *(18 marks)*

TRADE UNIONS AND EMPLOYMENT LAW

Starting points

Trade unions, industrial disputes and important organisations in the field of industrial relations (eg ACAS) were not a part of the AS business studies specification. This unit is an introduction to this important topic.

However, we did study the law in relation to other aspects of business activity. We discovered that UK businesses are subject to law passed by the European Union as well the government at Westminster. In addition judges can create laws as a result their decisions. An important aspect of our study of the law was the recognition that legal controls on businesses have advantages and disadvantages – this is true of employment law as well as legislation influencing other aspects of business activities.

Key terms

Collective agreements establish pay rates and working conditions in an organisation or industry. They are the outcome of collective bargaining between employers and the employee representatives.

Collective bargaining is negotiation between employers and the representatives of the workforce, usually trade union officials.

Trade unions are organisations of workers established to protect and improve the economic position and working conditions of their members.

The law is a framework of rules governing the way in which our society operates. These rules apply to businesses as well as individuals.

Union recognition: circumstances whereby the managers of a business accept the right of a particular trade union to negotiate on behalf of its members.

Trade unions

Trade unions are organisations of workers established to protect and improve the economic position and working conditions of their members. A number of different types of trade union exist, although a series of amalgamations over recent years has resulted in the distinctions between them becoming less clear. This has led to more unions falling into the 'general' category. Table 4.6 illustrates the types of trade union that operate in the UK.

Trade union numbers and membership

Mergers between unions have resulted in a smaller number of larger unions operating in the UK. Figure 4.7 shows the decline in the number of unions since 1976.

Trade unions are normally organised on a regional basis. For example, the Transport and General (T&G) operates in eight regions throughout the UK and Eire. Each region has a regional office staffed by full-time union employees (called organisers or officers). The region is made up of a number of branches (over 7000 in total in the case of the T&G) and each branch has an elected shop steward. The shop steward communicates with management on behalf of the union's members and reports back to members regarding management decisions. The head office has an administrative, statistical and legal staff and the senior officials of the union including, in the case of the T&G, general secretary Bill Morris. This structure serves the T&G's 900 000 members. Other major unions operate similar structures.

*P*OINTS TO PONDER

Spies working on behalf of the UK could soon have their own trade unions under reforms aimed at improving moral in the security services. MI5 and MI6 and considering ending their long-term ban on union recognition.

type of union	description	example(s)
craft unions	the oldest type of union, whose origins lie in traditional crafts	Musician's Union
industrial unions	these unions recruit members from a particular industry, but they may not represent all the employees within the industry	National Union of Teachers The National Union of Railwaymen
occupational unions	such unions recruit from similar occupations across a range of industries	National Union of Journalists
general unions	this category of unions is increasing in importance due to mergers between unions. They recruit members from a variety of occupations and industries	Transport & General (T&G) Unison

Table 4.6 *Types of trade unions*

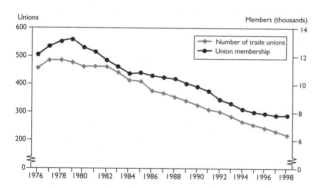

Figure 4.7 *Number of trade unions and union membership, Great Britain 1976–1998*

By the end of March 2000 there were 221 registered trade unions in the UK. Total membership of all trade unions was 7.8m in December 1998. This represented an increase of 12 000 from December 1997, the first rise in membership since 1984.

DTI [www.dti.gov.uk]

Objectives and functions of trade unions

Most trade unions in the UK have similar objectives. These focus on improving the economic position of their members by fulfilling the following:

- **maximising pay.** Unions engage in collective bargaining to provide their members with the highest possible rates of pay
- **achieving safe and secure working conditions**
- **attaining job security.** Arguably this is the most important objective of a modern trade union and one that is difficult to fulfil in the light of pressures resulting from globalisation and the increasing use of technology in the workplace
- **participating in and influencing decisions in the workplace.** Trade unions may achieve this through collective bargaining or through having representatives on works councils and other employer–employee committees.

In addition many unions have social objectives such as lobbying for higher social security benefits, improved employment legislation and improved quality provision by the National Health Service.

Trade unions achieve their objectives by carrying out a range of functions to the benefit of their members.

- Their most important and time-consuming function is protecting members' interests over issues such as discrimination, unfair dismissal and health and safety matters.
- They negotiate pay and conditions for their members through collective bargaining.
- Trade unions provide their members with a range

of personal services including legal advice, insurance, education, training and financial advice.

Union density

Union density is a term that refers to the proportion of a workforce that belongs to a trade union. Union density varies considerably from industry to industry. Only 6% of employees in hotels and restaurants are members of unions, compared with 61% in public administration and local government. Union density also varies according to age. Approximately 6% of employees aged under 20 are union members in contrast with 34% of those aged over 50.

When a business has a relatively high union density, there are a number of implications for the management of the business.

■ Decisions made by the business are more likely to be challenged, causing a more cautious approach by managers.
■ Decision making is likely to become more centralised creating common company policies in the field of industrial relations.
■ The management is more likely to have to reveal information about the company to trade union representatives.

Decline in trade union power

In March 2000 there were only 221 trade unions in the UK, with nearly eight million members. This represents a substantial change from 1979 when 13m Britons were represented by 487 trade unions. Declining membership and falling numbers of unions occurred steadily throughout the 1980s and most of the 1990s. Only since 1999 has union membership begun to recover. This period also saw a series of mergers amongst trade unions. One result is that today's unions are more general and represent a wider range of skills than was the case in the late 1970s.

These changes can be attributed to a number of causes. A predominant influence was probably a series of Acts of Parliament passed by Conservative governments during the 1980s gradually limiting the power and influence of trade unions. Conservative economic policy placed greater emphasis on controlling prices than on full employment thereby further weakening the power of trade unions.

The changing structure of industry has also contributed to the reduction of trade union influence. The decline of traditional industries such as mining, engineering and car manufacture, which had high levels of union density, resulted in the loss of thousands of union members. The industries that have developed in their place, mainly in the service sector, are not strongly unionised.

***P*OINTS TO PONDER**

58% of unions surveyed in 2000 said that their membership was rising, while 32% revealed that membership was unchanged. Changes in employment law (and especially the Employment Relations Act) have contributed to this increase in membership.

A further influence has been the internationalisation of UK industry. The UK has been highly successful in attracting investment from overseas. Foreign businesses have provided a catalyst to create a different industrial relations atmosphere. Conflict and disputes have been reduced and the emphasis has, in many cases, switched from collective agreements to individual ones. Unionised and non-unionised employees alike have accepted that in a global marketplace UK workers have to be competitive, otherwise businesses will move elsewhere. This new philosophy has been behind agreements such as single union deals and no strike agreements which are intended to avoid disputes and promote productivity.

Industrial disputes

Trade unions can use a variety of sanctions to place employers under pressure if negotiations do not reach a successful conclusion. Collectively these sanctions are termed industrial action:

- **strikes**. Workers can withdraw their labour so long as this course of action is agreed through a secret ballot. Strikes may be continuous or a succession of one-day actions
- **picketing**. This occurs when strikers stand at entrances to a place with an industrial dispute to attempt to persuade others not to cross the picket line, thereby breaking the strike action. Legislation restricts the number of people able to picket at any one time
- **work to rule**. Under this action unions dictate procedures to be followed by members in the course of working. This results in employees being less productive and output declining
- **sit in**. A sit in takes place when employees occupy a workplace for a specific period of time, thus causing production to be stopped
- **go slow**. Similar to a work to rule, this is a measure designed to slow production and reduce workers' productivity with adverse effects on the firm's profits
- **overtime bans**. Under this sanction employees are not prepared to work beyond their normal hours reducing the flexibility of the labour force. Overtime bans may mean employers have to recruit more employees incurring additional costs.

> **Key terms**
>
> *Arbitration* is the attempt to settle an industrial dispute through the use of a neutral third party.
> *Conciliation* is negotiations undertaken with the aim of reconciling differences between the parties to an industrial dispute.
> *Industrial action* is any activity organised by employees or their representatives as part of a protest against an employer during a dispute.
> *Industrial dispute* is a disagreement between an employer and employees (or their trade union representatives) over a range of matters, eg pay and working conditions.
> *A single union agreement* exists when an employer agrees to recognise only one union for the purpose of collective bargaining.

*P*OINTS TO PONDER

Evidence suggests that women are becoming the militant sex in the workplace. Female employees have initiated a series of disputes including one at British Airways. One striker commented 'women can be more determined, awkward and stubborn than men.'

Resolving industrial disputes

It is normal for industrial disputes to be resolved without unions taking any form of industrial action. The decline in industrial disputes in the UK over recent years has, in part, been a consequence of the effective use of measures outlined as follows.

1. Arbitration

Arbitration is a procedure for the settlement of disputes, under which the parties agree to be bound by the decision of an arbitrator whose decision is in some circumstances legally binding on both parties. The process of arbitration is governed by Arbitration Acts 1950–1996. There are three main types of arbitration.

1 Non-binding arbitration involves a neutral third party making an award to settle a dispute that the parties concerned can accept or not.
2 Binding arbitration means that the parties to the dispute have to take the award of the arbitrator.
3 Pendulum arbitration is a binding form of arbitration in which the arbitrator has to decide entirely for one side or the other. It is not an option to reach a compromise and select some middle ground. This system avoids excessive claims by unions or miserly offers by employers.

2. Conciliation

This is a method of resolving individual or collective disputes in which a neutral third party encourages the continuation of negotiations and the postponement (at least) of any form of industrial action. The conciliator's role does not involve making any judgement of the validity of the position of either party. The conciliator encourages the continued discussions in the hope that a compromise can be reached. Conciliation is sometimes called mediation.

Integrated Business: Honshu's decision

Honshu, the Korean computer manufacturer is committed to expanding its production capacity through the construction of a new factory in Europe. This will complement its existing production facilities in Wrexham, Brussels and Lisbon. The company, unlike most of its global competitors has a shortage of production capacity, and has decided that as part of its global strategy, output in Europe should be boosted.

Whilst the company has confirmed its expansion plans, the precise location of the new factory is unclear. The managers of Honshu (Europe) are currently drawing up a short-list of possible sites for consideration by the company's senior managers. A company spokesperson commented that this was an important decision. 'We are taking into account a wide range of factors before reaching a final decision. However, because the company believes that a reliable and committed workforce is essential for commercial success, the human element in the decision will be paramount.'

The company has gathered data relating to five countries in which it is most interested.

country	average increase in annual earnings (%)		number of working days lost through industrial disputes (000s)	
	1998	1999	1998	1999
Ireland	4.4	4.4	37	56
Italy	2.3	2.6	543	883
Finland	3.5	2.6	133	27
Spain	2.3	2.2	1263	1048
UK	4.6	4.9	282	242

Table 4.7 *Employment data for selected European countries 1998–1999*

Adapted from European Foundation for the Improvement of Living & Working Conditions [www.eiro.eurofound.ie]

1 How might a business cope in the short term with a shortage of productive capacity? *(8 marks)*
2 Assess the value of the data in table 4.7 to Honshu in taking its decision regarding the location of its new factory. *(12 marks)*
3 Honshu believes that 'a reliable and committed workforce is essential for commercial success'. To what extent do you agree with its view? *(15 marks)*
4 Discuss the other factors that Honshu should take into account before reaching a final decision. *(15 marks)*

No strike and single union agreements

The changing atmosphere within industrial relations has led to a number of developments that have limited the power and influence of trade unions within the workplace.

A 'no strike deal' is an agreement between employers and unions whereby in return for a pay and conditions package a union agrees to refrain from strike action for an agreed period. Often such agreements are accompanied by a commitment by both parties to go to binding arbitration in the event of a dispute. This reassures the union that it is not making itself too vulnerable by agreeing not to take industrial action. A no strike agreement can benefit a trade union in a number of ways.

- By presenting itself as non-confrontational the union may attract a greater number of members from within the workforce increasing its income and strength.
- A less confrontational stance might allow the union to appoint worker directors increasing the union's influence and role in decision making.
- Such agreements can improve the public perception of trade unions. This will assist the union in its activities in other businesses and industries and may persuade employers to recognise it.

A further advantage of no strike deals is that they

may lead to a single union agreement strengthening the position of the union within the business.

Single union agreements have become more common over the last 20 years. Under this type of deal employees agree to be represented by one union. This makes negotiation simpler for the employers (as there are only two parties to the discussions) whilst reducing the possibility of disputes between rival unions. Single union deals also assist in maintaining good communications between employers and employees lessening the possibility of industrial action.

Advisory, Conciliation and Arbitration Service (ACAS)

ACAS is an independent and impartial organisation established to prevent and resolve industrial disputes. ACAS's mission is to improve the performance and effectiveness of organisations by providing an independent and impartial service to prevent and resolve disputes and to build harmonious relationships at work. ACAS offers a number of services to employers and employees:

- preventing and resolving industrial disputes, particularly through the use of arbitration and conciliation
- resolving individual disputes over employment rights including individual cases of discrimination and unfair dismissal
- providing impartial information and advice on employment matters topics such as reducing absenteeism, employee sickness and payment systems
- improving the understanding of industrial relations.

ACAS was established in 1975 by the government during a period of industrial conflict to provide advice on industrial relations matters. Initially ACAS's role was mainly the resolution of industrial disputes. More recently the organisation has focused on improving business practices to reduce the possibility of industrial disputes. In the new Millennium demand for ACAS's services is greater than ever: the number of cases in which it is involved has almost tripled since 1979. Much of ACAS's work nowadays is conciliating in disputes

between an individual employee and his or her employer. This trend reflects the decreased influence of trade unions in modern businesses.

Industrial tribunals

Industrial tribunals are an informal courtroom where legal disputes over unfair dismissal or discrimination can be settled. Industrial tribunals were established in 1964 and are to be found in most major towns and cities in the UK. Each tribunal comprises three members: a legally trained chairperson, one employer representative and an employee representative. Most employee complaints are still settled by industrial tribunals.

Employment legislation

Key terms

Unfair dismissal is the termination of a worker's contract of employment without a legal reason.
Closed shop is a situation in which all the employees of a business are required to be members of a specific trade union.

Individual labour law

This aspect of employment legislation refers to the rights and obligations of individual employees. The amount and scope of individual labour law has increased in recent years, in part encouraged by the growing influence of the European Union on business matters in the UK.

A number of the most important Acts relating to individuals in employment are explained as follows.

- **Equal Pay Act, 1970**. This act rules that both sexes should be treated equally in all matters relating to employment. Equality in the workplace has been strengthened by European Union legislation, eg the 1975 Equal Pay Directive
- **Sex Discrimination Act, 1974.** This Act made discrimination on the grounds of sex or marital status illegal in recruitment, promotion, training

and dismissal. The Act created the Equal Opportunities Commission to monitor the effectiveness of the Equal Pay and Sex Discrimination Acts. The commission was given the tasks of encouraging the elimination of sexual discrimination in the workplace and promoting equal opportunities

- **Race Relations Act, 1976.** This legislation makes discrimination in relation to employment, against men or women on the grounds of colour, race, nationality or ethnic or national origin illegal. As in the case of sex discrimination, individuals have the right to take a claim for discrimination to an industrial tribunal. This Act also established the Commission for Racial Equality

- **Disability Discrimination Act, 1994.** Employers who treat a disabled person less favourably than others without proper reason are deemed to be behaving illegally under this Act. Employers are also required to make reasonable alterations to the working environment to assist those with disabilities in remaining employed

- **Working Time Regulations, 1998.** This European Union legislation (hence the term regulation) set a limit on the hours that employees could be required to work each week of 48 hours. Employees can opt to work longer hours if they wish, but employers cannot insist that they do so without inserting an appropriate clause in their contract of employment. The regulations also gave employees an entitlement to four weeks' paid annual leave.

EXAMINER'S ADVICE

Do not get too bogged down in the detail of these acts. The most important aspects of employment legislation are to understand its scope and to appreciate the impact it may have on businesses as well as their likely responses.

Key *issues*

Unfair dismissal is the termination of a worker's contract of employment without a legal reason. Legislation relating to unfair dismissal only relates to workers once they have been in a particular job for

one year or more. There are a limited number of reasons why an employee might be dismissed:

- where a job no longer exists – this is redundancy
- gross misconduct. Examples of this reason include theft from the employer or behaving violently at work
- failing to carry out duties in 'a satisfactory manner'
- another **substantial** reason, eg the ending of a temporary contract.

All other reasons for dismissal are considered unfair. Employees who think they have been unfairly dismissed can claim compensation by taking their case to an industrial tribunal.

Collective labour law

This group of laws apply to the operation of industrial relations and collective bargaining as well as the activities of trade unions. For many years the law did not play a significant role in employer–employee relationships. However, this philosophy was changed when the Conservative governments of the 1980s and early 1990s passed a series of Acts intended to restrict the power of trade unions:

- **Employment Act 1980.** Under this Act employers were no longer obliged to negotiate with unions – many unions were derecognised as a consequence. It also restricted picketing to employees' own place of work, thereby outlawing 'secondary picketing'. Closed shops were only permitted if supported by at least 80% of the workforce in a secret ballot.
- **Employment Act, 1982.** This Act increased the support for closed shops to 85% to make their continuation legal. It also made trade unions liable for damages if the union supported illegal industrial action
- **Trade Union Act, 1984.** This legislation made a secret ballot of employees a legal requirement before industrial action was lawful
- **Employment Act, 1988.** Protected union members from disciplinary action by their union for refusing to take part in strike action or

benefits	drawbacks
■ more motivated employees	■ increases costs of employment and production
■ increased flexibility, productivity and competitiveness	■ may require recruitment of non-productive personnel
■ more attractive to overseas investors	

Table 4.8 *A summary of the benefits and drawbacks of employment legislation to businesses*

picketing, despite a ballot in favour of industrial action

■ **Employment Act, 1990**. Closed shops were finally outlawed by this piece of legislation. Employees taking part in unofficial strike action could be dismissed without being able to make a claim of unfair dismissal

■ **Trade Union Reform and Employment Rights Act, 1993**. Unions were required to give employers a minimum of seven days' notice before taking official industrial action. It also abolished wages councils and minimum pay rates

■ **Minimum Wage Act, 1998**. The main elements of the new legislation are a general minimum wage rate of £3.60 per hour (raised to £3.70 in 2000) and a minimum rate of £3.00 an hour (£3.25) for all 18–21 year olds. Workers paid on a piece-rate basis and people employed on part-time or temporary contracts must receive the minimum wage

■ **Employment Relations Act, 2000**. Under this Act a trade union with a membership exceeding 50% of the employees in any particular business can demand union recognition and the right to introduce collective bargaining.

Impact of employment legislation on businesses

It is easy to assume that employment legislation simply constrains business activities and therefore has a purely negative effect on businesses. However, this is not the case. Employment legislation can have positive and negative effects on businesses and their activities.

Employment legislation can help to motivate the workforce. Employees who work in a safe and secure physical environment will be more contented and probably more productive. Employers will also avoid the costs, delays and bad publicity caused by

accidents at work or employee complaints about poor conditions. Furthermore, freedom from arbitrary dismissal may encourage a more co-operative, flexible and productive workforce enhancing the performance of the business.

Employment legislation restricting the powers of trade unions has encouraged the development of more flexible workforces. The ending of closed shops and the requirement for union recognition in many circumstances made it easier for businesses to implement changes in working practices improving the productivity and competitiveness of UK businesses. Firms were able to adopt single union deals, making collective bargaining simpler and ending damaging and costly demarcation disputes (disputes between unions concerning the respective roles of their members in the organisation).

Following the legislation of the 1980s and 1990s, the UK has some of the most employer-friendly employment legislation in the western world. This has helped the country to attract the lion's share of foreign investment entering Europe. The UK is an attractive site for overseas businesses because its favourable employment legislation helps to minimise labour costs. In 2000 the UK received 24% of all inward investment into the European Union.

However, in spite of the employer-friendly approach in the UK, employment legislation does increase costs above the level that would exist if no legislation were in place. To take an example, the national minimum wage, introduced in 1999, raised the wages of an estimated three million employees. It is estimated to have added approximately 1% to the nation's wage bill. Similarly the requirement (under the Disability Discrimination Act) to make 'reasonable' alterations to the working environment to enable the employment of disabled employees adds to costs of production.

Employment legislation also requires firms to employ greater numbers of non-productive workers such as human resource managers and safety officers. These employees add to the costs of production without making any direct contribution to the output of the business. Inevitably, costs increase as a consequence.

The effects of legislation may be greater on small firms who have fewer resources and are less able to keep up with changes in employment laws and may not be able to afford to respond in the appropriate manner. Larger firms have expert human resource specialists and are geared up for change. They may also be able to afford specialist employment lawyers to advise them on avoiding some of the effects of a new piece of employment legislation.

Progress questions

1 Distinguish between general and industrial trade unions. *(4 marks)*

2 Outline **two** objectives of trade unions in the UK. *(6 marks)*

3 Explain why trade union membership rose during 1999 and 2000 following many years of steady decline. *(7 marks)*

4 Why did the influence of trade unions diminish during the last 20 years of the twentieth century? *(8 marks)*

5 Explain the benefits that may arise from the use of binding arbitration to resolve an industrial dispute. *(8 marks)*

6 Outline **two** benefits a trade union might derive from negotiating a 'no strike' agreement. *(6 marks)*

7 Explain the difference between individual labour law and collective labour law. *(5 marks)*

8 Outline **two** types of discrimination that are illegal in relation to employment. *(6 marks)*

9 Explain the possible benefits to employers arising from the ending of closed shop arrangements. *(7 marks)*

10 In what ways might employment legislation assist in motivating employees? *(7 marks)*

Analysis and evaluation questions

1 Analyse the benefits to businesses arising from the employment legislation in the 1980s and 1990s that restricted the power of trade unions in the UK. *(12 marks)*

2 Blair and Brown plc, manufacturers of electronic components, have recently recognised the T&G union for the purposes of collective bargaining. Tony Brown commented 'We are a modern forward looking company and want to work hand in hand with our employees. Their interests are our interests.' Critically evaluate whether the interests of employers and employees in a large manufacturing business are likely to coincide. *(15 marks)*

3 The management team at Abdul Rasheed & Co have negotiated a no strike agreement with the single trade union in the factory. Discuss whether the existence of no strike agreement means that trade unions are no longer necessary. *(15 marks)*

4 'A well-managed firm looks after the interests of its employees because they are a very important asset to a successful business. Thus employment protection legislation is unnecessary.' Critically evaluate this view. *(15 marks)*

5 Examine whether the major burden of employment legislation falls upon small firms. *(12 marks)*

Case study

Council workers in Scotland have voted to strike over a pay row, the public services union Unison announced last night following an offer of a 2.5% pay rise. The union's members voted 16 128 votes to 12 672 to take action. The strikes will affect the council's ability to offer refuse collection, planning and leisure services as well as school meals.

Joe Di Paola, Unison's Scottish organiser for local government, said 'Central government has not funded staff pay increases for seven years and local government staff are fed up carrying the burden of cuts that local services have suffered.' A Unison spokesman said the recommended action was a one-day first strike, planned for August 29, followed by a two- and then a three-day stoppage.

The Scottish local authorities described the decision by members of Scotland's biggest local authority union as 'regrettable' adding that the pay offer was 'the most that councils can afford'. The local authorities have worked harmoniously with Unison for many years in spite of increasing difficulty in funding a full range of services.

The number of industrial disputes in Scotland has declined substantially since the early 1980s. The extension of employment legislation and implementation of new working practices have contributed to a huge reduction in the number of working days lost to industrial disputes.

Adapted from the Electronic Telegraph, *16 August 2000*

1 Outline **two** other sanctions that Unison might have used in this situation, apart from strike action.

(8 marks)

2 Examine the benefits arising from the legal requirement that a secret ballot is held prior to any strike action. *(10 marks)*

3 Discuss the possible advantages and disadvantages to local governments in Scotland from working together with Unison. *(15 marks)*

4 To what extent has recent employment protection legislation in the UK genuinely improved employer–employee relations? *(17 marks)*

HUMAN RESOURCE MANAGEMENT

Starting points

We introduced the topic of human resource management as part of AS level business studies. HRM is the process of making the most efficient use of an organisation's employees and covers a broad range of business activities:

■ assessing future labour needs
■ recruitment and selection
■ training
■ appraisal
■ motivation and reward of employees.

The question of rewarding employees through pay systems is an important element of AS business studies and encompasses methods of pay such as hourly rates, piece-work, salaries and performance related pay. It would be worthwhile to revisit this section before studying this unit in detail.

AS level business studies also considered the notion of HRM, and covered recruitment and selection. This unit will restate and develop further the concept of human resource management and look at appraisal and reward of employees in detail. HRM is best studied as a coherent whole, so it is important to gain an appreciation of the integrated and strategic nature of the whole process before considering the remaining components in detail.

What is human resource management?

Until recently most businesses have relied on the concept of personnel management. Latterly the influence of Japanese management techniques has encouraged the adoption of at least some elements of HRM.

HRM views activities relating to the workforce as integrated and vital in helping the organisation to achieve its corporate objectives. People are viewed as an important resource to be developed through training. Thus, policies relating to recruitment, pay and appraisal, for example, should be formulated as part of a coordinated human resource strategy. Human resource management is an all-embracing integrated approach that aims to make the best use of human resources in relation to the business's overall goals. Human resource management involves the strategic planning of the management of employees.

In comparison, personnel management considers the elements that comprise managing people (recruitment, selection, wages and so on) as separate elements. It does not take into account how these parts combine to assist in the achievement of organisational objectives. At its simplest, personnel management within businesses carries out a series of unrelated tasks.

The most enthusiastic supporters of HRM are foreign-owned companies operating in the EU. However, in spite of the potential benefits, many firms do not engage in human resource planning and management.

OneClickHR.com, a human resources software company, is developing a range of e-commerce services for small businesses. One of its offerings is a software package to assist small firms in implementing the principles of human resource management.

Why have firms adopted HRM?

A number of factors have persuaded UK businesses to implement human resource management.

■ A principal argument is that the Japanese have had apparent success in managing people using this technique. The Japanese have been seen to gain significant competitive advantage from managing a human resource that produces high quality products at minimum cost. It is human resource management that is credited with achieving this match between employee behaviour and organisational objectives.

■ Changes in organisational structure have led to many managers taking on responsibility for managing people within the organisation. Techniques such as delayering and the development of empowered teams have been an integral part of the implementation of human resource management. Acquiring, developing, motivating and rewarding employees are, it is argued, best done by managers and colleagues close to the employees in question. Under HRM managers can carry out many of the more routine tasks of traditional personnel management.

	'hard' HRM	'soft' HRM
Philosophy	employees are a resource like any other available to the business	sees employees as different, and more important, than any other resource available to managers
Time scale	HRM seen as a short-term policy: employees hired and fired as necessary	takes a long-term view of using the workforce as efficiently as possible to achieve long-term corporate objectives
Key features	■ employees paid as little as possible ■ employees only have limited control over working life ■ communication mainly downward in direction ■ leaders tend towards theory X view of workforce ■ employees recruited externally to fulfil human needs – giving short-term solution ■ judgemental appraisal	■ managers consult regularly and fully with employees ■ managers give control over working lives to employees through techniques such as delayering and empowerment ■ leaders tend towards theory Y view of workforce ■ emphasis on training and developing employees ■ employees promoted from within whenever possible – reflecting long-term desire to develop workforce ■ developmental appraisal
Associated leadership style	leaders operating this style of HRM are more likely to be at the autocratic end of the spectrum of leadership	leaders implementing 'soft' HRM are more likely to be democratic in nature
Motivational techniques used	probably mainly motivated by pay, with limited use of techniques such as delegation and teamworking	delegation, empowerment. Extensive use of techniques designed to give employees more authority

Table 4.9 *Approaches to human resource management*

■ The increasing popularity of psychological approaches to motivation has encouraged the adoption of HRM. Human resource management demands styles of working that meet the social and psychological needs of employees. The adoption of flatter organisational structures and psychological techniques of motivation are essential elements of HRM – organisations that adopt these techniques and structures would naturally move towards HRM.

Types of human resource management

The adoption of HRM by UK businesses is not as sweeping and as clear-cut as some might suggest. Surveys have indicated that many companies have opted to select only the elements of the human resource management package that fit in with their philosophies, management style and corporate objectives. For example, a firm might choose to implement rigorous selection and appraisal methods but ignore other aspects particularly developing employees through training.

There is not a single HRM policy. Different firms have interpreted the philosophy in different ways:

■ **'hard' HRM.** Some firms operate 'hard' HRM policies treating employees as a resource to be used optimally. Such firms regard employees as yet another resource to be deployed as efficiently as possible in pursuit of strategic targets. Employees are obtained as cheaply as possible, controlled and disposed of when necessary

■ **'soft' HRM.** Other firms use an HRM system that can be regarded as 'soft'. This approach is based on the notion that employees are perhaps the most valuable asset a business has and they should be developed to maximise their value to the organisation. This makes a long-term approach essential. Employees are seen as a resource to be valued and developed over time and in response to changing market conditions.

Planning the workforce

Workforce planning is one of the core activities of human resource management, whatever style is operated. Workforce planning entails a number of stages.

■ The starting point of workforce planning is to consider the overall or corporate objectives of the business.

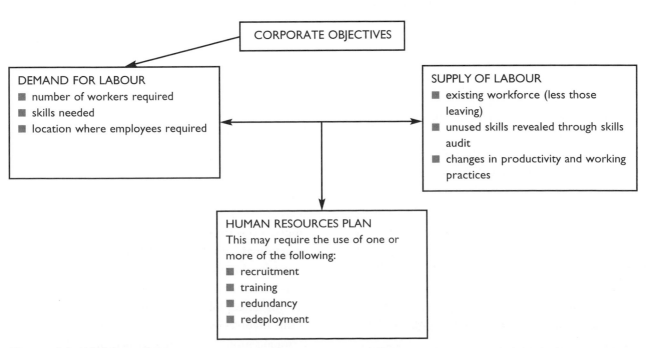

Figure 4.8 *Workforce planning*

- The next stage is to take a strategic view of employees, and to consider how human resources can be managed to assist in attaining the business's corporate objectives.
- This requires a judgement to be made about the size and type of workforce the organisation will require over future years.
- This desired workforce is compared with that currently available to the business.
- Once this comparison is complete the firm can decide upon policies (eg recruitment, training, redeployment and redundancy) necessary to convert the existing workforce into the desired one.

The plan will specify how the business will implement its human resource policies. An important element of the plan is a skills audit to identify the abilities and qualities of the existing workforce. This may highlight skills and experience of which managers were unaware.

Business in Focus

The increasing importance of e-commerce and information technology to many businesses in the western world has made traditional forms of work organisation appear obsolete, especially where a firm has an educated and well-trained workforce. As a result a growing number of companies in the UK, USA and Europe have introduced new human resource techniques underpinned by less hierarchical structures of decision making. They have emphasised the team approach, job rotation, performance-related pay, delegation of decision making and encouragement of employee financial shareholders.

   Evidence in the EU and the USA suggests that the adoption of a soft approach to human resource management can enhance productivity, profitability and share values. A survey in the USA has concluded that the implementation of soft human resource management is good for company performance.

The Financial Times

I Discuss why the adoption of a soft style of HRM appears to have improved the performance of a large number of companies.

Businesses require specific information when developing workforce plans.

- They need to research to provide sales forecasts for the next year or two. This will help identify the quantity and type of labour required.
- Data will be needed to show the number of employees likely to be leaving the labour force in general (and the firm in particular). Information will be required on potential entrants to the labour force.
- If wages are expected to rise then businesses may reduce their demand for labour and seek to make greater use of technology.
- The plan will reflect any anticipated changes in the output of the workforce due to changes in productivity or the length of the working week.
- Technological developments will impact on planning the workforce. Developments in this field may reduce the need for unskilled employees whilst creating employment for those with technical skills.

Workforce plans are also called human resource plans or manpower plans. Workforce planning teams are subject to a number of influences whilst drawing up their plans.

1. Corporate plans

These set out the goals of the entire organisation. Corporate plans relate to the business's mission statement. The goals included in corporate plans may include

- survival
- growth
- increased market share
- competing new markets (perhaps overseas)
- earning the highest possible profits.

A corporate plan suggesting expanding into a new market could, for example, have significant implications for employees. More employees might be required, possibly with different skills. If the expansion involves entering a market overseas, some employees may be redeployed. Finally, in some circumstances jobs may be lost as part of expansion if this involves joint ventures allowing some rationalisation and staffing reduction.

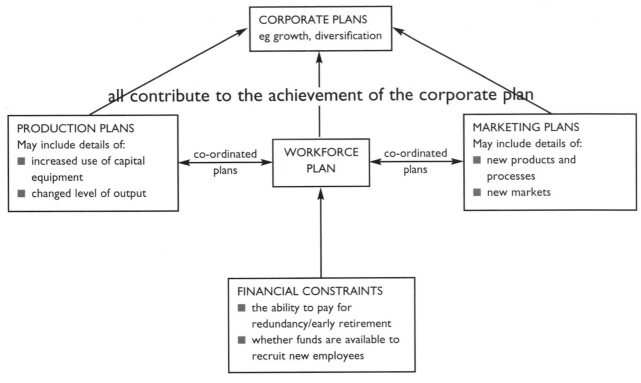

Figure 4.9 *Key influences on workforce planning*

2. Marketing plans

Marketing plans detail a firm's marketing objectives and how they intend to achieve these objectives (marketing strategy). The achievement of marketing objectives assists a firm in attaining its corporate objectives. If a firm plans to increase market share it may introduce new products. This might require the workforce plan to create a labour force with different skills through recruitment, training and redeployment.

3. Production plans

This type of plan details a business's objectives in relation to production. As with marketing plans the objectives in production plans are a central part of a firm's corporate strategy. Plans for production inform a business's workforce plan. Production may become capital intensive requiring fewer employees with greater skills. Alternatively a business might wish to give employees more responsibility for production as it adopts total quality management. This may require the

workforce plan to prepare for delayering and empowerment.

4. Financial constraints

Workforce planning operates within tight financial guidelines. Training, recruitment, redeployment and even redundancy are expensive. Firms operating a 'soft' approach to HRM may be prepared to grant a larger budget for workforce planning as they seek to develop their employees. On the other hand, advocates of 'hard' HRM would wish to effect workforce planning with minimal costs.

HRM and employee appraisal

Over 80% of UK firms are estimated to operate some sort of appraisal system. Many firms are extending appraisal schemes to part-time and peripheral employees. Effective appraisal systems can offer a number of benefits to businesses by helping managers and employees to focus on corporate targets. In addition many managers believe appraisal motivates those involved in the scheme. The type of appraisal system used is likely to reflect the firm's view of HRM.

Developmental appraisal

Developmental appraisal systems seek to increase the skills and productive capabilities of the workforce. The emphasis throughout the appraisal process is to identify an employee's training needs in relation to current and future roles within the business. By meeting these needs, employee performance can be enhanced. Douglas McGregor, in his support for the theory Y view of employees, commented that businesses could benefit from appraisal systems. Employee energy devoted to achieving organisational objectives coupled with a mutually supportive relationship between manager and subordinate can improve employee performance immeasurably. Finally, appraisal systems can encourage all employees to think strategically about their organisation.

Judgemental appraisal

However, other types of appraisal exist. Control systems of appraisal consider an employee's performance against targets agreed earlier. Employees meeting targets may be rewarded; those who do not may receive pay cuts. Such appraisal systems can limit individualism and creativity amongst employees and can be damaging to motivation and morale. Interestingly they are also based firmly on the premise that money is the major motivator. Judgemental appraisal can be seen as a mechanism restricting the degree of control employees have over their working lives.

Some managers express concern about the cost of appraisal, particularly complex systems that require interviews regularly. Any assessment of an appraisal system should be against the expressed objectives of the scheme. Is it to develop employees, or to ensure the most efficient use of the available workforce? The answer to this will depend upon a range of factors including leadership style, organisational culture, and, of course, the type of HRM operated within the enterprise.

HRM and employee reward systems

Employee reward systems are the mechanism used by firms to recompense employees for their labour services. They often comprise packages of pay and benefits.

The adoption of human resource management has seen a number of changes in reward systems including a move towards more individual arrangements of pay and benefits packages. This latter development has contributed to a decline in importance of trade unions in the workplace.

In a business environment subject to increasingly

rapid change, a number of factors influence businesses in the design of their reward systems for employees. Managers and shareholders expect that the reward system will prove cost-effective. Bonuses should encourage employees to work harder and strive to meet corporate objectives, not just be a payment for work they would have completed anyway. Pay rates should be set with a close eye on the labour market – enough to attract and keep good calibre applicants, but no higher.

Business in Focus

Shell is to fund the creation of a global e-university to deliver education and training to its worldwide workforce of 96 000 people. Shell is one of several companies investing in the enterprise along with all of Scotland's universities. Shell spends hundreds of millions of pounds each year on training and Scottish Knowledge, the company who will manage the e-university, expect to be training many of Shell's employees over the next few years.

A Shell spokesperson said the company recognised the necessity and benefits of providing high quality employee training. 'The development of the global university will allow our employees worldwide access to a huge range of education and training including technical courses and those on human resource management.'

Shell has not disclosed the extent of its investment in the e-university, though the figure is thought to be in the region of £4m.

The Scotsman

I Discuss the case for and against Shell investing its money in this way.

A good pay system (especially in a firm operating 'soft' human resource management) will consider employees and individuals and place less emphasis on collective bargaining. This may accompany a move towards local (rather than national) pay rates. This allows a more effective reward system offering greater pay to those who live in expensive areas of the country, eg London and the south-east.

Operating a flexible reward system able to recognise the differences of individual employees may be an important determinant for some businesses.

Businesses will want reward systems that encourage a reasonable turnover of labour. It can be unhealthy for a business if there is little or no turnover of labour. New staff bring fresh ideas and renewed enthusiasm into an organisation. Equally, a high rate of labour turnover can be harmful as experienced and highly trained employees leave and have to be replaced – often at great expense. Thus, a reward system should be designed to encourage a steady turnover of employees.

Any reward system should fit in with the organisation's leadership style, appraisal system and techniques designed to motivate and develop employees. In other words the reward system should be an integral and coherent part of the business's human resource management. There is little point in organising employees so as to provide them with some degree of control over their working lives and then operating a piece-rate pay system – or excluding training from any benefits package offered to employees. If the organisation seeks to empower employees, the reward system should support this aim. This might mean good rates of pay, but also the extensive use of non-financial rewards for employees. These could take the form of additional training, or being given greater authority, perhaps through promotion.

What is a 'good' reward system?

It is difficult to define the components of a 'good' reward system. To a great extent this depends upon what the management team considers to be the objectives of the reward system. It is possible to envisage two very diverse scenarios.

1 In a democratically led company seeking to operating a 'soft' HRM system and to delegate authority, the reward system may be intended to foster this process and to encourage staff to be independent, creative, to produce high quality products every time and to recognise and solve problems as they occur.

2 In an enterprise with a more autocratic leadership style, the objectives of the pay system could be

very different. The aim could be to use it to control the workforce: to ensure conformity and standard ways of completing tasks. Control could be achieved by withdrawing some benefits from employees who are deemed to have not to have met targets.

POINTS TO PONDER

Aspiring police chiefs on strategic management courses at the Police College at Bramshill are being introduced to the philosophy of human resource management. Senior police officers are taught the advantages of HRM alongside other techniques such as teamworking and managing internal and external stakeholders.

Measuring employee performance

Techniques designed to improve the performance of a workforce are of little value if managers are unable to assess the impact of changing policies. A number of measures are available to businesses to assess the performance of their employees.

Key performance indicators

1. Labour productivity

$$\text{Labour productivity} = \frac{\text{output per period}}{\text{number of employees at work}}$$

This is perhaps the most fundamental indicator of the performance of a group of employees. However, it is important to remember that productivity depends upon other factors such as the extent and quality of capital equipment available to the workforce as well as their talents and degree of motivation.

2. Absenteeism

$$\text{Absenteeism} = \frac{\text{number of staff absent (on one day)} \times 100}{\text{total number of staff}}$$

Absenteeism occurs for a variety of reasons,

including industrial accidents and illness. The term is frequently used to describe a situation where an employee is absent from work frequently and without good reason. Thus, it is used as a measure of the morale and motivation of a workforce. High levels of absenteeism can dramatically increase a business's costs.

3. Labour turnover

$$\text{Turnover} = \frac{\text{number of staff leaving during the year} \times 100}{\text{average number of staff}}$$

This ratio measures the proportion of a workforce leaving their employment at a business over some period of time, usually one year. Low wages and inadequate training leading to poor morale amongst employees may cause high levels of labour turnover. Another cause is ineffective recruitment procedures resulting in the appointment of inappropriate staff. Businesses require some level of labour turnover to bring new ideas into a business.

4. Health and safety

$$\text{Health and safety} = \frac{\text{number of working days lost per annum for health and safety reasons} \times 100}{\text{total number of possible working days}}$$

This measures the safety of the working environment. A dangerous working environment not only lowers employee morale but may also damage the performance of the workforce. Absence due to accidents and injuries in the workplace increases the labour costs incurred by a firm and can lead to adverse publicity.

Managers need to measure employee performance to assess the efficiency (and competitiveness) of the workforce. In service firms (where labour costs are a high proportion of total costs) this can be a particularly important factor. Measures of employee performance also help to assess the extent to which a workforce is motivated.

Human resource management and competitive advantage

Human resource management has the potential to provide businesses with a significant competitive advantage over rivals. Theory suggests that the implementation of HRM should make the organisation more competitive and to some extent this is borne out by the performance of Japanese companies.

Soft human resource management recognises the individual rather than producing personnel policies for the whole workforce. Reward systems, training and development, appraisal and communication are all geared to fulfilling the needs of the individual as well as those of the organisation. The key principle of HRM (or at least 'soft' HRM) is that each employee should be nurtured and developed in pursuit of the organisation's objectives. All aspects of the HRM 'package' should be coordinated to ensure coherence and to assist the attainment of strategic targets.

*P*OINTS TO PONDER

A survey conducted by the Cranfield School of Management found that, in spite of widespread support for the philosophy of human resource management amongst businesses and managers, the size and influence of HR departments did not increase during the 1990s. For example, in 1999 only 52% of companies had a seat on their board of directors for a senior HR director, the same figure as in 1990.

If an organisation is successful in operating its HRM policy, the outcome should be motivated and creative employees who are committed to the firm and who do not seek to leave. Such employees should be aware of the goals of the organisation and understand how they can contribute towards the attainment of organisational targets.

Under this scenario a business should incur less recruitment costs, enjoy higher levels of productivity and a reduction in faulty products. It may attract top-class applicants to vacancies because of its reputation as a caring and enlightened employer. All of these factors should make the organisation more competitive and better able to cope with the rigours of operating in international markets.

However, in the real world the case for HRM is not so clear-cut. Many businesses in the UK differ in their interpretation. Some see it as a confirmation of the value of employees who have to be developed to meet the needs of the organisation. Others take a 'hard' attitude viewing employees as simply another resource to be used as effectively as possible. The latter approach has a much more short-term focus. That different interpretations of the policy exist make it more difficult to assess its contribution to competitiveness. Its impact on competitiveness is more difficult to evaluate if its adoption is incomplete.

There are, however, theoretical arguments suggesting that human resource management may not enhance a business's competitiveness. Trade union recognition is a problem under HRM. The strategy requires people to be treated as individuals and as such to contribute to the attainment of corporate objectives. Yet, in spite of a decline in their importance during the 1980s and 1990s, unions have a long-established role in businesses in the UK. But there is an obvious tension in an organisation that attempts to deal with its employees on an individual basis within a framework of collective bargaining. This tension may manifest itself in employee dissatisfaction or, in extreme cases, in industrial action. Both scenarios could prove extremely damaging to a business's competitive performance.

Further problems may exist if the culture of the organisation is not suited to human resource management. Even 'hard' HRM implies some degree of delegation and at least a limited commitment to training. This can involve a degree of expenditure and some managers may oppose the lessening of control that HRM entails. Furthermore, the adoption of HRM may involve additional costs in the short term as managers and employees adjust to the new strategy and to revised roles within the organisation. The elevation of human resources to a strategic role may incite some opposition from those with responsibility for, say, marketing or finance. All of these factors can detract from the competitive performance of the organisation, especially in the short term.

Business in Focus

BP decided in 2000 to employ an outside firm to carry out all its human resource management functions. Increasing numbers of large companies are likely to meet their recruitment, training and other human resource management needs through outside firms. The Cranfield School of Management reports that this type of arrangement has increased by 40% in Europe over the period 1998–2000.

Some companies argue that outsourcing human resource management in this way allows them to use skills and knowledge not available within the company. Some critics argue that this is nothing more than another attempt to reduce operating costs. Supporters contend that this approach can result in businesses making a more effective use of their human resource.

1 Discuss whether it is possible for a business to operate a genuine 'soft' approach to human resource management by employing another firm to carry out activities such as recruitment and selection, training, appraisal and rewarding employees.

Progress questions

1 Distinguish between personnel management and human resource management. *(5 marks)*

2 Outline the elements that comprise human resource management. *(5 marks)*

3 Explain why many UK firms have decided to implement human resource management. *(7 marks)*

4 Explain the difference between 'soft' and 'hard' HRM. *(7 marks)*

5 Outline **two** external factors that might affect the workforce plan of a UK manufacturing business selling its products throughout Europe. *(6 marks)*

6 A manufacturing business has taken a decision to switch to capital-intensive production. How might a business's workforce plan assist in effecting this change successfully? *(8 marks)*

7 Outline the possible relationships between the style of HRM used by a business and the system of appraisal it operates. *(7 marks)*

8 Explain **two** ways in which the performance of a bank's workforce might be measured. *(8 marks)*

9 Franklins Supermarkets have a very low turnover of labour (less than 2% each year). Outline **one** advantage and **one** disadvantage that the company may experience as a result of this. *(6 marks)*

10 Outline the benefits a firm might receive from implementing human resource management. *(7 marks)*

Analysis and evaluation questions

1 Carbone & Caccachio Ltd manufacture a range of processed foods. The company is democratically led, uses autonomous work groups and is delayered. Analyse the benefits the firm might receive as a consequence of introducing human resource management. *(12 marks)*

2 The chief executive of a multinational commented recently 'My firm trades in a highly competitive market. Our "hard" version of human resource management is the best option in the circumstances.' Critically evaluate this view. *(15 marks)*

3 Most businesses use a mix of human and non-human resources to produce their goods and services. In the light of this, examine whether it is possible to measure the performance of the workforce accurately. *(12 marks)*

4 In the past three years there has been a 40% increase in the number of firms outsourcing their human resource management function. To what extent might this be expected to improve the competitiveness of a business trading in an international market? *(15 marks)*

5 Discuss whether the type of human resource management used by a business depends entirely upon the leadership style of the organisation. *(15 marks)*

Case study 1

Brown & Poulson plc has undergone a quiet revolution over the last two years. The company, one of the largest manufacturers of sports equipment in Europe, has elevated the role of human resources in the organisation, through the adoption of the philosophy of human resource management. The appointment of a director of human resources to the Poole-based company's board of directors emphasises the change taking place.

Recently appointed chief executive, Nicholas Kondratieff, believes that the workforce is a major contributor to the success of any business. 'Brown & Poulson's implementation of human resource management was overdue. We have lagged behind many of our major rivals, such as Nike, in terms of labour productivity and cost efficiency. I look forward to an improvement in the company's performance as a consequence of this decision.'

The company has introduced empowered teams in all areas of the business as an integral element of its style of HRM. The company is pursuing a policy of delayering throughout the organisation and has delegated much authority to teams and has worked to improve communication throughout the company. In the last financial year expenditure on training rose by 112% to equip employees with the skills necessary to carry out their enhanced roles. The company has recruited few employees from outside, preferring to develop its existing employees whenever possible.

Brown & Poulson are in the process of introducing an appraisal system to the company. The previous management team had always resisted the introduction of what they described as 'an expensive fad'. Nicholas Kondratieff and his fellow directors see a developmental appraisal system as a vital part of human resource management.

1 Explain the type of human resource management used by Brown & Poulson. *(8 marks)*

2 Examine how Brown & Poulson might measure the performance of their workforce. *(12 marks)*

3 Evaluate the possible implications for Brown & Poulson of the move from personnel management to human resource management. *(14 marks)*

4 Discuss whether the introduction of an appraisal system might assist the company in improving the performance of its workforce. *(16 marks)*

Case study 2

A year ago the outlook for car insurer Eagle Star Direct looked bleak. Losses at the company were running at £100m a year and its parent group, Zurich Financial Services, was seriously considering selling it off or even shutting it down. Some employees even suggested that the company give each of its 1.2m insured drivers £50 to switch to a rival insurer. They argued that the company's losses would be lower if this action was taken as compared with trading normally.

Eagle Star Direct sold most of its insurance as a result of customers telephoning staff at its call centres. At this time Eagle Star Direct had 1700 employees, a mix of brand names (Eagle Star and Zurich Municipal, for example), seven different call centre locations and a host of incompatible IT systems inherited from a variety of mergers. In short, Eagle Star Direct was on the ropes.

But just one year later Eagle Star Direct had moved back into profit. What is even more remarkable is that the turnaround was achieved without the widespread compulsory redundancies common at other companies when they 'downsize'. Neither did the company cut costs to such an extent that it is unable to trade successfully. Instead, it did what few companies do when facing severe financial problems: it asked its staff what it should do. Ian Owen, former managing director of Eagle Star Life (a sister company), was brought in to take control of the Direct division. 'My challenge was to put forward a strategy for the future and to turn a profit. To some it looked like an impossible challenge.'

The brands were merged into a single name: Eagle Star Direct. Seven IT systems were merged into one. Expensive television advertising campaigns were cut. Premiums charged to customers were increased by as much as 25%. 'Premiums were the lowest in the market, but expenses were out of control and there was little focus on customer service' says Owen. Eagle Star lost 200 000 customers, but says the figure has now stabilised at around one million, and its claim to be the best is now measured by the quality of customer service rather than purely on price.

But Owen's biggest challenge was to handle job losses without a collapse in staff morale. His first move was to tour the company's offices, stretching from Bournemouth in the south to Newcastle in the north, to speak to all 1700 staff. 'I thought it was crucial that everyone understood the situation the company was in. What I found was that there was a recognition that things had to change. The staff at our call centres were fantastic at coming up with ideas.'

The seven offices scattered throughout the UK were cut to three, resulting in the loss of 400 jobs. Yet the job of every member of staff was guaranteed. 'We said to everyone they had a job guaranteed for one year, and that if they were able to relocate, they would have a job guaranteed at that location.' Staff who did not relocate were offered redundancy pay of up to two years' salary. A 'war room' of 20–30 staff (some facing redundancy) was set up to implement fundamental change. Borrowing from a system used by Jack Welch at General Electric, 'town meetings' were held where staff most in the know (sometimes quite junior) were charged with making recommendations to senior management. Many recommendations highlighted ways to use labour more flexibly, assisting in reducing the company's operating costs. Some employees at Eagle Star Direct believe that creating a more flexible workforce was arguably the most important factor in turning around Eagle Star Direct.

Eagle Star Direct is heavily unionised, so the reaction of staff was crucial. Alan Wood, general secretary of the Union of Finance Services, which represents a large number of Eagle Star staff, says: 'The staff were saying "protect us from the worst", but they knew things had to be done.' He agrees that the company did all it could to ease the pain of the changes and recognised the role of the union as well as benefiting from its co-operation. 'Call

centres are run on a production line basis, and you can get British Leyland-style industrial relations if you are not careful. We've been through that phase and Eagle Star have been pretty good at working with us and allowing formal representation. When there is some grief, rather than letting it fester and then explode, it is taken up very quickly.' Wood noted that the changes in working practices were negotiated and introduced sensitively.

What management lessons are there to be learned from the Eagle Star experience? Owen says: 'When a company goes through downsizing, the big mistake is when no one can see the light at the end of the tunnel. You need to establish a common goal of where you are going, and get your staff behind it.'

The Guardian

1 a) Eagle Star Direct had gone through a series of mergers in the period leading up to the time when it experienced financial problems. Examine how mergers may make managing the workforce effectively a more difficult task.
   (8 marks)

   b) Evaluate the success of Eagle Star Direct in managing its human resources during a time of crisis. *(12 marks)*

2 a) Analyse the ways in which having a unionised workforce assisted the management team at Eagle Star Direct in improving the company's fortunes. *(6 marks)*

   b) Discuss whether unions have a role to play in a modern, democratically led organisation such as Eagle Star Direct. *(14 marks)*

3 a) How might individual bargaining have helped Eagle Star Direct to reduce its costs? *(7 marks)*

   b) 'Creating a more flexible workforce was arguably the most important factor in turning around Eagle Star Direct.' Critically evaluate this statement. *(13 marks)*

4 To what extent was the improvement in the performance of Eagle Star direct the result of effective communications at all levels within the organisation? *(20 marks)*

Operations Management

Introduction

The subject matter in operations management in A level business studies is divided between AS and A2. The AS course includes

- economies and diseconomies of scale
- capacity utilisation
- methods of production such as job, batch and flow
- quality control
- lean production (including topics such as just in time, cell production and kaizen).

The A2 course builds on the knowledge, concepts and skills you have acquired during the AS programme. It is worthwhile looking back over the AS materials before starting to study A2 operations management. More specific advice is given on any prior knowledge which is required at the beginning of each unit.

In the A2 course you will study the following:

- research and development
- critical path analysis
- the application of information technology within and between organisations
- location.

OPERATIONS MANAGEMENT

Starting points

The AS course covered a wide range of operations issues such as different methods of production (job, batch and flow) and the impact of the scale of production on unit costs. In this unit we begin by providing a short overview of the main elements of operations management and then consider a firm's location decision. This is a new topic which you will not have studied before at AS. As you study location try to identify links with other areas of the course – how might a location decision affect a firm's marketing activities, for example? How might the decision be affected by human resource issues?

Introduction to operations management

Operations management is the planning, organising and coordination of activities involved in the production of a firm's product or service. It is the management of the process which transforms inputs into outputs.

Operations management will include decisions regarding

- where to produce: what is the best location for the business?
- production facilities: what is the best scale of production? How large should the production plant be?
- production methods: what is the best method of production? What is the best way of combining the firm's resources? How should the production be organised? How should the production plant be laid out?
- where to purchase supplies from. How many stocks should the firm hold to meet production and sales demands?

Figure 5.1

The objectives of operations management include

- ensuring the firm can produce the quantities demanded by customers at the time they want them
- producing at an appropriate level of quality
- producing the goods as quickly as possible
- ensuring the goods are dependable
- ensuring the production system is as flexible as it needs to be, eg in terms of the range of products it has to provide
- ensuring the production is carried out as cost effectively as possible.

Obviously achieving these different objectives may lead to conflict; eg an improvement in quality may lead to an increase in costs. Adopting flow production techniques may lead to lower unit costs but reduces the amount of flexibility the firm has compared to, say, job production.

Key terms

Job production occurs when a firm produces one-off items which can be tailor-made to customer requirements.
Flow production occurs when each item moves continuously from one stage of a production process to the next.

Indicators of the effectiveness of operations management include

- productivity: eg the output per person, per factory or per machine
- unit costs ie the cost to produce one unit
- the number of defects ie what percentage of the units produced or services completed is faulty. How many goods are returned? What is the level of customer satisfaction or dissatisfaction?

Effective operations management should lead to better-quality products being produced more cheaply. Ineffective operations management, by comparison, is characterised by poor-quality products, delayed production and a failure to hit production targets.

EXAMINER'S ADVICE

Remember the constraints facing operations managers.

- *It may not be easy to produce more given the present level of capacity.*
- *Cutting costs may inevitably affect quality.*
- *The firm may not have the technology, skills or flexibility to produce the products that the marketing department wants.*

To achieve their goals operations managers must work closely with the other functions of the business. For example, the marketing function must specify exactly what customers want and what they are willing to pay; marketing will also help determine what needs to be produced when. Meanwhile the finance function will specify what equipment and processes can be afforded and the level of costs that the operations function must achieve. The human resources function will also need to work with operations to know what numbers of employees are required, what skills they must have and what training requirements there are.

The relationships between operations and the other functions is inevitably two-way. For example, the marketing department may set out what customers want but the production department must specify what it can actually produce. Similarly the desired level of operations might determine human resource requirements but the numbers and

For business success the activities of the different business functions must be integrated effectively.

Figure 5.2

skills of staff available also determine what it is feasible to produce.

Categorising operations systems

There are, of course, many different types of production processes – everything from an artist producing a few paintings a year to a bottling company turning out thousands of bottles every day. These systems can be categorised in a number of ways including

- volume: high-volume production includes chocolates and drinks; low-volume production includes an architect
- variety: high-variety operations include a tailor and a personal financial adviser who are capable of producing a wide range of products; low-variety operations include fast food restaurants which turn out a relatively limited variety of products
- variation in demand: products such as bakeries have relatively low fluctuations in demand; by comparison, the emergency services such as ambulance drivers have a big variation in demand throughout the week.

*P*OINTS TO PONDER: WHAT'S NEXT IN OPERATIONS?

The next phase of manufacturing is likely to involve **mass customisation** – this involves the production of customised items using mass production techniques as far as possible. A classic case of this is National Bicycles in Japan which has developed a system to make custom built bicycles

Business in Focus: Swatch

In the early 1980s the Swiss watch industry was almost dead. Cheap but often high quality products from Far Eastern manufacturers, such as Seiko and Casio, had almost destroyed the traditional Swiss industry. Trying to protect their investments the Swiss banks organised a merger of the two biggest companies to create the parent company called Swatch. Swatch saw the potential for a new plastic-cased watch which was already being developed within one of the merged companies. A major advantage was that it could be made in high volume at low cost. The quartz mechanism was built directly into the all plastic case and the number of parts was just 51, less than half the number in most watches. Fewer components meant the manufacture could be fully automated. This made Swatches cheap to produce even in Switzerland which had very high labour costs.

By the early 1990s Swatch had about 50% of the market. The ability to offer a good watch at a low price had enabled the watch to become a fashion accessory. This meant the company had to cope with increased demands for a variety of product designs. Through automation and standardisation of the internal mechanisms the company managed to increase variety without crippling increases in costs.

More recently Swatch has taken its skills in design and manufacture and applied them to car manufacturing in a good example of asset led marketing.

Operations Management, FT Pitman Publishing

1 What do you think are Swatch's main brand strengths?
2 What problems do you think Swatch might have encountered bringing about this transformation in its production methods?

for about 15% more than the price of a top of the range mass produced machine. The customer is measured in the shop on a special frame and chooses style, colour, brakes, tyres, pedals right down to his or her name to be painted on the finished bike (11m potential variations!). These details are faxed through to the plant and entered onto a host computer which generates bar code instructions for the tube cutting machine, painting robots and other processes. Each unique bicycle is delivered two weeks after the order. Other firms in other industries are following this principle. The appeal is: you sell the product then you build it so avoiding the risk of stock becoming obsolete. Obviously though it requires an incredibly flexible production system.

The Financial Times

Location

One of the first issues facing a new business will be where to locate its operations. This can involve high levels of investment and have a major impact on competitiveness. These decisions may involve several different elements: first which country, then which region and finally which specific plot of land. The decision on where to locate will affect a firm's costs (eg in terms of its overheads and ongoing running costs); it will also have an impact on its access to markets and the quality of the product, which will affect its revenue.

The decision on where to locate

The decision on where to locate will be a combination of quantitative and qualitative factors. This means that it is a combination of factors which can be measured such as the expected impact on costs and revenues (these are quantitative) as well as other factors which are less easy to quantify, such as the beauty of the surroundings and the quality of life in the area.

Factors affecting a firm's location may include

■ the costs of a particular location relative to other options. For example, the cost of land itself will vary from area to area; so will the cost of labour and services such as electricity. Taxation rates can also vary significantly from country to country. The decision to locate can therefore have a significant impact on a firm's profits.

The availability of lower-cost locations abroad has been a major factor for UK firms considering relocating to the Far East or eastern Europe. Low-wage employees and a much lower cost of living often make it very financially attractive for UK firms to be based overseas

■ the availability of government grants and incentives; if, for example, a government offers low rents or lower taxes to attract firms this can obviously act as an incentive to locate there. In the 1980s and 1990s the development agencies in regions of the UK, such as Wales and Scotland, were very effective at attracting overseas investment not just because of financial aid but also because of the general level of local and national government co-operation in areas such as planning permission. Governments often use a combination of push-and-pull techniques to get firms to locate in particular regions. Incentives such as grants help to pull firms to an area; refusing permission to build in other areas helps to push firms to locate where the government wants them to be

■ the infrastructure of the region. The availability of energy sources and transport facilities will affect the ease, speed and cost of production

■ the nature of the business itself. The extent to which a firm has freedom over the location decision depends in part on what it actually does. A self-employed website designer, for example, may be able to work from home. A fast food restaurant, by comparison, must be located somewhere near its customers whilst a mining company must base its production facilities where the actual minerals are

■ the location of the market. In some cases such as retailing it will often be important to be close to the market. A central high-street location is more likely to attract business than a site located several miles away from the main shopping areas. In other industries such as telephone banking it is not so important to be close to the customer

market access; the location of a firm may affect its ability to trade in particular markets. Firms based outside the European Union, for example, must pay a tax (a tariff) to sell their goods within the EU. Firms located within the EU do not have to pay this tax. This is one reason why many Japanese firms set up in the UK in the 1980s and 1990s because if they have UK production facilities using a proportion of UK components they can export to other EU states and not pay a tariff; this obviously makes their goods more competitive compared to exporting from Japan

exchange rates. In the late 1990s the UK had a very strong pound; this made it expensive for UK-based producers to export. On the other hand it meant UK firms had a strong purchasing power overseas which led some firms to relocate overseas at this time

political stability. The political climate can have an impact on the appeal of a certain area. The political troubles in Northern Ireland which led to several bombings deterred many investors in the 1980s and 1990s. The UK's reluctance to commit to the single currency meant some overseas investors were wary of locating in the UK because they were worried about the possible impact of being outside the 'euro zone'

resources. A firm may locate in a particular area because of the resources it offers. Microsoft located near Cambridge in the UK because it wanted easy access to top graduates and research facilities

image. A perfume company, for example, may benefit from being based in Paris or Milan but may not gain the same prestige from being located in Scunthorpe

the quality of life, eg how attractive is the area in itself? What are the facilities like? What is the standard of living like?

ethical issues. Some firms have avoided locating in low-wage areas for fear of being criticised for 'exploiting' local staff or of taking jobs away from the UK. In many cases firms expand in areas where they already have established links (and therefore feel some responsibility to the community) rather than take jobs elsewhere. The Body Shop set up one of its manufacturing operations at Easterhouse in Scotland specifically to bring jobs to a deprived area.

Business in Focus: Sony and the euro

In 2000 Sony, the Japanese consumer electronics manufacturer undertook a review of its operations in Britain because of a sharp deterioration in their profitability caused by the weakness of the European single currency compared to the pound and the yen which was hitting profitability of exports to Europe from Japan and Britain.

Sony has been making consumer electronics at its own factories in Britain since 1974. The two Welsh plants make colour TVs and computer display units. The company has also invested in new capacity to increase production of sophisticated digital television sets and state of the art professional cameras for use by television companies.

As part of the review Sony decided to shift production of high technology consumer electronics products from Japan to continental Europe (not the UK) to offset the recent sharp decline of the euro against the yen.

The Financial Times

1 Why do you think the pound might have been strong at this time?
2 What factors might have led Sony to choose Wales in the first place for two of its plants?

Quantitative analysis

The location decision can be absolutely critical to a firm because of its impact on costs and revenues and therefore profit. It can also be a difficult and expensive decision to change once it is made which makes it even more important to get it right first time. To help ensure the most financially attractive decision is made firms may use quantitative decision-making techniques. These may include

break-even analysis. A firm will want to know how many units must be sold in order to break even. It will also want to calculate the margin of safety ie how much sales could fall from its

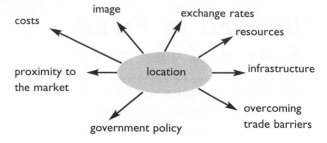

Figure 5.3 *Factors affecting location*

forecast figure before the firm starts to make a loss. If the fixed costs of a particular location are lower than another (perhaps because of lower rents) this will reduce the break-even level of output; similarly if the variable cost per unit is lower – eg due to cheaper wage rates – this will also reduce the break-even output. The lower the break-even the lower the risk to the firm in that fewer units have to be sold before a profit is made

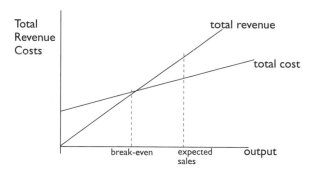

Figure 5.4

- investment appraisal. The decision to build in a particular location is often a large-scale investment and as such firms will undertake a detailed financial analysis of the expected payback period, the average rate of return and net present value. Given a choice a firm will usually choose the option with the quickest payback, the highest rate of return and the highest net present value. In reality the decision may not be that straightforward – eg one option may have a quicker payback but a lower rate of return. A firm will consider its expected sales relative to the break-even output of a particular location. The greater the margin of safety the less risk there is of locating in a particular place.

pOINTS TO PONDER

Perhaps rather surprisingly the base of the most valuable company in Europe and the seventh most valuable company in the world is Vodafone in Newbury, Berkshire. The company has market capitalisation of $256bn. It has 60 offices in Newbury spread all over different parts of the town, housing about 3000 of the 70 000 people who work for it.

Qualitative factors

Although firms are likely to examine the potential impact on revenues and costs of selecting a particular site the decision may also be affected by less measurable factors such as whether the location itself appeals to the managers and the quality of life in the area. For example, many Japanese firms have been attracted to the UK because of the importance of the English language in business. It is also because English is learnt in Japanese schools – this makes it easier for these firms to set up here than in France, for example.

Once a few firms have set up in a location this can also act as an incentive for others to locate there as they may think this proves it is safe and that networking (ie using the expertise and experience of others) will be easier. The growth of Hollywood as a film centre and Silicon Valley as a centre for computing is in part because the success of some firms has drawn in others.

Other possible qualitative factors which could attract managers to particular areas include the fact that they like the region or because they have particular attachments to the place. William Morris, for example, set up a car factory based in Oxford simply because he lived there. Managers might also choose a location because the name of the place enhances the product's image; a fashion house in New York sounds more exclusive than a fashion house in Grimsby. An advertising agency in London may have more appeal than one in Dundee. The reasons why a particular location is chosen are of course varied: in the case of call centres many firms have located in the north-east or north-west of the UK because callers like the accent of people from these areas more than the accents of people from the south-east. Although this factor may well impact on firm's profits it is difficult to place an absolute value on an accent and so this also counts as a qualitative factor!

*P*OINTS TO PONDER

Qualitative factors often have a major impact on where individuals and firms are located. Despite enormous success worldwide the members of the band U2 still spend a lot of time, and own businesses, in Dublin, the city in which they grew up. Similarly the band members of the Beautiful South have their headquarters in Hull where they first met.

Types of location decision

There are in fact many types of location decision which managers may have to consider. There is the initial decision of where to set up the business. In many ways this is the easiest decision in that the managers have no commitments to existing facilities. On the other hand it usually occurs at a time when money is tight and the firm will be heavily constrained by what it can afford. A key decision at this time is the desired capacity level – how big must the factory be? Or how much office space is needed? Managers may want to be optimistic about the possible growth of the business; at the same time they do not want to commit to large facilities and then find these are under-utilised.

Once a firm is established it may have to consider relocating at some point in its development. This occurs when a firm wants to move its facilities. This may be necessary because the initial reasons for choosing a place have now gone – eg government grants have been withdrawn or tax rates have been increased – or perhaps because the firm has outgrown its premises.

When relocation, a firm may have more experience of the type of facilities it needs compared to when it first chose its location; it may also have greater financial resources than when it started up. However, relocation brings with it all sorts of new problems including:

- staff who do not want to move (or the firm does not want to pay to relocate) – these may need compensation
- there could be a period of lost production time during the move
- there are costs of notifying customers and suppliers and administrative costs such as changing the firm's literature to include the new addresses.

A new location may also be part of an expansion process: a firm could be building new production facilities or opening up a new outlet, for example, The acquisition of new premises inevitably brings with it issues of management structure and control. A new facility will need controlling and the senior managers will need to decide on the best way of

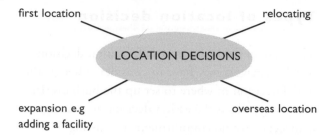

Figure 5.5 *Types of location decision*

structuring the business such as deciding what new jobs are created, what the reporting relationships will be and how to ensure effective communication.

Multinationals and overseas location

A multinational business is one which has bases in more than one country. Examples of multinationals are Shell, Ford, Coca-Cola and Exxon. Locating overseas naturally adds another dimension to any location decision. Many individuals in the UK, for example, have acquired properties in France or Italy either as a second home or to go and live there only to find it brings with it all sorts of problems they had not originally imagined. For example, acquiring properties abroad will involve an understanding of different legal requirements and processes. Overseas specialists will usually be necessary to make sense of the different requirements and to oversee the process of acquisition. Communicating and controlling facilities abroad may also prove more difficult simply due to the geographic distance between sites.

> **Key terms**
>
> *Multinational: this is a firm with production bases in more than one country.*

Why become multinational?

There are many reasons why firms might want to become multinational. These include

- to benefit from lower costs overseas
- to benefit from less regulation, eg fewer health and safety restrictions

- to benefit from a greater pool of labour, eg locating overseas may enable the firm to recruit more cheaply or to benefit from particular skills. The labour market may also be more flexible meaning that a firm can hire and fire staff more easily. The rights of employees in the UK, for example, have tended to be relatively low compared to those in other countries in the EU in terms of redundancy and dismissal rights and protection at work. This is one reason why the UK has been so attractive to overseas investors wanting to operate within the EU
- to benefit from particular resources such as minerals
- to benefit from market opportunities overseas. Firms may decide to expand overseas because the domestic market is saturated and there seems to be relatively slow growth compared to opportunities abroad or simply because a firm identifies attractive possibilities in foreign markets. Opening up new stores or new factories abroad therefore provides an opportunity for growth. This therefore creates the possibility of economies of scale. By operating on a larger scale worldwide a firm may benefit from purchasing economies reducing the cost per unit
- to be closer to their overseas customers; it may be easier to understand customer requirements and to provide a faster more efficient service
- to overcome protectionist trade barriers. Trading in China, for example, is very difficult unless a firm actually sets up there or at least has a form of partnership with a local firm. The Chinese government is eager to prevent what it regards as exploitation of the Chinese market unless western firms are actually investing into China at the same time
- to weaken trade union power. If a firm produces only in one country it is vulnerable to industrial action within that country. If, for example, there is a dispute with a trade union this could halt production completely; by having production facilities in several countries it is less likely production will ever be halted fully. Also it is more difficult for trade unions to organise themselves if they are in different countries so having, say, their factories in three different countries reduces the union power

Operations Management

163

compared to having all three factories in one country

■ to overcome exchange rate problems; by producing in the market where it sells, a firm will not face the difficulty of fluctuating exchange rates which can suddenly make exports from its home country seem uncompetitive.

Key terms

Protectionism: these are measures introduced by governments to prevent free trade. They include tariffs which are taxes on foreign goods and quotas which place a limit on the number of goods which can be imported from a foreign country.
Economies of scale: these occur when the unit cost falls as output increases. They provide larger firms with cost advantages.

Business in Focus: Market entry overseas: Boots in Japan

You cannot accuse Boots of being overhasty. While entering the Japanese market it took the firm over 14 months to open five stores. Meanwhile it has expanded elsewhere with enthusiasm – in Thailand it set up 70 stores in three years and in Taiwan it opened six stores in as many weeks. The Japanese market however remains difficult to enter due to its regulations, cultural norms and business practices. By adapting to Japanese practices Boots thinks it has found the way to succeed. To do this it decided local support was essential and therefore formed its first ever joint venture with Mitsubishi. Mitsubishi has proved a powerful ally for Boots in Japan; its international experience, local know how and the weight its name carries in Japan have been crucial in recruiting staff and dealing with bureaucracy.

The name has also allowed it to get the prime locations in towns. Building owners are usually suspicious of foreigners and unwilling to sell to them. The process of entering the Japanese market took three years in Japan (it usually takes Boots 18 months). The company had to reformulate over 2000 of its products to gain a Japanese licence. It also had to rethink some of its sales strategies. It has introduced seating at its cosmetics counters and changed the packaging to meet the Japanese preference for lavish presentation. Whereas its 'buy two get one free' has been tremendously successful in the UK it has failed miserably in Japan. At the same time it has learnt from the Japanese; for example, it has adopted lipstick amnesties where customers return old lipstick and get a replacement free. It has also adopted 'train highjacking' where a whole train or station is taken over to promote the firm. Boots estimate the Japanese health and beauty market is worth £17bn; four times the size of the market in the UK. One sixth of all over the counter medicines are consumed in Japan. With its mid-priced goods Boots thinks it has found a gap in the market which is dominated by exclusive department stores and discount drug stores and little in between. The company aims to find customers among Japanese women aged 18 to 35. They tend to be educated, influential in the health care market and have large disposable incomes and a willingness to experiment with new products. But they are very demanding.

The Financial Times

1 Why might Boots have chosen Japan as an area in which to expand?

Business in Focus: International strategies: Honda v Ford

Whilst all car companies have realised the potential gains from globalisation they have all tended to adopt different strategies. This can be seen by comparing the policies adopted by Ford and Honda.

Although Ford was one of the world's first multinationals it always used to operate on a regional basis and the management of each country had a considerable degree of independence when it came to production and marketing decisions. As a result the cars differed significantly from one country to another. Honda, by comparison, maintained a tight central control, designing and building cars in Japan and then selling them around the world. Although this approach did not seem to take much account of local differences, Honda was extremely flexible when it came to the actual design process. For example, Honda adopted simultaneous engineering and used multidisciplinary teams far earlier than western producers. This allowed it to respond more quickly to change. Interestingly in the 1990s both companies changed their approaches to try and gain some of the benefits of their competitor. At Ford, for example, the chief executive Alex Trotman introduced a radical programme of change known as Ford 2000. This replaced the old functional units with multidisciplinary teams. These are based in three vehicle centres which are each responsible for a particular type of vehicle. Small- and medium-sized cars, for example, are managed by a European team based in the UK and Germany. Honda, meanwhile, has decentralised much of its operations in recent years and as a result its cars are becoming less standardised as they are adjusted for local market conditions. Honda believes that eventually it will have four semi-autonomous divisions – namely Japan, the USA, Europe and Asia Pacific – and that cars will differ for each region.

Part of this change in the Honda approach is due to the fact that it now produces overseas. Nearly half of its worldwide sales of 2.1m in 1997 were produced in the USA and another 104 000 were made in the UK. Whilst encouraging greater regional variety Honda still believes it can gain from significant economies of scale by developing basic engineering structures which can be easily adjusted to regional characteristics. The basic body may be the same, for example, but there will be variations in styling and suspension settings.

1 With reference to this article do you think a global or a regional strategy is most likely to be successful for a car firm?

Is a low-cost location the best?

Although firms will often be seeking to increase efficiency and reduce their costs this does not necessarily mean they will always seek the lowest-cost location. Firstly, they may be influenced by qualitative factors – they may prefer to move to a location where they are familiar with the culture or language, for example. Secondly, they must consider the possible impact on quality. A cheaper location may not have the same access to high-quality resources. Thirdly, a firm's location may impact on its revenue; a high-street location may be expensive but attract far higher revenues and so prove more profitable.

The location decision must therefore involve an overview of many different factors including qualitative issues and overall profitability as well as costs.

Business in Focus: B&Q in China

In the rich world do it yourself has become a familiar pastime. But promoting it in China is no easy task … Most educated Chinese tend to recoil from the idea of manual work. Moreover there are few incentives to undertake DIY when there is a vast pool of migrant workers prepared to do jobs for less than 500 renminbi (£40) a month. Undaunted by these problems B&Q opened a warehouse store in Shanghai in June 1999, the first large British retailer to enter mainland China. To establish itself it has had to discover when it must adapt to the local market – and when it must insist on doing things differently.

B&Q, a subsidiary of the Kingfisher group, is the largest DIY operator in Europe. It first ventured into the Far East in 1996 when it opened a store in Taiwan. It has since opened eight stores in the country. The challenge is now to succeed in mainland China.

The B&Q Decorative Warehouse Store in Shanghai is a joint venture between B&Q International and a local concern Home Dec Building Materials. B&Q has a minority shareholding of 30% but has full operational control over the store. B&Q's timing into the Chinese market was good. Until the 1990s most urban Chinese lived in accommodation rented to them from their work units and had little incentive to decorate them. But the Chinese government is now promoting home ownership and a big decorating and furnishings market has developed.

Once the shell of the store building was complete it took just 12 weeks to prepare for opening day. The aim was to replicate as far as possible B&Q's UK store format: displays were erected by a team of store fitters and engineers from the UK.

B&Q's main competition is from Xinpin, a local private company, and the state owned Number Nine Department Store.

Practical problems make the development of the local market difficult. Even though a five day working week became standard in 1994 many Shanghainese commute long distances to work. Holidays are limited often to 10 days a year. Shanghai is China's most densely populated city and space is at a premium: few people have a spare room or garage that could serve as a workshop for DIY. The housing market is also radically different from that in the UK. New properties in China are empty shells with no flooring, no plaster on the walls or ceiling and no kitchen or bathroom units. To make such a place habitable goes well beyond the scope of ordinary DIY.

Typical customers are young couples who are about to marry or have just bought a flat. They are often accompanied by the person who will carry out the decoration work. The couple decide on the colours and styles of the product while the workman asks questions about the product use and quality. Customers often expect a sales assistant to accompany them whilst shopping and help them lift goods down from the shelf and carry them to the checkout.

B&Q Shanghai has the same personnel policies as in the UK. Staff refer to each other by their first names which is a radical departure in a hierarchy conscious China. The company also uses daily briefings to foster team spirit and the management style is more open and democratic than in many other Chinese companies. In its first big recruitment drive B&Q received more than 2000 applications for 160 vacancies. Many shop floor staff have the equivalent of a college degree. Staff are encouraged by the prospect of promotion as the firm grows within China.

However the challenge lies in extending its success in Shanghai to other cities; China is a country of significant regional differences in terms of labour markets, customer expectations and bureaucracy.

The Financial Times

1 What do you think will determine the success of B&Q in China?

Progress questions

	location A	location B
payback	5 years	6 years
average rate of return	12%	16%
net present value	£8m	£10m

1 Explain two ways in which the government might affect a firm's location decision. *(6 marks)*

2 Explain two possible factors, apart from the government, which might influence a firm's location decision. *(6 marks)*

3 What is meant by a multinational firm? *(2 marks)*

4 What is meant by protectionism? *(2 marks)*

5 Explain two possible reasons why a firm might want to become a multinational. *(6 marks)*

6 When making a location decision managers may consider both quantitative and qualitative factors. Using examples distinguish between quantitative and qualitative factors. *(4 marks)*

7 A firm's location decision may be influenced by its impact on the break-even output.

 a) What is meant by 'break-even output'? *(2 marks)*

 b) Explain how a location decision might influence the break-even output. *(6 marks)*

8 The location decision is an example of investment appraisal. Explain what is meant by 'investment appraisal'. *(2 marks)*

9 On the basis of the following data which location would you choose and why? *(6 marks)*

10 Explain two ways in which a firm's location decision may affect its competitiveness. *(6 marks)*

Analysis and evaluation questions

1 How important is the location decision in determining a firm's success? *(12 marks)*

2 Examine the quantitative factors a firm might take into account when deciding whether to relocate. *(8 marks)*

3 Are quantitative or qualitative factors more important when making location decisions? *(12 marks)*

4 Faversham Estate Agents Ltd is considering opening up new offices in France. Discuss the factors its managers might take into account when making this decision. *(12 marks)*

5 Hinds Electronics plc is considering relocating to eastern Europe. Examine the factors it might take into consideration when making this decision. *(8 marks)*

Case study 1

Buzz! Is an advertising agency recently set up by George Flame and Ahmed Gwadabe. George and Ahmed were at art college together when they were younger and have been friends ever since. For a while they had pursued their own careers working for different advertising agencies. Ahmed worked for one of the largest agencies in the country based in London. In the last few years he has handled some major accounts such as Heinz Beans and Palmolive Soap. George meanwhile has worked for a smaller agency based in Manchester which is where he used to live as a child. He has recently married and it was actually at his wedding that the idea of setting up an agency with Ahmed, who was his best man, first came about.

Both George and Ahmed are ambitious and although they have done well in their jobs they are eager to be their own bosses. After much hesitation and uncertainty they finally took the plunge and decided they would start afresh. Their idea is to target particular sectors such as schools, which have not traditionally been very interested in advertising, and to build up a reputation for being specialists in this field. They have both put their savings (what little they had) in a joint account and already decided on the name: Buzz! However, they have yet to agree on where the agency should be based – London? Manchester? Or somewhere else entirely?

1 Discuss the factors which might determine where Buzz! Is located. *(12 marks)*

Case study 2

In 1999 Lim Electronics, a South Korean firm, announced that it was looking for a location for a new factory outside of its home country. 'We are in the middle of a massive expansion programme and are now willing to operate as a multinational for the first time.' Lim's market share in most Asian markets is around 9%. Within the EU it is, on average, less than 3%.

Eager to attract new business the UK government has recently met with company representatives from Lim Electronics to discuss possible financial assistance. The company had also been meeting with representatives from other countries. 'Location is an important business financial decision and should not be taken lightly. Too many firms fail to pay sufficient attention to this decision. Just look at the number of cases of locational inertia and you can see what I mean. A good location ensures a firm's competitiveness.'

1 Examine the possible reasons why the UK government might offer financial assistance to attract Lim to this country. *(8 marks)*

2 Discuss the factors which might influence Lim's decision about where to locate its new factory. *(12 marks)*

3 To what extent does a good location ensure a firm's competitiveness? *(12 marks)*

PRODUCTIVE EFFICIENCY

Starting points

In this unit we will consider the determinants and the importance of productive efficiency ie ways in which firms can reduce their unit costs and why this matters. You will already have studied this topic before in the AS course. At that stage you focused on

- capacity utilisation – you considered how a low-capacity utilisation was likely to lead to high unit costs because resources were not being used efficiently
- economies and diseconomies of scale. You considered how a change in the scale of production can affect unit costs

- types of production – you studied the flexibility and efficiency of different types of production methods. Job production, for example, is very flexible but quite expensive whereas flow production is less flexible but leads to lower unit costs.

In this unit you will study the impact that research and development can have on a firm's productive efficiency.

Investment in research and development is often a key element of long-term success both in terms of improving a firm's efficiency and in generating new product developments to generate more sales.

Introduction

Productive efficiency is a measure of the success with which a firm turns its inputs into outputs. The more efficient a firm is the more output it generates with its inputs or the less inputs it uses to achieve a given level of output.

The efficiency of a firm is usually measured by the cost per unit. The more efficient a business is the lower the cost per unit; the less efficient it is the higher the cost per unit.

Figure 5.6

By improving its productive efficiency a firm can reduce its cost per unit. This means that

- it can then reduce the price per unit. This should lead to an increase in sales. The extent to which sales increase depends on the price elasticity of demand. By lowering its price the firm can offer better value for money and may achieve a competitive advantage over its competitors.

or

- it can maintain the same price and benefit from a

higher profit per unit. This profit can be invested into the firm or paid out to the owners.

𝓶 ATHS MOMENT

The price elasticity of demand

$$= \frac{\text{percentage change in demand}}{\text{percentage change in price}}$$

eg if a 5% price cut leads to a 10% increase in sales the price elasticity of demand

$$= \frac{+10}{-5} = -2$$

To become more efficient in production a firm will consider

- labour productivity. This measures the output per employee. Firms will usually try to increase the output per employee (provided that quality is maintained). An increase in productivity may be achieved through training, better capital equipment, better working practices (eg team working) or a change in management style

- the nature of the production process. Firms must consider the nature of their market and their customer requirements and decide on the most efficient process available. This may, for example, be job, batch or flow production. Flow production, for example, is more capital intensive than job production but is only likely to be efficient if there are high levels of demand for a relatively standardised product

- capacity utilisation ie the extent to which a firm is making full use of its resources. A firm's capacity measures the maximum output it can produce given its resources. Capacity utilisation measures a firm's actual output in relation to its capacity. The lower the capacity utilisation the less resources are being utilised and the higher the unit cost is likely to be because resources are not being used efficiently.

- the scale of production. A firm must decide on the most appropriate scale of production. Up to some level of output a firm may experience economies of scale; by expanding, the unit costs may fall due to, for example, purchasing or technical economies. However, if a firm gets too big it may suffer from diseconomies of scale ie unit costs may increase; this may be due to problems with communication, coordination and control as the firm gets too big.

m ATHS MOMENT

Capacity utilisation is measured by

$$\frac{\text{actual output}}{\text{maximum output}} \times 100$$

eg if present output is 40 000 units a year and the firm could produce 50 000 units with its resources its capacity utilisation is

$$\frac{40\,000}{50\,000} \times 100 = 80\%$$

Productive efficiency will therefore involve a number of factors such as employees' productivity, the nature of the production process, the scale of production and the capacity utilisation. It may also depend in the long term on the extent to which a firm undertakes research and development.

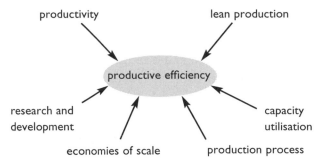

Figure 5.7

Research and development (R&D)

Research and development (R&D) is the generation and application of scientific knowledge to create a product or develop a new production process which can increase the firm's productive efficiency. If successful it leads to new ideas for products and new methods of production. For example, it may involve a team of employees at a confectionery company researching into a new flavour or a new variety of sweet and then trying out different versions until they have one they (and the customers) are happy with. Or it may involve another team focusing on new ways of producing the confectionery.

For R&D to be of any real value the various ideas and prototypes it generates must then be turned into a commercial reality. The process of turning an idea into a saleable product or service is known as innovation. Innovation is defined as 'the successful exploitation of new ideas'.

In some cases the process of R&D and innovation can take years (the development of Lusec, a drug designed to alleviate stomach ulcers took 20 years); in other cases it may be a matter of weeks or months – in the software industry, for example, new products are being developed very rapidly indeed.

The aim of research and development is to

■ develop products which have a unique selling point, allowing a business to differentiate itself from the competition and earn higher profit margins

■ develop better-quality products which meet customer needs more successfully

■ develop more efficient ways of producing to reduce the cost per unit.

Successful innovation allows firms to keep ahead of their competitors and to keep finding better ways of doing things. This is often the key to long-term success in a market. However, despite the importance of R&D many UK firms are criticised for failing to invest sufficiently in this area. This may be because investors in the UK often want short-term rewards and are not prepared to wait for the benefits which R&D might bring in the longer term. Also, spending on research and development can be a risky investment because so few ideas actually succeed in the marketplace; as a result managers may be wary of investing heavily in this area.

EXAMINER'S ADVICE

Students often confuse market research and research and development. Market research involves gaining an understanding of customer needs and the nature of the market. Research and development involves developing new products and new processes. Obviously the two are often linked: the research and development a firm undertakes will often be prompted by the findings of market research – having identified a niche in the market, for example, a firm might undertake research and development to produce exactly the right product to fulfil these needs.

Key terms

Research and development (R&D): this involves activities concerned with identifying new products and services and new ways of producing.
Innovation: this involves activities concerned with the successful exploitation of new ideas ie turning ideas into commercial successes.
Market research: this involves the gathering, analysing and presenting of information relevant to the marketing process.

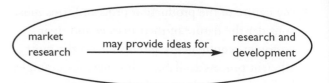

Figure 5.8

ⱣOINTS TO PONDER

In many cases a firm's research and development activities will be determined by the findings from market research. The company will identify what the market requires and as a result the firm will begin an R&D programme. However, on occasions a firm will develop something and then have to decide what to do with it! Famous examples of this include Post-it Stickers and Kevlar.

3M developed a particular type of glue which enabled you to stick something to something else, peel it off and use it again; the only problem was that it did not know what to do with this discovery. It was only when an employee started using the glue-on stickers to mark pages in his hymn book that the company started to realise its potential and eventually this led to Post-it stickers.

Dupont meanwhile developed one of the strongest man-made materials ever when it produced Kevlar. Originally Kevlar was developed for use in tyres but when tyre manufacturers chose steel radial instead the company had to look for new uses; these uses have included bullet proof vests for the army, producing a kind of rope to tie down oil rigs and use in sports equipment. As markets changed the company has had to find new uses for the product it developed.

ⱣOINTS TO PONDER

According to Lord Sainsbury, who was science minister for the UK, 'Business's ability to innovate is vital to its global competitiveness. It is only by continually developing new products, processes and services that business can gain the competitive edge necessary for the increasingly global economy. R&D is a key component of this, helping to generate the advances that lead to new value-added products and enabling people and capital to be more effective.'

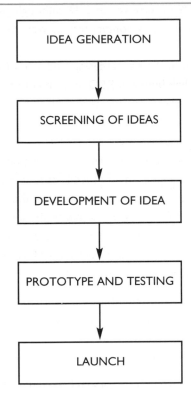

Figure 5.9 *The process of research and development through to product launch*

Sources of ideas

Firms may generate the ideas for research and development internally or externally. Internally ideas may simply come through discussion, employees' suggestion schemes or brainstorming activities. On the other hand ideas may be generated by a firm's own research department. Externally many new ideas are registered at the Patent Office; firms may pay a fee to the owner of a patent for the right to use their technology. Alternatively a firm might buy a franchise to produce under another firm's name; in return for a franchise a firm pays a fee and/or a percentage of its turnover. A firm's customers can also be a valuable external source of new ideas. You will notice that many companies have a customer phone line or a comments book to gain feedback from their consumers on their service and to discover more about what customers really want.

Business in Focus: Richer Sounds – generating ideas

Richer Sounds is a hi-fi retailer which was set up by Julian Richer in 1978 and which has now become one of the most successful retailing operations in the UK. It has been in the Guinness Book of records six years running for having the highest sales per square foot in the world. Colleagues (as all employees are called) are encouraged to contribute to the suggestions scheme. Every new idea that is submitted is personally read and acknowledged by Julian Richer and colleagues receive a small reward between £5 and £25 for each suggestion they submit. When the business started Julian calculates that he came up with about 90% of all the ideas within the firm and the colleagues came up with the remaining 10%. Nowadays thanks to the suggestion scheme this ratio has been reversed; colleagues submit about 20 ideas per year on average which is well above the usual rate of suggestions in other schemes.

According to Richer the key elements of an effective suggestion scheme are:

1 The most senior person in the organisation must be involved with the scheme.
2 Make it easy for people to enter their suggestions – on joining Richer Sounds colleagues are given a 'What can we do?' book that they can fill in.
3 Answer all suggestions.
4 Answer all suggestions quickly.
5 Encourage people to meet in small groups – every branch or department at Richer Sounds is meant to meet at least once a month after work; the company doesn't pay for their time but pays £5 a head for liquid refreshment.
6 Reward little and often.
7 Measure and the publish the results.
8 Use the ideas.

Research and development and quality

The quality of a product depends on its ability to meet customer requirements time and time again. Can a firm consistently deliver what customers want? This will depend on

- how well those needs have been defined to begin with (market research)
- how well the firm has designed the process for ease of manufacture
- how well designed the product or service is.

Research and development can therefore be extremely important in terms of ensuring a firm provides quality goods or services. It can help develop a product which meets customer need more precisely than the competition and it can help firms develop a system which is cost-effective and helps the organisation maintain quality easily.

Research and development and culture

Unfortunately simply investing in R&D does not guarantee that it will be successful; the process has to be managed carefully and almost inevitably firms must be prepared for some failures.

The success of R&D is often linked to the culture of the business. Firms which encourage employees to use their initiative and which are prepared to accept failure along with success are more likely to generate new ideas. Organisations which only reward employees for sticking to the rules and doing what they are told are less likely to have employees come to them with ideas.

Business in Focus: R&D Scoreboard

In the 1990s the Department of Trade and Industry in the UK set up the R&D Scoreboard to highlight the underspending by many UK companies on research and development and shame the directors into increasing their budgets to become more in line with their international

competitors. Since then UK firms have made progress – on average spending has increased from 1.7% of turnover to 3.4% although given more spending by competitors as well, the gap still remains.

Research shows increasing evidence of a positive link between R&D investment and future corporate performance as measured by sales growth and stock market value. This link is difficult to prove because there are so many variables and even if a link does exist there is a long time lag. However, if investment in R&D does increase the share price, as seems to be the case, the implication for investors is that in the long run shares in companies with big research and development budgets should outperform those with smaller budgets in this area.

1. Why do you think the average spending on R&D by UK firms has increased since the 1990s?

Protecting successful innovation

If a firm manages to develop new products and new processes successfully it will naturally want to protect these from being copied or imitated by competitors. If an innovation is genuinely new a firm may protect it by taking out a patent. Under the 1988 Copyright, Designs and Patents act the holder of a patent has the right to be the sole user of a process or manufacturer of a product for 20 years after it is registered.

The owner of a patent may sell the right to produce the product or use a process to others. This can be a valuable source of income to some organisations. If one firm suspects another of illegally producing a patented product or using its patented technology it can sue the offender. However, this can be costly and time consuming.

To protect a product or process worldwide a firm must register the patent in different countries; this can also be an expensive and slow process.

By comparison the work of artists, writers and musicians is automatically protected by copyright; copyrights do not have to be registered although once again it is up to the copyright holder to sue offenders.

company	R&D spend £000	as a % of sales
UK:		
AstraZeneca	1 813 613	15.8
Glaxo Wellcome	1 269 000	14.9
SmithKlineBeecham	1 018 000	12.1
British Aerospace	693 000	9.8
International:		
Ford Motor	7 100 000	4.4
General Motors	6 800 000	4.1
Daimler Chrysler	5 575 201	3.8
Siemens	5 049 119	7.3
IBM	5 039 000	5.8

Table 5.1 *Top five UK and international companies by R&D expenditure*

The Financial Times

Business in Focus: product failure – innovation

Unfortunately simply having an award winning design is no guarantee of success as shown by the problems of PCD Maltron. PCD Maltron has won many awards for its ergonomic keyboards since the company was established in 1977. But the commercial potential for the products which could have global applications still remains unfulfilled.

After over 20 years in the business Stephen Hobday has yet to progress much beyond the garden shed. Despite winning numerous awards the company's achievements in financial terms are somewhat poor.

Maltron keyboards are designed to prevent keyboard users suffering from Repetitive Strain Injury (RSI). Pain, weakness, numbness and many other RSI symptoms result from prolonged repetitive keyboard use. Estimates suggest 14m people have visited a doctor for RSI and another 40m have experienced the symptoms. The Maltron keyboard differs from conventional keyboards in that the keys are laid out to fit the shape of the user's hands rather than arranged in straight lines.

Although the idea may sound promising Hobday has failed to convince investors that the idea is worthy and has had to spend £40,000 of his own money establishing a new business from his house.

Maltron also designs keyboards for people who can only use one finger or a stick held in their mouths or for left handed people. The present 'qwerty' key layout was designed by Christopher Latham Sholes in 1867 to prevent the arms of a typewriter from jamming. 'People have got used to it but our own layout is much more efficient.' Past failures to patent ideas have also damaged the firm's prospects. American producers are already producing designs similar to Maltron's but at a lower price. About £20,000 a year is spent on advertising but the firm has no clear marketing strategy.

According to the DTI 'In many cases the people who come up with a brilliant idea are not the ones who take it on to commercial success. The process needs to be split and individuals need to understand where their function stops.'

The DTI also highlights the importance of corporate culture. 'People can be a fantastic driving force or a massive block. So many companies – both hierarchical and autocratic – have an ambience of ridiculing ideas or, if the ideas are progressive of dumping on them from a great height.' More successful companies 'tend to have very flat structures and an open style. People are empowered within defined areas and are allowed to take risks within reason. If the idea fails then it is perceived to be a learning process not a reason to cut off an employee's legs.' Teamwork is also a common thread running through companies that are turning products into a commercial success. 'Teams tend to be formed of their own accord – not by management – and dissolve when the project has run its course. Fluid teaming is endemic in more innovative products.'

The Sunday Times

1. According to the DTI 'In many cases the people who come up with a brilliant idea are not the ones who take it on to commercial success.' Why do you think this is?

Research and development and the product life cycle

Research and development occurs before a product is actually launched. At this stage a firm will be spending money on a project without earning any returns from it. This can cause cash flow problems; at the same time limited working capital may restrict the amount of investment a firm can actually undertake.

Once a product is launched a firm should already be considering the next stage in research and development; this may involve improving or modifying the product or developing a new product to generate sales when the original product enters the decline phase.

Of course firms usually have a range of different products rather than just one. Managers must

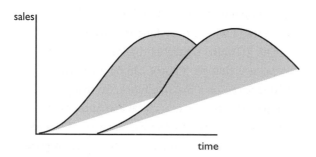

Figure 5.10 *Research and development can lead to new products being developed and launched*

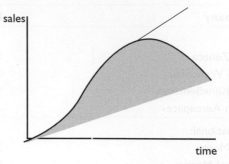

Figure 5.11 *Research and development can lead to extended sales through product modification*

therefore take an overview and plan for the portfolio of products as a whole; this can be helped via product portfolio analysis such as the Boston matrix. To ensure a balanced portfolio managers will often use the funds generated by the cash cows to invest into research and development to develop question marks and build them into stars.

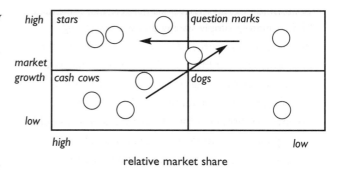

Figure 5.12

Research and development and product and process design

UK firms are often criticised for not paying enough attention to design issues when undertaking research and development. There is a tendency to rush the development of a product in order to get it launched. Unfortunately in the haste to get the product on sale not enough attention is paid to how it will be produced or exactly what it will do. This means it is often more expensive to produce an item than it could have been and that many products do not meet customer needs; this could help explain the high rate of failure of new products.

Good research and development will take into account a range of factors such as

- customer needs
- how the product or service is likely to be used
- competitors' offerings
- cost constraints (and quality and profit targets)
- ease of manufacture.

A well-designed product will not only meet customer requirements it will also be efficient and relatively easy to produce. By taking into account the production process (eg what components will be required, what machines are required, what skills are needed) a firm can make considerable cost and time savings and make the process much leaner.

How much should a firm spend on research and development?

Innovation can be an important means of gaining a competitive advantage. Washing powder tablets, pyramid tea bags, combined shampoo conditioners are all examples of how firms have gained market share through innovative products. To compete and remain ahead of the market a firm may decide to invest relatively heavily in research and development. However, this does involve risk: simply putting more money into this area does not in itself ensure success and may be wasted funds which could have been used elsewhere. There is therefore an opportunity cost which should be taken into account. To avoid the risk of investing in R&D a firm may pursue a 'me too strategy' whereby it imitates other firms rather than tries to break into new areas itself.

The amount a firm spends on research and development will therefore depend on its strategy. It will also depend on the nature of its market. In fast-changing markets such as consumer electronics the need to bring out new products is very strong – if you don't the chances are that your competitors will. Perhaps not surprisingly one of the biggest sectors for research and development spending is the pharmaceutical industry; to succeed in this market firms are continually striving to develop medicines which they can patent and which will bring them a

stream of future income. The firm which develops a cure for the common cold, for AIDS or for Alzheimer's will make a fortune. There may be less pressure to invest in a more protected market – where the need to innovate is less intense – or where the rate of change is slower.

*P*OINTS TO PONDER

In the 1980s the average amount spent on research and development by firms was 1.7%; it is now over 3.4%. This may be due to greater awareness of the importance of research and development to maintain competitiveness.

How can a firm ensure research and development leads to innovation?

The simple answer is it cannot. All a firm can do is try to create the conditions where innovation is more likely and try to manage the process as effectively as possible. This involves creating a climate where people want to try out new things and are not afraid of getting it wrong. It means creating a budgeting system which lets people have the resources to try out ideas and a remuneration system which rewards innovative behaviour rather than penalises it.

Innovation also requires the commitment of senior management throughout. It requires a willingness to question and explore and the necessary resources for employees to follow through ideas. It will also involve a good market awareness so that ideas are not simply developed for their own sake but are related to market requirements.

Business in Focus: innovation

The old ideas are often the best argues James Dyson the British designer best known for the invention of the bagless vacuum cleaner. Dyson has now announced a design for a new product which he believes will take the world of washing machines by storm. The new design threatens the big operators in the $20bn a year washing machine industry. Dyson Appliances, of which James Dyson is founder and owner, is to sell a front loading washing machine that replaces the conventional single drum design with two concentric drums rotating in opposite directions. Mr Dyson believes the design will replicate inside the drum the 'kneading' action of hand-washing in which clothes rub against each other. In the late 1800s some of the earliest manual washing machines used similar ideas. Using a concept patented in 1846 in the US early washing machines imitated the motion of the human hand on a washboard by using a lever to move one curved surface over another and rub clothes between two ribbed surfaces. The first electric powered automatic washing machines appeared in the early 20th century using propellor-like 'agitators to swirl water and clothing around a "top loading" washtub'.

The new Dyson is, by contrast, a front loader. It uses a tumbling action to bring the water into contact with the clothes. But the difference is that in the Dyson system an outer drum slides over a second cylinder that is slightly smaller in diameter and is roughly half as deep. When clothes are put inside, the 'contrarotating' action continually forces the articles against each other. The concept evolved from a £25m four year project by Mr Dyson's 350 strong research team.

Mr Dyson hopes the appliance, which he says cleans a given weight of clothes about twice as fast as comparable machines, will replicate the company's success with bagless cleaners. However the established firms are unlikely to be passive. Most of them have large research teams and have been investigating concepts such as 'waterless' machines using ultrasound or liquid carbon dioxide to clean clothes. Both ideas have been heavily tested but so far have been found to be less effective than water.

The Contrarotator will sell for about £700 and £1200 depending on the model. Whilst this is roughly twice the price of many UK machines and three times the price of those in the US Mr Dyson is calculating many consumers will be undeterred.

Cleaning up
Key dates in the history of washing machines:
1851 James King in the US patents first machine to use a drum
1908 Hurley Machine of Chicago brings out first electric washing machine
1922 Maytag of the US invents the agitator – a system that uses a propeller action to swirl clothing about in a tub full of water
1930s Front loading machine invented
1937 Bendix in the US introduces a wash/spin to remove water

The Financial Times

1 What do you think will determine the success of the new Dyson washing machine?

P OINTS TO PONDER

Can there be too much innovation? A study by CLK, a product development house, suggests that consumers are 'extremely irritated' by the wide range of products that can make buying a toothbrush or a shampoo into a real ordeal. Far from relishing the choice of say 50 competing chocolate bars or 100 slightly different computers consumers are bewildered and irritated by the time it now takes to make a shopping choice. Forty per cent of consumers said that British Telecom's package of offers and discount schemes was confusing while 50% said the same about the rapidly expanding choice of mobile phones on the market.

Why might firms fail to invest in research and development?

One reason why firms may fail to invest sufficiently in research and development may be that they cannot raise the necessary funds. R&D involves investment now in the hope of future returns. Firms which lack enough internal funds may struggle to borrow the money from banks. This may be because the banks are concerned that the research and development will not be successful and are not willing to take the risk. Alternatively the bank may be willing to lend but the rates of interest charged may be perceived as too high. Even if a firm does have the necessary finance itself some of the managers may be reluctant to use it in this area, preferring to use it elsewhere within the firm. For example, training or marketing may be seen as more of a priority than investing in research and development.

Another reason for the lack of research in the UK may be the pressure from investors for short-term rewards which may prevent managers from putting money into long-term projects. Investors may not be willing to wait for their rewards.

Firms may also be reluctant to invest because of the relatively low success rate; even if firms manage to get a product to the launch stage, for example, it still has a very low chance of success. Firms are naturally reluctant to put money into projects which have a high failure rate and may prefer to modify existing products instead.

People in business

Michael Dell and Dell

Michael Dell is in his thirties. He is the founder and chief executive of the world's biggest PC company which in 1999 had revenues of $23.5bn (£15.8bn) an increase of $7bn on the year before. He leads a private life and is the world's fourth richest businessman (his 14.3% of Dell is worth at least $21bn). 'We are the fastest growing and most profitable company in this sector' says Mr Dell. 'We're surviving pretty well with about 38% growth.'

The secret of success is no secret – do not let profit sucking middlemen take control. If you want to buy a Dell computer you ring them or go to the web site and order it. If you want 100 or 1000 Dell computers it's the same story.

Dell started young – as a 12-year-old he collected stamps at his home in Round Rock Texas. He then earned $2000 organising a stamp auction. Two years later he earned $18 000 selling newspapers. In 1982 aged 15 he took apart a computer for the first time. That was the year IBM launched its first PC. Three years later he drove to Austin University with three computers in the back of his car and soon had a sideline selling up to $80 000 of upgraded computers each year. Now he owns 14.3% of a company worth $148.5bn. He does not own a corporate jet, prefers not to be chauffeur driven, doesn't have any obvious trappings of wealth.

Dell has invested heavily in his back office and factory systems to streamline them and eliminate the human intervention that he discovered leads to faults! He focused on a process which limits the number of 'touches' that systems go through. 'We found every time there's a touch process (involving a human) there's an opportunity to insert a fault. So we reduced that. That's reduced the manufacturing time and improved quality and gives us better feedback about what the real problems might be.' On hard disks Dell was able to reduce the number of touches from more than 20 to 7. The Dell computer now has 10 to 12 touches in its manufacture. For the future Dell intends to expand into technical support and offer 'internet infrastructure support' to help people keep their web sites running smoothly.

The Independent

1 Has Michael Dell just been lucky?

Progress questions

1 Explain what is meant by the term 'research and development'. *(3 marks)*

2 What is meant by 'innovation'? Distinguish between research and development and innovation. *(4 marks)*

3 The managing director of Saski Ltd, a manufacturer of soft drink vending machines is considering how much money to invest in research and development in the coming year. Explain two factors which might determine how much a firm such as Saski invests in research and development. *(6 marks)*

4 Explain two possible benefits to a firm of greater levels of innovation. *(6 marks)*

5 Research and development begins with an idea. Identify two possible sources of ideas for research and development. *(2 marks)*

6 Explain two possible reasons why a firm's research and development may prove unsuccessful. *(6 marks)*

7 UK firms are often criticised for a lack of investment in research and development. Explain two possible reasons for this lack of investment. *(6 marks)*

8 Explain how firms may protect their findings from research and development from their competitors. *(3 marks)*

9 Explain two ways in which research and development within a firm might be linked to its marketing activities. *(6 marks)*

10 Distinguish between market research and research and development. *(3 marks)*

Analysis and evaluation questions

1 Examine the ways in which investment in research and development can improve a firm's competitiveness. *(8 marks)*

2 Examine the possible reasons why a firm might fail to exploit its investment in research and development. *(8 marks)*

3 How important is it for a firm to invest in research and development? *(12 marks)*

4 Which is more important to a firm: its marketing activities or its research and development activities? Justify your answer. *(12 marks)*

5 Why do so many new products fail? *(12 marks)*

Case study

Fujama plc, a specialist producer of cameras, recently announced a disappointing set of financial results in which its profits only rose by 2% instead of the 12% which had been promised at last year's annual general meeting. 'We have not done badly' said Mr Kitten, director of Fujama's UK division 'but the investors always want more – they are never happy. It is true our sales have declined this year due to factors beyond our control but due to effective cost control we have managed to boost our profits.' Part of the reason why the original target was not hit was due to the launch of a new model by one of its major competitors which took sales away from Fujama's best-selling product. 'The market is changing incredibly rapidly' said Mr Kitten. 'New products are coming out every few weeks; admittedly most of them fail but you've got to keep an eye on the market.'

Fujama had also experienced production problems at its main production plant. Problems with staff had led to a two-week stoppage earlier in the year and even now productivity levels remain relatively low.

At present the firm invests about 5% of its turnover in research and development.

1 Examine the possible benefits for a firm such as Fujama of undertaking research and development. *(8 marks)*

2 Should Fujama invest more money in research and development next year? *(12 marks)*

CRITICAL PATH OR NETWORK ANALYSIS

Starting points

In the last unit we studied how research and development can affect a firm's efficiency and competitiveness. In this unit we study a planning technique called critical path analysis. This is a new topic and you will not have studied it at AS; however, it does build on your AS work in that using critical path analysis is another way in which a firm may increase its productive efficiency.

In this unit you will study

■ what critical path analysis is
■ how to construct a network diagram
■ how to identify the critical path
■ the limitations of this technique.

Introduction

To achieve productive efficiency managers will want to plan projects as effectively as possible to ensure that time and resources are not wasted. They do not want to have people and machines sitting idle unnecessarily or materials delivered well before they are required. To help them in the planning process managers may use **network analysis**.

Network analysis is a method of organising the different activities involved in a particular process in order to find the most efficient means of completing the task. The aim is to complete the project in as short a time as possible. To do this a firm will determine the exact order in which activities have to be undertaken and identify which ones can be undertaken simultaneously to save time. Network analysis can be used in any type of project which involves several activities – anything from opening a new store to planning a new advertising campaign to organising the relocation of the firm. The technique was developed for DuPont in 1957 to speed up the building of a new plant.

To undertake network analysis managers must

■ identify all the different tasks involved in the process
■ estimate the expected length of time each task will take
■ determine the order in which tasks must be completed, eg in some cases particular tasks cannot be completed until another one has taken

place first (these are known as 'dependent' activities. In other cases activities can be undertaken simultaneously; these are known as 'parallel' activities because they can be undertaken at the same time as each other ('in parallel').

The next step is to construct a network chart. This is a diagrammatic representation of all the activities involved in the project, the order in which they must be undertaken and the times each one will take.

Key terms

A '**node**' is a circle representing the start and end of an activity.

When drawing a network diagram the following features are used.

■ A circle (called a 'node') represents the start and end of an activity.
■ A straight line represents the activity itself.

A line showing an activity is labelled in the following way: above the line the name of the activity is given; below the line the length of time the activity is expected to take is shown – this is known as the expected duration of the activity. In figure 5.13 activity B is expected to last ten days; activity A is expected to last four days; activity B can only be started when activity A is completed (that is why it only begins once A is complete).

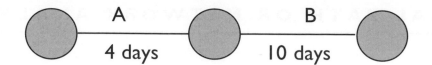

Figure 5.13

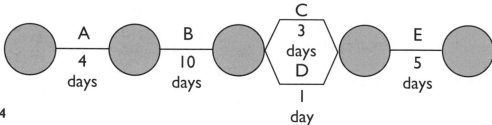

Figure 5.14

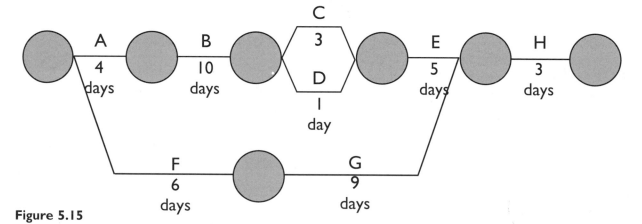

Figure 5.15

In figure 5.14 activities C and D can only be started after activity B has been completed. Activity E can only start when C and D are finished.

In figure 5.15 we have added in some more activities. You can see that

- activity F can start once A is completed
- G can start once F is completed
- H can start once E and G are completed.

All this information can be shown in a table (see table 5.2).
We now have a whole network diagram.

Remember the following rules when constructing a chart.

- The lines showing different activities must never cross.
- The lines showing activities should always begin and end at the mid-point of the nodes.
- The diagram must begin and end with one node.
- When drawing the activities and nodes do not put the end node on any activity until you are sure what comes next and whether anything else must also be completed before the following activity takes place.

EXAMINER'S ADVICE

If you are asked to construct a critical path analysis diagram (also called a network analysis) make sure you follow the rules. Many diagrams, like figure 5.16 contain fundamental errors. Look at the diagram to see some of the many mistakes which can be made.

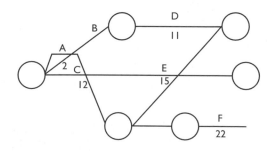

Figure 5.16

As you can see:
- *the lines denoting activities A, B and C cross*
- *there is no final node*
- *some activities are not labelled at all.*

Activity	preceded by	duration (days)
A		4
B	A	10
C	B	3
D	B	1
E	C and D	5
F	A	6
G	F	9
H	E and G	3

Table 5.2

Adding earliest start times and latest finish times

The next stage in producing a network chart is to show various information which can be calculated from the duration of each activity. This information is shown inside the node and to do this we now draw nodes in the following way:

The left-hand side shows the number of the node; this is used simply for reference and is done by numbering the nodes left to right.

The right-hand side of the node is used to show two other pieces of information known as the 'earliest start time' (EST) of the next activity and the 'latest finish time' (LFT) of the activity before.

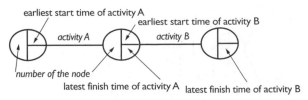

Figure 5.17

Earliest start times

The earliest start time (EST) is exactly what it says: it is the earliest time a particular activity can begin. This piece of information is shown in the top right of the node at the beginning of an activity.

As you can see in figure 5.18 the earliest times have now been added. To calculate these figures you take the earliest start time of the activity before and add on the duration of that activity.

The earliest time A can start is day 0 (this is the first activity in the project); this activity takes four days so the earliest time that B can start is day four. B takes ten days so the earliest C and D can start is $4 + 10 = 14$ days.

E can only start when C and D are *both* finished. C takes longer than D so the project must wait for this activity to be completed before moving on; the earliest that E can start is therefore $14 + 3 = 17$.

If you have a choice of numbers to add on to calculate the earliest start time choose the bigger number; the projects cannot continue until all previous dependent activities are finished so you must wait for the longest one to be completed. Before H can start, for example, it must wait for both E and G to be completed which means it cannot start until day 22.

By identifying the earliest start times a firm can see when materials are likely to be needed. This means that components and supplies can be ordered to arrive just in time to be used rather than arriving too early and be sitting around taking up space and costing money or arriving late delaying the whole project. Materials and resources for activity E, for example, do not need to be ready until day 17.

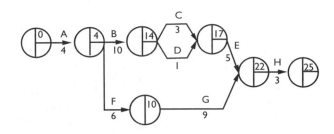

Figure 5.18

Calculating the earliest start time is therefore an important part of developing a lean approach to a project and ensuring people and materials are coordinated and ready at exactly the right moment.

Latest finish time

The bottom-right space of a node is used to show the latest finish time (LST) of an activity. Again this shows exactly what it says – the latest an activity can be finished without holding up the whole project.

Activity H must finish on day 25 – the day the whole project can be completed; since H takes three days it means the activities before must be finished by $25 - 3 =$ day 22 if the project is to be completed on time. Activity E must therefore be completed at the latest by day 22. Since E takes five days this means the activities before (C and D) must be finished by day 17. Given that C takes three days (which is the longer activity out of C and D) if this stage is to be completed by day 17 the stage before must be finished by day 14.

To work out the latest finish times, therefore you work right to left deducting the duration of a particular activity from its latest finish time to get the latest finish time of the one before. If there are two or more activities involved (such as C and D) choose the longer duration.

Rules

■ to calculate the earliest start time of an activity work *left to right* and add on the duration of the next activity to the previous earliest start time; if there is a choice choose the biggest number to add on.

■ to calculate the latest finish time of an activity work *right to left* and deduct its duration from the previous latest finish time; if there is a choice of numbers choose the largest number to deduct.

Total float time

Using the earliest start times and the latest finish times it is possible to calculate the total float time of an activity. The total float time shows how long an activity can overrun without holding up the whole project.

To calculate total float use the equation

Total float time = latest finish time − duration − earliest start time

For example if activity D has to be finished by day 17, can start on day 14 and lasts one day then the total float is $17 - 1 - 14 = 2$ days. This activity has two days' slack – it could overrun by two days and the project would still finish on time. By comparison if activity B has to be finished by day 14, can start on day four and lasts ten days, its float is $14 - 10 - 4 = 0$. There is no float – it must be completed on time or the whole project will be delayed. B is therefore known as a 'critical' activity because it has no total float. By identifying all of the critical activities the firm can see which activities must be finished on time; this is known as the critical path.

The critical path for the project in table 5.3 is ABCEH because these activities have no total float time. If they are delayed at all the whole project will be late and will not be finished in 25 days.

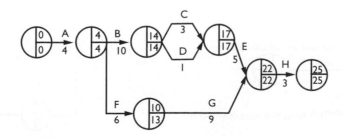

Figure 5.19

Activity	LFT	duration	EST	total float
A	4	4	0	0
B	14	10	4	0
C	17	3	14	0
D	17	1	14	2
E	22	5	17	0
F	13	6	4	3
G	22	9	10	3
H	25	3	22	0

Table 5.3

> ### Key terms
>
> **Total float**: *this shows the amount of time an activity can overrun without delaying the completion of the project as a whole. Critical activities have no total float time.*
>
> **Critical path**: *this identifies the activities which have no total float time; if these overrun at all the project as a whole will be delayed.*

By identifying the activities on the critical path managers can see exactly which activities are the priority in terms of making sure they stay on time; the critical path also shows the shortest time in which a project can be completed.

Benefits of critical path analysis

By undertaking a critical path analysis managers

- must consider exactly what activities are involved in a project. This is a useful exercise in itself because it helps to make sure that nothing is forgotten. It also means that managers are likely to consult all the different departments and functions involved and this can help to improve everyone's understanding of the issues and challenges involved in getting the project completed
- can calculate the earliest time when the project should be completed. This can be important information for customers (eg the firm can

announce a release date) and is important to help plan the launch arrangements. It can also help the managers decide whether a deadline can be hit or not

- can identify the 'critical' activities which must be completed in time to get the whole project finished as quickly as possible. This means that they can focus on these specific activities and make sure they do not overrun. At the same time the amount of float time on non-critical activities can be calculated. Whilst managers cannot ignore these activities entirely it may not matter so much if they overrun (provided they do not use up all their float time); it may even be possible to transfer labour and other resources from non-critical activities to critical ones to ensure the latter are completed promptly
- may be able to produce items or develop products more quickly than the competition providing it with a possible competitive advantage. By seeking to reduce the time taken for a project, network analysis is an important element of time-based management
- implement just-in-time ordering. Network analysis shows the earliest start times for each activity. Using this the firm can order materials and supplies to arrive exactly when they are needed and not before. This saves storage costs and also the opportunity cost of having money tied up in stocks. This can improve the firm's liquidity and free up cash which can be used elsewhere in the organisation.
- can use network analysis as a control mechanism to review progress and assess whether the project is on target. If there have been delays the effects of the earliest start times and latest finish times can be re-worked to see the effect on the completion of the project.

> ### Key terms
>
> **Working capital**: *this represents the day-to-day finances in the business. It is measured by current assets minus current liabilities.*
>
> **Time-based management**: *this represents techniques used to speed up the time taken to develop new products or processes such as simultaneous engineering.*

Problems of critical path analysis

Although critical path analysis can help business decision making it can have a number of drawbacks and limitations.

For example

- it relies on the estimates for the expected duration. If these prove to be inaccurate the calculations for earliest start times and latest finish times, and so the critical path analysis, may be wrongly identified. The estimates may be incorrect because some managers may exaggerate how long an activity takes to make it easier for them to complete within the agreed time. On the other hand some managers may be too optimistic, particularly if these activities have not been carried out before. A more complex version of critical path analysis called programme evaluation and review technique (PERT) includes a range of estimates for the durations of different activities; PERT produces a number of network diagrams based on optimistic, pessimistic and most likely durations of activities to take account of the fact that estimates cannot be completely relied on
- if JIT is used for the delivery of materials the ability to complete the project on time will depend on the reliability of suppliers. If they are late this will prevent the next activity starting on time. In 2000, for example, a petrol shortage led to many delays with deliveries and this would have delayed projects and prevented them finishing on time
- critical path analysis simply shows the quickest way to complete a project; it does not guarantee that this is the right project to be undertaking in the first place. It may be that the firm's resources could be used more effectively elsewhere
- all projects must be managed properly if they are to be completed on time. Drawing up a network diagram is only the starting point. Managers must agree on who is responsible for each stage of the project. They must be given the resources and budget to complete in the time agreed. There must be an effective review system to make sure the project is on schedule and to agree what action to take if it is not. A network diagram can

provide a valuable focal point for the management system but it is up to the managers to make sure that everything is implemented correctly and that each activity is completed on schedule.

EXAMINER'S ADVICE

When studying critical path analysis make sure you know

- *how to construct a network diagram*
- *what the critical path represents*
- *how critical path analysis can help a firm*
- *the limitations of critical path analysis.*

Other issues in critical path analysis

Before the project is started managers must agree on a definition of success. They must set out exactly what they want to achieve otherwise subordinates may cut corners to get the project done on time. The result may be that the project is completed quickly but that the quality is poor.

Managers must also agree on what resources and spending they are willing to commit to the project. Obviously the quickest way of completing a project will depend on what facilities and resources are available and how much the firm is willing to invest into getting it completed. With more people, more money and more machines the project could probably be speeded up. Whether particular activities can be conducted simultaneously will often depend on whether the firm has or is willing to invest in the necessary resources.

Managers will also be interested in the utilisation of resources throughout the project. It may be that certain activities could be undertaken simultaneously but that as a result some weeks would require very high levels of personnel whereas in other weeks very few people would be needed. If it adopted such an approach a firm may have to bring in extra staff for the busy week and pay its existing staff to do little in the other weeks. Rather than have such fluctuations in its staffing levels managers may want to shift activities around; this may mean that the project takes a bit longer but it may nevertheless be more desirable if it means that its full-time staff are fully employed each week.

Progress questions

1 What is meant by critical path analysis? *(2 marks)*
2 Distinguish between activities which are 'dependent' and activities which can be carried out in parallel. *(3 marks)*
3 What is a node? *(2 marks)*
4 What is meant by the earliest starting time? *(2 marks)*
5 What is meant by total float? *(2 marks)*
6 How can the critical path by identified? *(2 marks)*
7 Explain two possible ways in which critical path analysis might benefit an organisation. *(6 marks)*
8 Explain two possible problems in using critical path analysis. *(6 marks)*
9 In what ways can critical path analysis be linked to
   lean production
   time management
   working capital control? *(4 marks each)*
10 a) Using the information in the table construct a fully labelled network chart (including the earliest start time and latest finish times). *(8 marks)*
   b) Identify the critical path. *(1 mark)*

Activity	preceded by	duration (days)
A	–	5
B	A	10
C	–	4
D	A	15
E	B and D	7
F	C	14
G	E	20
H	F and G	2
I	B and D	5
J	H and I	18

Analysis and evaluation questions

1 Analyse the possible limitations of critical path analysis. *(8 marks)*
2 Examine the possible benefits to a firm of using critical path analysis. *(8 marks)*
3 How useful is critical path analysis to a firm when planning its operations? *(12 marks)*
4 To what extent can critical path analysis improve a firm's competitiveness? *(12 marks)*
5 Analyse the factors which might be involved in ensuring a project is managed successfully. *(8 marks)*

Case study

Sue Holland has a major project to complete in the next 40 days. She has been asked to have a new company website up and running ready to take orders on-line. This involves numerous tasks including agreeing the content of the site, getting the text written, getting an agency to work on the design, getting the domain name registered, alerting the search engines and so on.

She has listed all the various stages in the following table and estimated how long they should take (although she has never done this type of project before).

Activity	preceded by	expected duration (days)
A	–	10
B	A	5
C	–	4
D	B	8
E	B	2
F	C	19
G	D	11
H	E	8
I	G, H	5
J	I	16

1 a) Construct a network diagram for Sue. Make sure you fully label it including the earliest start time and latest finish time. *(8 marks)*

b) On the basis of your calculations how long should this project take to complete? *(1 mark)*

c) Calculate the total float on activity F. *(2 marks)*

2 Discuss the possible benefits to Sue of using critical path analysis. *(12 marks)*

INFORMATION TECHNOLOGY

Starting points

In the AS course you will have studied a part of operations management called 'controlling operations'. This involved topics such as stock control and quality control. As the name suggests this part of the specification involved topics which considered ways in which a firm could monitor its production and improve its efficiency. In this unit we study information technology (IT) and consider how IT can help a firm to control and improve its processes. You will probably be familiar with many of the different areas of IT such as the internet but you will not have studied the role of IT in operations management in AS.

In this unit we cover issues such as

- the importance of managing information
- the role of IT within marketing, operations, finance and human resource management.

Importance of information

The ability to manage information plays a crucial part in business success. Successful organisations understand their customers and their own activities. They keep up to date with market changes, anticipate future developments and keep stakeholder groups well informed. By comparison, unsuccessful organisations are slow to find out what is happening, do not communicate effectively and make poor decisions based on poor information.

Information technology plays a vital role in the management of information and the way in which it is used can provide a firm with a competitive advantage. Information technology (IT) involves the use of electronic means to help managers to gather, transmit and interpret information internally and externally. Examples of the use of information technology include word processors, spreadsheets, databases, bar code scanners, e-mails and the internet. Just think of when you have to undertake research for an assignment or a project: the person who can use the internet effectively, can find what he or she wants quickly and can usually find better sources of information than someone relying on their own research without the use if IT. Similarly managers who have good access to information will benefit from being better informed and making better decisions than their rivals. Not surprisingly then many firms are increasingly devoting resources to the management of information. There are, of course, numerous ways in which IT can be used.

- IT can be used to monitor customer buying. Firms can trace what particular customers buy (eg through their storecards) and which product lines are selling well. The use of information on customers can build up an ongoing understanding of what and when individuals buy. In some cases firms can build up such an effective profile of customers that they can tailor-make a service for each one – there are now book sites on the internet which will recommend books you are likely to want to read: you can also tailor-make your own electronic newspaper to reflect your interests. The process of building and updating a profile of each customer is called customer relationship management.
- IT can also be used to improve communications within a firm. This enables better decision making as managers can get the information they want when they want it. Intranets, e-mails and faxes all move information around the firm more easily; spreadsheets and databases enable the information to be processed more quickly.
- At Unipart, for example, employees on the

shop floor have terminals they can use to visit the company website to find answers to problems that they are facing for the first time but which have already been experienced elsewhere within the organisation. This means that time does not have to be wasted solving problems which have already been solved before. Consultancy firms such as Arthur Andersen place great store by their IT systems which enable them to tap into the experience of their consultants anywhere in the world. Management information systems (MIS) are IT systems developed to help managers access information more readily, eg an MIS might enable managers to quickly look up sales data or sales trends.

■ IT may also improve motivation as employees feel they can access the people they need to get a decision more easily and generally feel more involved in what is happening.

EXAMINER'S ADVICE

Don't forget how important it is to have accurate information. Think of all the topics you have studied in which the value of a particular technique depends on the underlying information. Techniques such as break-even analysis, investment appraisal, elasticity of demand and ratio analysis are only as useful as the data on which they are based. The effective management of information provides the organisation with the data it needs to make the right decision and therefore gives it a better chance of success.

Information technology and operations

The use of information technology can have a significant impact on a firm's operations enabling the firm to produce more efficiently and providing greater flexibility.

■ The use of computer aided design and computer aided manufacture (CAD and CAM), for example, lead to more versatile and less wasteful production; it can therefore be an important element of a lean production approach. IT also enables designers and engineers to undertake simultaneous engineering speeding up the development process and enabling firms to get new products to the market and new processes up and running before the competition.

■ Within the purchasing function an increasing number of firms are using web-based exchange systems for their purchases. By using the net firms can quickly compare prices and specifications from a range of suppliers to find the best deal. This can reduce costs and speed up the buying process.

■ IT can also improve stock control; the use of scanners within shops, for example, enables firms to know immediately what their stock levels are, reducing the need for as many manual checks. Also firms can use this system to automatically re-order supplies. With good IT links between a firm and its suppliers it is much easier to adopt a JIT system. In theory when a customer buys a product in the shop this will show up immediately on the stock system and another item will be ordered automatically from the supplier.

Key terms

Web-based exchange: this occurs when firms join together on the net to trade. Manufacturers can invite member suppliers to tender for orders.

Business in Focus

The internet is revolutionising the automotive industry. Mr Nasser, the chief executive of the Ford Motor company recently said that e-commerce promises 'nothing short of a total re-invention of this company … it will transform how we think, how we operate, how we design and manufacture. Above all it will change how our dealers communicate and connect with customers.' For example, by shifting their multi-billion dollar purchasing systems onto web-based exchanges encouraging suppliers to join them, they hope to save billions of dollars. They have also promised to turn cars into communication tools. Multi-media devices and wireless technology will make in-car equipment redundant. The big US car makers have all signed alliances with companies including Yahoo! Oracle CommerceOne and Microsoft. Ford has even signed a deal to install personal computers in the homes of all of its 350 000 employees. The manufacturers will also be affected by the rapid growth in on-line retailing which may mean the end of traditional dealerships.

1. What are the likely benefits for a firm such as Ford of using more IT?

Key terms

Computer-aided design (CAD): involves the use of computers to help in the production of designs, drawings and data for use in manufacturing.
Computer-aided manufacture (CAM) uses computers to support manufacturing processes such as computer numerically controlled machines (CNC), robots and automated handling systems. CADCAM (also known as computer aided engineering (CAE)) links product design and manufacturing through integrating CAD and CAM processes.
Materials requirement planning (MRP) is a computerised production scheduling system which looks at the future production schedule and from this derives a list of what components are needed at each stage and exactly when they will be required.

Information technology and planning

Rapid developments in IT have enabled firms to process data much more quickly and much more cheaply than in the past. This enables quicker and hopefully more accurate decision making. For example, IT tools such as spreadsheets have proved extremely useful when it comes both to monitoring the present situation and to planning ahead, so that managers can set budgets for different areas of the business and present levels of expenditure can then be compared easily with the set targets on an ongoing basis. The impact of any proposed changes in expenditure or revenue can be easily analysed

using spreadsheets enabling managers to answer 'what if?' type questions. IT can also be used for planning in many other areas of the firm such as sales forecasting and project planning (helping to produce network diagrams).

Information technology and location

Information technology is having a major impact on firms' location decisions. Increased use of IT means that more firms are now more footloose than before and do not need to be linked to any specific location. Internet banks, e-commerce firms and call centres, for example, are very free to locate themselves where they want rather than being tied to a particular location in the UK (or even the world). IT is also making it easier for employees to adopt 'teleworking' which means that they work from home; this frees up office space and so can significantly reduce a firm's facility costs. All sorts of employees can now work from home and only need to visit their offices relatively infrequently because they can keep in touch using IT. Sales representatives, journalists, authors, photographers, designers and so on can all send in their work from home. As well as cutting a firm's costs teleworking may motivate staff by cutting down on commuting time and giving them the sense of more control over their working life. Having said this some people enjoy the social interaction of an office or factory environment and prefer a clear division between work and home.

Key terms

Teleworking: occurs when employees work from home using information technology.

POINTS TO PONDER

Jack Welch, chairman of General Electric, wrote to his shareholders in 1996 saying 'information technology is making the huge transition from the function it was in the 1980s ... to the indispensable competitive tool, the central nervous system of virtually every operation in the company'.

Operations	Human resource planning
Stock control	teleworking
CAD/CAM	personnel record keeping
	workforce scheduling

Finance	Marketing
Cash flow forecasting	customer databases
Breakeven analysis	market research, eg through EPOS (electronic point of sale)
Investment analysis e.g. ratios and investment appraisal	New distribution/promotional channels – eg the internet

Table 5.4 *Examples of the use of IT within the functions of a firm*

Management of information technology

The rapid developments in IT (such as the internet) are creating incredible opportunities for firms which can seize the initiative. Organisations which appreciate the importance of information as a resource and as a competitive weapon can gain an advantage over their rivals. They can understand their markets and their own strengths more fully, they can react more quickly to change and they can exploit markets more effectively. They can find new ways of managing their operations, eg in terms of purchasing, producing and distributing their goods and services. The importance of information can be seen by the fact that several organisations have appointed 'knowledge managers' to manage the way information is gathered and distributed throughout the organisation.

Business in Focus: Sony's strategy and the internet

According to the Chairman and Chief Executive of Sony the world is passing through an age of meteors and dinosaurs. 'Sixty five million years ago a meteor hit the earth and the dinosaurs died immediately. The internet is like that meteor for the music industry' says the man who runs Sony's empire of consumer electronics, music and entertainment businesses.

With regard to the internet he says 'if we fail to adapt ourselves we will die.' 'The distribution of content has been changed enormously by the internet. Just look at the file sharing of Napster or Gnutella' he says referring to the computer technology that has enabled free exchange of music online. 'File sharing means we have to think about a fundamental change of the business model. It will not happen for three to five years but in the life of a company three to five years is not a very long time.' Sony's sales last year were £45bn. The company's chairman believes the technology of the internet favours a company that caters to many gateways to the connected world including games consoles (such as PlayStation2), hand held devices, mobile phones and personal computers. For the moment Sony is devoting its attention to its new piece of hardware PlayStation2. The games console combines two technologies that Sony hopes will take it into the next generation of consumer appliances: interactivity through the connection to the internet and enhanced graphics and functionality delivered by a supercharged computer chip. Sony aims to turn the games console into the interactive gateway to the home, combining its experience in products ranging from televisions to digital cameras to PCs and video consoles.

The Financial Times

1 Sony is switching many of its resources into developing internet-based products. Is it right to do so?

Problems of information technology

The greater use of information technology does not in itself solve a firm's problems. Whilst it provides the opportunity for firms to manage information more effectively its value depends on factors such as

■ how well trained staff are. Introducing IT is of limited use unless staff are able to use it properly

- the compatibility of different systems. Unfortunately many organisations have systems which are not particularly compatible with other stakeholders' systems such as their suppliers or within different sections of the firm. It is also common to find elements of a firm's IT system which do not work especially well together.

- what is done with the information. Simply generating more information does not in itself improve decision making. In fact it can make it worse because managers become bogged down in detail; before they do anything they request so much information that the final decision comes far too late.

Key *issues*

The internet promises a true revolution in business. It has already had a significant impact on the way in which business is done (eg e-commerce) and has led to the rapid growth of companies such as amazon.com and lastminute.com. The internet is transforming the way firms deal with their suppliers and their customers and offers tremendous opportunities if exploited effectively. At the same time it also threatens some firms which might be by-passed as customers deal direct with manufacturers or which might be slow to see the opportunities of the new technology.

Business in Focus

A British supermarket recently carried out an examination of its sales data in a certain store. Looking for unprofitable lines it discovered a certain type of fancy cheese that was bought by relatively few people each week. The answer seemed simple – axe the cheese. But then looking at the data the firm discovered that the few people who bought this cheese were people with much higher shopping bills than average. These same customers were also buying fine wines, expensive delicacies and gourmet foodstuffs. The company decided to keep the cheese so as to retain these high value customers.

This highlights the importance of 'data mining'. Using sophisticated software techniques to sift

through the enormous quantities of data a business can find hidden patterns to help a firm maximise its profits. Huge leaps in efficiency have been made possible by the availability of vastly increased processing power at relatively cheap prices.

Data mining has become much cheaper and much easier. Traditional retailers woke up to data mining several years ago resulting in the popularity of loyalty cards as a method of collecting data on customers which could then be used to target marketing at those most likely to respond. With the growth of e-commerce internet retailers also quickly realised the possible uses of forms of data mining. For example Amazon.com can make cross selling offers based on simple assumptions eg that someone buying a book on cat grooming would also be interested in pet toys. The chief operating officer of MicroStrategy a US data mining specialist says 'data mining is the key and the perfect example of how computers are helping us to be more efficient. The information has always been there, but the secret of technology is being able to unlock it.'

The Financial Times

I Discuss the ways in which a video retailer might use data mining.

EXAMINER'S ADVICE

Remember that information technology can help gather, analyse and transmit information but it is still up to the managers to use IT tools effectively and implement their decisions correctly. IT makes it easier to make better decisions but it does not guarantee the decisions are right or that they are then put into effect.

Internet

The internet is one particular area of information technology where the potential opportunities and threats can easily be seen. The rapid rise of many dot.com companies highlights the tremendous possibilities this technology opens up – new ways of marketing and completely new business models. At the same time the failure of so many of these new internet businesses also highlights the problems there can be in successfully exploiting any new technology.

The potential benefits of the internet include

- lower trading costs. E-commerce firms such as internet banks and internet travel companies do not need the same overheads as the traditional providers of such services, eg they do not need expensive high-street premises. This allows such firms to offer their services at a lower price
- 24-hour trading. An e-retailer can be trading all day every day enabling people to shop at their own convenience
- worldwide coverage. By using internet marketing firms can easily be accessible to customers all over the world. The internet is truly creating global markets. It is remarkably easy and cheap to establish a site and be trading all over the world in a very short period of time.

Business in Focus

Britain's £375m a year contact lens business is experiencing little growth because most opticians prefer to sell glasses according to Trevor Rowley, who launched PostOptics to sell lenses by mail order in 1998. He argues that opticians prefer to sell glasses for a few hundred pounds rather than lenses because the latter require constant healthcare monitoring. 'They simply find glasses much less work and hassle' says Rowley.

Had he not done so, he says, he would have remained a high street retailer facing an uncertain future as he was squeezed by the major players such as Boots and Dolland and Aitchinson which account for about 70% of the market of 2.5m users.

In just a few years PostOptics has emerged as one of Britain's largest independent retailers of lenses and accompanying solutions. Rowley claims his lenses cost on average one third less than those of his high street retailers. The company began simply selling cut price sterilising solutions

but expanded into lenses because profits were too low. He provides the lenses without the unprofitable advice and healthcare of the high street retailers. Some of Rowley's critics believe it is irresponsible to sell lenses through such channels and want tighter controls over the sale of such products over the internet. Regulations from the General Optical Council do exist but some commentators do not feel they go far enough.

Rowley says 'The internet is a great leveller. It exposes those who overcharge for their service and product. Those on the high street that don't do that have nothing to fear from us . .. The whole reason for launching PostOptics was that it became obvious to me that there was an enormous opportunity to change the traditional eye care market.' He worked on his plan for two years before launching the business. A year before the launch he employed a professional business manager something unheard of for a professional optician. He used existing staff, telephone lines and computers to cross subsidise the new business. Within a year it had built up a customer base of 5000 but was still not profitable until it sold lenses as well as solutions. Rowley realises competition is likely to follow but believes the market as a whole will grow rapidly.

The Sunday Times

1 Do you think products such as contact lenses should be allowed to be sold over the internet? Should the government intervene to prevent such sales? *(10 marks)*

2 What will determine whether the market for contact lenses grows or not? *(10 marks)*

However, whilst the appeal of e-commerce and on-line trading is undeniable firms must be cautious not to rush in without a proper business plan. Several firms including fairly high-profile businesses have struggled to make a profit in their first few years. The numbers buying off the internet are growing rapidly but remain relatively small compared to those buying through traditional distribution outlets and competition is increasing rapidly. In some cases e-retailers have failed to

attract sufficient trade to survive and have had to close. For example, Boo.com was a fashion website which attracted a lot of publicity but was not actually profitable and was forced to close in 2000. E-toys also closed its UK operations.

Whilst the internet offers firms new promotional and distribution opportunities it also provides consumers with the ability to rapidly search for alternatives and easily compare prices. This is likely to put downward pressure on firms' profit margins.

The impact of the internet will depend on how managers react to it and whether they can exploit its opportunities before others do while also maintaining an appropriate rate of return.

*P*OINTS TO PONDER

Being successful in business is often easier in hindsight. Cliff Stanford was an accountant who set up his own software house in 1979. In 1992 he set up the first dial-up internet service provider, Demon Internet. Unfortunately he did not fully appreciate the potential of the internet and said to his staff 'Don't waste too much time on the internet. It will be gone in another year.' He failed to realise that the World Wide Web would take off as quickly as it did.

Even so he still managed to sell the business for £30m!

Progress questions

1 What is meant by 'information technology'?
(2 marks)

2 Explain two ways in which the use of information technology might benefit a firm in its operations management. *(6 marks)*

3 Explain two ways in which information technology can benefit a firm's financial planning. *(6 marks)*

4 What is meant by teleworking? *(2 marks)*

5 Explain two ways in which teleworking might benefit a firm. *(6 marks)*

6 Explain two ways in which the greater use of information technology might improve a firm's communications. *(6 marks)*

7 Explain two factors which might determine how much a firm invests in information technology. *(6 marks)*

8 Explain two problems a firm might experience when introducing new information technology. *(6 marks)*

9 Explain two ways in which information technology might benefit a firm's marketing activities. *(6 marks)*

10 Explain two reasons why employees might resist the introduction of more information technology. *(6 marks)*

Analysis and evaluation questions

1 Analyse the ways in which information technology can benefit a firm's operations management. *(8 marks)*

2 Examine the possible benefits of information technology in the planning process. *(8 marks)*

3 Discuss the ways in which the use of information technology might benefit a firm. *(12 marks)*

4 Does the internet create opportunities or threats for a firm? *(12 marks)*

5 To what extent is the use of information technology the key to a firm's success? *(12 marks)*

Case study 1

Brainfest was a relatively small software company which specialised in computer security, eg it helped to protect other companies' databases from hackers. Brainfest was a leader in its field and had built a truly outstanding reputation for managing to stay one step ahead of 'the bad guys'.

Walking into the company's offices was something of an experience: the reception area contained numerous computer games (and these were also scattered all over the building for staff to use in their breaks). The company had a canteen on site which was very popular with staff partly due to the heavily subsidised meals and partly because of the amazingly good food it served. People would often meet up to discuss things in the canteen because it had such a friendly and trendy feel to it.

Visitors to the building were often surprised by how casually dressed everyone was. Suits were almost nowhere to be seen. The average age was also a shock to some – most of the staff were in their twenties and it was rare to find an employee over 40 years old.

Due to its incredible success in recent years the company had now outgrown its premises and needed somewhere bigger. The present offices were on the very outskirts of London and were all the firm could afford at the time. It had made it quite difficult to attract staff – many of whom wanted to be nearer the centre of the capital but the founders had no choice. The move will be coordinated by Jackie Schnell who has created a small project team to make sure it works smoothly. Not surprisingly she is using all the latest techniques and software to help her control everything but at the heart of it all is good old-fashioned critical path analysis.

According to Brian Mudowlski, the company's founder – an American who came to the UK in his twenties and has stayed ever since – Brainfest's success is due to its staff and its culture. 'We hire the best, pay the best and ensure we provide an environment which is buzzing' he says. It is certainly unusual. This year's Christmas party was held in Lapland, for example, and at the end of each week there is a 'beer bust' when all the staff get together for a drink. Obviously as the firm has got bigger some of these events have got more difficult to organise. Also

Brian is concerned that the firm may be losing its innovative edge. 'We still invest heavily in research and development but I am not sure we are achieving the same levels of innovation as we did.' According to outsiders Brian himself is one of the key reasons for the firm's success – his vision, technical expertise and energy have led the way and have brought people to the firm who just want to work with him. Having said this his own involvement has been gradually diminishing – partly this is inevitable because it has grown and partly because he now has other priorities such as his family and children. 'I still live for the business but appreciate there are other things as well.'

Brian is also considering setting up a second branch in the USA. 'At the moment all our clients are UK-based – in fact they are all located in the south. The US market has always seemed quite attractive to me and I think we might benefit from being out there. The USA is always one step ahead of the UK in this field and by competing head-on it might spur us on.'

Perhaps not surprisingly for a firm at the cutting edge of technology its own use of it is quite staggering to outsiders. For example, Brian has managed to create almost paperless offices – all documents are transferred onto computer. Information technology runs through almost every aspect of the business.

1 a) Discuss the factors which might determine the new location for a firm such as Brainfest.

   (12 marks)

   b) Examine the ways in which critical path analysis might help Jackie in organising the relocation of Brainfest. *(8 marks)*

2 a) Analyse the possible reasons why Brainfest invests heavily in research and development.

   (8 marks)

   b) Consider the ways in which the managers of Brainfest can ensure it continues to enjoy a high level of innovation in the future. *(12 marks)*

3 a) Outline the possible operations objectives a firm such as Brainfest might set itself. *(8 marks)*

   b) Discuss the ways in which the use of information technology might benefit a firm such as Brainfest. *(12 marks)*

4 Discuss the factors Brainfest might consider before opening up a branch in the USA. *(20 marks)*

Case study 2

Pablo Santo believes he knows the key to business success: information management. 'First of all you need to understand your customers and that means keeping in touch with them. Then you need to get everyone within the firm working together and that means keeping them informed. Also the more you keep in touch with your staff the more you learn from them and the better you get. Managing information helps us in all areas of our business and keeps us one step ahead of the competition.'

Pablo is the boss of a large European producer of confectionery called Sertar. Since he has been the managing director he has undertaken significant investment in information technology. At times this has met with resistance within the firm from managers who think there are more pressing priorities and that at times the investment has been too fast. 'Having the technology to manage information is not enough in itself and even if you do have all the information you want that does not ensure the business will succeed. You can't forget the product itself, for example' said one.

1 Some of the managers at Sertar resisted the introduction of information technology. Analyse the possible reasons why some managers may resist the introduction of information technology. *(8 marks)*

2 Discuss the ways in which information technology may benefit a firm such as Sertar. *(12 marks)*

CHAPTER 6

External Influences

Introduction

As with all topics in A2 business studied you will have studied some elements of this subject during your AS level course. The major elements you will have studied are as follows:

- markets and the different types and degrees of competition that exist within them
- a number of important macroeconomic issues including the business (or trade) cycle, interest rates, exchange rates, inflation and unemployment. The emphasis in studying these elements of economics was on the effects they can have on businesses and how businesses may respond to changes in their economic environment
- the scope of UK and EU laws in the fields of health and safety, employment protection, consumer protection and the promotion of free and fair competition in markets. Once again the focus of this section was on the effects of legislation, rather than detailed study of the laws themselves

- social responsibilities and business ethics
- technological change.

The A2 specification for business studies builds upon the subject knowledge and skills acquired during the AS programme. In particular the basic knowledge acquired about the economic, social and legal environments will be developed further considering how they affect the ability of firms to compete in international markets and to meet their corporate objectives. It is worthwhile looking back over your AS materials before starting to study A2 external influences. More specific advice is given on any prior knowledge required at the outset of each unit.

During your A2 programme you will study the topics set out as follows:

- economic opportunities and constraints
- governmental opportunities and constraints
- social and political opportunities and constraints.

It is valuable to view these external influences as providing firms with opportunities as well as imposing constraints.

ECONOMIC OPPORTUNITIES AND CONSTRAINTS

Starting points

As part of the AS course we studied in detail a number of factors that affect the economic environment in which firms operate. Key areas of study included the following:

- the business or trade cycle. All nations suffer fluctuations in the level of activity within their economies. At times spending, output and employment all rise; during other periods the opposite is true. This is the business cycle under which economies regularly pass through recognisable stages including booms and slumps
- since May 1997 the Monetary Policy Committee at the Bank of England has had responsibility for setting interest rates. The authorities use interest rates extensively to manage the economic environment. Interest rates have a wide impact affecting spending decisions by businesses and individuals alike
- the UK is a relatively 'open' economy, meaning that it exports a high proportion (approximately 33% of the UK's production of goods and services were destined for overseas markets in 2000) of the goods and services produced. The country imports goods and services to a similar

value. Because of this openness the exchange rate is an important factor for the business community. Changes in the exchange rate can affect selling prices and costs and have the potential to have a profound effect on the activities of most businesses

- inflation is the change in price levels occurring over some period of time. As with the exchange rate this can affect the competitiveness and performance of UK firms through its impact upon prices and costs
- unemployment represents a waste of human resources. Unemployment can have a double impact upon businesses. The level of demand for a business's products may be affected by a change in the level of unemployment. Unemployment affects the amount of money consumers have available as well as their confidence in taking spending decisions.

EXAMINER'S ADVICE

The AS specification contained a great deal of fundamental information relating to economic factors that shape the environment in which businesses operate. It is worth revisiting this material briefly before studying this unit in detail.

Key terms

Interest rates are the price paid for borrowed money.
*An **exchange rate** is the price of one currency expressed in terms of another. For example, the pound might be worth 1.5 euros.*
*The **business cycle** is a regular change in the level of economic activity within a country highlighted by boom, recession, slump and upswing.*
Inflation is a persistent rise in the general price level and an associated fall in the value of money.
***Unemployment** exists when people who are seeking work are unable to find any employment.*

The study of these topics encompassed the nature of the economic variables and gave some overview of their individual effects upon business and consumers. This unit will build upon the work undertaken in the AS course. The stage of the business cycle, and changes in key economic variables such as inflation, unemployment, exchange and interest rates have considerable implications for strategic decisions within businesses. The economic factors also have important interrelationships of considerable significance for businesses when planning and implementing business strategy. This unit will look at these issues in some detail.

Economic environment and business strategy

A business's strategy is simply the long-term plans through which it seeks to attain its corporate objectives — ie the objectives of the whole business. For example, a business may have growth as a major corporate objective and will develop plans to achieve the desired rate of growth. These plans may include

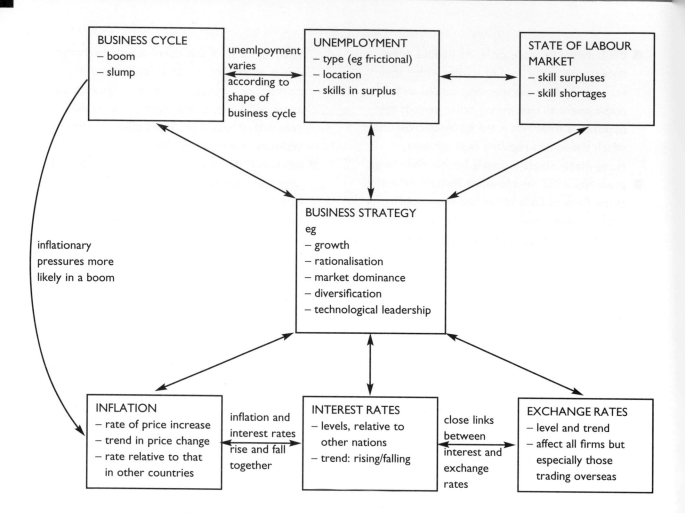

Figure 6.1 *Business strategy in an integrated business environment*

Factors such as interest and exchange rates, the business cycle, inflation and unemployment combine to shape one aspect of the environment within which businesses operate. Thus, as the economy moves through the various stages of the trade cycle rates of inflation and unemployment may change. Equally interest rates may be adjusted to dampen the effects of the business cycle creating further implications for firms. Finally, the strategic decisions taken by businesses in response to opportunities and constraints that appear in the economic environment also determine that environment. Thus a decision to rationalise because the economy is moving into recession may contribute to the economic downturn.

increasing innovation as part of the development of new products, entering new markets or pursuing a policy of takeovers and mergers. Figure 6.1 summarises the major economic variables that might impact upon strategic planning and decision making. The diagram also emphasises the interrelationships that exist between the elements that make up the economic environment for businesses.

Interest rates

Since the early 1990s successive governments have

relied heavily upon interest rates to manage the economy. In May 1997 the newly elected Labour government handed control of interest rates to the Bank of England. This decision was intended to allow a longer-term strategy to operate with regard to interest rates without governments altering rates for political (rather than economic) reasons. The Bank's Monetary Policy Committee meets regularly to determine the level of the UK's base rate on which all other rates in the economy depend.

Interest rates affect businesses in a number of ways. It is not simply a case of whether they rise or fall: businesses also take into account the overall

	1.	2.	3.	4.
RISING INTEREST RATES	1. UK interest rates rise relative to those in other countries	2. UK becomes attractive to foreign investors as higher rates offered by financial institutions	3. Foreign investors purchase pounds to enable investments in UK financial institutions	4. Demand for pounds rises. The price of pounds – the exchange rate – also rises
FALLING INTEREST RATES	1. UK interest rates fall relative to those in other countries	2. UK becomes less attractive to foreign investors due to falling returns offered by financial institutions	3. Foreign investors sell pounds (to buy other currencies) to allow them to invest in other countries	4. Supply of pound rises. The price of pounds – the exchange rate – falls

Figure 6.2 *Interest rates and exchange rates*

level of rates. Thus a small increase in interest rates may have little impact if rates are low. This is unlikely to be the case when rates are high before the change is introduced.

- A change in interest rates will affect a firm's decisions on investment and expansion. Thus rising rates may cause the postponement or cancellation of investment plans. Businesses may decide to invest in other countries if they feel that interest rates may be volatile or high relative to other countries.
- Changing interest rates affect consumers' spending decisions. As a result of increasing interest rates consumers may decide to save more (attracted by high rates) or to delay spending decisions requiring borrowing. Purchases of products such as cars, white goods (fridges and cookers, for example) and televisions are sensitive to changes in interest rates. Consumers may demand more of these products when interest rates fall.
- Interest rates also affect the value of the pound in terms of other currencies. Increases in interest rates tend to exert upward pressure on exchange rates; similarly falling rates encourage the value of the pound to decline. Thus rising interest rates may make it more difficult for exporters to sell their products overseas. We will consider the

effects of exchange rates on business strategy more fully later in this unit. Figure 6.2 illustrates the relationship between interest rates and exchange rates.

Businesses tend to take a long-term view of interest rates. Rates can be altered each month, and strategic decisions are rarely taken on the basis of factors that may alter again within a month or two. However, a country with a reputation for having persistently high rates, or for interest rate volatility, may be unattractive to businesses. Volatile rates make long-term planning more difficult. Unpredictable changes in internet rates may have significant effects on domestic demand and the exchange rate (in turn affecting overseas consumers). In these circumstances firms may seek to relocate overseas and diversify into products for which demand is less dependent upon interest rates.

Exchange rates

For an open economy such as the UK, exchange rates are an important issue. Exchange rates affect the prices UK businesses pay for raw materials and components purchased overseas and also for the revenue received from products sold in foreign markets.

Integrated Business: little optimism in the north of England

Business optimism among manufacturers in the industrial heartlands of the north of England has declined sharply over the past few months. This region of the UK contains few of the 'newer' manufacturing industries such as electrical engineering. Those regions relying on more traditional manufacturing industries are experiencing difficulty in competing in markets within the UK and overseas.

Even the prospects of a reduction in interest rates has not cheered northern businesses. Economists and industrialists agreed the prospect of a 0.25% cut in interest rates would be of little help to firms in depressed areas. Nigel Sherlock, president of the north-east Chamber of Commerce, said 'Whether rates fall or not is a marginal point, though it may change sentiment and encourage exporters. The maximum effect of a rate cut on growth kicks in only after one year. In any case a quarter-point cut won't do very much, though it's a start.'

The north-east also recorded the largest falls in output and new orders of all regions in the UK during the summer of 2000. Local industrialists blamed the decline largely on sterling's strength against the euro, which has made exports less competitive. But Sherlock said recent high-profile local successes, including the announcement by US company Atmel that it would reopen the former Siemens semiconductor plant on Tyneside, suggested the tide was turning.

The Financial Times

1 Discuss the case for and against multinational manufacturing companies such as Atmel locating in economically depressed regions of the UK.
2 To what extent might changes in interest rates prove effective in bringing prosperity to regions such as the north-east of England?

Key issues: the euro

On 1 January 1999 a single European currency – the euro – was introduced into 11 European Union countries. Austria, Belgium, Finland, France, Germany, Ireland, Italy, Luxembourg, the Netherlands, Portugal and Spain all adopted the new currency. The UK has delayed a decision on when (or if) to join the single currency. The 11 countries have locked the foreign exchange values of their national currencies to the euro and share the new currency. Euro notes and coins will become available on 1 January 2002 and until then participating states will use their domestic currency. By 30 June 1992 old banknotes and coins will be withdrawn from circulation.

Convergence between the economies of participating countries is viewed as an absolutely necessary condition for a single currency. The economic criteria to be met are set out as follows:

■ annual inflation of less than 2.7%
■ government deficits (government income less than spending) of below 3% of gross domestic product
■ national debt to be less than 60% of gross domestic product
■ long-term interest rates below 6.8%

There are a number of sound arguments for the UK joining the euro. The biggest potential beneficiaries could be UK businesses.

■ Cheaper transaction costs would result for UK companies if the euro replaced sterling. No longer would it be necessary to exchange currencies when trading with other countries using the euro meaning the commission charges would be avoided.
■ Being within the euro zone would assist the UK in attracting inward investment which is vital for jobs and prosperity.
■ A major benefit would arise from the stable exchange rates that would operate throughout Europe. Trading in euros would remove the risk of adverse exchange rate movements and potential loss of earnings from international trade.
■ Prices would become transparent. As all goods and services would henceforth be priced in the same currency through much of Europe comparing the prices of suppliers would become a simple process.

Fluctuations in exchange rates create a great deal of uncertainty for businesses trading internationally. When exchange rates are volatile, businesses become uncertain about earnings from overseas trade. This adds to the risk businesses incur as part of their trading activities.

Exchange rate changes can create uncertainty for a number of reasons.

- If firms agree deals priced in foreign currencies, they may receive more or less revenue from a particular transaction than expected if the exchange rate alters in the intervening period. Thus, a deal to sell whisky to Japan, may give Scottish distillers less revenue than anticipated if the contract is agreed in terms of yen and the pound then rises in value against the Japanese yen. In these circumstances the amount of yen stated in the contract will convert into a smaller number of pounds, causing a shortfall for the exporter.
- Changing exchange rates can affect prices and sales in overseas markets, even if the exporter avoids direct exchange risk by insisting on payment in domestic currency. For example, a London-based clothes designer may sell clothes overseas, but stipulate that they are paid in pounds sterling. A rise in the value of the pound may mean that foreign retailers are forced to increase the prices of the clothes to maintain profit margins. As a consequence sales may be lower than expected giving the London-based design company less revenue than forecast.
- Competitors may respond in unexpected ways to exchange rate changes. Foreign firms may reduce prices to offset the effects of an exchange rate change, putting rivals under pressure to do the same or lose market share.

Firms like to operate in a relatively risk-free environment and to reduce uncertainty. The undesirable consequences of exchange rate changes can be reduced through the use of techniques such as forward foreign currency markets. This sets a guaranteed exchange rate at some future date (when transactions are completed) meaning that the amount received from overseas trading is more certain. However, fixing an exchange rate in this way does not guarantee a particular level of sales. Furthermore, the bank arranging this service may require a fee.

EXAMINER'S ADVICE

When examining the possible effects of changes in the exchange rate it is important to consider the likely price elasticity of demand for the products in question. Products with elastic demand will be more affected by changes in the exchange rate with demand proving very sensitive to price fluctuations.

Exchange rate changes are more of a problem in markets where fierce price competition occurs. In these circumstances demand is more likely to be price elastic and businesses are under pressure to respond quickly to any change in exchange rates.

*P*OINTS TO PONDER

Camelot is planning to increase the price of its £1 ticket for the first time when – as the company expects – the government drops the pound in favour of the euro.

The lottery operator has been reluctant to raise the price because of the ease and convenience of paying a pound coin for a ticket. Senior Camelot executives believe that the prospect of a two-euro note or coin (worth £1.27 at current exchange rates) provides an ideal opportunity to raise the price.

Businesses may respond to the pressures of exchange rate changes by seeking to create productive capacity in overseas markets to avoid the effects of changing currency values. A number of foreign motor manufacturers located in the UK have revealed that they are considering relocating in the euro zone in Europe to avoid the difficulties imposed by fluctuations in the value of the pound against the euro. In particular Toyota have argued strongly for the UK to adopt the euro to eliminate exchange rate risk.

Rising value of the pound	Falling value of the pound
A single pound purchases greater amounts of foreign currencies (eg £1 rises from being worth 1.5 euros to be the equivalent of 1.75 euros).	A single pound purchases lesser amounts of foreign currencies (eg £1 declines from being worth 1.5 euros to be the equivalent of 1.25 euros).
the effects ...	**the effects ...**
A pen produced in the UK under these circumstances and priced at £10 will rise in price from E15 [10 × 1.5] to E16.50 [10 × 1.75] when sold in France. At the same time a French wine priced at E18 will fall in price in the UK from £12 [18/1.5] to £10.29 [18/1.75].	In these circumstances the same UK-manufactured pen priced at £10 will fall in price from E15 [10 × 1.5] to E12.50 [10 × 1.25]. A French wine priced at E18 per bottle in France will experience a rise in price in the UK from £12 [18/1.5] to £14.40 [18/1.25].

Table 6.1

An alternative approach, currently used by Toyota, is to require suppliers to price their products in a different currency. The company, which sells cars throughout Europe, has announced that it intends to pay UK suppliers in euros. As a result fluctuations in the exchange rate will have less impact on the company as it pays suppliers in the same currency that it receives from European customers.

Inflation

Inflation in the UK has been at low levels over recent years. This has offered UK businesses a number of advantages.

- Costs are much easier to control in periods when prices are rising slowly.
- Pricing strategies are easier to establish (and simpler for consumers to understand) when inflation is low.

How might UK firms respond to a rising value of the pound?	How might UK firms respond to a falling value of the pound?
EXPORTERS	EXPORTERS
■ allow prices to rise in foreign markets reducing probable sales. Remember exporters receive the same price in pounds for each overseas sale, but will sell less in this situation ■ leave prices unchanged in overseas markets in terms of foreign currency. Sales should be unchanged but the exporter will receive fewer pounds from each sale. Neither of these options is attractive to exporters – rising exchange rates are bad news.	■ could allow prices to fall in overseas markets as a result of the exchange rate change. They will receive the same amount in pounds from each sale but should achieve higher sales ■ increase their prices to maintain price levels in terms of the foreign currency. Sales should remain constant (depending on competitors' actions) and revenue should rise in pounds as a result.
DOMESTIC PRODUCERS	DOMESTIC PRODUCERS
■ reduce prices to compete with cheaper imports ■ enjoy the benefits of cheaper imports of materials and components ■ emphasise other elements in the marketing mix, eg the quality of the product.	■ enjoy increased sales as a result of rising prices of competitors' imported products, assuming foreign businesses do not hold prices down ■ increase prices (to some extent) to enjoy increased revenues from each sale ■ must beware the increased cost of imported raw materials and components.

Table 6.2 *Changes in exchange rates*

- If UK inflation is lower than that experienced by other nations, businesses may receive a competitive advantage. Rival firms located in other countries may face increased costs and face pressure to increase their prices in an attempt to maintain profit margins.
- Sales forecasts are more likely to prove accurate during periods of relatively low inflation. During bouts of inflation consumers may switch to cheaper overseas products or decide to save against an uncertain future.
- Government policies to reduce inflation may have adverse effects on businesses, reducing the levels of expenditure on the business's products.

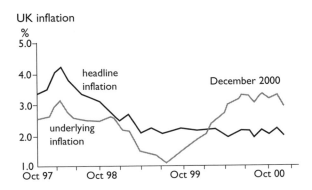

Figure 6.3 *UK inflation 1997–2000*

Headline inflation reflects the rate of inflation faced by consumers, whilst the underlying rate of inflation excludes changes in mortgage interest rates which can have a significant impact on price changes.

BBC News 16 January 2001 www.bbc.co.uk

In an environment of relatively stable prices businesses may be willing to expand capacity through investment and to develop new products. Price stability removes an element of risk from business planning, engenders confidence amongst senior managers and may result in more positive business strategies. Arguably, the low rate of inflation enjoyed by the UK over recent years, has been one factor encouraging foreign firms to locate in this country.

However, businesses' responses to a period of inflation will depend upon the perceived cause of inflation, the level of inflation and the confidence they have in the government's ability to control price rises. Inflation caused by high levels of demand (so-called demand-pull inflation) may encourage firms to expand to meet the high and potentially profitable levels of demand. Even cost-push inflation (fuelled, for example, by high wage claims) may not be regarded as too damaging, if the resulting inflation is at a low level and the government appears capable of preventing price increases from accelerating.

Business cycle

The business cycle is a permanent feature of the economic environment for firms. All that changes is the stage of the cycle through which the economy is passing. The effects of changes in the business cycle vary from industry to industry. Firms selling income elastic goods such as designer clothes and foreign holidays (where demand is sensitive to changes in income) may find that sales rise in a boom and fall during recession. Conversely, businesses selling staple products such as foodstuffs where demand is income inelastic, may be relatively unaffected by the business cycle.

It is possible to argue that the business cycle will

Firms supplying these products may be significantly affected by the business cycle	Firms supplying these products are unlikely to be affected to a great extent by the business cycle – in fact demand may rise for some of these products in a recession/slump
■ champagne ■ sports and leisure goods ■ restaurant meals ■ jewellery ■ household furniture	■ coal ■ bread ■ cigarettes and tobacco ■ petrol ■ fresh vegetables

Table 6.3 *Products affected and unaffected by the business cycle*

only provoke short-term responses in many firms, because its effects are relatively short-lived. Booms and slumps do not last forever and businesses can take actions to see them through difficult trading periods. During boom periods managers may increase prices to restrict demand and increase profitability; they may subcontract work to other firms or seek supplies from overseas. Equally in conditions of recession or slump, lay-offs may occur or short-time working may take place whilst overseas markets are targeted to increase sales. Well-managed firms will predict the onset of a boom or slump and take appropriate action in advance. Short-term responses may be all that are required if governments are successful in eradicating the more extreme effects of the business cycle.

Decisions of a more strategic nature may be more likely if the effects of the business cycle are prolonged. A deep and lasting recession may persuade firms to close factories or to relocate overseas. A lengthy period of prosperity may encourage the innovation of new products as consumers' income rises and the expansion of productive capacity.

Labour market

Unemployment is perhaps the most obvious manifestation of the workings of the labour market. Since the early 1990s unemployment has fallen almost continuously in the UK. By 2001 the jobless total was hovering at about 1m – the lowest figure for 20 years. Unemployment at such a low level can lead to severe shortages of skilled labour. A report in 2000 suggested that nearly 25% of employers struggle to fill job vacancies. The report explained that shortages of skilled personnel are affecting businesses at all levels and in all industries.

*P*OINTS TO PONDER

A dot.com company is offering £50 000 to anyone who can recommend a team of ten people to join the business. Entranet, an e-business solutions supplier based near Reading, will give the money to any person who suggests a team of programmers or creative developers.

Falling unemployment and accompanying skill shortages create problems that take time to solve. Businesses look to the government to assist through the provision of state training schemes and the development of relevant vocational courses in schools and colleges. Recent UK governments have attempted to support industry in these ways.

Business in Focus

The National Health Service is planning to develop a new kind of medical practitioner to help overcome the shortage of doctors and lengthening waiting lists. The intention is to create a 'skilled practitioner' who would receive two years' formal training and a further two years' on-the-job training. This would qualify skilled practitioners to carry out minor surgery such as the removal of cataracts from patients' eyes.

The proposal has attracted a mixed reception. Supporters suggest that it will mean patients will receive treatment more promptly and that the time of highly skilled surgeons will not be used up in treating relatively minor ailments. However, the Royal College of Nursing has expressed doubts. They are unsure whether the new type of employee would have sufficient skills to carry out surgery and favour enhancing the role of nurses within the NHS.

l   Identify two NHS stakeholders who may have an interest in this proposal. Discuss the arguments for and against the creation of skilled practitioners from their perspectives.

However, businesses can take action.

- Skill shortages encourage the development of capital-intensive methods of production in manufacturing and service industries. Using technology to replace labour can boost productivity thereby enhancing international competitiveness.
- Businesses may relocate to take advantage of more plentiful and cheaper sources of skilled labour. However, this may require location outside Europe as most of the EU is experiencing similar skill shortages.

Businesses may invest in training schemes to develop the required skills in their employees. This may entail giving relatively junior or unskilled employees additional skills to enable them to carry out a wider range of activities. This can be a risky approach, however, as unscrupulous competitors may entice away skilled employees once training is completed.

POINTS TO PONDER

Skilled stonemasons brought to the UK from India were reported in October 2000 to be earning just £3 a day, or approximately 30 pence an hour. But the workers are still earning twice the rate available in India.

The skills shortage creates difficulties for many businesses, but opportunities for others. Recruitment agencies and firms providing training for other businesses may enjoy increasing demands for their services during a period of skill shortages.

International competitiveness

Key terms

International competitiveness is the extent to which a business can match the standards achieved by rival firms from overseas.
Economic growth is an increase in the real value of goods and services produced by a nation's economy.
Globalisation is the tendency for many markets to become worldwide in extent. Globalisation leads to businesses trading throughout the world, rather than in a single country or region.

Competitiveness, whether international, national or local, may have a number of elements. Competitive firms may be able to produce products cheaply, but they also have to be competitive in non-price terms. Competitiveness can relate to the quality of the goods and the consumers' perception of the business as well as how effective a business is at marketing its products.

The factors determining international competitiveness relate to all aspects of the operation of a business.

- The efficiency with which the business produces its products. Businesses that achieve high levels of productivity through the use of highly trained employees, effective production systems and efficient technology are likely to be able to supply products at highly competitive prices. In markets where demand is price elastic this may be a very important element of international competitiveness.
- Quality is important to consumers throughout the world; quality in this context may relate to the design of the product, its functions and features as well as durability and meeting delivery dates. Certain products are able to compete globally on the basis of being high quality and this may allow firms supplying these products to charge a premium price. BMW and Sony are internationally competitive in this respect.
- Competitiveness may also relate to image in certain industries. Firms may need to be seen to be ethical, or to demonstrate concern for the environment. For example, senior managers at Shell, the Anglo-Dutch oil company, argue that the public image of oil companies (given their huge potential to cause pollution) is an important competitive weapon.
- Marketing contributes to competitiveness. Competitive firms communicate effectively with actual and potential consumers. They use market research to discover consumers' needs, develop appropriate products and inform consumers of their existence. Internationally competitive firms (eg the fast food chain McDonalds) are able to enter new markets successfully.

However, some elements of international competitiveness depend upon the actions of governments. Only governments can create a stable economic environment, eliminate the more extreme effects of the business cycle and dampen volatile exchange rates and help to create a suitably educated and skilled workforce. The extent to which any government succeeds in these aims will have an

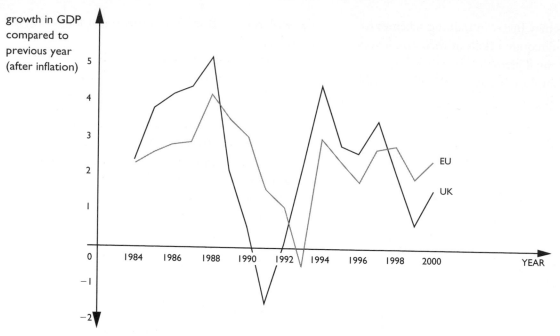

OECD

Figure 6.4 *Economic growth rates for UK and EU, 1984–2000*

important influence on the international competitiveness of domestic businesses.

Economic growth

Economic growth is an increase in the value of goods and services produced by a nation's economy. It is normally measured by an increase in gross domestic product (GDP). In the financial year 1999–2000 the GDP of the UK was £903 426m. The population of the UK is approximately 59m giving a GDP per head, or per capita, equal to £15 312. Governments seek to increase this figure over time as it represents a rise in the country's standard of living.

Most countries' economies experience economic growth over a period of time, though in the short term, economies may stagnate or even decline in size. Figure 6.4 illustrates the economic growth rates for the UK and the European Union from 1984 until 2000.

Governments aim to maintain steady and sustained economic growth over a period of time. However, this is a difficult target to achieve, as the operation of the business cycle tends to create the fluctuations apparent in figure 6.4. Governments use counter-cyclical policies (including control via interest rates and taxation levels) to attempt to

eliminate the more extreme fluctuations. High rates of economic growth are not desirable, as they tend to result in slumps whereby economic growth may become negative. This can be seen in the period 1988–1991 in figure 6.4.

Governments can stimulate growth as a consequence of their economic policies. Short-term growth can be encouraged by cuts in interest rates and taxation which fuel borrowing and spending, prompting greater output and hence economic growth. The danger is, however, that firms and individuals purchase products from overseas, promoting growth in foreign economies. Supply-side policies may be implemented to achieve sustained economic growth. This type of policy entails increasing the productive capability of the economy by improving the skills of the workforce, encouraging more people into employment and promoting competition within markets to increase output and GDP.

The case for economic growth is not clear-cut. Growth brings disadvantages as well as advantages. These arguments are summarised in table 6.4.

Globalisation and growth

The fact that economic growth is not always an advantage has been highlighted in the well-publicised opposition to further economic

the benefits	the drawbacks
■ high rates of economic growth provide the government with increased tax revenues permitting greater expenditure on health, education and transport benefiting all businesses and citizens in the UK and encouraging further growth	■ not all regions within an economy benefit equally during periods of economic growth. Firms selling in the south of England are likely to enjoy increases sales whilst those in less prosperous regions such as Wales and the north of England may only see a marginal increase in revenues
■ growth provides opportunities to all in society. Individuals benefit from greater chances of promotion; high levels of consumer spending encourage enterprise. Businesses small and large may thrive in a growing environment	■ growth may result in shortages of labour and other materials. This may result in higher wages and prices fuelling inflation and creating uncertainty amongst the business community
■ businesses generally enjoy higher sales and increased profits. Expansion is likely for firms selling income elastic products such as cars and foreign holidays. Growth creates new markets for products	■ growth places individuals and businesses under pressure. Workloads increase and decisions may be rushed. In these circumstances it may prove impossible to maintain the quality of management and businesses may lose coordination and a clear sense of direction

Table 6.4 *The benefits and drawbacks of economic growth for businesses*

development and especially to globalisation. Opponents of uncontrolled economic growth argue that other factors such as a clean environment, the protection of plants and wildlife and adequate leisure time contribute to the standard of living as much (and maybe more than) consumer products. As societies become richer this argument may become even more persuasive.

Business in Focus

Jose Bove, the French anti-globalisation campaigner was sentenced to three months in prison for his attack on a McDonald's fast food outlet in August last year. The sentence, handed down by a court in southern France, was tougher than that demanded by the prosecutor at the trial of the radical farmers' leader.

Bove and nine other members of his farmers' union, the Peasant Confederation, were accused of attacking a half-built McDonald's branch in the town, which lies in a region famous for its pungent Roquefort cheese, to protest against US duties on French cheeses. During his trial, Bove told the court that the attack was aimed at highlighting the injustices of the world trading system.

Bove said he would appeal against the guilty verdict, adding that the decision would not stop him from continuing his battle against multinationals such as McDonalds, which he claims pose a threat to small farmers, good food and a way of life.

The farmers' protests have struck a chord with people throughout Europe who fear continued economic growth and the increasing dominance of multinational corporations. McDonalds has been the focus of much criticism for its apparent arrogance in ignoring cultural differences through its imposition of standardised products worldwide.

1 Discuss whether it is possible for a multinational business such as McDonalds to operate a form of local globalisation whereby it recognises the cultural and social differences in the markets in which it trades.

Opportunities in the European Union

The European Union currently has 15 member states constituting a market of over 360m people – larger than the markets of Japan and the USA added together! Negotiations have already begun heralding the entry of new states into the union. Thirteen countries have made applications to join the EU. They are Bulgaria, Cyprus, the Czech Republic, Estonia, Hungary, Latvia, Lithuania, Malta, Poland, Romania, the Slovak Republic, Slovenia and Turkey. If all these countries become members the land area of the union will increase by 34% and its overall population will increase by 105m to 465m.

The enlargement of the EU offers businesses considerable opportunities. At its simplest there are over 100m extra consumers freely available to businesses in the UK and other established EU member states. Firms may expect to achieve increased sales and perhaps to benefit from economies of scale in supplying an enlarged market. High-technology and service industries (eg telecommunications and banking) are likely to face relatively little direct competition from these countries.

Furthermore, firms may choose to locate in countries such as Romania and Hungary to benefit from lower costs and, initially at least, fewer controls on business activity. The states of eastern Europe may prove particularly attractive to manufacturers seeking to expand or transfer their European productive capacity.

There is, of course, a downside to the expansions of the EU. Greater competition is likely to appear in some industries where the relatively undeveloped economies of eastern and southern Europe have an advantage. Analysts fear that western Europe's agricultural industry may be threatened by a surge of cheap imports from the new member states. The productive potential of Poland's agricultural industry alone is awesome. Jobs may also be lost in economies where labour is relatively expensive as the competition from the east increases.

Pan-European strategy

The increasing size of the EU market will place firms under greater pressure to develop strategies to sell their products successfully in up to 28 diverse countries. A single strategy is unlikely to suffice.

Managers responsible for developing strategies to sell products throughout Europe will need to consider a number of issues.

- The acceptance that Europe is not a single market, not even 28 countries, but a series of localities all of which are different in some way and need different products and different approaches to marketing. This means that differences in products and marketing campaigns are essential, making it more difficult to achieve economies of scale.
- Increasing Europe's borders has made it bigger, more varied and more difficult to sell to successfully as languages and cultures become more diverse.
- Market intelligence becomes less available as one moves east and south. This makes it more difficult for managers to assess market and production potential within the proposed new member states of the EU. For example, pricing can be a difficult issue: firms wish to generate the highest sales possible, but to avoid allegations of dumping cheap goods.

Business in Focus

Vodafone is the largest mobile phone company in the world and the UK's largest business. The company is aiming to maintain its pre-eminent position through an aggressive strategy of growth. Its intention is to dominate the global mobile telecommunications market.

The company has taken over a number of companies overseas as part of its expansion strategy. After a struggle Vodafone took over German mobile phone giant Mannesmann and has since agreed deals in most other major European countries to provide itself with a comprehensive European network. The final element was put in place following a deal whereby Vodafone purchased a 25% share in Swisscom – Switzerland's largest mobile phone company.

Alongside this Vodafone has pursued a global strategy negotiating joint ventures in South America and, in November 2000, took a £1.7bn stake in China Mobile (Hong Kong), the world's second biggest mobile phone operator with nearly 40m subscribers.

1 Business analysts were nervous about Vodafone's purchase of part of China Mobile (Hong Kong) and the company's share price fell when the deal was announced. Evaluate the case for and against a high-technology company seeking global domination.

Institutions of the European Union

Businesses trading within the European Union are likely to be affected by a number of institutions.

1 European Commission

The commission proposes EU policy and legislation that is then passed onto the Council of Ministers. The commission also executes the decisions taken by the Council of Ministers.

From 2005 the expected 28 member states of the EU will each have a single commissioner. All the commissioners are obliged to be independent and to act only in the interests of the EU.

2 Council of Ministers

This is the union's decision-making body. It agrees or adopts legislation on the basis of proposals from the commission. It meets in Brussels and, less frequently, in Luxembourg. Each member state acts as president of the council for six months. Meetings are held each April, June and October and one minister from each country attends. The minister attending from any country depends upon the matter under discussion. For example, if the union's budget is being discussed then finance ministers will attend.

Twice yearly, heads of government meet in what is known as the **European Council**. This was established in 1974 and sets broad guidelines for future action by the union.

3 European Parliament

The European Parliament meets in Strasbourg in eastern France. It has 626 members (members of the European Parliament or MEPs) of whom 87 are from the UK. The Parliament's opinion is needed on proposals before the council can adopt them. It is a supervisory body with the power to approve and dismiss the European Commission. The Parliament votes on the commission's programmes and monitors day-to-day management of European policies. In spite of this the Parliament currently has little authority or power.

4 European Court of Justice

The Court of Justice consists of 15 judges – one from each member state. The court rules on interpretation and application of EU legislation. Its aim is to ensure that the law is observed in line with the Treaty of Rome. The court also deals with disputes between member states. Judgements from the court are binding in each member state and its rulings take primacy over national legislation.

5 European Central Bank

In January 1999, the European Central Bank (ECB), based in Frankfurt in Germany, took responsibility for the conduct of monetary policy in the 11 countries taking part in the first wave of European Monetary Union (EMU). The bank sets interest rates for the countries using the single currency, the euro. It also is the sole issuer of Europe's currency, the euro. The UK has not yet decided to join the euro and does not have a say in the running of the bank.

The single European currency

On 1 January 1999 a single European currency – the euro – was introduced into 11 European Union countries. The UK has delayed a decision on when (or if) to join the single currency. The 11 countries have locked the foreign exchange values of their national currencies to the euro and share the new currency. Euro notes and coins will become available on 1 January 2002. By 30 June 1992 old banknotes and coins will be withdrawn from circulation.

*P*OINTS TO PONDER

Vauxhall, the car manufacturer, estimates that the UK's failure to sign up for the euro is costing the company £10m a year in currency transaction costs.

The 11 countries will also share a single interest rate, set by the European Central Bank (ECB), and a single foreign exchange rate policy. The ECB will be responsible for the monetary policy of these 'euro zone' countries.

The single currency will sharpen competition throughout Europe and it will influence the markets in three important ways:

1 **cheaper transaction costs**. The single currency will allow countries in the euro zone to trade with each other within changing currencies. This will reduce (but not remove) the transaction costs. It will cost less for companies to make payments between countries within the euro zone. Firms in the euro zone will notice the greatest difference. However, businesses from outside the euro zone which trade with companies inside it will also notice the effects.

2 **stable exchange rates**. The single currency will remove exchange rates between countries in the euro zone. This may lead to better decision making for its companies. If UK companies purchase products priced in euro the exchange rate risk may be transferred to them.

3 **transparent price differences**. The single currency will make price differences in the countries in the euro zone more obvious. This may affect companies who charge different prices for their products in countries within the euro zone. On the other hand, companies buying from the euro zone will be able to compare prices more easily. Either way, this will intensify competition.

Business in Focus

Various UK businesses have already been affected by the adoption of the euro by 11 EU states, in spite of the UK's indecision over whether and when to join:

■ **exporters and importers**: UK exporters and importers are already using the euro. Even exporters used to quoting in sterling have been asked to quote in euros from customers in the euro zone

■ **multinationals**: Some multinationals that operate in Europe have used the euro since 1 January 1999, to simplify their accounts and finances. Some have required their UK suppliers to use the euro too

■ **UK firms in supply chains**: Many UK firms find themselves being asked to deal in euros if they are in supply chains headed by multinational companies

■ **retail banking**: Most banks offer euro accounts for businesses

■ **wholesale financial markets**: Financial markets started to use the euro instead of the currencies it replaced on 1 January 1999

■ **subsidiaries**: Subsidiaries owned by a parent company based in the euro zone have found that its group's accounts changed to the euro.

Progress questions

1 What is meant by the term business strategy?
(3 marks)

2 Explain two ways in which a UK-based manufacturing business, trading throughout the EU, might be affected by a fall in UK interest rates.
(7 marks)

3 Outline why a business would be more likely to monitor long-term changes in interest rates.
(7 marks)

4 Explain the circumstances in which inflation may pose problems for businesses.
(8 marks)

5 Examine the ways in which an international airline may respond to the threat of a prolonged and deep slump.
(9 marks)

6 Consider the possible responses of a large insurance company to a steady fall in the rate of unemployment.
(8 marks)

7 Explain **two** factors determining the international competitiveness of a business that are beyond the control of that business.
(6 marks)

8 Outline why some groups are fiercely opposed to the process of globalisation.
(6 marks)

9 Explain two ways in which a firm might need to alter its marketing when adopting a pan-European strategy.
(7 marks)

10 Outline why the adoption of the euro by the UK would place the country's businesses under more intense competitive pressure.
(8 marks)

Analysis and evaluation questions

1 'Rapid rates of economic growth bring few benefits to businesses and cause great problems.' To what extent do you agree with this statement? *(15 marks)*

2 Analyse the ways in which a small East Anglian food processing business might be affected if the UK decides to adopt the euro.
(12 marks)

3 The chief executive of a car manufacturing business recently commented that the major determinant of her company's international competitiveness was the exchange rate of the pound. Critically evaluate this statement.
(15 marks)

4 Some multinationals such as Sony and, more recently Coca-Cola, have adopted the principle of global localisation recognising that markets across the globe have distinct differences. Discuss the importance of this approach in the twenty-first century.
(15 marks)

5 Examine the importance of stable interest rates to a firm trading throughout Europe.
(12 marks)

Case study

In 2001 the management team at Nissan reached a very important decision: the new Nissan Micra is to be built in the UK preserving many thousands of jobs in the north-east of England. The workforce at Nissan has agreed to a new, more flexible shift pattern. The company intends to boost production gradually to half a million vehicles per year, making the factory the largest car assembly operation in the UK, and one of the largest in Europe. The additional labour required will come mainly from using existing employees more efficiently.

Nissan's factory in Sunderland is the most productive car plant in western Europe. It is highly regarded and highly efficient. Businesses such as Nissan, who opt to locate in the UK, also receive other benefits, in spite of complaining about the level of bureaucracy. The UK has a very flexible labour market and a significant lack of laws relating to businesses when compared with other countries in the EU. This factor makes it much easier for firms in the UK to change the scale of their organisation.

In spite of the advantages of locating in the UK, a grant of £40m from the UK government was required to help ensure that the Micra was made in the UK. Furthermore, Nissan is looking to protect sales in Europe from changes in the value of the euro by purchasing a high proportion of the car's components from the euro zone.

The company expects the UK to continue to enjoy steady rates of economic growth over the next few years, bringing a range of benefits to the company. Nissan's decision has also gone some way to restore confidence in the UK's car manufacturing industry.

1 Explain what is meant by the phrase '... the most productive car plant in western Europe'. *(6 marks)*

2 Analyse how locating in the UK might contribute to the international competitiveness of Nissan. *(12 marks)*

3 **a)** Explain why purchasing a high proportion of components from the euro zone might protect Nissan from changes in the value of the euro against the pound. *(6 marks)*

b) To what extent is Nissan able to protect itself from exchange rate fluctuations? *(10 marks)*

4 Discuss the advantages and disadvantages to Nissan of increasing its output in an economy where unemployment is already low and more economic growth is forecast. *(16 marks)*

GOVERNMENT POLICIES AFFECTING BUSINESSES

Starting points

The topics covered in this unit were not a part of the AS specification. However, it is worthwhile reading the units in the AS text on competition, interest rates and exchange rates, and inflation and unemployment to provide a background to a study of government policies. In particular it is worth revisiting the unit on the business cycle that explains the fluctuations that normally occur in the level of the UK's economic activity over time. Many of the government's policies are designed to dampen the fluctuations that occur as a result of the business cycle. Others are intended to regulate the degree of competition within markets. Reading these units will help you to understand the economic objectives that the government targets in its management of the economy.

Introduction

Key terms

Economic policy: *a series of actions (such as changing interest rates and altering rates of taxation) through which the authorities attempt to create the best possible economic environment for businesses and individuals.*

The **economy**: *the complex interaction of millions of consumers, thousands of businesses and governments in supplying a wide range of goods and services.*

Economic activity: *the level of production, spending and employment occurring in an economy at a given point in time.*

Balance of payments: *a record of a country's trade and financial transactions with the rest of the world over a specified period of time, normally a year.*

Balance of payments (current account): *a financial record of a nation's trade in goods and services with the rest of the world over a specified period of time, normally a year.*

The operation of the UK's economy affects everyone and every business in the country. Changes in the level of production, employment or prices can have significant consequences for managers, for employees and for consumers. However, we cannot consider the UK economy in isolation. The UK is a part of the wider EU economy and is an important component of the global economy that is assuming ever greater importance. Not surprisingly the government has a number of objectives for the economy and all of its policies are intended to fulfil these objectives.

As early as 1945 the government had established economic objectives that still broadly apply today. These objectives are as follows:

- price stability. This means controlling the rate of inflation as measured by the retail price index. In the 1980s the UK suffered high rates of inflation, but they have declined steadily since that time. Since 2000 inflation has been around 2.5–3%. Having an inflation rate below that of other nations offers firms a potential price advantage

- steady and sustained growth in the economy allowing greater levels of production. Economic growth offers firms and individuals the potential for increased incomes and greater prosperity. Most western economies (including the UK) aim for a growth rate of 3–4%, although some developing economies such as Singapore have achieved annual rates in excess of 10%

- a low rate of unemployment. It is impossible to have everyone in the economy employed. Unemployment in 2001 is hovering around the 1m mark, a relatively low figure when compared with over 3m unemployed in the 1980s. Unemployment represents a major waste of resources by an economy

- a balanced balance of payments avoiding long-term deficits and surpluses. Governments usually aim to avoid deficits on the current account of the balance of payments. This means the value of goods and services sold overseas should at least be equal to the value of imports of goods and services. On occasions governments seek to avoid the exchange rate rising which can contribute to a balance of payments deficit on the current account.

The Bank of England has responsibility for operating some of the government's economic policies, which we shall consider in more detail later in this unit. The bank recently restated the government's economic objectives.

The Government's central economic policy objective is to achieve high and stable levels of growth and employment. Price stability is a precondition for these high and stable levels of employment and growth . . . In the past inflation has contributed to the UK's poor economic performance, not least by holding back the long-term investment that is the foundation for a successful economy.

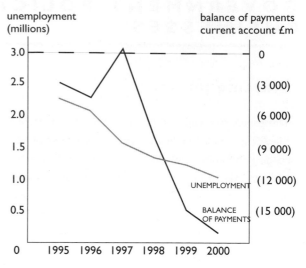

Figure 6.6 *Performance of the UK economy, unemployment and the balance of payments 1995–2000 The figures for the balance of payments relate to the current account only (imports and exports of goods and services), showing the net balance in £m. A negative figure indicates greater expenditure on imports compared with earnings from export sales. The unemployment data relates to the number claiming unemployment benefit on an annual average.*

www.statistics.gov.uk and Labour Market Trends, January 2001

Figures 6.5 and 6.6 illustrate the performance of the UK economy over recent years. Most governments would be satisfied if they could manage the economy to achieve the following targets in relation to the economy:

- the rate of inflation below the government's 2001 target of 2.5% annually
- less than 5% of the workforce unemployed
- steady economic growth at rates of 2–3% each year
- avoiding large deficits on the current account of the balance of payments as a result of the value of imports of goods and services exceeding exports of the same.

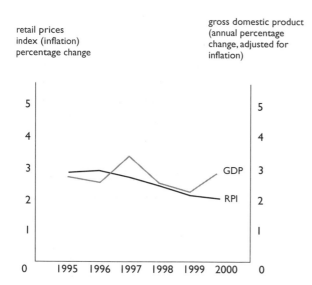

Figure 6.5 *Performance of the UK economy, GDP and inflation 1995–2000*
The data for GDP (gross domestic product) provides an indication of the growth occurring in the UK economy over the period in question. The data shows the annual percentage increase compared with the previous year. Inflation is measured by the retail prices index (RPI). This also shows the percentage increase, year on year.

www.statistics.gov.uk

However, managing the economy to achieve these objectives simultaneously is not an easy task. Many governments over recent years have failed to achieve these objectives. In part this is because in introducing policies to attain one objective, others become less achievable. There is a trade-off as illustrated in figure 6.7. Government economic policies designed to achieve objectives such as higher rates of economic growth and reductions in unemployment can have undesirable consequences. A consequence of higher growth and lower unemployment might be increasing inflation as shortages of raw materials, factories and offices as well as skilled labour force up prices. Another result might be increasing imports as individuals and consumers spend increasing sums of money on imports causing a balance of payments problem.

Possible objectives	TYPE OF GOVERNMENT POLICY	possible objectives
low unemployment		price stability
	expansionary government ← policies increasing level of economic activity	contractionary government → policies reducing level of economic activity
high rates of economic growth		'balanced' balance of payments (current account)

Figure 6.7 *Government policies and economic objectives*

Government policies

> **Key terms**
>
> **Direct taxes**: *taxes on income and wealth, eg income tax, corporation tax and inheritance tax.*
> **Indirect taxes**: *taxes on spending, eg value added tax.*
> **Interest rates**: *the price of borrowed money.*
> **Fiscal policy**: *the use of taxation and public expenditure to manage the level of economic activity.*
> **Monetary policy**: *controlling the amount of money and/or interest rates within the economy in order to achieve the desired level of economic activity.*
> **Privatisation**: *the process of transferring organisations from the state to the ownership and control of individuals and other businesses.*

The government operates a number of different policies with the aim of providing the best possible economic environment for UK businesses. This entails adjusting the level of activity in the economy to avoid the excesses of booms and slumps. The government's economic policies can be divided into two categories:

1 monetary policy. Using this policy the government (or the Bank of England acting on its behalf) manipulates the amount of money and/or interest rates within the economy in order to achieve the desired level of economic activity.
2 fiscal policy. This refers to the government's use of taxation and public expenditure to manage the economy. By adjusting the levels of taxation and government expenditure, the government can alter the level of activity within the economy.

> **EXAMINER'S ADVICE**
>
> *It is important to avoid getting too involved in the detail of economic policy. Examiners in business studies set questions on the impact of economic policies on business and their responses to a changing economic environment. Your study should reflect this.*

Monetary policy

This type of economic policy involves adjusting the amount of money in circulation and hence the level of spending and economic activity. Monetary policy can make use of one or more of the following:

- altering interest rates
- controlling the money supply
- manipulating the exchange rate.

Although at times all three techniques have been used, more recently governments have tended to rely upon altering interest rates to manage the economy. Since May 1997 the Monetary Policy Committee of the Bank of England has had responsibility for setting interest rates. The Monetary Policy Committee sets interest rates monthly with the aim of achieving the government's target for inflation whilst attaining long-term growth in the economy. Table 6.5 highlights the aims that may lie behind the authorities altering interest rates and, importantly, the implications for individuals and businesses.

rising interest rates	falling interest rates
The likely objectives of increasing interest rates include the following:	Reductions in interest rates may be introduced with the following objectives in mind:
■ reducing the level of consumer spending	■ reducing levels of unemployment
■ limiting inflationary pressure in the economy	■ stimulating the level of production in the economy
■ slowing the level of economic growth (as measured by GDP)	■ promoting exports sales by reducing the exchange value of the pound
■ avoiding increasing imports creating a deficit on the balance of payments	■ increasing rates of economic growth in the economy
In general higher interest rates will assist in dampening down an economic boom.	Reducing interest rates can assist an economy in recovering from a slump.
The implications of rising interest rates are considerable:	The consequences for businesses and individuals of falling interest rates include the following:
■ many businesses may experience falling sales as consumers increase savings	■ demand and sales are likely to increase
■ demand for products purchased on credit may decline significantly	■ production is likely to be stimulated by increasing employment
■ businesses cancelling or deferring investment plans	■ export sales of price sensitive products may increase whilst imports become less competitive
■ firms reduce borrowing by eg cutting levels of stocks	■ businesses may undertake increased investment promoting growth in industries such as construction.
■ increased value of sterling increasing the prices of exports while reducing import prices.	

Table 6.5 *Changes in interest rates – objectives and implications*

Broadly speaking, rises in interest rates depress the level of economic activity and reductions promote an expansion of economic activity.

Effects of changes in interest rates

The impact of rising interest rates will depend upon the size of the change as well as the initial rate. A small increase at a relatively high level of rates will have little impact whilst a larger increase from a low base rate will have a significant impact.

Not all businesses are affected equally. We can identify several categories of businesses that are particularly susceptible to changes in interest rates.

■ Small firms are often affected greatly by changes in interest rates as they have smaller financial reserves and a relatively greater need for borrowing. The Bank of England estimates that every 1% rise in interest rates costs the UK's 1.5m small firms an extra £200m in interest rate payments. Significant rises in interest rates can lead to substantial increases in bankruptcies amongst small firms.

■ Even larger firms with high levels of borrowing (and therefore high levels of gearing) can be affected by alterations in interest rates. For example, a rise in rates can lead to a hefty increase in interest payments forcing firms to reduce costs elsewhere or to pass on the extra expenses in the form of higher prices – if this is possible. Alternatively a cut in interest rates offers a substantial reduction in expenses to such firms improving their competitiveness.

■ Firms trading overseas are affected by alterations in interest rates. Rising interest rates tend to lead to an increase in the exchange rates as individuals and businesses overseas purchase sterling to invest in UK financial institutions to benefit from higher rates. A fall in interest rates would have the opposite effect. The relationship is shown in detail in figure 6.2 in the previous unit.

*P*OINTS TO PONDER

The Bank of England held interest rates steady at 6% in December 2000 for the tenth time in a row, marking the longest period of stable borrowing rates since the 1980s. This follows a period in which the bank was criticised for changing rates too regularly.

other economic variables	rising interest rates	falling interest rates
unemployment	unemployment increases as levels of production decline	unemployment declines as the level of economic activity rises
inflation	falling demand and output reduces inflationary pressure	increasing output and spending causes prices to rise fuelling inflation
economic growth	will slow as businesses cut output and investment and spending declines	is stimulated by cheaper loans and rising business investment and increasing consumer expenditure
exchange rates	value of the pound is likely to rise	exchange value of the pound generally falls
balance of payments (current account)	fewer imports purchased improving the current account balance	increased spending will 'suck in' imports worsening current account balance

Table 6.6 *Interest rates and other economic variables*

However, it is not only the direct effects of altering interest rates that affect businesses. The use of interest rate policy by the authorities can have a profound impact upon the general economic environment in which businesses operate. The Bank of England's Monetary Policy Committee changes interest rates to assist the government in achieving its economic objectives. This means that altering rates affects the level of unemployment, inflation and growth existing in the economy. They also change managers' expectations of these key economic variables affecting their day-to-day and strategic decisions.

Table 6.6 illustrates the relationship that exists between the level of interest rates and key economic variables such as economic growth and unemployment.

Fiscal policy

Fiscal policy is the use of government expenditure and taxation as a means of controlling the level of activity within the economy. In particular a government's fiscal policy is the relationship between the level of government expenditure and the amount raised in taxation in any given year. The fiscal year runs from 6 April to 5 April the following year.

The balance between taxation and government expenditure is determined annually when the Chancellor of the Exchequer announces the annual budget. The government can operate two broad types of fiscal policy:

1 expansionary fiscal policy. This entails cutting taxation and/or increasing government expenditure on items such as health, education, social services, defence and transport. The effect will be to increase the amount the government borrows to fund its expenditure (known as the public sector borrowing requirement or PSBR) or to reduce the surplus held in the government's coffers at the end of the fiscal year.
2 contractionary fiscal policy. This is brought about by reducing government expenditure or increasing taxation, or by both policies simultaneously. The effect is to increase the government's PSBR or to reduce its surplus on its budget for the fiscal year.

Figure 6.8 summarises the operation of fiscal policy. Fiscal policy can help to stabilise the economy (avoiding the worst effects of the business cycle) through the operation of the 'automatic stabilisers'. For example, lower unemployment when the level of economic activity is high means temporarily lower social security spending, higher income tax receipts and higher National Insurance contributions. Higher company profits generate higher corporation tax receipts, and higher spending by consumers yields higher VAT receipts and excise duties. These factors together will have a contractionary effect, dampening an economic boom.

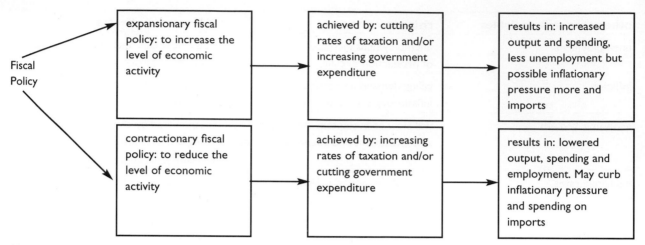

Figure 6.8 *Operation of fiscal policy*

Tax and expenditure policies can have immediate effects on the level of economic activity, although the precise effects will depend upon the types of tax altered and the nature of government expenditure:

- **direct taxes**. These are taxes on income and expenditure and include income tax and corporation tax (levied on company profits). Direct taxes take a larger amount from individuals earning high salaries and companies announcing handsome profits. The government can forecast with some accuracy the effects arising from an increase (or reduction) in income tax. Although the overall effect may be predicted, the implications for individual businesses will vary according to the type of product supplied. Firms supplying luxury goods (long-haul foreign holidays, for example) might be significantly affected by a change in income tax rates, especially for those earning higher incomes, whilst those selling basic foodstuffs may be relatively unaffected

- **indirect taxes**. VAT (value added tax) and other taxes on spending are classified as indirect. Changes in this type of taxation can have a rapid effect on the level of economic activity, although its effects are difficult to predict. An increase in VAT will cut consumer spending, reducing demand for goods and services and eventually lower the level of economic activity. However, the extent of the fall in demand will depend upon the price elasticity of demand for the goods in question. Consumers will continue to purchase essentials such as fuel and food, although

demand for products associated with DIY, for example, may decline. An important side effect of increasing indirect taxes is that it is inflationary.

*P*OINTS TO PONDER

The European Union announced in January 2001 that the UK government's fiscal policy would need to alter significantly if the euro is to be adopted. A report by the European Parliament argued that the UK would have to cut public spending substantially or raise income tax by 2 pence in the pound.

Government expenditure is the other half of fiscal policy. Governments may spend more in two broad categories:

1. **transfer payments**. This is expenditure on unemployment benefit, pensions and other social security payments. Changes in expenditure on these items will have a rapid impact as they are received by relatively poor members of society who will most likely spend the increase or cut back if necessary almost immediately. An increase in transfer payments often results in substantial increases in demand for basic goods such as food, public transport and gas.

2. **the infrastructure**. Governments improve the infrastructure though their spending on housing, roads and flood protection. Investment in these areas can increase the level of economic activity by boosting demand for the services of

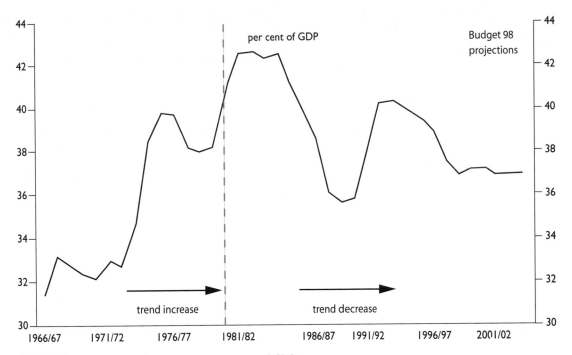

Figure 6.9 *Public sector expenditure as a percentage of GDP*

HM Treasury [www.treasury.gov.uk]

construction firms whilst reducing costs for other firms. A new road, for example, might cut a business's transport costs. This, however, is a much slower method of altering the level of economic activity.

Fiscal policy has not been an important part of the economic armoury of recent governments. Government expenditure fluctuates with the business cycle because of the automatic stabilisers discussed earlier, but generally the trend has been to have a relatively neutral fiscal policy (neither expansionary nor contractionary) and to rely upon the use of interest rates to control the economy. Figure 6.9 shows that there has been a decreasing trend in public expenditure over recent years, reflecting a change in philosophy about government intervention in the economy and the lessening importance of fiscal policy.

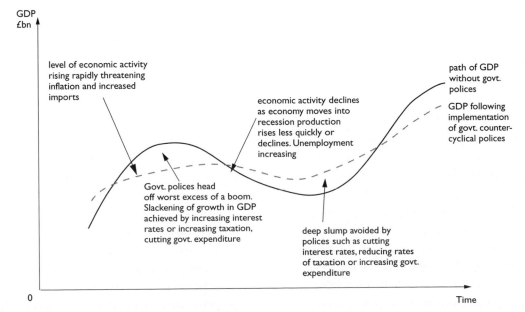

Figure 6.10 *Government economic policies at work*

EU and government policies

At the time of writing the UK has not reached a decision on when to join the European single currency – the euro. The government states that it will adopt the euro 'when the conditions are right'. To operate a single currency in 15 or more countries requires the economies to be at similar stages in the business cycle and to pursue common economic policies to avoid their economies becoming unsynchronised. When (and if) the UK does adopt the euro the government at Westminster will lose a substantial degree of control over economic policies. The European Central Bank (the EU's equivalent of the Bank of England) will set interest rates for all member states. Fiscal policy may be decided domestically, but will be subject to the overall control of the EU.

Privatisation

This is the process of transferring organisations from the state to the ownership and control of individuals and other businesses. In the 1980s and 1990s many major state enterprises were sold into the *private sector*, shown as follows.

1981	Cable & Wireless
1982	Amersham International, Britoil
1983	Associated British Ports
1984	Enterprise Oil, Jaguar, British Telecom
1986	British Gas
1987	British Airways, Rolls Royce, British Airports Authority
1988	British Steel
1989	Water companies
1990	Electricity distribution companies
1991	Electricity generators

By November 1990, one in four of the population owned shares and more than 40 former state-owned businesses had been privatised, a process which affected more than 600 000 workers in former nationalised industries. The UK began a worldwide fashion for privatising former state-owned businesses; since 1990 the policy that has been copied by governments across the globe. The arguments in favour of privatisation are formidable.

■ By removing potentially inefficient monopolies privatisation offers consumers the possibilities of lower prices and better-quality products. Businesses in competitive markets cannot afford to be inefficient. The policy is based on the unshakeable belief in the superiority of private enterprise.

■ Private businesses are more likely to pursue long-term policies to increase the prosperity of the businesses, to the benefit of all in society. In contrast, the objectives of the former nationalised industries were unclear and inconsistent – often little more than breaking even.

■ The process of privatisation has provided huge sums of revenue for the government. By 2000 the figure exceeded £40bn. This has enabled the government to reduce its borrowing and to cut taxes. The proceeds from privatisation played an important part in creating a society in which enterprise was valued and rewarded.

*P*OINTS TO PONDER

The policy of privatisation has reached the far corners of the globe. Iraq, under dictator Saddam Hussein, has officially approved a policy of privatisation as a means of avoiding sanctions imposed by the United Nations.

However, the drawbacks of privatisation have become increasingly apparent.

■ Critics have argued that privatisation has not, in fact, resulted in more efficient industries. The establishment of watchdogs such as OFGAS and OFTEL have highlighted that left to their own devices the newly privatised companies might exploit consumers through excessive prices and poor-quality products. Furthermore, the well-publicised problems facing the UK's railways have provided further ammunition for those opposed to privatisation.

■ Some economists have argued that having thousands of UK citizens as shareholders in privatised businesses will not encourage long-term strategies to be adopted by the businesses. Shareholders, having limited understanding of business, will look for a quick return. This will encourage managers to maximise short-term profits – a policy not necessarily in the long-term interests of the company or the economy.

The perceived shortcomings of privatisation have led to a mild backlash against the policy. Countries such as New Zealand have created new nationalised industries, and even California has taken steps in this direction. Government proposals to privatise the London Underground and the UK's air traffic control have encountered much opposition. It may be that nationalisation is no longer a dirty word.

Government intervention

> **Key terms**
>
> **Government intervention**: the involvement of the state in business matters such as passing legislation, controlling business activities, supporting businesses and shaping the economic environment in which businesses trade.
>
> **Laissez-faire**: a policy in which governments reduce taxes and spend less on supporting the activities of businesses.

The issue of privatisation is at the forefront of the debate about the extent to which the government should intervene in the economy. The Conservative governments of the 1980s and 1990s argued that the state's role in the economy should be minimised to allow markets and businesses to operate with the maximum degree of freedom. In part this was achieved through the policy of privatisation, but also by the reduction in government subsidies and grants to industry and by legislation limiting the state's role in business matters. For instance, wages councils (responsible for setting the wages of many low-paid workers) were abolished and regulations governing markets such as telecommunications and financial services were relaxed allowing new suppliers and greater competition. This approach to managing the business environment is described as laissez-faire and puts faith in a greater degree of self-regulation by businesses.

Business in Focus: minimum wage successful

Sceptics who predicted that job losses would be the result of implementing the national minimum wage have been proved wrong. More than 2m workers have benefited from the new pay floor, especially women and part-time workers. The government has taken the decision to increase the wage to £3.70 per hour, and meet the trade union demand to increase the rate.

Even the Confederation of British Industry has admitted that the increase in pay rates has not affected businesses in the ways it expected. They have cautiously supported a rise of 20 pence in the rate. The question is whether the government will follow other European nations in introducing a mechanism whereby the minimum wage is automatically upgraded in line with average earnings.

In the meantime the minimum wage has been declared a success: raising the incomes and living standards of the poorest in society without damaging the competitiveness of UK businesses.

1 Discuss whether the apparent success of the minimum wage suggests that the government should play a larger part in establishing pay rates for other groups such as directors.

There are, not surprisingly, advantages and disadvantages to businesses arising from trading under a government that takes a laissez-faire approach to economic management.

EXAMINER'S ADVICE

The case for and against government intervention in the economy is an integrating topic within A level business studies. It is a topic that ranges across the entire external influences syllabus, bringing together topics such as the economic, legal and political environments.

Businesses benefit through less interference in their activities. Government intervention tends to raise costs (insisting on the employment of safety officers, for example) reducing the competitiveness of UK businesses. This can be a major handicap for firms operating in highly price-competitive markets where small cost differentials can lead to substantial loss of sales. By removing the requirement to pay national rates of pay, wages may fall in poor regions such as the north of England and Wales attracting new businesses and making existing businesses more competitive. Supporters of the laissez-faire approach argue that the UK has been extremely successful in attracting overseas producers because of the lack of regulation of businesses. They contend that governments cannot prevent the operation of global market forces, and that it is a waste of money to try. Finally, the laissez-faire approach helps to promote an entrepreneurial society in which individuals take responsibility for their own economic welfare and are more creative and hard working as a result to the benefit of all in society.

Business in Focus: Corus closes down amid protests

Corus, the Anglo-Dutch steel maker, provoked the fury of the government, MPs and trade unions yesterday by announcing more than 6000 job losses aimed at stemming losses running at more than £1m a day.

Ministers led a blistering attack on the company after being kept in the dark until yesterday morning about the scale of the redundancies. But Sir Brian Moffat, Corus chairman, defended his actions. He said 'We were not prepared to go into details with the government before first talking to our employees.'

The government urged the company to reconsider, but Corus insisted that the cuts were needed to make it competitive again. Wales will be hardest hit, with 1340 redundancies at the huge plant in Llanwern, near Newport, in south Wales. The nearby factory at Ebbw Vale will close altogether with the loss of 780 jobs, while redundancies will also hit factories at Shotton in north Wales and at Redcar in Teesside.

Stephen Byers, the trade and industry secretary, described the closure as a 'bitter blow' to the communities affected. But the government was left on the sidelines, unable to soften the blow, after Corus refused to give ministers advance notice of its plans and rejected all offers of help.

Downing Street said the company's behaviour meant that ministers had not been able to make plans for emergency action to help those being made redundant. Moffat blamed the strength of the pound against the euro and overcapacity in the steel industry in Europe for the cutbacks.

The Guardian

I To what extent does the trend towards globalisation mean that the economic policies of any single government are of little relevance to multinational businesses?

However, many individuals and groups oppose the laissez-faire style of economic management. They argue that it is vital that governments support struggling industries in poor regions to prevent heavy unemployment and poverty. The threatened closure of the Rover car manufacturing plant in the Midlands in 2000 would have led to thousands of job losses and much hardship. Governments should recognise that economic change is inevitable, and attempt to soften the blow of economic restructuring of this type. Allowing businesses to regulate their own activities with minimal interference from the authorities is likely to result in unscrupulous businesses exploiting workers (through low wages and poor conditions) and consumers – by charging excessive prices. Some controls, it is argued, are essential to prevent this happening, particularly where a business faces little competition and exploits its monopoly power.

POINTS TO PONDER

A laissez-faire approach has many implications. Top directors in the UK's biggest companies gave themselves pay rises of more than 26% in 1999 – ten times the rate of inflation. Over 30 executives earned more than £1m. The average pay received by the UK's best-paid executives was £960 000.

Progress questions

1 Explain the economic objectives pursued by UK governments over recent years. *(7 marks)*

2 Outline the difficulties a government might encounter when attempting to achieve its economic objectives simultaneously. *(7 marks)*

3 Distinguish between monetary policy and fiscal policy. *(4 marks)*

4 Outline the possible effects of a fall in interest rates on a business manufacturing consumer durables such as televisions and freezers. *(6 marks)*

5 Explain the general effects on the business community of an increase in interest rates. *(7 marks)*

6 Why might a fall in interest rates lead to a decline in the exchange value of the pound? *(4 marks)*

7 Outline how a government might use fiscal policy to increase the level of economic activity. *(7 marks)*

8 Explain why the effects of changes in indirect taxes may be difficult to predict. *(6 marks)*

9 State **two** advantages and **two** disadvantages arising as a result of the privatisation of the electricity supply industry. *(4 marks)*

10 Explain **two** arguments in favour of the government adopting a laissez-faire approach to economic management. *(6 marks)*

Analysis and evaluation questions

1 'Many businesses are relatively unaffected by changes in interest rates.' To what extent do you agree with this statement? *(15 marks)*

2 Examine the effects on a manufacturing firm trading throughout Europe of a significant fall in the level of interest rates in the UK. *(12 marks)*

3 Analyse whether fiscal policy can only be used by governments who believe in intervening in the operation of the economy. *(12 marks)*

4 Discuss whether privatisation is only of value if it creates competition within an industry. *(15 marks)*

5 'Government intervention to support "lame duck" businesses is pointless in the global economy. It cannot prevent the operation of international forces.' Critically evaluate this statement. *(15 marks)*

Case study

Rolls Royce has confirmed that it will be producing engines for super jumbo airliners following the announcement that the government has invested £250m in the project. The project to manufacture the engines is expected to cost over £1bn. The government's support for Rolls Royce comes 14 years after a Conservative government privatised the company. In this respect the decision represents a public move away from a laissez-faire approach to managing the economy.

The public money will safeguard 7000 jobs over the next few years, many in the Derby area. It will not, however, reverse the 1300 redundancies planned for the company's Coventry factory. Workers in Coventry have confirmed that they will take strike action over the proposed job losses.

The government support must be confirmed by the European Commission and is sure to provoke criticism from competitors such as General Electric in the USA. A government spokesperson commented that the investment proved 'the government's commitment to help highly-skilled high-tech companies become more competitive internationally'.

Rolls Royce chairman John Rose said moving ahead with the production of engines for the super jumbo would secure 7000 jobs directly and indirectly. A spokesman later added that 70% of Rolls Royce engines were sourced outside the company and at least 20% of the content of an engine historically came from the USA. Rolls Royce hopes to use the public money to help it to attract further money from the private sector.

The Guardian

1 a) Explain what is meant by '… a move away from a laissez-faire approach to managing the economy'. *(4 marks)*

   b) Discuss whether the government's decision to offer financial support to Rolls Royce indicates that the policy of privatisation has failed. *(11 marks)*

2 Outline the effects of the government's action upon the level of economic activity in the UK. *(8 marks)*

3 Examine the reasons why the government may have decided to support Rolls Royce in this way. *(11 marks)*

4 Discuss whether government support for Rolls Royce will genuinely make the business 'more competitive internationally'. *(16 marks)*

SOCIAL ENVIRONMENT

Starting points

This section builds upon the work started at AS level. As part of the AS external influences module we considered the nature of social responsibilities and the groups within society to whom firms are responsible. This unit briefly recaps this information before building upon it. It also develops the issue of ethical behaviour within business. It would be of value to re-read the AS section on ethics to reacquaint yourself with what constitutes ethical behaviour and its potential for conflict with profits.

The remaining sections of this unit represent entirely new material. It examines environmental factors in the form of constraints (including the activities of pressure groups) as well as opportunities. This section will include consideration of social audits. Finally the unit will cover political change.

Key terms

Shareholder concept: the main responsibility of managers is to the shareholders (or other owners) of the company.

Social responsibilities are the duties a business has towards employees, customers, society and the environment.

Stakeholders are individuals or groups with a direct interest in an organisation's performance.

Stakeholder concept: view that the managers of businesses are responsible to a wide range of groups including their customers, employees, suppliers and society in general.

Introduction

Stakeholders are individuals or groups within society who have an interest in an organisation's operation and performance. Stakeholders include shareholders, employees, customers, suppliers, creditors and the local community. The interest that stakeholders have in a business will vary according to the nature of the group.

EXAMINER'S ADVICE

Do not confuse the stakeholders and shareholders. Stakeholders is a much broader term encompassing various groups including, of course, shareholders.

Over recent years businesses have become much more aware of the expectations of stakeholder groups. In the past managers were expected to operate businesses largely in the interest of the shareholders. A growing awareness of business activities and the rise of consumerism has complicated the task of the management team. Today's managers have to attempt to meet the conflicting demands of a number of stakeholder groups.

Social responsibility

Social responsibility is a business philosophy that emphasises that firms should behave as good citizens. They should not merely operate within the law, but should consider the effects of their activities on society as a whole.

Meeting social responsibilities has many implications for businesses:

- taking into account the impact of their activities on the local community – protecting employment and avoiding noise pollution, for instance
- producing in a way that avoids pollution or the reckless use of finite resources
- treating employees fairly and not simply meeting the demands of employment legislation
- considering the likely sources of supplies (and whether they are sustainable) and the ways in which suppliers meet their social responsibilities.

Some businesses willingly accept these responsibilities partly because their managers want to

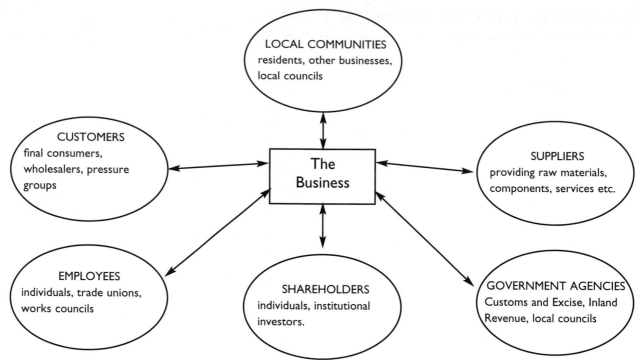

Figure 6.11 *Examples of a business's stakeholders*

do so, partly because they fear a negative public image. It can be argued that socially responsible behaviour can pay off for businesses in the long term, but may entail additional short-term expenditure.

POINTS TO PONDER

The country's largest insurance company, CGNU, is putting the finishing touches to a new policy. Called 'socially responsible investment', it means that companies in which the group has invested £200bn will in future be judged on how they make their money – and not just how much they make.

Areas of social responsibility

The nature of a business's social responsibility will vary according to the nature of the business. A petrochemicals company is more likely to be concerned with polluting the environment than a building society. On the other hand, in an age of rapid developments in information technology, building societies may see their social responsibility to be the maintenance of employment. We can

Business in Focus

Consumerism has developed for a number of reasons. Advances in technology have meant that many modern goods are highly sophisticated. This has created a need for advice and support for consumers who often spend large sums of money on products such as computers and cars. This development has also been fuelled by fears about the growing power of big business and the possibility of this power being abused.

Consumerism has led to the creation of organisations to protect the consumer in many countries. An example of this type of organisation in the UK is the Consumer Association. They test new products and support members who have complaints about the behaviour of businesses or the quality of goods and services. The Consumer Association also publishes *Which?*, a magazine providing information on the comparative performance of a wide range of products.

1 In many markets, firms are becoming fewer and larger. In view of this, discuss whether the consumer is really becoming more powerful.

identify a number of key elements of social responsibility, beyond the responsibilities a business has to its shareholders.

1 Responsibilities to consumers

The consumer has become a force to be reckoned with over recent decades and this has been reflected in the development of consumerism. Increasingly consumers have been better informed about products and services and prepared to complain when businesses let them down. The rise of consumerism has meant that businesses have been required to behave more responsibly by looking after the interests of the consumer.

2 Responsibilities to employees

Businesses have a variety of responsibilities to their employees that are not a legal requirement. For

Business in Focus

Reebok, the second largest manufacturer of training shoes in the USA, has published a highly self-critical report on its Indonesian factories. The company, based in Massachusetts, employs 10 000 workers in Indonesia.

Reebok employed an independent organisation to conduct the report into working conditions in its Far East factories. The report identified a number of problems:

■ health and safety issues including labels missing from dangerous chemicals, and workers suffering skin complaints due to inadequate protective clothing
■ poor working conditions with insufficient toilets for employees
■ communication problems: safety notices were written in English, for example
■ few women in senior management positions, even though 80% of the workforce is female.

Reebok has spent £300 000 improving conditions in its Indonesian factories and is continuing to review other overseas factories. Reebok is clear about the reasons for publicising the report and highlighting its desire to improve conditions. 'As concern for human rights issues grows among consumers,

particularly younger consumers, we believe our leadership and reputation will translate into greater preference for our brands and products.'

The Guardian

1 Explain **two** advantages that Reebok might receive as a result of establishing a factory in Indonesia.
2 Do you think that Reebok has taken this action because it is genuinely concerned about its employees in Indonesia, or because it hopes to improve its profits in the future by appearing socially responsible to informed and caring western consumers?

example, firms should provide their employees with training to develop their skills as fully as possible and make sure that the rights of employees in Third World countries (where employment legislation may not exist) are protected fully. This may mean paying higher wages and incurring additional employment costs.

3 Responsibilities to the local community

Firms can benefit from the goodwill of the local community. They can encourage this by meeting their responsibilities to this particular stakeholder group. This may entail providing secure employment, using local suppliers whenever possible and ensuring that the business's operation and possible expansion does not damage the local environment.

4 Responsibilities to customers

Customers are critical to businesses. Offering high-quality customer service, supplying high-quality products that are well designed and durable and at fair and reasonable prices should create satisfied customers and quite possibly generate repeat business.

5 Responsibilities to suppliers

Businesses can promote good relations with suppliers by paying promptly, placing regular orders and offering long-term contracts for supply. These are not legal requirements, and might result in higher prices for materials and components, but may also assist suppliers to meet their own responsibilities, eg in the maintenance of employment.

POINTS TO PONDER

A MORI poll conducted in 2000 revealed that 38% of senior business executives in 350 large UK companies believed that UK firms should pay more attention to social responsibilities. The equivalent figure for 1999 was 35%.

Business and social responsibilities

Stakeholder and shareholder concepts

The importance of social responsibility to businesses is a matter of considerable debate. Businesses accept the need to make a profit for their owners and the need to operate within the law. More contentious is the expectation that a competitive business will take into account the obligations it may have to society in general. This is known as the stakeholder concept whereby a business takes into account the needs of its stakeholders – and not just its shareholders.

In spite of the growing popularity of the stakeholder concept, there are opponents to the philosophy. A school of thought exists that supports what is known as the shareholder concept. This view advocates the management of businesses to meet their responsibilities to shareholders, by maximising profits. This should result in increasing share prices and higher dividend payments. The needs of other stakeholders are regarded as of secondary importance.

In what ways can businesses accept their social responsibilities?

Businesses can take a variety of decisions and actions allowing them to meet their responsibilities to their stakeholders in general.

■ For manufacturing businesses the impact of their sources of supply can be considerable. Using

Business in Focus: the ultimate shareholder view

Milton Friedman, the famous free market economist, and professor of economics at the University of Chicago holds extreme views on the shareholder/stakeholder division. Friedman has argued that a business can best meet its social responsibilities by making the largest possible profit and then using its resources as efficiently as possible whilst operating within the law. Friedman contends that any other approach will result in society suffering a lower standard of living, although this argument ignores that business activities impose many external costs on society such as pollution and noise.

sustainable sources for resources means that future generations will have access to the same materials. Body Shop International's refusal to use any materials that are unsustainable or any components that have been tested on animals reflects a sense of responsibility to many relatively poor Third World communities and to animals.

■ Many manufacturers have considerable potential to pollute the environment. Altering production processes (sometimes at considerable cost) can reduce or eliminate many forms of pollution. One of the UK's largest chemical firms, ICI, recently faced protests from pressure groups concerned about the scale of its pollution. The company has been cited as 'Britain's worst polluter'. ICI confirmed that it has reviewed production techniques and methods of waste disposal to minimise the possibility of further pollution.

■ Socially responsible firms put employees before profits. Maintaining employment, even when the level of sales is not sufficient to justify this, is an important means of fulfilling social responsibilities, as is the continuation of unprofitable factories to avoid creating unemployment blackspots. These types of policies are only really sustainable in the short term, unless the business in question is earning handsome profits elsewhere.

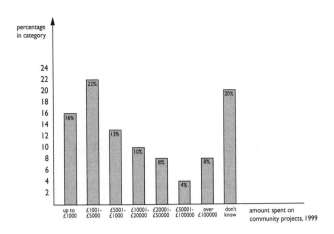

Figure 6.12 *Expenditure by small and medium-sized businesses in the UK on community projects, 1999*

Mori, Jan/Feb 2000

■ Choosing suppliers is an increasingly important issue for firms who are keen to confirm that their raw materials and components come from socially responsible firms. Many firms operate a code of conduct for suppliers, including restaurant chain McDonalds. The fast food company operates a code of conduct prohibiting suppliers from using child labour and insisting upon basic health and safety standards. The company has a contractual right to inspect suppliers' premises to ensure the code of conduct is implemented.

■ Supporting the local community is an important way of fulfilling social responsibilities. It can provide the public with a clear perception of the 'caring' side of modern businesses. Birmingham Midshires Building Society won an award in 2000 for its support for an imaginative scheme providing facilities for youngsters to play football after dark to discourage them from engaging in criminal activities. Over 70% of the UK's best-known companies (those making up the FTSE 100) are members of *Business in the Community*. This organisation exists to assist member companies in 'continually improving, measuring and reporting the impact that their business has on their environment, workplace, marketplace and community'.

POINTS TO PONDER

The Italian clothing firm Benetton faces a publicity storm following renewed allegations that a Turkish factory licensed to make its clothes has used child labour. An international trade union inquiry alleges that at least 25 children below Turkey's legal minimum working age of 14 have been employed at a textile factory in Istanbul. The supplier produces clothes carrying the Benetton label that earn £500 000 a year in royalties for the Italian company.

Why should businesses accept social responsibilities?

It is easy to argue that by meeting their social responsibilities businesses are likely to reduce profitability. Providing workers with ongoing training, investing in facilities for the local community, trading with suppliers who do not use cheap child labour and only engaging in non-polluting production techniques will all increase costs, reducing a business's profitability and limiting its international competitiveness.

POINTS TO PONDER

'In the future, the successful company will not be judged solely in terms of the financial bottom line. Some would argue that this is already the case. Responsibilities to the environment, to the health, safety and welfare of our staff, and to wider society will form an integral part of the way in which we do business.'

Dr Chris Fay, Shell UK chairman and chief executive

However, this is a relatively simple view and there are more subtle arguments in favour of businesses fulfilling their obligations to society.

■ Some businesses have a high profile with regard to issues of social responsibility. Thus the public sees Shell and BP as having enormous potential to pollute. The directors of these companies have recognised this and regard socially responsible behaviour as an important competitive weapon.

As an example Shell supports education and produces much valuable material for use in schools and colleges. In particular the company gives information on environmental matters. Clearly both Shell and BP hope that being seen to be socially responsible will improve their sales.

- Sometimes behaving in a socially responsible manner may reduce costs. Treating employees with respect and paying slightly above the going rate may improve motivation and performance and reduce labour turnover. For businesses where labour represents a high proportion of total costs (banking and insurance, for example) this could represent an important saving.

- In markets where little product differentiation occurs, adopting a socially responsible stance may improve sales and profits. The Co-operative Bank is alone in the banking sector in promoting its ethical and socially responsible views. In recent years its profits have risen significantly.

It may be that social responsibility might reduce profits in the short term, but over a longer timescale the marketing advantages may dominate and profits could increase.

Increasingly, however, analysts are not assessing businesses solely in terms of profits. It can be argued that businesses should also be judged in terms of their records on pollution, consideration of their employees and support for the community. A small proportion of businesses are engaging in social responsibility reporting. This form of reporting includes the costs to the business of acting in a socially responsible manner (charitable donations for example) and the benefits received, which are usually difficult to quantify in monetary terms. A few businesses include their social reports within their annual reports. A 'successful' business might not be the most profitable, but the one of most

Business in Focus: Marks & Spencer

UK clothing manufacturers were left reeling after M&S sacked William Baird, its fourth biggest supplier, putting 4360 UK jobs at risk and 2900 overseas. Peter Salsbury, M&S's chief executive, told its supplier of 30 years that it was ending its relationship with the company from next autumn. The decision affects 16 factories in the UK. Baird said it expected 'significant redundancies and restructuring costs'.

The news hit the whole clothing sector amid fears that other M&S suppliers would also lose business. A M&S spokesperson said 'We have been looking how we can get more buying efficiencies into the supply chain. This is overwhelmingly the largest consequence of the action we are taking.'

David Suddens, Baird's chief executive, said M&S's decision came as 'a bolt from the blue' and marked a watershed for the UK clothing industry. He said it had 'survived rather better' than the rest of the textile industry 'because of the support given by M&S'. Two years ago M&S sourced 70% of its clothing from UK factories, though that has since fallen to about 55%. Suddens commented that the need to satisfy impatient shareholders lay behind M&S's decision.

M&S promised to do everything possible to make this less painful but admitted that more M&S clothing would be sourced overseas. Observers feared other UK suppliers might be threatened. One commented 'If you're willing to take that kind of action with your fourth biggest supplier, you're not going to worry too much about a smaller one.'

Adapted from the Electronic Telegraph

I Discuss the likely effects of this decision on the performance of Marks & Spencer in the short and long term.

value to all sections of the community in which it trades.

Business ethics

Business ethics can provide moral guidelines for decision making by organisations. An ethical decision means doing what is morally right; it is not a matter of merely calculating the costs and benefits associated with a decision. Individuals' ethical values vary. Ethical values are shaped by a number of factors including the values and norms of parents or guardians, those of religion, and the values of the society in which a person lives and works. Most actions and activities in the business world have an ethical dimension.

> **Key terms**
>
> **Ethics** are the shared attitudes and principles held by the employees within a business.
> An **ethical code of practice** states how a business believes its employees should respond to situations that might challenge the values of the business.
> An **ethical stance** refers to a business that has introduced an ethical policy.

What are ethical decisions?

Ethical behaviour requires businesses to operate within certain moral guidelines and to do 'the right thing' when taking decisions. What exactly is ethical behaviour? This is a tricky question. An ethical decision would take into account the moral dimension, but not everyone would agree what is ethical. Some may argue that it is not ethically wrong for supermarkets to charge high prices for basic foodstuffs; others would disagree. Different moral values make a decision as to whether a business is behaving ethically a tricky one to reach.

The following scenarios arguably illustrate examples of diverse businesses taking moral decisions.

- The frozen food retailer Iceland has recently taken over the Booker cash and carry business. Iceland has not sold tobacco for some time because of the health risk associated with the product. Following the takeover, the retailer is considering removing tobacco from all Booker outlets, denying itself the opportunity to sell a profitable product.
- The Bank of Scotland and the Alliance & Leicester have agreed to invest in establishing the 'universal bank' to provide basic banking services for up to 3m people in the UK who are excluded from the current banking system. This decision is likely to cost the banks between £5m and £10m.
- The Japanese multinational Mitsubishi has reached an agreement with a pressure group

committing itself to use wood only from environmentally responsible sources. This decision is expected to increase the company's costs, but to help to protect the remaining rainforest.

Each of these decisions could be judged to be financially disadvantageous to the business in question. It is therefore possible to argue that they have been taken because the businesses believe that it is the morally correct course of action. However, some may contend that there are 'hidden' commercial benefits from each of the decisions.

Changing views towards ethical behaviour

A series of accidents and incidents during the 1980s and 1990s fuelled a call for businesses to behave in more ethical ways and to introduce morality into decision making. Serious accidents such as the leaking of toxic gas from Union Carbide's plant in Bhopal, India in 1984 (an estimated 7000 died and 500 000 were injured) and the sinking in 1987 of P&O's Herald of Free Enterprise outside Zeebrugge harbour leading to the loss of 194 lives have led to criticisms of business practice. Firms were viewed as more interested in profits than in behaving in a responsible manner. The air of mistrust deepened with a series of business scandals including the fraudulent use of the Mirror Group's Pension Fund by Robert Maxwell.

*P*OINTS TO PONDER

Islamic investors in the UK now have the opportunity to invest in the Stock Exchange without compromising their principles. The high-street bank HSBC has just launched an investment fund that follows strict Shariah principles that forbid Muslims from investing in areas such as the arms trade, gambling, pornography, alcohol and banking.

The call for a more moral approach to business was reinforced by the report of the Cadbury Committee in 1992. A key recommendation of the committee was to strengthen the role of non-executive directors in the hope that they would ensure greater morality in corporate decision making. Non-executive directors do not take an active role in the management of the company and are well placed to control unethical and undesirable practices.

Since that time many businesses have recognised that standards expected of businesses have risen and that a clear competitive advantage can be gained from adopting an ethical stance. Over 70% of the UK's larger businesses operated some form of ethical practice by 2000. And the ethical approach was not limited to large firms. A Mori survey in 2000 found that over 60% of small- and medium-sized businesses consider that they operate ethical policies to some degree. Some businesses have adopted highly ethical stances and have publicised their change of strategy. For other companies this ethical approach has represented a unique selling point in markets containing many similar businesses selling undifferentiated products.

> ### Key terms
>
> **Environmental responsibility** entails businesses choosing to adopt processes and procedures designed to minimise harmful effects on the environment, eg placing filters on coal-fired power stations to reduce emissions.
> **Pressure groups** are groups of people with common interests who act together to further that interest.

Creating an ethical business culture

An ethical business culture exists when all employees in a business behave in a moral manner as a normal part of their working lives. This offers businesses a number of advantages in terms of marketing, particularly in relation to corporate image. Furthermore, businesses with a reputation for ethical behaviour may be more successful in attracting high-quality employees.

However, although senior managers may appreciate the benefits of changing the corporate culture to enable the adoption of an ethical stance, it may be less apparent to employees further down the organisational hierarchy.

The first issue to be resolved is the introduction of an ethical policy into the organisation. The Institute of Business Ethics offers advice to managers seeking to make this change. This information is highlighted as follows.

Six key stages in implementing an ethical culture within a business

1 **Find a champion** – make sure that the change has the public support of the Chief Executive.
2 **Discover the issues** – discover the ethical issues employees are likely to encounter.
3 **Benchmarking** – look at the policies introduced by other firms and copy good practice.
4 **Test the idea** – try the new approach out on a small part of the business first. This will help to iron out teething problems.
5 **Code of conduct** – issue this to everyone to make sure that all employees, suppliers and interested parties are aware of what is expected of them when taking decisions.
6 **Make it work** – ethical elements should be introduced into training programmes and especially into induction programmes.

Some businesses have enjoyed great success in developing ethical values within their organisations. Texas Instruments (better known as TI) took the approach of ensuring the organisation behaved ethically by encouraging each individual employee to be ethical in all aspects of their work. This extended to issuing individual employees with cards offering advice on what to do when faced with ethical dilemmas and identifying more senior staff able to offer support.

Introducing ethical approaches and codes of conduct can conflict with existing policies. In some senses a democratically led organisation with high-quality, two-way communication lends itself to implementing change. Such an organisation might be more responsive to a new culture although there is potential for conflict in a business managed in this way. Firstly in a democratically managed business, employees are unlikely to respond well to a new culture imposed upon them without consultation. Indeed they may wish to play a substantial role in shaping the new culture, which

Business in Focus: changing employee attitudes

Research by the Industrial Society in 2001 has revealed that UK employees are increasingly aware of the values of the company for whom they work. A survey of over 250 employees showed that more than 50% of those questioned elected to work for their particular company because they 'believed in what it does and what it stands for'. Over 80% of UK professionals would not work for an organisation whose values they did not believe in, while 99% care whether their employer behaves responsibly. Historically, it was consumers who tried to alter businesses' ethics. Nowadays employees are more influential.

These findings challenge the conventional view that successful recruitment depends upon potential employees being offered suitable pay and benefits packages. The Industrial Society comments that 'Other priorities such as ethics and corporate reputations are playing a more important role nowadays.'

1 To what extent might this increased employee awareness of corporate values benefit UK businesses?

might conflict with the objectives of the senior managers.

Secondly, in an organisation with a high degree of delegation employees take responsibility for some decisions and may, if empowered, have considerable responsibility for controlling their daily work. Imposing a new and uniform culture in such an environment may prove difficult. Employees may resent any loss of independence in how they conduct their working lives. This can be a tricky dilemma for even the most highly skilled managers.

Is ethical behaviour simply another form of public relations?

Certainly businesses would like to be perceived as more ethical. There is little doubt that some businesses have adopted a more ethical stance that is genuine. Companies such as Body Shop and the Co-operative Bank have based much of their marketing on their strong moral principles. This can prove to be a profitable decision as well as a moral one. Ethics is seen as good business by many firms at a time when a more informed public demands moral behaviour by firms.

The danger for businesses adopting token ethical stances is that the attentions of the media and pressure groups might reveal the superficial nature of their principles. This could be a public relations nightmare causing substantial damage to the business's public image and profits. However, for firms in the tertiary sector, the temptation to pay lip service to ethical behaviour may prove irresistible.

For many firms however, the decision on their ethical position will depend upon an assessment of the potential costs and benefits. If the costs of ethical behaviour exceed the benefits, a superficial adoption of moral principles is the most likely outcome. However, if a commercial advantage can be gained without incurring too many additional costs, then a complete change of corporate philosophy might result.

Environmental threats and opportunities

The media take a great interest in business activities in relation to the environment. When firms are found to be guilty of some act of pollution adverse publicity is likely to follow. Society expects higher standards of environmental performance than in the past.

*P*OINTS TO PONDER

Scientists have announced that one of the major sources of gas pollution in Ireland is the methane produced by cows. They have recommended reducing the number of cattle in Ireland from the current figure of 11m.

Key terms

Environmental audits *(green audits) assess the impact of an organisation on the environment in which it operates.*

External costs *are the costs of production (often associated with pollution) borne by third parties such as local residents.*

Market failure *occurs when a market does not operate efficiently and results in under or overproduction of particular products.*

Resource management *is a method of decision making concerned with the allocation and conservation of natural resources.*

Social audits *are independent investigations into the impact of a firm's activities upon society in general.*

Social costs *are the entire costs of production of a product that is borne by society. They are, in effect, the total of private (or internal) costs and external costs.*

There are many potential causes of damage to the environment. The major environmental concern identified by the government is global warming. This is caused by the release of a concoction of industrial gases (principally carbon dioxide) that has formed a layer around the earth. This layer allows the sun's rays in but prevents heat escaping causing the so-called 'greenhouse effect'. Other problems include the pollution of rivers and land and the dumping of waste, some of which is toxic and harmful to wildlife and humans alike.

Businesses contribute in many ways to the creation of environmental damage:

- the emission of gas through production processes
- pollution caused by transporting raw materials and products, particularly using road vehicles which emit noxious gases and create congestion and noise. A report by the EU suggested that pollution from vehicles in the UK could be responsible for up to 40 000 deaths amongst elderly people each year
- the pollution of the sea by businesses using it as a 'free' dumping ground. The North Sea is one of the most polluted stretches of water in the world
- destruction of natural environments as a result of activities such as logging (cutting down trees for commercial purposes as in the Amazon rainforest) and the building of homes on greenfield sites.

The Environment Agency is intent on identifying the companies responsible for the worst cases of pollution in the hope that adverse publicity will improve standards of environmental care. In 2000 the chemicals company ICI was named as the country's worst polluter. The firm, which has an annual turnover of £9bn, was fined almost £400 000 for spilling in excess of 400 tons of chemicals into the environment.

Costs of polluting the environment

Businesses are acutely aware of their private costs, ie the costs of production they have to pay themselves, such as expenses for raw materials and wages. These are easy to calculate and form part of the assessment of profitability. However, environmental pressure

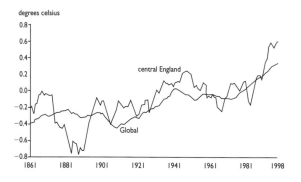

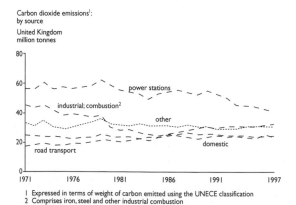

1 Expressed in terms of weight of carbon emitted using the UNECE classification
2 Comprises iron, steel and other industrial combustion

Figure 6.13 *Global warming and gas emissions*

Social Trends, 2000

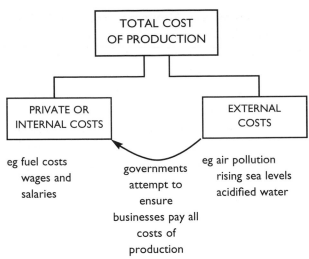

Figure 6.14 *Internal and external costs of production*

1 the Environmental Protection Act, 1991. This introduced the notion of integrated pollution control recognising that to control only a single source of pollution is worthless as damage to one part of the environment means damage to it all. This Act requires businesses to minimise pollution as a whole.

2 the Environment Act, 1995. This legislation established the Environment Agency with a brief of coordinating and overseeing environmental protection. The Act also covered the control of pollution, the conservation of the environment and made provision for restoring contaminated land and abandoned mines.

The government imposes fines on firms who breach legislation relating to the protection of the environment. These are intended to force firms to bear the full costs of their production (including external costs) although environmental pressure groups and other critics believe that the sums are not sufficient to deter major businesses with budgets of billions of pounds annually. The government also attempts to encourage 'greener' methods of production through the provision of grants. The government has created the Carbon Trust, which since April 2001 has given capital grants to firms who invest in energy-saving technologies. The intention is to slow the onset of global warming by reducing emissions of carbon dioxide. In a similar vein, government funding is also supporting the development of environmentally friendly offshore wind farms to generate 'clean' electricity.

groups and others have pressed for businesses to acknowledge the costs they create for other groups in society –the external costs of production.

Noise, congestion, air and water pollution all impose costs on other individuals and groups in society. A firm extracting gravel from a quarry may create a number of external costs. These could include congestion on local roads caused by their lorries. This would impose costs in terms of delay and noise pollution on local residents. The destruction of land caused by the quarrying could create an eyesore for people living nearby and may reduce the value of their properties. Dust may be discharged into the atmosphere. The quarrying firm will not automatically pay for these costs. It requires government action to ensure that they pay these external costs as well as their internal ones.

Thus, the total costs of production equal internal or private costs plus external costs borne by third parties. By ensuring that firms pay all the costs associated with the production of a product, governments can avoid what is termed market failure. Market failure could occur as a result of pollution because suppliers may not be charged the full costs of production and oversupply might result, as profits are high.

Methods of controlling pollution

The government has passed a series of Acts of Parliament designed to protect the environment. Two acts are of particular importance:

POINTS TO PONDER

Research by the Department of the Environment indicates that the external costs associated with air travel are about £3 per passenger on short-haul flights and approximately £20 per passenger on longer journeys. External costs associated with air travel include noise, congestion around airports and air pollution.

The EU has also passed hundreds of directives relating to environmental protection. The UK is also a signatory to a number of international agreements intended to provide environmental protection on a global scale. For example, the UK government has attended a number of Earth Summits at which targets for reducing the production of carbon dioxide have been agreed.

The desire of the general public for firms to protect the environment is also an important factor. Firms who harm the environment risk falling sales as a consequence of adverse publicity and damage to their corporate image. Indeed firms perceived as environmentally friendly may gain a substantial competitive advantage.

Implications of environmental control for businesses

The need to alter business practice to take account of environmental protection has implications for most aspects of business activity:

- **production**. Firms face pressure to redesign products to use less materials and packaging and to make these materials biodegradable or recyclable. These requirements affect all types of businesses. For example, house builders are under great pressure to build on brownfield sites (land previously used for building, often in cities and towns) and to protect the countryside by minimising the use of greenfield sites. Strict controls on production techniques are intended to minimise pollution

- **purchasing**. Businesses are encouraged to seek sources of supply that are sustainable and do not damage the environment or to use recycled materials. For example, the paper industry makes a great deal of use of recycled materials and uses this as part of its promotion

- **marketing**. Businesses use their 'green credentials' as an important component of their marketing strategy. Adverts will make reference to environmental protection and even projects to improve the environment. Packaging will confirm the company's concern to avoid pollution. This is particularly important to firms that are seen to have great potential to pollute (BP and Shell, for example) or for those who use this aspect of their operations as a USP – Body Shop International is an example of the latter

- **human resources**. New processes and procedures in manufacturing make some jobs and skills obsolete creating a need for redundancies or retraining. Environmental management has resulted in many businesses needing employees with new skills requiring a retraining programme or recruitment. Environmental managers seek to minimise the effects of the business's activities on the environment and to ensure that the firm meets new legislative requirements as they emerge. Businesses may also seek to hire employees skilled in resource management and having the ability to influence corporate decisions to ensure the development of management strategies designed for the most efficient use of scarce natural resources.

The implications of environmental protection are profound especially for the so-called polluting sector – eg chemicals and oil extraction and refining. They require a corporate response from senior managers within a business. But as with many external

Business in Focus

A Swedish company, Naty, has developed what is described as the first environmentally friendly disposable nappy. The *Nature Boy and Girl* unisex nappy carries the slogan 'Mother Nature says: thank you' and is for sale in UK supermarkets.

The nappy is made from 70% renewable materials (GM-free cotton grown in Italy) compared with only 30–35% for other brands of disposable nappy. The remainder of the nappy is made from a biodegradable plastic manufactured from GM-free maize. The eco-friendly nappy uses about half the amount of chemicals used in more conventional disposable nappies and contributes less to the greenhouse effect if burned.

However, the company's new product has met with opposition. Opponents remarked that it may use a high proportion of sustainable raw materials but would contribute to what is a large waste disposal problem.

1 Discuss the ways in which Naty might respond to the criticism of its product by environmental pressure groups.

influences the environment provides opportunities for businesses as well as constraints.

New markets have been created for businesses supplying training in environmental management. Firms also offer to supply environmental control equipment to adapt production processes to minimise the possibility of environmental harm. Equally a market exists for testing equipment to monitor emissions or the toxicity of waste products. Finally, businesses can use environmental policies as a means of obtaining a competitive advantage. BMW, for example, promotes itself as a manufacturer of cars that are almost entirely recyclable. This could prove attractive to environmentally aware consumers.

Social and environmental audits

Social auditing is not a new concept; firms in Holland used the technique as long ago as 1966. However, there is currently an increasing level of interest in social auditing as organisations of all sizes are being compelled by stakeholders to be more accountable. The social audit assesses the social impact and ethical behaviour of an organisation in relation to its aims, and those of its stakeholders. Stakeholders may include nearby residents, consumers, creditors and staff. The best and most successful organisations recognise that they will only prosper in the long term if they satisfy the aspirations of their stakeholders or at least are seen to be doing so. To satisfy this intensifying scrutiny demands more accountability.

Social auditing is an important non-financial measure of the efficiency of a business and one that is likely to become more common in the future. Many pressure groups have called for a wider form of reporting of a business's activities. The government has supported calls for so-called 'triple bottom line' reporting whereby businesses account for their financial, social and environmental performance. The government's trade secretary stated in 2001 that it was likely that legislation would be passed to require firms to conduct social audits.

Social auditing is being practised by a number of high-profile organisations seeking to enhance reputations for being socially responsible. Examples

Business in Focus: BP Amoco – social reporting

Our terms of reference agreed with BP Amoco were:

- Discuss with BP Amoco's senior managers non-financial policies (Health & Safety & Environment, Ethical Conduct, Employees and Relationships) to understand the 1999 objectives and priorities, the means of accomplishing these objectives, and the degree to which these objectives were met.
- Review a selection of publicly available information relevant to BP Amoco's adherence, as a check on the appropriateness of the information reported and statements made in the report. Test evidence supporting the report's data statements and assertions at a sample of BP Amoco sites.
- Review relevant documents such as the 1999 Board minutes and 1999 Ethics and Environment Assurance Committee minutes to assess management awareness and commitment to policies.
- Review data relating to Health & Safety to confirm it has been collected and reported accurately by the company.

Ernst & Young, Auditors

BP Amoco website

include Ben and Jerry's (US ice cream manufacturer), and Tradecraft plc in the UK.

Social audits have several elements. Firstly, firms are required to draw up and implement policies stating the ways in which they will conduct the aspects of their business which impact upon society generally. This may include issues such as the following:

- using sustainable sources of raw materials
- ensuring suppliers trade ethically avoiding, for example, the use of child labour
- operating an extensive health and safety policy above the legal requirements thereby protecting the well-being of employees
- engaging in a continuous process of

environmental management and monitoring the effects of production on the environment

■ trading ethically and taking account of the moral dimension in decision making.

Secondly, an independent body monitors the effectiveness of these policies and the effects on society generally. The Ernst & Young report reproduces a small part of the social report from BP Amoco. In this, auditors Ernst & Young (a firm providing a range of accountancy and related professional services) have challenged BP's account of its social performance to provide detailed feedback on the success of the company's social and environmental policies and to make recommendations for future action.

Finally, once the social audit is complete firms review their social and environmental policies in the light of the information from the auditors. In most cases the social audit is published in a process known as social reporting.

Some firms, mainly those with potential to inflict enormous pollution on society conduct environmental audits which are similar in nature and approach but focus solely on aspects of company policy with potential to harm the environment. These are also published.

Social audits can be a valuable exercise for firms to conduct. Audits may identify anti-social (or potentially anti-social) behaviour as problems arise. This helps to promote the corporate image of the business as a caring and responsible organisation. However, conducting an audit of this kind is not a guarantee that a firm is socially responsible. Managers must ensure that social policies are carried out effectively at all levels within the organisation and that employees are committed to them. Sufficient resources must be devoted to ensuring that the business remains socially responsible and problems identified in social audits should be resolved speedily. The danger of a less active approach is that social audits publicise weaknesses and firms are seen not to respond with damaging consequences for their corporate image.

*P*OINTS TO PONDER

Social reports produced by companies such as Barclays

and Ford have been condemned as 'corporate spin' by the New Economics Foundation, an organisation which has developed modern methods of social accounting. It quotes Procter & Gamble (P & G) as an example of poor practice in relation to social reporting.

What the company said: 'An employee should be able to answer "Yes" to the questions: is this the right thing to do, will this action uphold P & G's reputation as an ethical company'? – from the P & G code of conduct.

What the company does: P & G continues to trade in Burma while many other companies have pulled out because of the continued abuse of human rights by the Burmese government.

Pressure groups

Key terms

Direct action is any action taken to restrict the normal trading activity of the firm or firms who are the subject of the protest.
Lobbying is an attempt to persuade a person in a position of power to a particular viewpoint.
Pressure groups are collections of people who combine to bring about change.

A pressure group is a collection of people who combine to bring about change. Various types of pressure groups exist:

■ environmental groups, eg Greenpeace and Friends of the Earth
■ groups concerned with consumer issues such as the controversy surrounding fuel prices in the UK. An alliance of farmers and road haulage operators blockaded fuel depots with conspicuous success in the autumn of 2000 as a protest against high fuel prices, although the Consumers' Association is probably better known.
■ businesses lobbying government for changes in policy or legislation. The Confederation of British Industry (CBI) is a well-known group
■ issues concerning the welfare of animals – eg Compassion in World Farming (CIWF) who campaign against the export of live animals

- trade unions who campaign on behalf of their members, eg the National Union of Teachers.

Pressure groups in action

Pressure groups operate with the aim of making politicians, businesses and the general public aware of the issues and their opinions in order to bring about some specific change. For example, several pressure groups are currently campaigning against the use of genetically modified ingredients in foodstuffs. By their actions groups such as Greenpeace hope to influence the views of consumers and governments against these products. In this way they can affect the actions of the major companies. One of the largest multinational companies involved in developing GM foods is Monsanto. In October 1999 senior advisors told the Monsanto board of directors that the company was regarded as socially irresponsible and that the European public had been alienated by their attempts to develop GM products. The company responded to the advice and promised to halt trials and to consult European consumers.

Pressure groups can use two main tactics in attempting to achieve their aims:

1 **lobbying**. Pressure groups can campaign through the use of techniques such as leafleting, petitions and demonstrations. This process, known as lobbying, is undertaken with the intention of winning the support of the public and, critically, politicians with the power to effect change. This relatively gentle process is arguably more likely to gain the support of the general public, but can be very expensive for pressure groups as well as slow. However, it is often an essential component of bringing about change even if direct action is more likely to attract the attention of the media.

2 **direct action**. This can take many forms including

- picketing factories and retail outlets
- boycotting the products of companies concerned
- occupying business premises and public buildings
- violent and illegal actions such as letter bombs

Direct action is undertaken for two purposes. First, by preventing the organisation or organisations at the centre of the protest from carrying on their normal commercial activities the group puts pressure on the managers and directors of the business. Second, direct action, and particularly spectacular direct action, is likely to attract the attention of the media. This offers pressure groups a further opportunity to win public sympathy for their cause.

Business in Focus: Greenpeace protesters win GM case

In September 2000 the executive director of Greenpeace and 27 other environmental activists were cleared of causing criminal damage in a field of genetically modified maize in Norfolk. The executive director, Lord Melchett and his fellow protestors were acquitted after a retrial, accused of trampling several acres of GM crops in Lyng, Norfolk in July 1999. After the acquittal Melchett said the verdict sent a clear message to the government. 'The time has come for Mr Blair and the chemical companies to stop growing GM crops. People don't want to eat GM food: supermarkets won't sell GM food and now the time has come for people to stop planting GM food.'

A spokesperson on behalf of the biotechnology company Aventis, who were testing the crop, condemned the verdict. The company expressed its disappointment that a small minority of protestors could take direct action rather than relying upon strength of argument. The spokesperson said the protestors should wait for the outcome of the trials before reaching a decision regarding GM crops.

1 Discuss the ways in which the direct action of Greenpeace and the subsequent court case might influence the decisions of large multinational biotechnology companies such as Aventis.

What influences the success of pressure groups?

A number of factors contribute to the chance of pressure group campaigns succeeding:

- the amount of publicity that activities of the pressure group might attract, and the amount the managers of affected businesses believe it may attract in the future
- the degree of public sympathy for the campaign. If the businesses in question believe the protestors are winning public support and that sales may be affected they are more likely to respond to the demands of the activists. Some of the UK's high-street banks have abandoned their branch closure programme following highly vocal protests by local community groups
- the alternative products available to consumers – if no close substitutes exist then the business may be relatively unaffected. In this case it might decide to sit out the protests
- the potential damage to the business's corporate image as a result of the activities of the pressure group. If the business operates in a highly competitive market with little product differentiation, then being seen to be responsive

to the views of the public might be advantageous, so long as the costs to the business are not too great. In effect the business will compare the net cost of not responding to that of giving in (to some degree) to the protests. If the business projects itself as socially responsible, then it will be under greater pressure to react positively to pressure from organised groups.

Political change

Political developments can offer opportunities as well as posing threats to businesses. The anticipated increase in the membership of the European Union from the current 15 countries to 28 will open up huge new markets for UK business. These new markets total 105m consumers and will not be protected by tariffs or quotas. But this political development also has drawbacks. It will open up UK markets to producers from countries such as Poland and Turkey. These countries are likely to have significant advantages in terms of labour costs and may be more price competitive than UK manufacturing firms.

Progress questions

1 Explain **two** advantages that a business might receive from operating in a socially responsible manner. *(6 marks)*

2 Outline the responsibilities a business in the tertiary sector might have to **two** stakeholder groups. *(6 marks)*

3 Distinguish between the stakeholder concept and the shareholder concept. *(4 marks)*

4 Examine the ways in which a multinational manufacturing business might fulfil its social responsibilities. *(8 marks)*

5 Explain the differences between a business operating ethically and one operating legally. *(6 marks)*

6 Outline **two** difficulties a firm practising empowerment might encounter in introducing an ethical code of conduct. *(8 marks)*

7 Distinguish between internal or private costs and external costs. *(4 marks)*

8 Why might the existence of external costs result in the overproduction of a product? *(6 marks)*

9 Explain methods available to a pressure group in attempting to achieve its objectives. *(6 marks)*

10 Explain **two** factors that might contribute to the possible success of Greenpeace's campaign against genetically modified food. *(6 marks)*

Analysis and evaluation questions

1 'Firms become socially responsible because it improves their public image, not through a genuine desire to meet the needs of all their stakeholders.' To what extent do you agree with this statement? *(15 marks)*

2 'Ethical businesses cannot meet their responsibilities to their shareholders.' Critically evaluate this statement. *(15 marks)*

3 Examine whether concern for public image, rather than the fear of legal sanctions, is the main motive persuading businesses to adopt environmentally friendly policies. *(12 marks)*

4 Consider the arguments for and against the use of direct action by pressure groups campaigning against experiments on animals. *(12 marks)*

5 Discuss whether social audits and reporting are likely to alter the policies multinational businesses pursue. *(15 marks)*

Case study 1

Nestlé, the Swiss-based group, has been criticised by the Advertising Standards Authority (ASA) over the company's claim in a 1996 advert to have socially responsible involvement in developing countries. The decision marks the end of a three-year battle over the advert and a significant point in the long-running war of words between Nestlé and various pressure groups.

The decision by the ASA represents a victory for Baby Milk Action, a pressure group which has pursued Nestlé for the promotion and sale of baby milk powder to mothers in Third World countries. The pressure group has criticised the company for

unethical business behaviour. Baby Milk Action condemned the firm for selling a product to poor communities when the majority of mothers were able to feed their babies naturally. This latter course of action is described as more nutritious and hygienic.

The World Health Organisation estimates that more than 1 m babies a year die from diarrhoea picked up from unhygienic bottle feeding. WHO operates a code of conduct, which Nestlé has supported since 1984, aimed at restricting the use of manufactured baby milk powder and strictly controlling its marketing.

Nestlé insisted that it is a 'responsible and responsive company'. However, this dispute over the ethics of selling an unnecessary product to poor Third World mothers began in 1977 and is the basis of the world's longest-running consumer boycott.

Adapted from the Guardian, 12 May 1999

1 **a)** What is meant by the term 'unethical business behaviour'? *(4 marks)*
   b) Explain the difficulties in developing a uniform ethical policy through a large and diverse multinational business. *(6 marks)*
2 Examine the strategies open to Baby Milk Action and other pressure groups in their long-running dispute with Nestlé. *(10 marks)*
3 Discuss the actions that Nestlé might take in the future to enhance its image as a socially responsible company. *(14 marks)*
4 Nestlé is a multinational giant selling in markets throughout the world. To what extent does its size and global dimension protect it from criticisms by UK-based pressure groups? *(16 marks)*

Case study 2

Vasa Zbyslaw could not conceal his delight. 'We have had our best trading year so far; our critics will have to eat their words now' he gloated. 'I knew that our strategy of offering highly competitive prices combined with unrivalled standards of customer service would help us to win market share from *British Airways* and the other big boys. We are now recognised as the market leader in low-cost air travel in the UK. This will keep the shareholders happy.

The contented look on the faces of the directors of *Chiltern Airlines* hid the stress of five years of hard work and some worrying periods when the company was unprofitable and survival seemed unlikely. Vasa and Selena Patel had been the driving force behind the creation of *Chiltern Airlines* in the early 1990s, recognising that a niche existed in the UK for cheap air travel between major towns and cities. Vasa argued that, in spite of privatisation, the UK's rail network was expensive, unreliable and had a poor safety record. 'Business people and tourists want a reliable and quick service. They want to arrive on time and not to be held up by the wrong type of snow or cows on the line. If we can offer a

low-cost service with a clear focus on high-quality customer service, I think we are bound to succeed.'

And he had been proved right. The company had won the right to offer flights between a number of major UK towns and cities. The company had taken time to establish itself, slowly gaining a reputation for providing low-cost travel. During its growth stage the management team had created a democratic leadership style encouraging effective communication at all levels within the organisation. The tough competition assisted the managers in establishing a task-centred culture in which employees had a high degree of control over their working lives. Vasa and Selena believed that a committed and motivated workforce was a cornerstone of a successful business.

Vasa and Selena worked hard to develop a well-deserved reputation for excellent customer service. 'This will make us stand out from the competition' Selena remarked. 'We should have been able to operate on more routes but for government restrictions on flight paths and night flying because of possible noise pollution. This has reduced our potential to earn profits. However, being perceived as socially responsible is more important than short-term profitability.

Selena was keen to build upon the company's image and to build a reputation for ethical trading activities. 'There are a number of advantages to this' she argued. 'We could utilise this as a unique selling point. None of our competition has a highly publicised ethical stance.' Vasa was less convinced. 'I accept that there are considerable marketing advantages from playing the ethical card, but I foresee practical problems in changing the culture of the company. It is ironic but the culture and leadership style we have developed would possibly hinder us in adopting an ethical code of conduct.'

However, both Vasa and Selena acknowledge that the commitment of the UK government to maintain interest rates at low levels has benefited *Chiltern* in a number of ways. 'The government's policies on fuel prices and other taxes haven't always helped, especially imposition of airport tax' Vasa mused. 'However, low interest rates have helped encourage the development of the market for budget flights as well as benefiting our company. Freeing up competition in the national and international air travel market has also helped in many ways.'

Fierce rivalry in the marketplace

The market for cheap air travel has become increasingly competitive as new firms entered the market. Vasa and Selena were particularly worried by the creation of *Go* in November 1996. This company is a subsidiary of *British Airways* formed to offer budget flights throughout Europe. Even with the backing of the mighty *British Airways*, *Go* initially struggled to earn a profit. In 1999 the company announced a £12m loss reflecting the difficulty of attracting sufficient customers to make profits in such a low-price market. The arrival of other new firms, eg *Buzz*, meant that in spite of the rapid growth of the market spare capacity existed in the supply of low-cost flights.

Having celebrated the increased level of profits *Chiltern's* board of directors turned their attention to the strategic issue of European expansion. Some of *Chiltern's* directors favoured seeking to move into European routes. Selena believed that with ever closer links with Europe the move into the European market was a natural development. 'We will need to introduce changes in most aspects of our operation to succeed in the tough European market. We will need to consider the implications for our marketing and our financial plans in

particular. The government's reluctance to join the single European currency does not encourage this move as it introduces more financial risk into operating flights from, say London to Berlin.'

However, a majority of directors feel that whilst any expansion plans involve risk and that the company cannot simply rest on its laurels, growth is considered to be particularly important at a time when the market is growing.

1 Chiltern Airways trades in a highly competitive market. It faces competition from low-priced rivals such as Go and EasyJet as well as from major national airlines such as British Airways. Discuss the possible ways in which Chiltern Airlines might improve its competitiveness. *(14 marks)*

2 Vasa commented 'Government policy has helped rather than hindered our strategy of expansion.' To what extent do you agree with his statement?
(18 marks)

3 Chiltern Airways is considering a decision to enter the European market. Evaluate the case for and against such a decision. *(18 marks)*

4 Assess the case for and against Selena's view that '… being perceived as socially responsible is more important than short-term profitability.'
(16 marks)

5 Chiltern Airlines anticipate difficulties in introducing an ethical code into the business. Critically assess this view. *(14 marks)*

Objectives and Strategy

Introduction

In the part of the specification of the AS called 'Objectives and strategy' you will have studied

- starting up a firm; this involved considering how an entrepreneur would identify a new market opportunity and protect a good idea. It also included a study of different types of enterprise such as sole traders, private and public limited companies. You will also have studied the problems of starting up in business
- business objectives. In this part of the course you will have studied the typical objectives of a firm and the aims of different stakeholder groups
- business strategy – this involved a study of SWOT analysis.

The A2 specification builds on the AS work you

have done. It is worthwhile looking back over your AS materials before beginning this part of the A2 course. In particular it is worth reviewing the objectives and strategy sections. More specific advice is given on any prior knowledge you will need at the beginning of each unit.

During the A2 course you will study

- the impact on firms of changing size. This includes a study of how firms grow (such as takeovers and mergers) and an analysis of the problems they face as they get bigger
- the mission statements and the importance of organisational culture
- decision-making techniques. This includes scientific decision making and decision trees
- contingency planning. This involves planning for crises.

OBJECTIVES AND STRATEGY

Starting points

In this unit we consider the issues involved in business growth. In the AS the focus was on how firms start up and the problems of starting up. We now consider why a firm might want to grow, how it might finance such growth and the problems of managing a larger organisation.

Several of the topics will be new to you but will build on areas of the specification you covered at

AS level. For example, the financing of growth requires an understanding of different sources of finance which was covered in the finance section of the AS course. You may also want to revisit topics such as economies of scale and the difference between private and public companies as they are developed in this unit.

Introduction

A firm's objective is its overall target. Once a firm has established its objective it can then decide on the best way of achieving this – its strategy. Different organisations will have different objectives, For example, firms might seek to innovate or to diversify. One of the most common objectives of firms is to increase in size.

Growth

Many owners and managers will want their firms to grow. This is because

- larger firms may benefit from economies of scale. This may mean lower unit costs and can result in higher profit margins or lower prices
- larger firms have more power over their markets. For example, they may be able to negotiate better deals with their suppliers and distributors; they may also be able to bargain for better positioning for their advertisements
- larger firms tend to be safer from takeover simply because they are more expensive to buy. Managers who are interested in their own job security will therefore have an incentive to make their firms bigger and as a result protect their own jobs
- larger firms have more status. Managers will often want the praise and recognition that comes with building up a business.

The growth of a business may come internally or externally. Internal growth occurs when the firm sells more of its products. External growth occurs when a firm acquires or joins up with another.

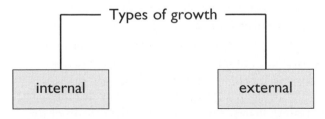

Figure 7.1

Internal growth is often slower – it may take some time to penetrate a market and increase sales. External growth is naturally faster and more sudden because a firm acquires another organisation's sales in one go.

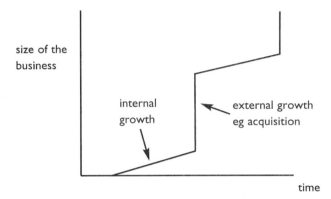

Figure 7.2

Business in Focus: entrepreneurs who have made it!

- Childhood friends Ben Cohen and Jerry Greenfield set up a premium ice cream company in Vermont in the late 1970s. Their somewhat quirky approach in which they maintained very clear social and ethical values paid off when they sold the business to Unilever in 2000 for $326m.
- Ben Way, a dyslexic 19-year-old, was awarded the British Entrepreneur of the Year award in 1999. He had recently won a £25m contract to develop an e-commerce programme. He was totally self-taught and started his business from his bedroom when he was 15.
- In the early 1990s Trevor Bayliss developed the wind-up radio for sale to Third World countries. Winding up the radio generates enough power for 40 minutes of listening. Over 20 000 a month are now produced in South Africa.
- In 1978 James Dyson started work on a vacuum cleaner which would use a new technology entirely. Over 5000 prototypes later he launched the world's first bagless vacuum cleaner.

I Do you think there is a certain type of person who is most likely to be successful as an entrepreneur? What do you think are the characteristics of an entrepreneur?

Business in Focus: fast growth

The fastest growth company in the UK in 2000 was Dataworkforce, a telecoms recruitment agency. The business was founded by Neil Franklin who is now its president. Although his academic record at school was not particularly impressive this has been more than made up for by an outstanding business career.

The recruitment company was started in his South London flat in 1995 with £5000 of his savings. It now supplies telecommunications engineers all over the world and has increased sales by 273% a year. The company's sales are now over £20m.

Franklin claims his success is due to two main factors: an unflinching focus on the customer and investment in research in a rapidly changing sector. 'I always try to meet my customers face to face' says Franklin. 'I will fly anywhere in the world to meet clients. They are often surprised to find the chairman of the company on their doorstep. And that makes them remember you.'

Rather than build up a large and indiscriminate database of personnel Dataworkforce has built up a small list of top performers. It uses mainly former military personnel who are 'technically proficient, used to taking orders and prepared to work anywhere in the world at a moment's notice'. Franklin then researches target companies and works out ways he can add value for them; the work may involve installing a mobile phone network in south-east China or laying cables across the Atlantic. At any moment the company has around 400 engineers in over 50 countries.

The Sunday Times

I Why do managers want their firms to grow? What do you think determines how fast a firm grows?

Financing growth

In order to grow, a firm will need to have the finance necessary to acquire resources such as new premises or equipment or to hire new staff. This finance can come from internal and external sources. Internal sources of finance include

- retained profits: the firm can invest its profits into stocks and new equipment
- the sale of assets: if firms have assets which are not being used (such as land) it may sell these to raise cash.

External sources include

- overdrafts: this is a short-term form of finance which can be called in at any time by the bank
- mortgages: this is finance acquired using property as collateral
- loans: this is long-term borrowing in which a firm agrees to pay back the borrowed money over an agreed period of time.

All of these forms of borrowing mean the firm is committed to interest repayments. This can cause problems if the firm's performance is poor since it may struggle to repay its interest.

Key terms

Internal finance comes from within the firm, eg from retained profits or asset sales.
External finance comes from outside the firm, eg from the sale of shares or loans.

Alternatively a firm may raise money externally by issuing shares. This means that the control of the business is diluted amongst more owners.

Growth and cash flow

The expansion of a business may bring many benefits in the long term but can also lead to cash flow problems in the short term. As a firm expands it will be buying new fixed assets, purchasing stocks and investing in areas such as new product development. These all lead to cash outflows. Over time this investment should lead to more sales and cash inflows but in the short term the business may have to plan carefully to avoid cash flow problems. Its options may include

- arranging a loan
- ensuring debtors pay on time
- delaying payment to suppliers as long as possible.

If a firm does grow too fast and fails to manage its cash flow effectively this is known as 'overtrading'. Overtrading occurs when a firm has too much money invested in building up stocks or has spent too much acquiring bigger premises and as a result has liquidity problems.

Key terms

Overtrading occurs when there are liquidity problems caused by expanding too rapidly.

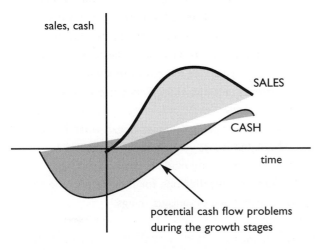

Figure 7.3

Adjustment during growth

As an organisation grows, its managers must examine the firm's structure and the roles of people within the business. Many firms start off as sole traders. The founder is the boss and he or she makes all the major decisions. This type of enterprise is able to respond quickly to market conditions and the founder has complete control. He or she can make decisions without having to consult others and has a clear overview of the business situation.

The next stage as a firm grows usually involves more people being hired to deal with the additional business. At this stage there may well be a good team spirit. Individuals share out tasks amongst themselves and can communicate easily with each other to sort out any problems. Employees feel they are all working towards the same goals. Individuals share jobs, help each other out and generally deal with things as and when they come up; there may not be formal job descriptions at this stage.

If, however, growth continues it may be necessary to develop a more formal structure within the organisation. To avoid too many people doing the same thing or to avoid things not getting done at all it usually becomes necessary to clearly define what each job involves. More rigid job descriptions become the norm and a more formal structure evolves with defined lines of accountability.

At this point the people at the top of the organisation are less directly involved with the day-to-day work. Their approach must be less hands-on simply because they cannot do it all themselves; this means that the senior managers must learn how to delegate and let others do the front-line work for them. In larger organisations managers must focus on the overall planning, coordinating and controlling rather than the actual doing.

For some managers the transition from the 'boss' (the person who does things himself or herself) to 'manager' or 'leader' – the person who focuses on the overall direction of the business and delegates day-to-day tasks to others – can be a very difficult one; they can find it hard to remove themselves from direct contact with the job and their customers. In many firms the senior managers continue to intervene too much even though the business has grown because they cannot 'let go'; the danger of being too interventionist is that they undermine their subordinates. Furthermore, managers who cannot relinquish control inevitably place a block on the size of the firm – if they always want to know exactly what is going on, the business as a whole cannot grow very big.

Keeping control of a growing business

As an organisation grows it naturally becomes more difficult for managers to keep control of all of its activities. There are more people to manage, more products to oversee and more things to do. Managers must therefore develop ways of keeping everyone informed and focused and ensuring that employees know exactly what is happening and how their actions contribute to the success of the organisation as a whole.

To help coordination and maintain control within the firm managers often introduce procedures such as budgeting, appraisal systems and management by objectives. Budgeting helps managers to plan and monitor what is being spent, appraisals provide a good opportunity to review what has been happening and set new targets for the future whilst a system of management by objectives helps to ensure everyone is working towards the same goals. Without such systems running throughout the organisation, there may be no clear direction.

Good communication is of course also essential. Employees, suppliers and investors must be kept informed so they are clear about what is happening at the moment within the firm and where the business wants to go next. Good communication is also needed to keep the organisation in close contact with its customers so it can meet their needs precisely.

EXAMINER'S ADVICE

It is important to remember the problems involved when a business grows. Many students assume that 'bigger is better' without considering the challenges this brings.

From private limited company to public limited company

When people first set up in business they often operate as sole traders. This means that they have

People in business: Malcolm Walker

Malcolm Walker was brought up in a Yorkshire mining village. He left school at 17 with O level woodwork and is now head of Iceland, the UK's frozen food retailer.

The company has over 700 stores nationwide – a far cry from the shop Mr Walker rented in 1970. At that stage he sold unpackaged frozen peas and fish fingers by the scoopful out of plastic washing up bowls from a couple of freezers bought on hire purchase. Short, with a shock of dark hair, a wide and ready grin and a strong Yorkshire accent Mr Walker hates 'pretension and snobbery' whether in the City or among 'foodies'.

In recent years he has made some significant developments in the firm's strategy first announcing it would remove genetically modified ingredients

long before other retailers and then banning artificial flavours and preservatives from its products. What Mr Walker realises is that business 'is not complicated. When you boil it down it is about perseverance.' And he is not afraid to try things others laugh at. In 1996 he launched a free home delivery service for customers who spent more than £25 in the shop. Rivals said it was financial suicide.

His money making schemes began when he was at school. In his last year there he organised a dance for charity and made a small profit. 'So I decided to do another one for me and become an impressario. I like organising things.'

The Financial Times

unlimited liability and that they are both the owner and the manager of the business. As a firm develops, the owners of a business will often form a private limited company (Ltd).

A private limited company is owned by shareholders and has limited liability. This means that the liability of the investors is limited to the amount that they initially invested and that their personal assets cannot be taken to meet the company's debts. Without limited liability it would be very difficult for companies to attract investors; shareholders would be afraid that they would lose all of their personal assets if the company failed. The existence of limited liability means that investors know the maximum that they can lose if it all goes wrong.

To set up a private limited company the owners of a business must complete the Articles and Memorandum of Association; these two documents set out the formal details of the company, such as its name, registered office and objectives. They also set out the internal rules of the business including any restrictions on the sales of shares, eg they may specify that shares are only sold within the family.

Subject to the restrictions in the Articles of Association the owners of shares in a private limited company can sell their shares to other investors but they are not allowed to advertise them for sale. This can make it difficult to sell such shares quickly.

If a firm wants access to far more potential shareholders it can become a public limited company (known as a plc). By becoming a plc a firm is allowed to advertise its shares to outside investors and to have its shares traded on the Stock Exchange. The Stock Exchange is a market for buyers and sellers of public limited companies' shares.

Given that a plc's shares are quoted on the Stock Exchange it makes it much easier for investors to sell them on if they want to because there is easy access to far more potential buyers. Unlike private limited companies the owners of plcs cannot place restrictions on who the shares are sold to. The market for plc shares is therefore 'liquid' – because they can easily be turned into cash – and as a result they are often more attractive to investors.

From the perspective of a business, becoming a plc means it can sell shares to the general public and can therefore raise more finance for its projects. From the perspective of investors it provides them with the opportunity to make profits through share dividends and/or an increase in the share price whilst also enabling them to hold a relatively liquid asset.

There is, however, no guarantee that a private company which decides to become a plc will actually be able to sell shares to the general public. This will naturally depend on the price of the shares and the timing of the sale; if there are more attractive alternatives elsewhere a firm may struggle to find buyers at the given price. This is why companies employ specialists such as merchant

private limited company	public limited company
has 'Ltd' after its name	has 'plc' after its name
can place restrictions on sales of shares	no restrictions on sale of shares
shares cannot be advertised	shares can be sold on the Stock Exchange
limited liability	limited liability

Table 7.1 *Comparison of private limited companies and public limited companies*

Key terms

*A **private limited company (Ltd)** is owned by shareholders and has limited liability; its shares cannot be sold on the Stock Exchange.*
*A **public limited company (plc)** is also owned by shareholders but its shares can be sold on the Stock Exchange.*
***Flotation:** this occurs when a private limited company becomes a public limited company.*

EXAMINER'S ADVICE

Remember that the overwhelming majority of companies in the UK are private limited companies. Most companies do not need the finance which might be available through the Stock Exchange – they can finance their plans without it – and/or they do not want the extra burdens of being a plc.

bankers and brokers to advise them on how to sell shares to the public.

Problems of being a public limited company

Although plcs have access to more finance and generally receive more media attention that Ltds (because more of the public own shares in them) there are several disadvantages of becoming a plc.

■ Plcs are more heavily regulated than Ltds, eg they have to publish far more detailed accounts – these reports are available to the public including competitors.
■ Because there are no restrictions on who the shares are sold to a plc is more vulnerable to takeover. There is no guarantee that shares will be held by family members or friends; they may well be held by other firms looking to gain control.
■ Because the shares are traded daily the share price will fluctuate according to supply and demand. If demand is particularly low (perhaps because of poor results or a rumour of future bad news) the share price is likely to fall and the company will be vulnerable to takeover. Managers often have to take actions to keep the share price up even if these actions are not necessarily in the best long-term interests of the firm, eg they may use inferior components to cut costs and boost short-term profits even if this damages the long-term brand image.

Short-termism

UK firms are often criticised for a short-termist approach. This means that managers often plan for the short term rather than the long term. Many managers argue this is necessary because they are under great pressure from shareholders to deliver short-term rewards. Most shareholders in the UK are financial institutions such as pension funds; these institutions often want quick returns to pay out to their own investors. As a result UK managers may be less willing to invest in projects which have a long-

term pay off; investment in new product development, research and development, training and brand building, for example, may be avoided because they eat up funds in the short term. This may make it much more difficult for UK firms to compete over time because they lack the necessary investment.

In some other countries such as Germany the shareholders tend to be individuals and organisations who are involved with the firm in some way, e.g. they may be the firm's suppliers or distributors. As a result these investors are generally eager to see the firm prosper in the long term because they themselves will benefit from the increase in business. This means that this type of investor is likely to look more favourably on long-term projects which put the firm in a much stronger long-term position even if the returns are not particularly high in the short term.

Retrenchment

Not all firms will be growing: at any moment some will be reducing the scale of their operations; this is known as 'retrenchment'. Retrenchment may be a deliberate policy by a firm or it may be forced on the business due to its poor performance.

A firm may deliberately reduce its operations if

■ it is suffering from diseconomies of scale. A firm may have grown too big and, consequently, may be experiencing problems with communication, control and motivation. There may be too many levels of hierarchy so that messages get distorted, communication between sites may be difficult and employees may feel alienated because they feel the senior management do not pay them enough attention. By scaling down its operations a firm may hope to achieve a more manageable size and reduce the unit costs
■ it feels it has lost focus. A firm may be operating in too many different markets or have too wide a product range. As a result decision making may be slow or inappropriate and a firm may lose its competitive edge because it is trying to do too much at any moment. A reduction in the number of the firm's offerings may result in better decision making and greater competitiveness.

In some cases retrenchment may be forced on a firm. This may be because of

- changes in the competitive nature of the market, eg the entry of a large competitor able to offer lower prices may force an existing firm out of the market
- changes in social trends, eg a movement away from certain types of products which are regarded as unhealthy or environmentally unfriendly
- new product development
- changes in the economy, eg a recession, high interest rates or a strong pound may cause a firm to reduce its output.

Business in Focus

In 2000 C&A announced it was withdrawing from the UK market having incurred losses of £250m since 1995. The endless rows of rather bland, synthetic sweaters, skirts and trousers which defined C&A's image throughout the Nineties were designed to a pan-European formula which was snubbed by the British who had a range of more exciting shops to choose from. In the rest of Europe, however, C&A has continued to flourish but the UK withdrawal became almost inevitable. So what went wrong?

In 1998 with sales falling the company tried to revamp its image spending more than £6.5m on aspirational television advertising featuring glamorous models and the promise of something rather wonderful. However what happened was that whilst the layout changed, the clothes remained the same. Ironically, new designs are now coming through and being snapped up just as the stores are about to close. Also the company has given each store's staff more control over what is stocked – they have reversed the changed layouts which were full of empty spaces and packed the shops with goods. This has led to a revival in the company's fortunes in the UK albeit too late. A C&A spokesman says 'the power has been given back to the shopfloor and we are giving customers what they want again. Other companies should learn from us if they are thinking about bringing in expensive consultants. If they want to know what the customers want they should ask the people who work on the shopfloor.' The company is helping staff to find new jobs, training them in interview skills and CV writing. The company's property arm is leasing the store sites throughout the UK to new companies including Next and Matalan. Meanwhile redundancy payments will generally be about twice the statutory minimum and staff and managers are now receiving monthly bonuses directly linked to their store's turnover. It is a winning formula in that things are better than they have been for years. Sadly it is too late for the company's 4,800 staff.

The Times

Progress questions

1 Wilson Ltd is a small family company which produces indoor exercise equipment such as rowing machines. Explain two possible sources of internal finance the firm might use to expand.
(6 marks)

2 Splash plc is a UK producer of sportswear. Explain two external sources of finance the firm might use to expand.
(6 marks)

3 What is meant by overtrading?
(2 marks)

4 Distinguish between private limited companies and public limited companies.
(3 marks)

5 Explain the business significance of 'limited liability'.
(4 marks)

6 Explain two problems a firm might face when expanding rapidly.
(6 marks)

7 Explain two reasons why a private limited company might want to become a public limited company.
(6 marks)

8 Explain the possible reasons why a firm which is expanding might experience cash flow problems.
(6 marks)

9 What is meant by 'retrenchment'? *(2 marks)*
10 Explain two reasons why a firm might adopt a strategy of retrenchment. *(6 marks)*

Analysis and evaluation questions

1 Examine the possible problems a firm might face if it grows rapidly. *(12 marks)*
2 Joely Pavrotti has just been appointed the managing director of an advertising agency called Pow! She is determined to turn the agency into one of the fastest growing in the country. Consider the ways in which Pow! might finance its growth. *(12 marks)*
3 The owners of Javeed Ltd, a family-owned retail business, are considering turning the company into a plc. Examine the factors they might take into account before making this decision. *(8 marks)*
4 To what extent is it better for a firm to operate internationally rather than just nationally? *(12 marks)*

Case study 1

Julia Sanders runs a company which offers a cleaning service for offices. She started out as a cleaner herself but was soon so busy that she took on an assistant and it grew from there. She now has customers within a 50-mile radius, employs 40 staff and has a turnover of several million. 'It's sort of grown without me even thinking about it' she said in a recent interview with a local newspaper when she was voted local businessperson of the year. 'I've never really thought of why I've been so successful – I've been too busy running the business!' However, the workload has taken its toll and she recently had to take a few days off work to relax. 'My doctor told me to take it easy for a while but I couldn't stay off work for too long or I'd go mad. I've got to do something to keep busy.'

Julia has a 80% share in the business; the only other shareholder is her husband, Tom, who now works in the business as well. Tom believes that Julia should relax more; he's even suggested she should try selling the business! 'The kids are not interested in taking it over; I think we might as well sell it and enjoy the proceeds. Nearly everything we've earned has gone back into the company. Why not get something out of it and enjoy ourselves a little?'

Julia was having none of this – in her view the company was ready to float and become a plc. 'I have great plans for the firm but we need much more investment. So far we've grown bit by bit. I want to do it properly now and become a national business with an instantly recognised brand name. Those few days off have given me time to think it through; I know where we should go next and think we should do it as a plc. I know it will be a bit different but with me still in control we'll continue to provide the quality of service that has made us so successful in the past. I'm not worried about profits in the short run necessarily but we'll get there in the end.'

1 Analyse the differences between a private limited company and a public limited company. *(8 marks)*
2 Should Julia try to float her business? *(12 marks)*

Case study 2

'Looking back we were too successful' says Pete. Pete had left school at 16 and gone to work for his father as a builder. Over the years he had gained a great deal of experience and eventually he decided to set up on his own. His particular area of interest was in fitting new kitchens and he felt there was a demand for good-quality workmanship. He set up in the mid-1980s just as the property boom was happening. He soon found he was swamped by orders not only to fit kitchens but also to design them to begin with. He worked closely with the clients and made sure he delivered on time and produced a high-quality piece of work. As the orders came in Pete soon found he could not cope with all the business and so he hired others to help him complete the work. Finding people was easy but Pete found it difficult to keep an eye on their work all the time and at times felt that the standards of work were slipping. Some days he found himself working harder than ever to check that their work had been done properly! He was also getting swamped by all the paperwork. His dad had done all this before and now he was responsible for it he realised how time consuming it was. Even when recession hit, Pete found his business was extremely busy – even if people were not moving house they often decided to improve their kitchen and his firm seemed to be top of the list when it came to choosing a kitchen fitter! He was employing a team of over 20 people working on several different jobs at once. He had never been more successful or more stressed! He seemed to spend most of his time organising things and missed not doing the work himself. Much of his day was spent filling in forms, talking to his employees or chasing up new business rather than fitting kitchens which is what he thought he was good at. His dad had advised him to get others in to help on the management side of the business but Pete was reluctant to share control.

In early 2001 after over ten years of success the business collapsed. Pete had failed to keep on top of things and found the firm had major cashflow problems – he was owed money on several big contracts and could not pay either the suppliers or the employees. To some extent Pete had seen this coming but had felt unable to do much about it. He had tried to chase up the money he was owed and plan things a bit more but he had found he just didn't have the time to keep on top of things.

1 With reference to the case study outline the problems which face a growing firm.   *(8 marks)*
2 To what extent was the collapse of Pete's business inevitable?   *(12 marks)*

CHANGE IN OWNERSHIP

Starting points

This unit focuses on the ways in which a firm might expand. This includes mergers, takeovers and management buy outs. You will not have studied these topics at AS level although when we consider issues such as the benefits and problems of such types of growth you may want to revisit economies and diseconomies of sale. These were covered in the operations part of the AS specification.

The unit also covers international expansion and management buy outs.

Internal and external growth

External growth occurs when a firm decides to expand by joining together with another. This may occur either by a takeover or a merger. A takeover occurs when one firm gains control of another by acquiring a controlling interest in its shares. A merger occurs when one firm joins together with another one to form a new combined enterprise. Mergers and acquisitions are both forms of integration.

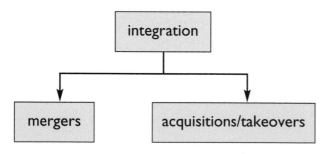

Figure 7.22 *Forms of integration*

If one business wants to take over another it must buy up 51% of the other firm's shares so that it has a majority vote. It may buy these shares either by using cash or by offering its own shares in return (this is known as a paper offer). The attacking company will make an offer to the shareholders of the victim company. The directors of the targeted company will decide whether or not they think the bid is fair and whether or not to recommend to

their own shareholders that they should accept it; if they reject the offer the takeover becomes a 'hostile bid'.

If there are not enough shareholders willing to accept the offer the attacking company may decide to increase the amount it offers for each share. There is, however, a strict timetable that the attacking company has to follow so it cannot keep increasing its offer indefinitely.

In a merger the two (or more) firms agree to form a new enterprise; shares in each of the individual companies are exchanged for shares in the new business.

> ### Key terms
>
> A **takeover** occurs when one firm gains control of another.
> A **merger** occurs when two or more firms join together to create one new united organisation.

Types of integration

There are three types of integration:

1 horizontal
2 vertical
3 conglomerate.

Horizontal integration occurs when one firm joins with another at the same stage of the same production process. For example, when Ford took over Volvo this was an example of horizontal integration because they are both car manufacturers.

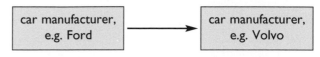

Figure 7.23

The possible reasons for this type of integration include

■ greater market share; by combining together the two firms will have a greater share of the market and as a result they are likely to have more power over other members of the supply chain, such as suppliers and distributors

■ economies of scale; larger-scale production may bring a reduction in unit costs due to financial, production or purchasing economies

■ the opportunity to enter a different segment of the market and thereby spread risks to some extent.

Vertical integration occurs when one firm joins with another at a different stage of the same production process. Forward vertical integration occurs when one firm joins with another business at a later stage in the same production process.

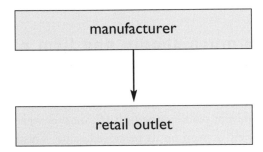

Figure 7.24 *Forward vertical integration*

Backward vertical integration occurs when one firm joins with another business at an earlier stage in the same production process.

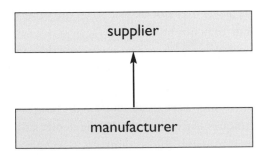

Figure 7.25 *Backward vertical integration*

Firms may undertake vertical integration in order to

■ gain control over supplies. This may be important for a firm to ensure it can maintain its suppliers (eg in times of shortage) or if it is essential to maintain the quality of its supplies. By gaining control of its inputs a firm may also be able to deny competitors the supplies they want

■ guarantee access to the market. By buying up retailers, for example, manufacturers may ensure their products actually get to the market and are displayed and promoted in the way they want.

A conglomerate merger occurs when firms in different markets join together, eg if a chocolate company joins with a paint company. Tomkins plc was one of the last big conglomerates in the UK and at one time sold guns, Mother's Pride bread and bicycles!

A firm may become a conglomerate in order to spread its risk. By operating in several markets or countries a firm is less vulnerable to changes in any one market. However, in some ways conglomerate mergers are much riskier than other forms of integration because managers may be entering markets in which they have relatively little experience.

Problems following a merger or takeover

Although in theory integration can offer many potential advantages such as economies of scale, many mergers and takeovers are relatively unsuccessful. One of the main problems following integration is coping with the different cultures of the organisations involved. Employees are likely to have different values regarding key areas such as customer service, quality, investment and training and this can cause conflict. Employees from one organisation may find that behaviour which was praised and rewarded in the past is now criticised. There will also be adjustment problems regarding pay and conditions – eg employees in one of the organisations may have a significantly better remuneration scheme than in the other – either the firm increases the rewards for one (which is expensive) or tries to negotiate the rewards of the other downwards (which will be unpopular).

Many firms also find that they experience diseconomies of scale following integration. Despite improvements in information technology communication can be a problem and there can be a lack of a common sense of purpose. The result is often a lack of coordination and demotivation.

Business in Focus: Glaxo

1 Discuss the possible benefits of the merger with SmithKline Beecham for Glaxo. *(20 marks)*
2 Consider the possible reasons why Glaxo invests so much in R&D. *(15 marks)*
3 Discuss the possible value to Glaxo of creating small profit centres within the firm. *(15 marks)*

After months of trying to organise and gain clearance from the regulatory authorities GlaxoSmithKline finally become one of the world's top drug companies in December 2000. The merger of Glaxo Wellcome and SmithKline Beecham creates a pharmaceuticals giant with sales of nearly £19bn and a market value of £130bn. It has 15,000 scientists and will spend nearly £7.5bn a year on the search for new drugs. Its massive sales force will dwarf most competitors in most of the 60 countries in which it operates. Only Pfizer of the US which in 2000 took over Warner Lambert for £60bn will be bigger.

The merger goes a long way towards creating Sir Richard Sykes' vision of a 'mega company'. As Glaxo chairman his view was that the industry would move towards a situation in which half a dozen companies had about a 10% share of the global prescription market; double the size of today's leaders. Along with Pfizer GlaxoSmithKline (which will also be known as GSK) will have about 7% of the global drugs market leaving others such as Merck of the US, Novartis of Switzerland and AstraZeneca of the UK with around 4.5%. Investors will expect GSK to use its huge R&D budget to produce a steady flow of blockbuster drugs.

To help bring this about the company is completely transforming the way R&D is organised with small units being created as separate profit centres which will compete for funds from GSK headquarters and pass on promising ideas to a central drug development unit. The company is hoping to instil competition without losing cooperation and also hopes to avoid the bureaucracy created in many large organisations. At the moment GSK has very few drugs in the pipeline that look like blockbusters. If it cannot develop them it will have to bring in drugs invented outside the company (as Pfizer has done on many occasions recently). The new chief executive of the combined operation must decide if a 7% market share is enough or whether to pursue Sir Richard's 10%. Also he must decide how to gain more of a foothold in Japan where the company needs more critical mass and whether to stay in consumer health.

Market share (%)
GlaxoSmithKline 7
Pfizer 6.7

The Financial Times

Furthermore many of the supposed benefits of integration do not appear – computer systems turn out to be incompatible, employees do not cooperate and share information and the business lacks focus or control. As a result integrated companies can find that their costs increase and that the returns generated are lower than would have been expected if they had remained single.

How much should one firm pay for another when undertaking a takeover?

The amount paid by one firm for another will ultimately depend on its perceived value. This in turn depends on the assets of the target firm and how the attacker believes these can be utilised. A starting point in a bid may be the target company's balance sheet – this shows the 'book value' of a company. However, the book value will not necessarily reflect the actual value of the firm because

- some assets may not be valued eg the value of brands may not be included
- some assets – such as property – may be valued at historical cost (ie the price paid for them) rather than their current value
- the firm may have used window-dressing techniques (such as changing the depreciation policy) to flatter the accounts.

These other factors may well be reflected in the current share price and therefore the market value of the business.

However, to make sure that the victim company's shareholders are willing to sell their shares the attacker is likely to have to pay a premium (ie to offer more than the existing share price). The amount of premium the bidder is willing to pay will depend on the extent to which they believe there will be gains such as economies of scale or synergy; the bigger the perceived gains the more they are likely to pay.

When deciding what a firm is worth there is inevitably a degree of risk. The risk involved will depend partly on whether it is a hostile or a welcome bid. If the bid is welcomed by the directors of the target company they will be willing to share information with the bidder. If the bid is hostile the attacking company will have no inside knowledge of the target firm and so may or may not be paying more than it should.

Takeovers, mergers and the government

A government might encourage firms to take over or merge with each other because this may lead to economies of scale. This in turn may lead to lower prices for consumers. Given the increasing globalisation of markets it may be important for UK firms to grow in size to be able to compete internationally. On the other hand the government may be concerned if firms get too big because this may lead to monopoly power and the exploitation of consumers. Given the possibility that integration may lead to an abuse of power the government reserves the right to investigate firms which have more than 25% market share or proposed mergers and acquisitions which might lead to this market share. The government investigates via the Competition Commission. Each case is investigated on its own merits and there is no assumption that monopoly power is undesirable – indeed it is up to the government to prove a firm is acting against the public interest before action can be taken. Possible courses of action include preventing integration from going ahead or forcing a dominant firm to sell off part of its business.

Going international

As well as growing within their domestic market firms can also grow by expanding overseas. The benefits of this are that it provides new market opportunities. If, for example, the domestic market is saturated, selling overseas can provide new

growth. Imagine you sell telephones; the UK market is fairly saturated so the majority of the sales which now occur are when people upgrade or replace a broken phone. In other countries with a lower standard of living the telephone market may still be in the growth phase of its life cycle.

The decision to sell overseas can be a difficult one to take. Along with all the usual problems of expansion a firm may face additional challenges such as dealing with exchange rate fluctuations and coping with new legislation. A firm will also have to familiarise itself with market conditions and consumer behaviour which can vary radically from one country to another.

Typically firms begin to sell abroad by exporting. They continue to produce in the UK but sell some of their products to overseas customers. If, however, demand from abroad continues to grow a firm may extend its operations by using an overseas agent. An agent will represent the business overseas and try to generate more sales on its behalf. An agent is likely to have more insight into the market than the UK firm and this should help to boost sales. Agents do not take ownership of the goods or services – they are paid on commission.

Instead of using agents a firm may join up with a local producer and either give or sell a licence to allow the products to be made there. The advantage of this approach is that the firm can benefit from local knowledge and skills as well as having lower distribution costs by producing in the region. In some cases linking up with a local firm may be the only way to enter a market because the foreign government may insist that local businesses are involved.

Alternatively a business may set up its own factory abroad and produce for itself. This is likely to involve high levels of investment and so will only be undertaken by firms if they are sure that demand will be sustained and profitable.

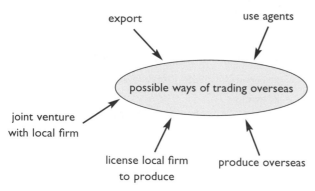

Figure 7.26

Business in Focus: from national to international

The Gerdau group is a century old family run steel company. Even when the rest of the steel industry in Brazil was struggling in the 1990s, because of the strong Brazilian currency, Gerdau maintained high profits. Underlying the strong performance is an international expansion that has reduced Gerdau's exposure to the risks of operating in Brazil. In a country where companies have traditionally focused on the domestic market Gerdau has pioneered globalisation, transforming itself from a local nail manufacturer at the beginning of the century into a global steel manufacturer.

Gerdau's international expansion began in the mid-1980s when it had reached the limits of its growth in Brazil where it had had 50% growth in steel products. A collapse in the domestic steel market exposed the company's dependence on Brazil and reinforced its desire to diversify.

Interestingly it decided to diversify internationally not into another market. This was not an obvious move – with cheap and readily available raw materials and power as well as an advanced infrastructure Brazil has many advantages for the production of steel over other countries. Gerdau forfeited these advantages by moving production abroad although this did serve to overcome trade barriers. The company decided to expand into America on the basis that European production costs were high and Asia too culturally different.

Gerdau first acquired a steel company in Uruguay in 1985 and Chile in 1995 and Argentina in 1997. It then bought some American steel mills in 1999.

The company has grown cautiously step by step carefully weighing up the benefits and risks at each stage. One of its chief criteria is logistics. Its nine mini mills are strategically situated to supply regional markets at lower costs than its competitors. 'Market proximity was one of the main considerations in our search for new plants abroad. All of our mills share that characteristic' says the company's president. The company exports its management style with reward programmes and an organisational structure built around teams designed to promote innovation and quality. In return the company has benefited from acquiring technological know how abroad. 'We never acquired a company because we sat on a pile of cash. It was to grow and also to learn.' As a result of foreign acquisitions foreign sales now make up 51% of the firm's total sales volume.

The Financial Times

1 What do you think has made Gerdau's expansion so successful?

Management buy outs

A management buy out occurs when the managers of a business take it over by buying a controlling interest in its shares. This may occur because the original owners feel the performance of the organisation is likely to deteriorate in the future whereas the managers may be convinced that they can still turn the business around. Alternatively the existing shareholders may want the firm to concentrate on other areas of the business and so be willing to sell off one particular part of the overall company.

Several management buy outs have occurred as a result of privatisation, where government has sold off a business to transfer it from the public sector to the private sector. Selling a firm to the existing managers is often the quickest and easiest way of privatising it.

To finance a buy out managers often have to borrow the money; they are unlikely to have enough personal funds to finance the deal themselves. This means that many buy outs have high gearing and the new owners face relatively high interest payments. This can put a great deal of pressure on the managers to ensure the business performs well to cover these repayments.

Buy outs can also be stressful for managers because by taking over the company they become totally responsible for the success (or failure) of the business. Rather than reporting to the owners, the managers must make all the decisions themselves; if the business does fail they are personally losing money. This means their role within the firm has changed and this can put a great deal of pressure on them. On the other hand if the firm does succeed they now keep all the rewards because they own it – this can obviously be very motivating. Previously if the business did well the profits belonged to the owners not them; now the rewards are theirs!

Key terms

Management buy out: *this occurs when the existing managers of a firm buy a controlling interest in the business in which they work.*
Gearing *measures the amount a firm has borrowed compared to the capital employed. High gearing means the borrowing is a high percentage of the total long-term sources of finance.*

Progress questions

1 Distinguish between a takeover and a merger.
(3 marks)

2 Explain two possible reasons why one firm might horizontally integrate with another. (6 marks)

3 Explain two possible reasons why one firm might vertically integrate with another. (6 marks)

4 What is meant by a conglomerate merger? (2 marks)

5 What is a management buy out? (2 marks)

6 Explain two possible reasons why managers might decide to buy out their company. (6 marks)

7 Explain two possible problems managers might face having undertaken a management buy out.
(6 marks)

8 Explain two possible problems a firm might face after a takeover. (6 marks)

9 Explain two ways in which a firm might finance a takeover. (6 marks)

10 Identify two different groups which might be affected by a takeover. Explain one way in which each group might be affected. (6 marks)

Analysis and evaluation questions

1 Examine the possible problems a firm might face following a takeover of another business. (8 marks)

2 Consider the factors a firm might consider before undertaking a takeover. (12 marks)

3 Discuss the possible reasons why the managers of a firm might take over the business. (12 marks)

4 Examine the factors which might determine the success of a merger. (12 marks)

5 Discuss the possible problems of a management buy out. (12 marks)

Case study 1

Sean and Frank Keegan run an agency for actors. Most of their clients manage to get small parts in the theatre or on TV but they also have several 'stars' who have landed big TV or film roles.

Sean and Frank are twins and their agency is called 'Brothers in Arms'. They set up the business in the 1970s when they had been unable to get enough acting parts for themselves! The agency had built up quite a reputation not least because of the charms and endless socialising of Sean and Frank. Whenever there was a showbusiness party to be at they were there. They seemed to know almost everyone who was anyone in British TV and theatre – at least they claimed they did. They also looked after their clients very well. They had what one called 'the personal touch'; 'when they spoke to you you felt really important – you were sure that one day you would make it and they would help you to get there.' Not that their success was down to luck – Sean and Frank worked extremely hard; even when they were at parties they were endlessly trying to get their clients parts. But now they had decided to call it a day. They both wanted to enjoy some of their wealth and even though they loved their work they knew the only way to do this was to stop completely. On 5 July, their birthday, they decided to sell the business and move overseas. With typical generosity they decided to offer it to their own staff first. The four most senior staff were Melanie, Jav, Vipul and Moira. They had all been at the agency for over ten years each and had gradually taken on more and more responsibility. Melanie was aged 53 and had been considering retiring early until this offer came along. Jav was younger and had been getting frustrated that there seemed nowhere else to go in the business. He had considered setting up his own agency but was not sure if he was really brave enough to go it alone. Moira was also ambitious but was busy writing her own soap opera which she hoped to get produced in the future. Vipul was less ambitious. He saw work as a means of earning money to finance his hobbies and his family life. He was 40 and enjoying life to the full at the moment.

1 Should Melanie, Jav, Vipul and Moira buy out the business? *(12 marks)*

Case study 2

LMB Bank plc had been eager to buy Courts Bank for several months. Finally in August 2001 it launched its bid. It offered £7.20 for each share. 'We believe there is a strong commercial logic behind this bid and are confident of success' said Mike McGinty the chief executive of LMB.

LMB is largely based in the south of England and has been particularly strong in the small-business sector. Courts by comparison was more prominent in Scotland where it had an extensive high-street presence. Attempts by Courts to break into new markets overseas by undertaking its own takeovers had largely been unsuccessful' now it found itself the victim not the aggressor!

The director of Courts strongly advised its shareholders to oppose the bid. 'This bid is in no-one's interests. We have various plans for the future of the bank including the development of e-banking and are convinced that if we are left to act independently the returns to shareholders can return to the high levels of the past.'

The management team at LMB are well known for their aggressive approach to cost cutting. In the last few years they have brought about major reductions in the cost to turnover ratio whilst at the same time boosting the revenue of the firm. According to Mike 'The managers at Courts have taken their eye off the ball for too long and their shareholders have suffered as a result. We intend to boost shareholder value once again.'

1 Analyse the possible reasons why LMB wants to take over Courts. *(8 marks)*

2 Discuss the possible factors which might determine the price LMB offers for each share of Courts. *(12 marks)*

3 Assuming the takeover goes ahead consider the factors which might determine success of the new business. *(12 marks)*

BUSINESS OBJECTIVES

Starting points

In this unit you will learn about the mission statement of a firm. This sets out the overall aim of a firm. Although you may not have studied mission statements before, the topic is very closely linked with business objectives. The objectives of a firm should relate directly to its mission statement. Before starting this unit it is therefore worth reviewing your materials on objectives from the AS course. We will also study organisational culture in this section. This is a very important topic which involves the ways in which people within the firm think and behave. Organisational culture links up with many other areas of the course and has a big impact on a firm's success.

Mission statements

A mission statement sets out what a firm is trying to achieve ie the reason why it exists. For example, a firm may set out to be 'the lowest-cost producer in the industry' or to 'maximise the returns for our shareholders'. By setting out a mission everyone within the firm knows what they should ultimately be trying to do. All of their actions should be directed towards the same thing. This should make decision making easier: when faced with a series of options managers can compare them in relation to the overall objective of the business. Mission statements can also motivate people – they know exactly why they are there and what the business is trying to achieve and this can give them a sense of belonging and direction.

*P*OINTS TO PONDER

Lego's mission is to 'nurture the child in all of us'.

However, some mission statements are so unrealistic that employees pay little attention to them. In other organisations managers clearly ignore the mission statement and so other employees lose faith in it as well. Imagine that the mission of your organisation was supposed to be 'to delight all of our customers' but every time you had an idea to improve customer service it was ruled out on the grounds of cost; you would soon realise that what the managers said they wanted to do was not the same as what they actually wanted to do. A mission statement will only have value therefore if the behaviour of everyone within the firm supports it. In these circumstances it can be a powerful way of uniting people and developing a corporate spirit.

Key terms

A **mission statement** sets out the reason why the organisation exists. One of the most famous mission statements occurred in Star Trek where the star ship Enterprise's mission was 'to boldly go where no man has gone before'.

*P*OINTS TO PONDER

'A company that attempts the impossible, thinks the unthinkable and achieves the incredible.'

(United Technologies: next things first.)

Once a firm has established its mission it can set its objectives. The objectives turn the mission statement into something which is more quantifiable. Rather than simply being a statement of intent an objective sets out clearly what has to be achieved.

To be effective objectives must be

- **S**pecific ie they must define exactly what the firm is measuring such as sales or profits
- **M**easurable ie they must include a quantifiable target, eg a 10% increase
- **A**greed. If targets are simply imposed on people they are likely to resent them; if however, the targets are discussed and mutually agreed people are more likely to be committed to them

People in business Schultz and Starbucks

Howard Schultz is the chairman and chief global strategist of the Starbuck's coffee chain who has built a personal fortune of around £160m. He is the driving force behind the chain's ferocious expansion opening branches in Beijing, Shanghai, Tokyo, Kuwait, Korea and Saudi Arabia. There are now more than 2,300 Starbucks worldwide. The mission of the business is to provide 'the Third Place' which is an oasis for contemplation – a stress-free place between home and work. 'The beverage is just a vehicle for crafting an experience. It's theatrical presentation – the music, the lighting, the atmosphere, the people – so that when people walk into our stores they feel better about themselves ... coffee has been a stimulus to conversation for hundreds of years.' Schultz has said he wants to reach McDonald's 25,000 branch target but does not believe the companies are comparable. 'McDonald's is in the fast food business and we don't think that's the business we're in. We're in the business of creating an experience around coffee and culture and the sense of community and the Third Place.'

After college Schultz spent three years in the marketing department of Xerox before joining Hammarplast, a Swedish housewares company. In 1982 he jumped ship to Starbucks which was then a distributor of coffee beans. Having visited Italy in 1983 where he saw the cafe culture in action he knew this was the way forward. His colleagues were not convinced so he left to start Il Giornale a café selling Starbucks coffee until they relented and hired him back.

The Guardian

Is Starbucks anything more than a coffee shop?

- **R**ealistic. If the objectives are unrealistic (eg they are too ambitious) people may not even bother to try and achieve them. To motivate people the targets must be seen as attainable
- **T**ime specific. Employees need to know how long they have to achieve the target – eg do they have two or three years?

An example of a good objective would be: 'to increase profits by 25% over the next four years'. By comparison a bad objective would be 'to do much better' – it is not clear what 'doing better' actually means, how it will be measured or how long you have.

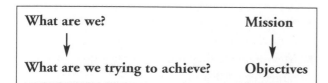

What are we?	Mission
↓	↓
What are we trying to achieve?	Objectives

The nature of the mission statement and the firm's objectives will be influenced by the organisation's culture.

Organisational culture

The culture of an organisation consists of the values, attitudes and beliefs of the people who work within it. Every organisation has its own unique culture and this has a big effect on its success. Imagine that you went on a tour of 200 schools and colleges around the country; each one would have its own way of doing things. In some, sport might be regarded very highly; in others it would be less important. In some there may be a very strong emphasis on doing the work neatly; in others the content may be thought of as much more important than the presentation. Some schools might be very formal; others might be more relaxed. Some might be focused almost entirely on exam grades; others

> **Key terms**
>
> An **organisation's culture** is determined by the values, attitudes and beliefs of the people who work within it.

might be more interested in the overall education a student receives. Think about your own school or college – how does it differ from others in the area? What do the staff and students seem to value most?

Just as schools differ so do businesses. In some firms the emphasis is on getting the job done – it does not matter what you do (providing it's legal) as long as you get results. If you upset people along the way so be it. In other organisations the emphasis is much more on working as a team and keeping up good relations with others; it is felt that it is not worth doing some things if you upset others as a result. In some firms new ideas are welcomed; the managers encourage you to try things out even if you fail occasionally. In other organisations you are expected to do what you are told and no more; if you start to question this you are seen as a troublemaker.

All of these differences are due to the organisational culture ie it depends on what managers within the firm regard as important.

There are hundreds of ways in which differences in the culture of organisations may be measured. Typical examples include

- task v people cultures. Does the job (task) come first? Or do people matter more?
- customer v firm cultures. How important is the customer? Does the customer really come first? Is the firm product oriented or market oriented?
- innovative v conservative cultures: does the firm like to carry on doing things the way they have always been done or is it open to new ideas? Does it welcome change or is it afraid of it?

Business in Focus: Southwest Airlines

'We started back in 1971 with three planes serving three Texas cities ... today we've got over 300 airplanes in 55 cities. We like mavericks – people who have a sense of humor. We've always done it differently. You know, we don't assign seats. Used to be we only had about four people on the whole plane, so the idea of assigned seats just made people laugh. Now the reason is you can turn the airplanes quicker at the gate. And if you can turn an airplane quicker, you can have it fly more routes each day. That generates more revenue, so you can offer lower fares.' (Herb Kelleher, CEO, Southwest Airlines)

Twenty-nine years ago, Rollin King and Herb Kelleher got together and decided to start a different kind of airline. They began with one simple notion: if you get your passengers to their destinations when they want to get there, on time, at the lowest possible fares, and make darn sure they have a good time doing it, people will fly your airline.

Southwest was launched with a 'love' them under the slogan 'Somebody up there loves you.' Its air hostesses wore hot pants and white PVC go-go boots. Drinks were Love Potions, peanuts were Love Bites and tickets came from Love Machines. Today Mr Kelleher has taken to extremes the notion that work can be fun. At the company's Dallas headquarters everyone, Mr Kelleher included, wears casual clothes, the practical jokes are incessant and the working routine is frequently interrupted by birthday celebrations or awards. The same spirit is at large on the company's aircraft, where the flight attendants play tricks on the passengers and turn the safety instructions into an excuse for a comic turn. One example: 'Those of you who wish to smoke will please file out to our lounge on the wing, where you can enjoy our feature movie presentation, Gone with the Wind.'

But there is a serious side to his approach. He believes that in a successful business the employees, not the customers, come first. The reasoning behind this philosophy is that if a company's employees are happy everything else will fall into place.

The Financial Times

1 What do you think was the main reason for the success of Southwest airlines?

***P*OINTS TO PONDER**

The army has a very formal culture in which orders are generally expected to be obeyed without question. The army has a tall hierarchy with narrow spans of control. This ensures a high level of supervision to make sure errors are not made and people do as they are told. Individuals are addressed by their full title (captain, major, colonel) and whoever has the highest rank will have the overriding authority. The Special Air Services – the SAS – by comparison is much more task focused. Individuals are member of the SAS because of their particular expertise. Members call each other by first names not their official titles and the importance of someone in the team depends on their ability to contribute to a particular mission. Far more than the regular army the SAS needs individuals to be able to react and make their own decisions in unusual situations. To achieve its own unique aims and to reflect the nature of its people (highly skilled and highly motivated) the culture of the SAS must be different. It deliberately sets out to distinguish the way it operates from the rest of the army.

Why does culture matter?

The culture of an organisation influences the way in which people work. People who join a new business often adapt to the existing culture just to fit in and be accepted. It takes a very strong character indeed to be willing to stand out and act differently especially if he or she is new to an organisation.

The culture will affect individuals' behaviour in all sorts of ways: it will affect how much effort they make to complete a job correctly, how they treat customers and the importance they place on teamwork. Walk into some stores and it is immediately clear that the culture of the organisation is very focused on the customers and on ensuring a high-quality service. In other shops there seems to be very little interest indeed in meeting the customer's needs.

If a manager wants to improve the performance of his or her business this often involves a culture change. In such a situation it is important that employees appreciate the need for the change. If the manager can build the idea of improvement into the culture of the firm then providing a better service will become the norm. If, on the other hand, complacency and inefficiency is the normal form of behaviour the manager may have to fight hard to change the way the firm operates.

Business in Focus

'After 15 years of consistent success we endured a year of dramatic setbacks. Those events provided us with a clear wake-up call that told us we had to rethink our approach for the new century...The world was demanding greater flexibility, responsiveness and local sensitivity while we were further centralising decision making and standardising our practices, moving further away from our traditional multi-local approach. We were operating as a big, slow, insulated insensitive 'global' company and we were doing it in a new era when nimbleness, speed, transparency and local sensitivity had become absolutely essential to success.

- Think local, act local. Many people say Coca-Cola is the brand with the greatest worldwide relevance. We know instinctively, however, that the global success for Coca-Cola is the direct result of people drinking it one bottle at a time in their own local communities. So we are placing responsibility and accountability in the hands of our colleagues who are closest to those billions of individuals.
- Focus as a marketing company. Disciplined focus is absolutely critical. All our success flows from the strength of our brands and our ability to relate to people.
- Lead as model citizens. In every community where we sell our brands we must remember we do not do business in markets; we do business in societies.

In our recent past we succeeded because we understood and appealed to global commonalities. In our future we'll succeed because we will also understand and appeal to local differences. The twenty-first century demands nothing less.

Douglas Daft chairman and chief executive of Coca-Cola,
27 March 2000

As the article shows Coca-Cola's culture and approach had become out of line with the attitudes of its customers all over the world. Coca-Cola had to rethink its own attitudes and consequently its strategy.

1 Discuss the possible benefits to Coca-Cola of thinking local and acting local?   *(15 marks)*

Business in Focus: Marks & Spencer

After years of being one of the country's favourite companies it is now attacked on all sides for poor quality and over priced goods. M&S needs to fight hard to protect its traditional image of better quality which might justify a price premium. It is a long time since any self respecting teenager went into an M&S store to buy clothes. Now even parents have learned to say no. Shoppers in their thirties and forties used to dress like their parents. Now many of them want to dress like their kids.

M&S is now focusing on its major stores; analysts believe the company makes most of its profits from around 40 stores. It then has another 270 stores which are less successful. In the past the company tended to focus on adding stores without really considering the success of each one; it only recent started to charge a notional rent to its stores. The company is now said to be considering closing some of its less profitable stores (something it did not really consider in the past). The rot at M&S began in 1998 when it announced a 23% fall in half year profits and warned of further bad news. In the event pre-tax profits fell from £1.2bn to £546m then fell again to £418m the next year. The share price meanwhile fell from £6.65 to £7. The biggest problems were in M&S's core area of British retailing although its overseas operations were also disappointing. It had, for example, failed to make much success of Brooks Brothers in North America. It is also planning to sell a food chain it bought in America and has had to close several large stores in continental Europe. The grand plan for international expansion has failed it seems.

Heads have rolled. Sir Richard Greenbury, the firm's autocratic boss, was forced to step down earlier this year. His successor had bold plans to overhaul the company's supply chain and buy more from abroad. He was later fired. Behind the problems were two key faults:

Firstly the rigid top down culture assumed 'head office knows best.' This was fine so long as customers kept coming and competitors lagged behind but it also made it difficult to question the M&S way of doing things. Only now is M&S ending many outmoded working practices which only existed because someone at head office decided they were useful many years ago.

Secondly top management was always recruited internally. People tended to join M&S from school and work their way up. Few senior appointments were made from outside the company. Arguably this led the company to missing out on many changes going on in the industry such as retail revolution in the mid 1990s when companies such as Gap and Next shook up the industry with attractive displays and marketing gimmicks. Their supply chains were overhauled to provide what customers were actually buying – a surprisingly radical idea at the time!

M&S stuck to its outdated business model. It clung to its 'buy British' policy and based its buying too much on what its buyers guessed about what ranges of clothing would be in demand rather than reacting quickly to the results of the tills. Meanwhile its competitors were putting together global purchasing networks which were not only more responsive but were also not linked into high costs linked to the strength of sterling.

In clothing M&S also faced the underlying problem that overall demand has at best stabilised and may be set to decline. This is because changing demographics mean that an ever higher share of consumer spending is being done by affluent over 45s. They are less inclined to spend a high proportion of their disposable income on clothes.

The results of M&S' rigid management were not limited to clothes. The company got an enormous boost 30 years ago when it spotted a gap in the food market and started selling fancy convenience foods. Whilst food takes up about 15% of its floor space it accounts for about 40% of its turnover. However the company gradually lost its competitive advantage as other stores imitated its formula. M&S has been forced to respond to their innovation by copying in-house bakeries, delicatessens and meat counters.

A good example of M&S' isolation from what was needed in the market was its refusal for more than 20 years to accept credit cards, launching its own store card instead. This was the cornerstone of a new financial services division also selling personal loans, insurance and unit trust investments. Eventually in April 2000 it accepted credit cards; it suffered again because it had to give 3% of its revenues to the credit card companies but failed to generate the necessary increase in sales to offset this. At the moment takeover specialists do not think M&S looks that attractive – even if you took it over and broke it up the costs of doing so would be extremely high. M&S has over 75,000 staff who would have to be made redundant and whilst the properties the company owns may be in attractive sites it may be difficult to sell them all off at the same time and so the sales could involve lots of time-consuming individual deals.

The Economist

EXAMINER'S ADVICE

The culture of an organisation can have a tremendous impact on its success. It can influence employees' commitment to work, the emphasis on quality and their openness to change. The power of culture should not be underestimated! There are many opportunities for you to bring the idea of culture into your answers so look out for them. The right culture can be a strength of the firm; an inappropriate culture can limit its success.

POINTS TO PONDER

The film *A Few Good Men* starring Jack Nicholson and Demi Moore focuses on the culture in the US marines. Two marines are accused of murdering another soldier but their defence is that they were simply following the orders of their superior without question, which is what they were trained to do. Their code they say is to respect 'their unit, the corps and God and country' in that order.

Changing culture

The culture of an organisation is often a reason for poor performance: people have come to accept poor quality or they do not try particularly hard to get things right. They accept second best, they fail to look for new ideas or new ways of doing things. In this situation management has the difficult task of trying to bring about cultural change. This can be very hard because it means changing the way people think and what they value. In some cases you may be directly challenging the way things have always been done, what people believe in and asking people to change the way they behave.

One way of speeding up the process is to get rid of the 'old guard' and bring in new people with new ideas and ways of doing things. Culture change is often associated with a new chief executive; if a school is failing the government will bring in a new headmaster or headmistress to bring about change. One reason why greenfield sites are attractive to firms is that they do not bring with them a workforce which has a set way of doing things. Japanese firms setting up in the UK in the 1970s and 1908s deliberately chose areas which had no previous associations with their type of business. This meant they could introduce their own ways of doing things without meeting resistance from employees who thought they knew how to do it a different way.

Key terms

Greenfield site: *this is an area which has no previous link with a particular type of industry.*

Culture change may also require a change in the reward system. If you want people to think and behave differently you must reward them accordingly. In the appraisal system or just in day-to-day comments you must acknowledge the behaviour which you like and encourage them; you must also point out and penalise people if the behaviour is wrong.

Culture change will also require some form of education or training programme to explain to people why it is being done and what the benefits are. People will also need reassuring that they will be able to adjust to the new approach and that they will be able to prosper under the new systems.

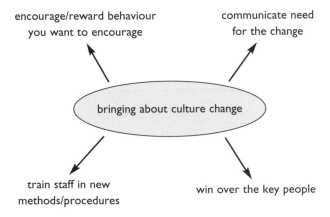

Figure 7.27

Entrepreneurial culture

The concept of culture applies as much to countries as it does to organisations. The UK has been criticised by many commentators for its lack of an enterprise culture. Despite enormous progress in the last 20 years it still remains quite difficult to be an entrepreneur in the UK and this is partly due to the attitudes of people in the country.

- Banks are reluctant to lend to entrepreneurs; they remain quite conservative, preferring established firms to start ups.
- If people fail in business it is difficult for them to start up again; once you have been a bankrupt in the UK it is extremely difficult to raise finance again. In the USA business failure is seen as almost inevitable at some point in your life. It is much more common the USA and regarded as perfectly natural for people to set up several businesses during their life.

The failure to encourage and support entrepreneurs means the UK is not as innovative as it might be and this costs jobs, exports and earnings.

Business in Focus

Every time Kenneth Davies calls a board meeting for his company, Everwhite Plastics, an insolvency practitioner from the Department of Trade and Industry has to be present. Davies' problems stem from 1989 when he became director of a Welsh construction company. He says he 'never saw the accounts or signed cheques'; he simply got on with what he was good at – managing large construction projects and making sales. He left the husband and wife team who owned the company to run the finances. But when the company collapsed in the early 1990s recession the DTI sought to ban Davies from becoming a director again. Eventually after many legal battles Davies was granted an exemption from the ban. Today his business is one of Britain's fastest growing private companies. Its sales are now over £6m with 65 people employed in an area that has 20% unemployment. Davies paid a high price when his business went under – he lost his home and his marriage broke up. He had difficulty opening a bank account and getting another mortgage. But now he is eager to get a second business going. Like many entrepreneurs he is always restless and has a huge appetite for risk. He continually has new ideas. In an enterprise economy such personalities are essential and this requires a culture which allows people to try more than once. To generate a genuine enterprise culture the British attitude to failure must change. Given that 45% of start up businesses fail within three years, failure has to become regarded as acceptable. Dan Wagner, head of Dialog, the on-line business provider says 'In America to have started a business that fails is seen as an honourable battle scar or a rite of passage. Nobody questions the right to try again.'

Would be American entrepreneurs have a head start on their British peers simply by virtue of numbers. They are likely to have more role models and the infrastructure of support permeates their culture. They also have less to fear if it goes wrong – friends, family, business angels and banks seem less likely to penalise them. Interestingly in America at any one time 8% of people are engaged in starting their own business. In Britain the figure is 3%. In Germany, France, Denmark and Finland it is less than 2%. 'You have to remember that the average duration of a business in America is the same as the duration of a job: four to five years. People will give it a go, and if it doesn't make money they will stop and do something else' says Reynolds the London Business School's entrepreneur professor.

The Sunday Times

1 Arguably the culture in the UK does less to encourage entrepreneurs than in other countries such as the USA. What are the possible implications of this for the UK?

Progress questions

1 What is meant by a mission statement? *(2 marks)*
2 Explain two possible benefits for a firm of introducing a mission statement. *(6 marks)*
3 Explain two factors which might determine the nature of a firm's mission statement. *(6 marks)*
4 What is meant by an organisation's 'culture'? *(2 marks)*
5 Explain two possible ways in which the culture of a firm might affect its performance. *(6 marks)*
6 Explain the possible problems of changing an organisation's culture. *(6 marks)*
7 How might a firm build an innovative culture? *(6 marks)*
8 Explain two ways in which a manager might bring about a cultural change. *(6 marks)*
9 Explain two reasons why employees might resist a manger's attempt to change their organisation's manager. *(6 marks)*
10 Explain two reasons why an organisation's culture might change. *(6 marks)*

Analysis and evaluation questions

1 Examine the possible benefits to an organisation of having a mission statement. *(8 marks)*
2 Analyse the ways in which an organisation's culture might affect its performance. *(8 marks)*
3 To what extent does the culture of an organisation determine its success? *(12 marks)*
4 Discuss the possible problems involved in trying to change an organisation's culture. *(12 marks)*
5 To what extent can the introduction of a mission statement improve a firm's performance? *(12 marks)*

Case study

When Franco Zeferelli took over at Chelten Sixth Form College he felt that there had been a lack of leadership in the past. Results had been declining, staff had been leaving and there was a general sense of decline and disillusionment. Franco spent the first few weeks after his appointment meeting the staff and students and getting to know how the college worked. He also went out of his way to invite in parents and find out their views as well.

From his discussions Franco felt that the culture of the organisation was rather negative. Talking to his senior staff Franco said 'People seem to accept second best and don't strive to be excellent. The message we are sending out is that it is OK to do the bare minimum. Students pick up on this and it affects their attitude to work as well. Everyone who works here seems to think that we simply exist to get by rather than to excel. I want to put some energy back into the place and make us more ambitious. The culture of the place must change.' One of Franco's ideas is to produce a mission statement for the college. He sees this as a valuable exercise both internally and in terms of the college's external image.

Franco had originally worked in marketing and had run his own successful marketing consultancy for many years. After ten years' running a business he had decided to go into education and quickly worked his way up into management there. This was his first appointment as a principal.

1 Consider the problems Franco might face changing the culture of the college. *(12 marks)*
2 To what extent might the introduction of a mission statement benefit the college? *(12 marks)*

BUSINESS STRATEGY

Starting points

In this unit we study the way in which firms make decisions. This includes scientific decision making and decision tree diagrams. It overlaps with scientific marketing which was covered in the marketing section of the A2 course. The topics in this section do not particularly build on AS work, although the way on which decisions are made and the quality of decisions clearly affect all areas of the specification.

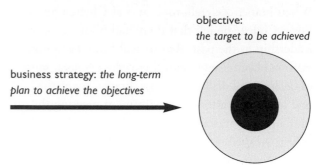

Figure 7.28

Management and decisions

Management is all about making decisions. Managers are in charge of various resources (such as people, money, machines and materials) and must decide how to use these most effectively. This involves hundreds of decisions every week.

Making the right decision is crucial to effective management and to a successful business. Managers must be able to offer customers the right products at the right price in the right place and in the right way; to do this they must get their decisions right. No manager will get everything right all of the time but the good managers are the ones who get it right most of the time and who make sure the big decisions are correct.

Strategic and tactical decisions

The business strategy is the long-term plan to achieve the business objectives. For example, if a firm's target was to increase profits it might try and do this by reducing costs or by increasing revenue; these would be two strategies to achieve the same goal. Similarly if a firm was trying to boost overall sales the managers might take a strategic decision to do this by trying to sell more of its existing products or by increasing sales of new products; again these would be two different ways of achieving the same end goal.

Strategic decisions tend to be long term, involve a major commitment of resources and are difficult to reverse. For example, the decision to invest in new product development is likely to involve a high level of finance and take several years. Strategic decisions also tend to involve a high level of uncertainty. Over time market conditions often change significantly and so firms must change their strategies to cope with unfamiliar conditions.

The value of producing a clear strategy is that it sets out the firm's overall plan; this helps employees develop their own plans to implement the strategy. If you know the firm wants to diversify, for example, you know that it is realistic to consider market opportunities in new segments of the market. If you know the strategy is to boost the firm's market presence in a particular region you will know it is worth putting more resources into this area.

The decisions made about how to implement the strategy are called 'tactical decisions'. Compared to strategic decisions tactics tend to be

- short term
- involve less resources
- made more regularly and involve less uncertainty.

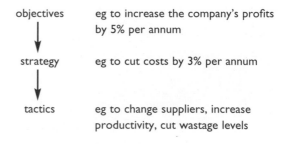

Figure 7.29

strategic decisions	tactical decisions
long term	short term
involve high commitment of resources	less resources involved
difficult to reverse	easier to reverse
usually taken by senior management	usually taken by more junior management

Table 7.2 *Strategic versus tactical decisions*

Making a decision

There are many different ways of making a decision: in some cases managers will research the decision thoroughly – they will gather data and analyse it before deciding what to do; in other cases they may rely on their own experience from the past or on their gut feeling. It depends on what the decision is, the risk involved and their own personality. If, for example, the decision concerns the purchase of new production equipment and involves hundreds and thousands of pounds a manager will probably research the decision very carefully; with an unfamiliar decision involving high levels of resources managers would not want to risk getting it wrong. If, however, the decision simply involves ordering some more supplies of pens for the office the manager might be more inclined to use his or her experience. The same is probably true of your own decision taking – if you are spending a few hundred pounds on a new PC you will probably research the decision much more than if you feel thirsty and want to buy a soft drink.

When you gather data and analyse it before making a decision this is known as a scientific approach to decision making. It is scientific because it is rational and logical and is based on data. Many of the mathematical topics you have studied are to

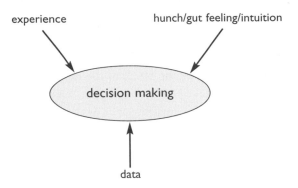

Figure 7.30

help managers analyse the data as part of scientific decision making. Break-even analysis, ratio analysis, investment appraisal and correlation analysis, for example, are all ways in which managers analyse the data to try and make the right decision.

Scientific decision making should reduce the risk of error because decisions are based on information. On the other hand the usefulness of this method will inevitably depend on the quality of the data. The better the information the more likely it is the right decision will be made; this is why market research is important and why managers need to

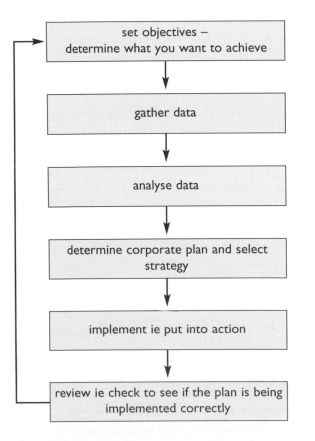

Figure 7.31 *A model of scientific decision making*

ensure they have effective ways of gathering, analysing and circulating information within the organisation to ensure each manager has the information he or she needs at the right time.

Decision trees

A decision tree is a mathematical model which can be used by managers to help them make the right decision.

Imagine that a manager is trying to decide whether to cut the price of a product or increase the amount of money spent on advertising. These options can be illustrated as follows.

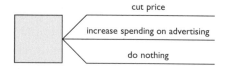

Figure 7.32

The square shows that a decision has to be made and the lines coming from it show the possible choices facing the firm. Note that there is a third line saying 'do nothing'; this is because managers always have the option of doing nothing at all so you should always include this as an option when drawing a decision tree.

Whenever you choose a particular course of action such as advertising or cutting the price there will be a range of possible outcomes. For example, if the firm advertises its products there may be a big increase in sales or a small increase in sales; similarly if the price is cut this may have a big or a small impact on sales. These possible outcomes can be illustrated on the decision tree as follows.

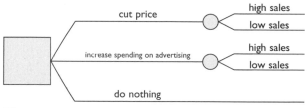

Figure 7.33

The circles show that different outcomes are possible; these are then illustrated by the lines coming out of the circles.

At the moment the decision tree simply illustrates the options and the possible outcomes. To make it more useful and to help managers make the decision we can add in some numerical data.

First, we need to know how likely it is that the predicted increase in sales will be 'high' or 'low' for each option. This is known as the probability of a particular outcome. The value of the probability can range from 0 to 1. The bigger the number the more likely it is that an event will happen. If the number is 1 this means the event is certain to happen.

𝑚 ATHS MOMENT

The probability of an event is the likelihood of its occurring. Probability can have a value between 0 and 1. The bigger the number the more likely it is that an event will occur.

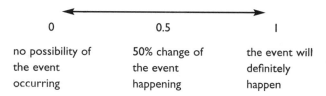

Figure 7.34

If all the outcomes of an event are considered their probabilities must add up to 1 eg if the probability of it raining tomorrow is estimated to be 0.4 then the probability of it not raining must be 0.6. Combined, the probabilities = 1 because it must either rain or not rain. Similarly if we estimate that following a change in design the probability that sales will increase is 0.5, and the probability that sales will fall is 0.3 then the probability that sales stay the same must be 0.7.

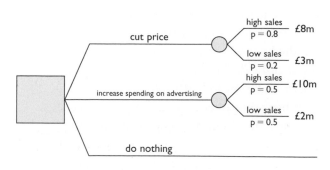

Figure 7.35

In figure 7.35 we have now added the probabilities of each outcome (where 'p' shows the probability). For example, the managers have estimated that if the firm advertises there is a 0.5 chance of a big increase in sales and a 0.5 chance of a small increase in sales; in other words there is a 50% chance of a big increase in sales and a 50% chance of a small increase. In the case of a price cut however, the manager has estimated that there is a 0.8 chance of a big increase (ie an 80% chance) and a 0.2 (or 20% chance) of a small increase.

We have also added in the estimated benefits of each outcome. For example, if the firm advertises and there is a big increase in sales the benefit will be an increase in profits of £10m. A small increase would increase profits by £2m.

The diagram now shows

- the three possible decisions the firm could take (cutting price, increasing advertising or doing nothing)
- the outcomes of each one (eg high sales or low sales)
- the probability of each outcome (eg 0.5)
- the financial consequences of each outcome (eg an increase in profits).

The next step is to work out 'the expected value' of each decision. This is basically a weighted average of the outcomes taking account of the probability of each one. Although the firm may gain £10m by advertising – this is only 50% likely; there is also a 50% change that it will gain £2m. So what, on average will it gain? Imagine if this decision was made over and over again. Fifty per cent of the time the firm would gain £10m; 50% of the time it would gain £2m so on average it would gain £6m.

This can be calculated using the equation

$$\text{Expected Value} = (\text{probability}_1 \times \text{outcome}_1) + (\text{probability}_2 \times \text{outcome}_2) + \ldots$$

[where 1 represents the first outcome and 2 represents the second outcome and so on].

That is, to calculate the expected value we multiply the probability of each outcome with the financial consequences of the outcome and add them all up. This shows how much the firm would earn on average if the decision was taken repeatedly.

Expected Value of advertising =
$(0.5 \times £10m) + (0.5 \times £2m) = £5m + £1m = £6m$

If we look at the option of cutting the price we can see there is an 80% chance of earning £8m and a 20% chance of £3m. This means on most occasions the firm would earn £8m but there is a 20% probability of earning £3m. Once again we calculate the expected value using the equation

Expected Value =
$(0.8 \times £8m) + (0.2 \times £3m) = £6.4m + £0.6m = £7m$

This has a higher expected value than advertising and so on this basis the manager would choose this option. The expected values are shown on the decision tree diagram above the outcome circles; the options which are not chosen are shown using a double-crossed line.

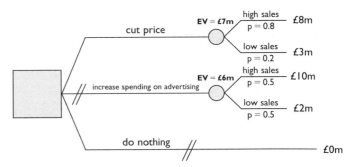

Figure 7.36

Using decision trees can be very useful for managers because it

- makes them think about the different options they have and consider the possible consequences of each one
- forces them to quantify the impact of each decision
- helps them to logically compare the options open to them.

However, decision trees do have various limitations and drawbacks.

- Decision trees use estimates of the probability of different outcomes and the financial consequences of each outcome. The value of decision tree analysis depends heavily on how accurate these estimates are.
- Decision trees only include financial and

quantifiable data; they do not include qualitative issues such as the workforce's reaction to different options or the impact on the firm's image.

Developing decision tree analysis

In the examples used so far we have only considered two possible outcomes following any decision and we have assumed the outcomes are positive. In reality there may be several different outcomes following any decision; it is also possible that a particular decision leads to losses if things go wrong. One further addition to our analysis is to include an initial costs of undertaking a particular course of action such as the costs of research and development

or the costs of building a distribution network. When deciding which course of action to choose a firm will consider the expected profit once the initial costs have been chosen.

Figure 7.38 incorporates the new elements mentioned.

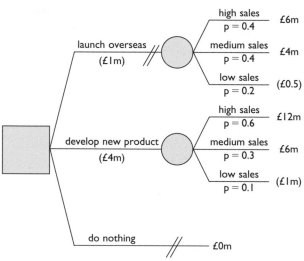

Figure 7.38

Launch overseas

Expected value = (0.4 × £6m) + (0.4 × £4m) + (0.2 × −£0.5m) = £2.4m + £1.6m − £0.1m = £3.9m

Initial cost = £1m
Expected net profit = £3.9m − £1m = £2.9m

Develop new product

Expected value = (0.6 × £12m) + (0.3 × £6m) + (0.1 × −£1m) = £7.2m + £1.8m − £0.1m = £8.9m

Initial cost = £4m
Expected net profit = £8.9m − £4m = £4.9m

One further refinement to decision tree diagrams is to add in more than one decision on the chart. It is possible, for example, that one decision may lead to others. For example, if a firm decides to enter an overseas market and it is successful, this may lead to a further decision about whether or not to enter a second market overseas as illustrated in figure 7.39.

In figure 7.39 the firm will choose to enter one overseas market but will not enter a second one.

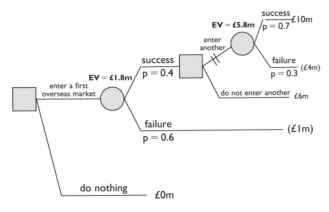

Figure 7.39

The role of risk

It is important to remember that the expected value shows how much the firm would earn on average if the decision was repeated time and time again. In reality it may well be a one-off decision and therefore only one of the outcomes will actually occur. In our first example advertising will either lead to a £10m gain or a £2m gain. The expected value of £6m is a weighted average but in fact the firm will earn £10m **or** £2m – it will not actually earn £6m. This may have an impact on the decision a firm makes. In figure 7.40, for example, a firm can choose between modifying an existing product or developing a new product. Each option has two possible outcomes.

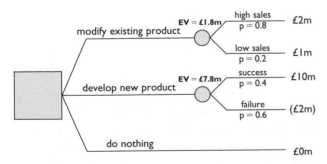

Figure 7.40

The expected value of modifying an existing product is

$(0.8 \times £2m) + (0.2 \times £1m) = £1.8m$

The expected value of developing a new product is

$(0.4 \times £10m) + (0.6 \times -£2m) = £2.8m$

Although developing a new product has a higher expected value than modifying an existing product the firm may choose the latter rather than the former. This is because there is a possibility of losing much more money if the new product fails than could be lost by modifying the product. If managers dislike risk they may choose to make modifications to the existing product because this limits the downside if it all fails. On average if the decision was repeated time and time again developing a new product would be the best decision on financial grounds but as a one-off decision the firm may prefer to play safe and choose to modify the existing product.

Corporate plan

A corporate plan is a long-term strategy by which a business hopes to achieve its objectives. The plan therefore depends on what the firm is trying to achieve. It will also depend on the firm's resources and the environment in which it operates.

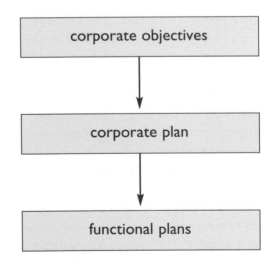

Figure 7.41

> **Key terms**
>
> The **corporate plan** sets out the overall strategy of the firm to fulfil its objectives.

The corporate plan sets out the firm's overall strategy; from this the plans for all the different functions of the business (eg marketing, finance, people and operations) will then be derived. The corporate plan basically sets out how the firm is going to get to where it wants to get to. Once this has been decided each section of the business can plan how it will contribute to the overall strategy.

The value of planning is that it makes sure that managers are looking ahead and thinking about what they want to achieve and how to achieve it rather than just drifting along. Producing the plan is also a useful exercise because it forces managers to consider the organisation's strengths and weaknesses in relation to its environment and to think about how all the different elements of the firm interrelate.

However, corporate planning can have drawbacks. There is a danger that a plan which sets out what a firm is going to do for, say, the next five years is soon out of date. If managers keep pursuing the original plan when all around them has changed there is a danger that they will actually be doing the wrong thing. It may be necessary therefore to ensure the firm has a flexible approach to planning and keeps revisiting the original plan to ensure it remains viable and relevant.

Contingency planning

Contingency planning occurs when a firm prepares for unlikely events. Most firms undertake some form of contingency planning, eg they will have fire practices in case there is a fire and they are likely to take back-up copies of the data held on their

People in business: Michael Porter

Michael Porter is a business guru. His book Competitive Strategy published 20 years ago has become a management bible. It has been printed in over 50 editions and translated into over 17 languages. Porter is a professor at Harvard Business School as well as a business adviser to many major corporations and governments. Commenting recently on this work which has led to executives everywhere coming up with so called strategies:

'the word strategy is used promiscuously. The truth is that in any industry very few companies have a strategy. The rest are just imitators, following the pack.' To produce a real strategy rather than just adopting best practice (eg cutting costs and improving products) a firm must be able to demonstrate it is trying to deliver distinctive values that are different from its competitors.

It has to carry out a set of activities to deliver the product in a different way from competitors. A strategy should involve trade offs where a company has to sacrifice some of its subsidiaries or opportunities to focus on its strategy. A strategy must also fit – all the company's activities must be consistent. A strategy must also have continuity – there is no point in having one strategy in 2000 if you have a different one in 2001.

Asked whether strategic planning does in fact make good business Porter says '...on the evidence of loads of personal evidence from hundreds of companies over the years, there are a tremendous number of managers who find that having a structure to look at competition has been enormously beneficial. There are many elements that make a good CEO and strategic analysis is not 100% of it. But the best CEOs are able to give a clear purpose to their organisations. You find they endlessly repeat their strategy to their employees.'

The Sunday Telegraph

1 According to Porter what is a strategy? How useful does Porter think strategic planning is?

computers at regular intervals in case the systems crash. However, managers must decide exactly which events are worth preparing for and how many resources to put into contingency planning. Should the firm have back-up plans in case there are problems with suppliers? Does it need to plan what to do if employees walk out on strike? What about planning for a situation where a competitor makes a takeover bid?

To decide on which events to plan for, a firm will consider

- how likely is a particular event to happen?
- what is the potential damage if it does occur?

The greater the likelihood of an event and the greater the potential damage if it does occur the more likely a firm is to plan for it. Food manufacturers, for example, are likely to plan for a situation where their products are contaminated and they have to recall them.

The need for contingency planning highlights the dynamic nature of business and the need to be prepared for the unexpected. Obviously a firm cannot prepare for every emergency but it is worth highlighting the biggest risks and preparing for these. Firms must continually examine their own operations and their environment to check they are prepared for possible changes in the future; in this way managers will be proactive – anticipating and preparing for change – rather than reactive – having to react to crises as they develop.

The impact of a crisis

When a disaster does occur such as a fault in the product or a fire at the factory this can cause panic. Hopefully the firm will have a contingency plan which it can put into action but even so this is likely to be a stressful time. It is easy to rush into a decision at times like these because of the pressure to do something and be seen to be doing something – this can lead to rushed and inappropriate decision making; on the other hand if you delay too long the crisis may get worse. As well as sorting out the crisis itself the firm may have to handle the press as well. When managing a crisis it is important

- to identify the 'facts' as soon as possible. What is

Business in Focus: contingency planning at Guinness

To the outside world the £23bn merger between Grand Metropolitan and Guinness was put together in record time. It was formally announced just five weeks after the GrandMet chairman put the idea to Guinness' chairman. But the reality was the product of several years of secret planning and preparation by a team at Guinness. In 1994 Guinness put together a 'virtual' law team to anticipate and prepare for possible developments in the industry.

The project began with an analysis of the industry 'from top to bottom'. When this was complete the team had collected 16,000 lever arch files which they housed on one complete floor of a City office block. 'By the end we could tell you how many bottles of port were sold in Iceland in each outlet, where those outlets were, whose port it was and at what price' they said.

The next step was to build models for every conceivable transaction from merger, takeover to joint venture. Documentation was put together for each one of these options for each of its main competitors down to the number eight by size in the world.

Then they set about working out their response if they were not leading the consolidation. When the suggestion of a GrandMet Guinness deal came up the team were already ready. When asked whether this was an expensive way of doing things Guinness said 'Yes and no. It was expensive when nothing was happening but once the button was pushed it was very cheap. Instead of lots of people scrabbling around doing work which may or may not be required it's all there.'

The Financial Times

1 How much should a firm spend preparing for a possible takeover bid? *(15 marks)*

Business in Focus: crisis at Ford

In 2000 Jac Nasser the chief executive of the Ford Motor Company appeared on US network and cable television in a campaign to restore confidence in the world's second largest carmaker.

In an unprecedented advertising blitz Mr Nasser has been telling viewers 'I want all of our owners to know that there are two things we never take lightly – your safety and your trust.' These appearances have been prompted by growing protests over the fatal tyre failures on Ford's best selling sports utility vehicle, the Explorer. In one of the biggest product recalls seen by the industry in recent years Ford pledged to replace the 6.5m Firestone tyres supplied by Bridgestone, the Japanese tyre manufacturer. According to US federal authorities faulty Firestone tyres on Ford's off road Explorer have been linked to more than 60 road deaths. Put simply Ford has been accused of fitting a product liable to 'tread separation' and catastrophic blow outs that could cause the Explorer to flip over at speed. The stakes are high: analysts believe that Explorers account for more than 20% of Ford's $7.24bn net income.

Following the crisis Ford set up a so called 'war room' in Detroit to oversee the crisis. In addition to a national broadcast and print campaign the company set up 24 hour hotlines. It also dramatically increased orders for replacement tyres from Goodyear and Michelin and halted Explorer production at three US plants enabling 700,000 tyres earmarked for new cars to be used in recall. Ford's action contrasted sharply with Mitsubishi Motors in Japan which recently admitted it had concealed customer complaints for more than 30 years. Mitsubishi failed to report defects including failing brakes, malfunctioning clutches and faulty fuel tanks and tried to cover up problems without a product wide recall.

Industry analysts say the contrasting styles illustrate different corporate cultures in which Japanese firms are loathe to admit engineering problems whereas US firms prefer to get the problem out in the open. Mitsubishi ended up recalling 600,000 vehicles in an exercise which cost $70m. For Bridgestone and Ford the cost was estimated to be between $300m and $500m. But financial cost is not the real issue – the real dilemma is always how to restore confidence in a product or as with Firestone an entire brand once it has been tainted. Jac Nasser has said 'you have my personal guarantee that all the resources of the Ford Motor Company are directed to resolve this situation.'

The Financial Times

1 Do you think Ford should be held responsible for the problem with Bridgestone tyres?
2 If you discover a problem with one of your products, is it better to keep it quiet or let the public know?

the scale of the problem? How many people are likely to be affected?

■ to establish good communication systems; managers must make sure that everyone is 'on line' and reacting in the same way. If, for example, different managers are giving the press different information following a scare about the safety of the product this will create the impression they are not in control and the public may lose faith.

Managing change

Although it is a cliché one of the constants of the business world is that firms will face change: the only thing you can be certain of is that things will be different in the future. Change may be internal eg employees' needs and expectations may change over time – or external – eg changes in the economy.

To be successful firms have to try and anticipate change rather than always reacting to it. This means they need to be proactive rather than reactive. To anticipate change firms need good information systems – they need to be regularly monitoring the environments in which they operate. Gathering information may be done in many ways, eg it may be done through market research to find out changes in market conditions or through great employee participation to identify changes in the workplace. A successful firm is likely to be well informed so that it is less likely to be caught by surprise. Even then sudden events or crises can occur and in this situation contingency planning and a flexible approach can help.

Change may be incremental ie a gradual move away from one type of product to another by customers, or dramatic – eg a change in legislation bans the product. It may be anticipated – eg changes in regulations may be announced a long time in advance – or unanticipated – eg a problem is found with the safety of a product. Obviously incremental change which is anticipated is easier to plan for than an unanticipated dramatic change.

When bringing about change firms must consider issues such as

- the final destination – is it clear to everyone what you are trying to achieve?
- resources – do you have the finance to bring about the change you want?
- reactions of others – how will employees and competitors react?
- what are the conditions for success – what will you have to get right to make sure the plan succeeds?

Resistance to change

Managers often find that employees are resistant to change. This is usually for the following reasons.

- They do not understand the purpose of the change – why is it happening? What are the managers trying to achieve? Why is it necessary?
- They do not trust the managers. The managers may have explained the change but employees do not believe them – they suspect the end result is likely to be more work, less pay and fewer jobs!
- They do not agree with the change. They understand what it is and why it is being done but they do not think it is the right solution. They may have (or think they have) a better answer.

- They will be worse off as a result. They understand the change and why it is happening but they do not actually like it. It may mean a loss of status or benefits or simply involve a lot of extra and undesired work.

To ease the process of change managers should

- make sure people understand the logic and need for change
- think about the timing – the process of change can sometimes seem to go on for too long and you lose people's enthusiasm; at the same time sudden change can appear frightening to people so managers need to ensure people feel comfortable with the pace of change
- make sure people feel able to cope with the change – this may involve extra training to ensure they have the necessary skills or demonstrating how such change has been successful elsewhere
- show vision and commitment. Bringing about change will usually involve leadership. Managers must show they know where the business is going as a result of the change and why it is necessary. They must show their commitment to the project (in words, deeds and resources) or others will lose confidence.

An organisation which is happy to change and in which change and progress are a key part of the culture is more likely to succeed than one which continues to do things the same way regardless. Markets, technology, regulations and products are changing and developing at an incredible rate; successful firms must be flexible to such change, ready to adapt their products and processes to new conditions. This involves a workforce which is open and actively seeking new ways of doing things. In some cases it may even involve a complete change in what the organisation does and how it does it. Firms such as 3M and IBM have succeeded by reinventing themselves to change with the times. Change therefore has to be anticipated and embraced; firms ignore it at their peril.

Progress questions

1 Outline the stages of the scientific decision-making model (4 marks)

2 Explain two possible benefits of adopting a scientific approach to decision making. (6 marks)

3 A manager estimates that following an advertising campaign the probability that sales will increase is 0.4, the probability that they will fall is 0.1. What is the expected probability that sales will stay the same? Explain your answer. (3 marks)

4 Sue Ryder is trying to decide which of the following courses of action she should take:

   a) Expand internationally. This is expected to cost £2m; she estimates a 0.8 chance of success and a 0.2 chance of failure. Success would lead to a profit of £5m; failure would lead to a loss of £3m.

   b) Invest in new products. The initial cost would be £4m. The probability of success is estimated to be 0.5 and would bring profits of £6m. If the product fails the expected loss is £0.5m.

   c) Do nothing. This would cost nothing and bring no change in profits or losses.

   Construct a decision tree to illustrate the situation in question 4. Which decision would you choose and why? (6 marks)

5 Distinguish between 'strategic' and 'tactical' decisions. (3 marks)

6 What is meant by a corporate plan? (2 marks)

7 Explain two factors which might influence a firm's corporate plan. (6 marks)

8 What is meant by a contingency plan? (2 marks)

9 Explain two reasons why a firm might undertake contingency planning. (6 marks)

10 Explain the possible reasons why a firm's workforce might resist the modernisation of the production process. (6 marks)

Analysis and evaluation questions

1 Is scientific decision making useful? (12 marks)

2 Analyse the possible benefits to managers of using decision trees. (8 marks)

3 Discuss the possible implications for a firm of a sudden change in the number of competitors in its market. (12 marks)

4 How important is corporate planning? (12 marks)

5 To what extent should a firm invest in contingency planning? (12 marks)

Case study I

'You should have known something like this was going to happen. Something like this always happens to us. Why didn't you plan for it?' screamed Isobel. Isobel was married to Mark. They had both been working in a hospital but had been bored by their jobs. A year ago they had decided to set up a shop together. They had no previous business experience but lots of enthusiasm. Mark had a contact in Greece who produced pots. They had met when Mark and Isobel were on holiday several years ago; they had all got on well and had kept in touch ever since.

When Mark and Isobel decided to go into business together they contacted their friend in Greece and arranged to buy pots from him which they would sell in their shop. They decided to call the shop 'Lots of Pots' and armed with a business plan eventually convinced the bank to lend them enough money to set up. Unfortunately from the very first moment the shop opened times had been tough. Mark and Isobel had struggled to attract sufficient numbers to break even despite working almost 16 hours a day either selling in the shop or trying to generate business.

Along the way there had been various disasters which made Isobel think they were cursed. Weeks after moving in there was a flood in the shop because the roof leaked. Then a big DIY store nearby started selling its own range of pots at cheaper prices. Then just last month Mark tripped on the shop's front step and in the fall broke his leg. It was still in plaster.

And now just as things looked as if they might be looking up – last week they had had their best week ever in terms of sales – their delivery of pots failed to turn up. When they tried to get hold of their friend in Greece to find out what had happened there was no answer. After two days of telephoning anyone and everyone they knew in Greece Mark and Isobel have now learnt that their supplier has gone bankrupt and has disappeared, leaving many creditors behind him. 'What do we do now? Not only do we have no pots to sell but that rat has got our money as well. Why did you agree to pay him up front? You must be mad. You never plan for anything properly – you just think everything will be alright. Well Einstein what are we going to do next?'

1 To what extent should Mark have planned for the problems his business faced?

Case study 2

Lulu Rocher is facing a difficult decision. Should she put money into launching a new product or should she spend it modifying the existing product range? She knows she has to do something because the sales of the Beauty cosmetics range have been rather disappointing recently. Lulu is the marketing director of the cosmetics division of Portello, a company which produces a wide range of products from toilet rolls to toothpaste. Lulu has to produce a proposal to the directors of the company outlining her plans for the cosmetics.

She has estimated the costs and expected profits shown as follows:

- launching a new product: initial cost £4m; likelihood of success 0.3; likelihood of failure 0.7; the expected profit if the product is successful is £18m; if the product fails the company could lose £2m
- modifying the existing range: initial cost £1m; the likelihood of a significant increase in sales is 0.6; the likelihood of a relatively low increase in sales is 0.4; the expected profit if sales are much higher is £3m; if the sales increase is relatively low the expected profit will be £1.2m.

1 a) Construct a decision tree highlighting the options facing Lulu.
(5 marks)

b On the basis of your decision tree which choice should Lulu take? Justify your answer.
(5 marks)

2 Discuss the value to Lulu of using decision tree analysis.
(12 marks)

Case study 3

Frank Zappa was the founder of Solutions, a management consultancy firm. Frank had worked for one of the world's biggest management consultancy firms for many years and had been highly successful. He had been promoted rapidly and had been rewarded well. However, this had not been enough for Frank – he wanted to run his own firm. At the age of 38 to the amazement of his colleagues he left his well-paid, secure job and decided to start up his own firm. He approached several contacts from his previous job for finance and was soon trading as Solutions Ltd. He managed to convince several colleagues to come with him – they were attracted by the challenge and the chance to build something from scratch.

From the beginning Frank made it clear that this consultancy was to be different – eg there was no dress code and no fixed hours – people came and went as they wanted. Staff were encouraged to 'think outside of the box' meaning that he wanted them to find original solutions to problems. 'If all we can do is come up with the same as everyone else we won't survive – we need to think of solutions the competition could not even dream of!'

The company's mission was 'Turning problems into profits' – Frank wanted companies in trouble to approach his business and he would show them how to turn the business around.

'In those days there was a real buzz about the place. We were often working 50 or 60 hours a week but we hardly seemed to notice. We were all in it together – trying to prove ourselves and trying to prove we were the best. We worked hard and played hard. We would finish late at night and then all go out and party. Then we'd be up early the next day and start again! And it paid off. We did some excellent work – often coming up with some of our best ideas when we were out in the evening! What was good in the early years was that everyone felt involved and able to contribute. We had employed some excellent people and they paid us back with some truly brilliant work. It didn't matter how long you'd been with us, what else you'd done or even how old you were – if you could help solve a particular problem you were on board.'

The company had some great successes early on and attracted a great deal of publicity – the result was that it was almost overwhelmed by demand for its services. In some ways this success was almost its undoing – the rapid growth brought a number of problems which Frank and his team struggled to cope with. 'We wanted to be out there solving problems for others not staying at home looking after our own business. We took our eye off the ball.'

As part of the rapid expansion Solutions took over another consultancy called Seton which specialised in different sectors. 'We thought this would add breadth to our operations. We looked like similar companies from the outside. It looked cheap at the price and had already had some success – I thought we could take it further. We thought some of their experiences and their general approach could be valuable. As it turned out we did not quite get what we had expected. From the outside and from talking to a few people at the top they seemed to be on our wavelength. When we actually got to see them in action these guys were so different it was scary. We like to base our decisions on facts. We research everything thoroughly so we know the problem inside out and then we let our minds run loose. We come up with innovative solutions but always come back to what the numbers say. Whenever we can we use quantitative techniques like decision trees to weigh up our options and make sure we get it right. At Seton they seemed to make it up as they go along. Give them a problem and they would try and solve it but they never seemed to look at the facts. They definitely had some star players but as a whole they played a high-risk game. There was no doubt we had to try and change things a bit to bring them in line with our culture. Most of them didn't like it but we knew how we wanted things done and over time I think we won.'

Interestingly, although Solutions encouraged its staff to contribute and Frank liked to see himself as someone who was always prepared to listen the firm still depended heavily on him for the overall direction. Even though it had grown so much in such a short period of time Frank remained a central figure and whether this was done consciously or not his views often dominated. In part this was because he was so good at his job ('A genius at work' had been the lead article on Frank in a recent management magazine) – others naturally looked to him for advice and guidance. Frank had typically been the first to see the need for a contingency plan in the event that something happened to him unexpectedly or if an emergency developed and he was not on hand to deal with it.

1 a) Analyse the ways in which the culture at Solutions may have contributed to its success in the early years. *(8 marks)*

   b) Consider the difficulties Solutions may have changing the culture at Seton after the takeover. *(12 marks)*

2 a) Examine the possible benefits for Solutions of horizontal integration with Seton. *(8 marks)*

   b) Discuss the problems which Solutions might have experienced as a result of rapid growth in its early years. *(12 marks)*

3 a) Examine the possible benefits to the managers of Solutions of using decision trees when making decisions. *(8 marks)*

   b) Frank believes that 'all the best decisions are based on data not intuition.' To what extent do you agree with this view? *(12 marks)*

4 a) From the very beginning Frank outlined a mission for the business. Examine the factors which might determine the value of a mission statement for an organisation such as Frank's. *(8 marks)*

   b) Discuss the possible value of contingency planning for Solutions for a situation when Frank was unexpectedly unavailable. *(12 marks)*

Case study 4

Karen Carpenter was something of an entrepreneur. She always had several business ideas on the go at once. If you asked her what she did it was always 'some of this and some of that'. She was always on the look out for a new idea; some worked, some failed but even if she was knocked back Karen would always get up and try again. And she had certainly been successful over the years. Her most recent venture was importing outdoor heaters. These were large gas heaters bought mainly by cafes and restaurants; they generated a considerable amount of heat allowing people to sit out relatively late at night. This meant the cafes and restaurants could use the space outside for much more of the day and evening and for more of the year.

Karen had set up a new company called Night Heat to concentrate on the import and selling of the product. The heaters were stylishly designed and had proved very popular on the Continent where Karen had first seen them. In the UK the company focused initially on wholesalers in the south-east area whom Karen knew well from another of her business ventures selling kitchen equipment in the region. The Night Heaters generated quite a lot of interest which was soon followed up by a relatively high number of orders.

However, in recent months the major national DIY retailers had started importing their own versions of the Night Heater. According to Karen these were 'not as well designed, were not as effective at heating the surrounding area and would use up the gas more quickly. Also if they go wrong there's very little they can do about it whereas we can service the heaters for our customers.' However, the competitors products were 10–15% cheaper to buy because of the purchasing power of the big retailers.

Looking at the latest sales figures Karen knew that something had to be done. 'We need to rethink our marketing strategy' says Karen 'and cut the price until we win back our market share. I am convinced the answer lies in lower prices. At the same time we should expand into new areas quickly and try to sell direct to the end users.'

Karen was also concerned about the working capital of the business and the fact that her new plan would need substantial finance. 'We need money, but if investors look at our figures I think we'll struggle to get it' she said. 'Why not window dress the accounts?' suggested her friend Cath. 'You might be right' said Karen. 'I feel certain all we need

is a bit more time and a bit more money to make this work. If we can get through this next few months the rewards will come flooding in, I'm sure.'

Meanwhile Karen is also working on another project to set up a company selling holidays over the internet. She has found two people with a background in this sector who will run the company but apart from that will be starting from scratch.

Night Heat's profit and loss statement for the year ending 1 September XXXX

	£
Turnover	80 000
Operating profit	2000

Balance sheet as at 1 September XXXX

Fixed assets	37 000
Current assets	30 000
Current liabilities	27 000
Net assets employed	**40 000**
Issued share capital	5000
Reserves	500
Long-term liabilities	34 500
Capital employed	**40 000**

1 a) Examine the factors which might influence Karen's marketing strategy for the Night Heater. *(8 marks)*

   b) Evaluate the new marketing strategy proposed by Karen. *(12 marks)*

2 a) Examine the ways in which Karen might improve the working capital of Night Heat. *(8 marks)*

   b) Discuss the ways in which Night Heat could window dress its accounts. *(12 marks)*

3 Consider the human resource issues involved if Karen does decide that Night Heat should 'expand into new areas quickly and try to sell direct to the end users'. *(20 marks)*

4 a) Examine the ways in which critical path analysis might help Karen establish her new internet travel company. *(8 marks)*

   b) Discuss the factors which might determine the location of her new internet business. *(12 marks)*

INDEX

Acknowledgements:

The author and publisher would like to acknowledge the following for use of copyright material:

The Economist, page 265; *The Financial Times*, pages 16, 21, 31, 161, 163, 165, 176, 190, 258, 263, 278; *The Guardian*, pages 118, 153; *The Times* and *The Sunday Times*, pages 173, 192.

Orders: please contact Bookpoint Ltd, 130 Milton Park, Abingdon, Oxon OX14 4SB. Telephone:(44) 01235 827720, Fax: (44) 01235 400454.
Lines are open from 9.00–6.00, Monday to Saturday, with a 24 hour message answering service.
You can also order through our website: www.hodderheadline.co.uk

British Library Cataloguing in Publication Data
A catalogue record for this title is available from The British Library

ISBN 0 340 801468

First published 2001
Impression number   10 9 8 7 6
Year   2005 2004 2003

Typeset by Fakenham Photosetting, Fakenham, Norfolk.
Printed in Great Britain for Hodder & Stoughton Educational, a division of Hoddor Headline, 338 Euston Road,
London NW1 3BH by Martins the Printers, Berwick upon Tweed.